Interpersonal
Neurobiology and
Clinical Practice

The Norton Series on Interpersonal Neurobiology
Louis Cozolino, PhD, Series Editor
Allan N. Schore, PhD, Series Editor, 2007–2014
Daniel J. Siegel, MD, Founding Editor

The field of mental health is in a tremendously exciting period of growth and conceptual reorganization. Independent findings from a variety of scientific endeavors are converging in an interdisciplinary view of the mind and mental well-being. An interpersonal neurobiology of human development enables us to understand that the structure and function of the mind and brain are shaped by experiences, especially those involving emotional relationships.

The Norton Series on Interpersonal Neurobiology provides cutting-edge, multidisciplinary views that further our understanding of the complex neurobiology of the human mind. By drawing on a wide range of traditionally independent fields of research—such as neurobiology, genetics, memory, attachment, complex systems, anthropology, and evolutionary psychology—these texts offer mental health professionals a review and synthesis of scientific findings often inaccessible to clinicians. The books advance our understanding of human experience by finding the unity of knowledge, or consilience, that emerges with the translation of findings from numerous domains of study into a common language and conceptual framework. The series integrates the best of modern science with the healing art of psychotherapy.

A Norton Professional Book

Interpersonal Neurobiology and Clinical Practice

edited by Daniel J. Siegel,
Allan N. Schore,
and Louis Cozolino

W. W. NORTON & COMPANY
Independent Publishers Since 1923

Note to Readers: Many of the authors featured in *Interpersonal Neurobiology and Clinical Practice* include their experiences and the experiences of others in the form of examples, narratives, and quotes to illustrate key concepts and theories. This information is edited for content, and names, other than those of the authors, have been changed; certain individuals referred to are composites. Any resemblance to a specific person is entirely coincidental. Standards of clinical practice and protocol change over time, and no technique or recommendation is guaranteed to be safe or effective in all circumstances.

Contents

Contributors

Daniel J. Siegel, M.D., is a clinical professor of psychiatry at the UCLA School of Medicine and the founding co-director of the Mindful Awareness Research Center at UCLA. He is also the Executive Director of the Mindsight Institute which focuses on the development of mindsight, and teaches insight, empathy, and integration in individuals, families, and communities. Dr. Siegel has published extensively for both the professional and lay audiences. His five *New York Times* bestsellers are: *Aware: The Science and Practice of Presence, Mind: A Journey to the Heart of Being Human, Brainstorm: The Power and Purpose of the Teenage Brain*, and two books with Tina Payne Bryson, Ph.D.: *The Whole-Brain Child*, and *No-Drama Discipline*. His other books include: *The Developing Mind, The Pocket Guide to Interpersonal Neurobiology, Mindsight, The Mindful Brain*, and *The Mindful Therapist*. He has also written *The Yes Brain* and *The Power of Showing Up* with Tina Payne Bryson, Ph.D. Dr. Siegel also serves as the Founding Editor for the Norton Professional Series on Interpersonal Neurobiology which currently contains over seventy textbooks. For more information about his educational programs and resources, please visit: www.DrDanSiegel.com and www.mindsightinstitute.com.

Allan N. Schore, Ph.D., is on the clinical faculty of the Department of Psychiatry and Biobehavioral Sciences, UCLA School of Medicine. He is the author of six seminal volumes, including *Affect Regulation and the Origin of the Self* (Classic Edition), and two recently published books, *Right Brain Psychotherapy* and *The Development of the Unconscious Mind*, as well as numerous peer reviewed articles and chapters. His contributions appear in multiple disciplines, including neuroscience, psychotherapy, psychoanalysis, psychiatry, developmental psychology, infant mental health, attachment theory, trauma studies, behavioral biology, clinical psychology, and clinical social work. He is the past editor of the Norton Series on Interpersonal Neurobiology, and has received a number of honors for his work, including an Award for Outstanding Contributions to Practice in Trauma Psychology from the Division of Trauma Psychology, the Scientific Award from the Division of Psychoanalysis of the American Psychological Association, Honorary Membership by the American Psychoanalytic Association, and the Reiss-Davis Child Study Center Award for outstanding contributions to Child and Adolescent Mental Health. He has extensively lectured internationally, and has had a private psychotherapy practice for more than four decades.

Louis Cozolino, Ph.D, has diverse clinical and research interests and holds degrees in philosophy, theology, and clinical psychology. His primary interests are in the areas of the synthesis of neuroscience with psychotherapy, education, management, and executive functioning. He is the author of ten books including *The Neuroscience of Psychotherapy, The Neuroscience of Human Relationships, Attachment-Based Teaching, The Making of a Therapist*, and *Why Therapy Works*. He has also authored and co-authored articles and book chapters on child abuse, schizophrenia, education, language, and cognition. Dr. Cozolino lectures around the world on brain development, evolution, and psychotherapy and maintains a clinical and consulting practice in Los Angeles and New York.

Carly Samuelson is a writer for Cozolino & Co. who specializes in Interpersonal Neurobiology. She attended graduate school at Pepperdine University, where she earned a Master of Arts degree in Psychology and began her work with Dr. Lou Cozolino. Prior to continuing her education, Carly studied journalism and worked as a writer and producer of television.

Chloe Drulis is a writer for Cozolino & Co. and a Master's student in Clinical Psychology at Pepperdine University. She is trained in play-based therapeutic intervention and began her career working with children at Therapeutic Play LA in Los Angeles. This inspired her future academic pursuits on the subject of Interpersonal Neurobiology, including her work with Dr. Lou Cozolino.

Stephen W. Porges, Ph.D., is Distinguished University Scientist at Indiana University where he is the founding director of the Traumatic Stress Research Consortium in the Kinsey Institute. He is Professor of Psychiatry at the University of North Carolina, and Professor Emeritus at both the University of Illinois at Chicago and the University of Maryland. He served as president of the Society for Psychophysiological Research and the Federation of Associations in Behavioral & Brain Sciences. He is the originator of Polyvagal Theory, a theory that emphasizes the importance of physiological state in the expression of behavioral and mental health problems.

Kathy Steele, MN, CS, is in private practice in Atlanta, Georgia and is an Adjunct Faculty at Emory University. Kathy is a Fellow and a past President of the International Society for the Study of Trauma and Dissociation (ISSTD), and is the recipient of a number of awards for her clinical and published works, including the 2010 Lifetime Achievement Award from ISSTD. She has (co)authored numerous publications in the field of trauma and dissociation, including three books, and lectures internationally on topics related to trauma, dissociation, attachment, and therapeutic resistance and impasses.

Bonnie Badenoch, Ph.D., LMFT, is a mentor, teacher, and author who delights in integrating the discoveries of interpersonal neurobiology and relational neuroscience into the art of therapy. She helps others cultivate their capacity for true presence as the foundation of healing, both in the counseling room and in daily life. Her home is in the Pacific Northwest where she writes, gardens, hikes, and relishes time with her wife, family, and friends. She is the author of *Being a Brain-Wise Therapist* (2008), *The Brain-Savvy Therapist's Workbook* (2011), and *The Heart of Trauma* (2017).

Richard A. Chefetz, M.D., is psychiatrist in private practice in Washington, D.C., past President of the International Society for the Study of Trauma and Dissociation (2002-3), and co-founder and chair of their Psychotherapy Training Program (2000-8). He is also a Distinguished Visiting Lecturer at the William Alanson White Institute of Psychiatry, Psychoanalysis, and Psychology. He is faculty at the Washington School of Psychiatry, the Institute of Contemporary Psychotherapy & Psychoanalysis, and the Washington-Baltimore Center for Psychoanalysis. In 2015, he published *Intensive Psychotherapy for Persistent Dissociative Process: The Fear of Feeling Real*, with W. W. Norton, in the Interpersonal Neurobiology series.

Daniel Hill, Ph.D., is a psychoanalyst, educator, and a leading proponent of the affect regulation model. He is the author of *Affect Regulation Theory: A Clinical Model* (2015). His publications and presentations include topics ranging from the clinical use of multiple models to religious fundamentalism. He was the founder/director of PsyBC and CSAR (1996-2017). For the past 15 years Dr. Hill has conducted on-going study groups focused on an in depth understanding of the regulation of affect. He is in private practice in NYC where he is on the faculties of the National Institute of the Psychotherapies and the New York University Postdoctoral Program in Psychoanalysis and Psychotherapy. Dr. Hill can be contacted at danhill@psybc.com.

Pat Ogden, Ph.D., is a pioneer in somatic psychology, the creator of the Sensorimotor Psychotherapy method, and founder of the Sensorimotor Psychotherapy Institute (sensorimotor.org). Dr. Ogden is co-founder of the Hakomi Institute, past faculty of Naropa University, a clinician, consultant, international lecturer and groundbreaking author in somatic psychology. Her current interests include couple therapy, child and family therapy, social justice, diversity, inclusion, consciousness, and the philosophical/ spiritual principles that underlie her work.

Oliver J. Morgan, Ph.D., is Professor of Counseling and Human Services at the University of Scranton. He teaches and publishes extensively in addiction studies. His most recent book, *Addiction, Attachment, Trauma, and Recovery: The Power of Connection* was awarded the Independent Press Award in 2020.

Terry Marks-Tarlow, Ph.D., is a clinical psychologist in private practice in Santa Monica, California. She is Adjunct Professor at Pacifica Graduate Institute, Santa Barbara, and the California School of Integral Studies, San Francisco, as well as Visiting Professor at Universita Niccolo Cusano London. She teaches and trains nationally and internationally on interpersonal neurobiology, nonlinear dynamics, creativity, and clinical intuition. She illustrates her own books, which include *Clinical Intuition in Psychotherapy* (Norton, 2012), *A Fractal Epistemology for a Scientific Psychology* (Cambridge Scholars, 2020) and *Mythic Imagination Today* (Brill Press, 2021).

Daniel Hughes, Ph.D., is a clinical psychologist in South Portland, Maine, who founded and developed Dyadic Developmental Psychotherapy (DDP), the treatment of children who have experienced intrafamilial relational trauma. The treatment model has expanded to become a general model of family therapy. Dan has conducted seminars and spoken at conferences throughout the United States and internationally. He is engaged in the training and supervision of therapists in his treatment model, along with consultations to various agencies and professionals. He is the author of many books and articles. His website is www.danielhughes.org. The website for DDP is ddpnetwork.org

Preface

by *Daniel J. Siegel, MD*
Founding Series Editor
The Norton Series on Interpersonal Neurobiology

What an honor to invite you to join us in this collection of contributions from clinicians and scientists exploring how to bring the foundations of a wide range of research disciplines to the practice of psychotherapy and other ways we promote well-being in our world.

Along with the series editors, Lou Cozolino and Allan Schore, and the many authors in this compendium and the Norton Series on Interpersonal Neurobiology, the goal to provide a science foundation to the broad field of clinical practice has been a driving force in our collective teachings over the past twenty years. Whatever the particular focus of help and healing you may have in your professional work, our hope is that this approach will offer accessible, practical, and impactful ways to translate cutting edge rigorous science into clinical understanding and interventions that help bring health into our world. "Consilience" is the term sociobiologist E. O. Wilson offers for us to name the pursuit of common ground across usually independent disciplines of knowledge. Here you'll find a consilient way to weave a wide range of sciences into a useful framework for your work to help others grow.

Bonnie Badenoch invites us to explore the central importance of therapeutic presence and its healing properties in our therapeutic relationship. Richard Chefetz takes us on a deep dive into the important developmental role shame plays in our clients' lives and offers clinical examples of how we may help heal these attachment wounds so prevalent in modern times. Lou

Cozolino and his colleagues offer us an insightful overview of the centrality of executive functions in our lives and how, with proper therapeutic intervention, we can help others develop more flexible and adaptive regulatory capacities with these prefrontally mediated capacities that can grow across a lifespan. Dan Hill extends these important abilities into a view of the central organizing role of regulation and dysregulation in how we can both understand our clients' challenges and how to help them move to more effective ways of using consciousness to empower their regulatory skills. Another Dan, Daniel Hughes, gives us timely insights into the teleconference setting of how we might use the resonance or synchrony between individuals to view emotional growth, and how this can be facilitated even in the virtual setting of contemporary psychotherapy in the face of distance, or a pandemic. Terry Marks-Tarlow take us further down this important path to understand synchrony in exploring how the nervous system functions in oscillating harmonics, not only within the individual, but how these can be entrained within a relationship that can promote growth and healing. Oliver Morgan takes the baton of this weaving of neural functioning and relational connections at the heart of Interpersonal Neurobiology in focusing our attention on addiction and the power of relationships to impair or repair our mental lives. Pat Ogden invites us into the powerful work of sensorimotor psychotherapy by examining the deep philosophical and neural underpinnings of how being mindful of the body plays a foundational role in the therapeutic process. Stephen Porges applies his polyvagal theory perspective on the challenges to well-being in the face of the persistent and pervasive threats of the COVID-19 pandemic and how we might offer ways to move from the reactive states of fight-flight-freeze-or-faint into the receptive state of openness and social engagement. Allan Schore provides a deep dive into how the therapeutic relationship can enable us to focus on early attachment experiences and how moving with a patient into earlier states of development may be necessary to then repair those ruptures in attuned, growth-promoting ways of being that can now, finally, facilitate freedom and development for the individual. Kathy Steele weaves the powerful work of our dear colleague, the late Jaak Panksepp, another IPNB series author, as she illuminates how the subcortical motivational states influence how we adapt to trauma and how the clinician can use this understanding in practical ways to promote well-being and healing. Finally, the chapter I offer invites us to consider how the foundational framework of IPNB can be used not only in the clinical setting, but also to be more broadly applied to promote well-being in families, communities, schools, nations, and our larger natural environment by exploring the central role of integration as a key mechanism underlying health and flourishing.

I invite you to take in each of these contributions knowing that you have at your fingertips a solid scientific foundation for however you personally and professionally can help bring more well-being into the world. It is with deep gratitude for each of our contributing authors that I welcome you to *Interpersonal Neurobiology and Clinical Practice*. May you find helpful practices and pearls of wisdom in the reading ahead.

Interpersonal Neurobiology and Clinical Practice

1

Interpersonal Neurobiology
From the Inside Out

A Brief Overview of a Consilient Approach to Personal, Public, and Planetary Flourishing

Daniel J. Siegel

IN THIS BRIEF CHAPTER, WE WILL EXPLORE THE HISTORY OF INTERPERSONAL neurobiology (IPNB) and its implications for our professional work, personal lives, public policy, and scientific understanding of health, the mind, and the cultivation of well-being in our waiting world.

Introduction: Five Foundations of IPNB

The term "interpersonal neurobiology" was coined in the early 1990s to attempt to describe an approach of identifying the common ground across disparate scientific disciplines and building a conceptual framework from their usually independent ways of studying, measuring, conceiving, and describing the nature of reality (see Siegel, 1999, 2012, 2020). E. O. Wilson (1998) terms this strategy for understanding the world from a range of perspectives "consilience." The framework of IPNB offers individuals a consilient opportunity to "see the whole elephant" of the world, building on the hard-earned discoveries from the wide range of science to construct a multidisciplinary perspective on processes such as the mind, mental health, and the fundamental properties underlying the emergence of living systems.

As the many innovative chapters of this volume attest, the broad framework of IPNB offers many windows, focusing in this compendium on the field of mental health and the art of psychotherapy, to draw upon science to provide new insights into the nature of the mind and novel approaches to helping reduce the suffering of others and to cultivate flourishing in life. In this way, we can see how there are many strategies for drawing upon a consilient approach to science and then applying this strategy in unique ways to support one another in bringing more well-being into our lives. IPNB is not a form of therapy; it is a consilient framework for understanding reality that can inform therapy, as well as a broad range of additional human endeavors that support mental health, education, parenting, public policy, and planetary well-being.

In the broad field of mental health, with its wide range of individual disciplines including psychology, nursing, social work, master's-level therapy fields, and psychiatry, we do not have a common curriculum, nor a common grounding in science, that joins our fields in the professional effort to understand the mind and to heal mental suffering. Amazingly, surveying over 100,000 mental health professionals in person from around the globe from our various disciplines reveals that over 95% have indicated that in their formal educational programs to enter the field, they were not given any definition of what the mind actually is, nor what a healthy mind might be. IPNB provides a consilient framework that addresses this issue by offering a definition of the mind and of what a healthy mind might be considered to be—and then shows how to cultivate well-being and human flourishing beyond just reducing mental suffering.

While the offerings in IPNB are varied in their focus for mental health practitioners, they all build on the fundamental principles of this framework. The first principle is to link empirical research from a range of fields published in peer-reviewed journals to the practice of psychotherapy and the understanding of mental health and mental suffering. Reading the now over 75 books in the Norton Series on Interpersonal Neurobiology, or diving into the chapters of the authors in this volume, you as a reader may discover that IPNB also provides another foundation beyond this first one of drawing upon science: the importance of relationships in mental health. That is the second fundamental principle of IPNB: Relationships are not icing on the cake of a life well-lived; they are not even dessert—they instead can be seen as the main course.

A third fundamental principle is that what happens in our relationships, what we can simply label with the spatial identifier "inter," is directly related to what happens inside our body, the "inner." Here you can see that we use the body as a referential indicator of the location of what is being discussed. This is at the heart of what the term IPNB begins with, the word "interpersonal." The "inter" of this word is the between; the "personal" indicates the inner. When the term IPNB was created, the feeling, the intention, the motivation of the words was to begin with this inner-inter focus.

A fourth principle, embedded in the second part of the name IPNB, is the neuroscience underlying the processes of mind and mental health. Yes, understanding the whole nervous system within the body is one part of how IPNB begins to explore life. Yet while neurobiology is a branch of biology, one of the major disciplines of science IPNB draws upon, one that studies life in its many manifestations, the initial intention of this part of the IPNB name was not to limit the framework to this specific branch of biology; instead, it was to begin with that field—especially inspired and motivated in the cultural context at the beginning of the 1990s, the Decade of the Brain. If we could begin the naming process again, it might be more accurate to choose a different second word—perhaps just "science" or "knowing" or some broader linguistic symbol that would invite equal participation of all the ways of studying the nature of reality beyond merely a branch of biology. We begin with science, our first principle, but IPNB now weaves in a wide range of human endeavors to understand and improve the world, such as contemplative practice, art, music, literature, history, political movements, public policy, environmental protection, social justice, parenting, education, and many other fundamental aspects of being a human member of life on this planet.

A fifth foundational notion of IPNB is that as a framework of understanding, not a specific way of doing something (like therapy or education or parenting), it invites individuals to explore the tenets of its consilient approach and then extend them in their own specific and unique ways. In this fifth principle, IPNB is a working framework that can and should continually challenge itself to test the validity of its tenets and continue to grow and develop as new knowledge emerges and as new applications are innovatively created. You can then see how a given chapter, book, or workshop that uses IPNB as a foundational framework may provide initial common ground but then offer very differentiated strategies of cultivating health. At first, such different-appearing approaches may seem troubling; yet when these five foundational principles are honored and the individualized yet rigorous applications are explored and validated as effective, we can then open our minds to the infinite capacity to expand and evolve our fields of knowledge.

One Approach to IPNB: A Dozen Integrative Principles

Building upon these initial five foundations of the framework, a dozen consilient ideas have been uncovered by exploring a broad range of sciences including anthropology, sociology, linguistics, psychology, biology, chemistry, physics, and mathematics. Seeking out the common ground across these independent pursuits has led to a set of principles for one approach to IPNB. It is important to emphasize that this is just one way of building and extending the working framework of IPNB; there are many ways of taking a consilient approach to reality and then drawing upon this emerging view in distinct ways. What follows in the remainder of this brief chapter is my particular way of applying these ideas in a range of human endeavors. Rather than finding references throughout this concise overview, please refer to *The Mindful Therapist* or *Mindsight* (Siegel, 2010a, 2010b) for direct therapeutic applications; the *Pocket Guide to Interpersonal Neurobiology* (Siegel, 2012) for a linking of these ideas in a nonlinear format; *Mind* (Siegel, 2017) for a personal journey through these ideas; and *The Developing Mind, Third Edition* (Siegel, 2020) for extensively referenced discussions.

Mind is broader than the brain and bigger than the body.

While this IPNB principle may evoke confusion, or even irritation, in various scholars, this notion is at the heart of viewing how the inner and the inter could be fundamentally part of the same process. But what in the world might be both inside and between?

Energy and information flow is fundamental to mind.

Physics studies energy, and energy is a process explored, if not directly named, by the major scientific disciplines. For example, the brain in the head (we also have brains in our gut and in our heart) functions by means of electrochemical energy flow patterns within the skull. Interpersonal relationships involve communication that is based on the sharing of energy and information flow.

Energy comes in many forms—electrical, chemical, light, sound—and has a range of contours, locations, intensities, and frequencies. If you add "forms" at the end of this sequence, you come to a helpful acronym, CLIFF, describing how energy manifests in our lives. When energy, in whatever form, is in a particular pattern that symbolizes something other than the energy flow itself, such as the term "hello," we call this energy-in-formation simply, "information." If you see the word "goodbye," it is also a form of light (or sound if you are listening to this aloud), but the pattern of letters symbolizes not a greeting when we meet, but one when we leave one another.

As energy patterns change, we call this "flow." In this manner, we can define a fundamental unit of a system of mind as this: energy and information flow. Pure energy is the flow as a conduit; information is the flow of energy as a constructor. Constructive information processing includes the levels of category, concept, and symbol.

> Energy and information flow occurs within an individual,
> and between the individual and the world of other
> people and the planet—the world of nature.

This IPNB principle highlights the reality that neither skull nor skin is an impermeable barrier that blocks the flow of energy and information. Whether you are a therapist, an educator, a parent, or a policy maker, or are involved in environmental protection or social justice, taking on this perspective of inner and inter as locations of energy and information flow will help set the stage for how the mind plays a part in each of these pursuits.

> "Mind" involves at least four facets: subjective experience,
> consciousness, information processing, and self-organization.

Each of these four facets may be emergent properties of the system of energy and information flow that is both embodied (the inner) and relational (the inter). In mathematics, collections of elements are called a complex system when they have the three characteristics of being open (to influences from outside themselves); capable of being chaotic (roughly, becoming random); and nonlinear (meaning a small input at one time leads to relatively large and difficult-to-predict outcomes). Mathematics reveals that complex systems have emergent properties—the interaction of the elements of the system gives rise to something greater than the individual components of the system. Our hypothesis at the heart of this principle is that the four facets of mind may each be emergent properties of the complex system of embodied and relational energy and information flow.

One facet of mind can be defined this way: An emergent,
self-organizing, embodied, and relational process that
regulates the flow of energy and information.

This fourth facet of mind is seen as the known emergent property of
the self-organization of complex systems. The complex system in question
is both embodied and relational energy and information flow: The mind is
both inner and inter.

A healthy mind is one that cultivates
integration, within and between.

Optimal self-organization, the fourth facet of mind, leads to the flow
of the system with the five qualities of FACES: flexible, adaptive, coherent
(resilient over time), energized, and stable (reliable, not rigid). Imagine a
river, bounded on one side by chaos and on the other by a bank of rigidity.
The flow of the river itself is that of harmony, the FACES flow that emerges
with optimal self-organization. In a consilient manner, various symptoms
of various syndromes of mental unhealth—known as psychiatric disorders
or mental disorders or emotional disorders—can be reframed as examples
of chaos, rigidity, or both. This prevalent pattern, that each example of
mental suffering seems to fit into the chaos and/or rigidity experience, can
be seen as consistent with impairments in optimal self-organization. But
how does the central flow of optimal self-organization arise? It arises with
the linkage of differentiated parts of a system, a process we can simply
call integration. When integration—the linkage of differentiated parts of
a complex system—arises, a FACES flow emerges, and chaos or rigidity is
not an ingrained feature of the flow of the system. A mind that cultivates
integration within and between is a healthy mind.

Mental unhealth emerges with impaired integration.

Chaos and rigidity can be seen as impairments to mental health. Related
notions include dysregulation or dysfunction. Sometimes the terms
"hypoarousal" or "hyperarousal" are used to describe being dysregulated. In
the brain, regulation depends on the linkage of differentiated parts; major
forms of psychopathology each reveal impaired neural integration. In contrast,
studies of well-being are correlated with neural and relational integration.

In the study of parent-child relationships as an example of inter-integration, secure attachment can be viewed as a form of interpersonal integration, whereas insecure forms of attachment, with their expression of various aspects of chaos or rigidity, can be seen as the outcomes of limitations to the differentiation and linkage needed for integrative communication.

This principle suggests that clinical assessment, or self-assessment, in the evaluation of mental health can begin by asking the question, what forms of chaos or rigidity may be present in an individual's life? Are there periods of a FACES flow of being flexible, adaptive, coherent, energized, and stable? Are there periodic or extended times when chaos and rigidity instead prevail? Pervasive, persistent, extensive, or frequent times of chaos and rigidity would be seen as the hallmarks of impediments to integration, the basis of mental suffering.

Relational and neural integration are mutually reinforcing.

A range of studies consiliently suggest that relational integration involving the honoring of differences and the cultivation of compassionate linking communication stimulates the growth of integration in the brains of those in the relationship. Likewise, neural integration seems to underly the capacity for compassionate communication and the mindsight ability to see the mind—the subjective experience—of another with respect and kindness. In this way, inner and inter-integration mutually reinforce each other.

Where attention goes, neural firing flows, and neural connection grows.

The mental process of attention directs how energy and information flow through a system. That system may be the physical brain, or it may be within relationships—just as the way these words direct your attention as a reader is influenced by the choice of words and when to use them by the writer in the reader-author relationship inherent in reading.

Neural firing is the electrochemical energy flow within the nervous system. Sometimes that flow interconnecting activated neurons has symbolic value, and we can call this flow of energy "information"—a neural representation as it "re-presents" that something in neural code.

Repeated neural firing activates genes to turn on protein synthesis and can lead to alteration in neural structures. This can include the modification of existing neural connections known as synapses, the growth of new synapses, the growth of new neurons, the laying down of myelin to enhance neural connectivity and communication, and even the alteration of the epigenetic (on top of gene molecules) regulators that shape how the brain will grow in response to future experience.

In this way we can see how mind—including the facet of regulating energy and information flow as a self-organizing process—can directly alter neural firing, connectivity, and structure. This is how experience—energy flow—is remembered and influences growth and development.

> Mind in its regulatory role both monitors and modifies energy and information flow, and these are learnable mindsight skills.

The fourth facet of mind as self-organization suggests that, like any regulatory process, that which is being regulated is both monitored, tracked, or sensed on the one hand, and then modified, transformed, or shaped on the other. This dual process of regulation suggests that to strengthen the mind, mind training can directly reinforce these two functions.

Monitoring energy and information flow can be stabilized so that what is perceived is seen with more depth, clarity, detail, and focus. Stabilizing the monitoring capacity of mind entails at least three aspects, what can metaphorically be considered a tripod of the mind with the three legs of openness, objectivity, and observation.

Openness is the state of being receptive to whatever arises without filtering away unwanted elements, such as emotions, memories, or thoughts.

Objectivity entails sensing mental experiences as objects of the mind and not the totality of one's experience or identity.

Observation involves the capacity to have a witness aspect of consciousness, one that is a bit distant from experience but can be fully aware of what arises in the focal attention that may drive energy and information flow into awareness.

> The term "mindsight" can refer to the capacity to have insight into one's own inner state of energy flow, to sense that in others as empathy, and to modify that flow within and between toward integration.

Once the mind has strengthened this mindsight tripod of monitoring, it can now take the details of what is experienced and modify the experience toward integration. This modifying, shaping, or transforming function addresses the question, how can an individual cultivate mental health?

One way to address this is the cultivation of integration across a set of domains.

There are nine domains of integration.

The term "integration" used here is specifically defined as the linkage of differentiated parts of a system. For complex systems as described above, this linking of differentiated parts is the mathematically determined process underlying the unfolding of optimal self-organization resulting in the FACES flow of the system bounded on either side by chaos or rigidity.

In this perspective from IPNB, integration is viewed as the foundation of health. Impediments to health, revealed as chaos and/or rigidity, can emerge in a variety of domains. Here nine domains are briefly named and defined; extensive discussion of each of these domains is beyond the scope of this highlighting chapter. The final domain is explored in more detail at the end of our overview.

Integration of Consciousness

Consciousness includes the experience of being aware (or knowing) and that of which we are aware (the knowns). Differentiating the knowns from one another and from knowing itself and then linking these components of consciousness to one another constitutes the foundations of the integration of consciousness. A practice known as the Wheel of Awareness offers one of many ways to integrate consciousness.

Vertical Integration

Energy flow from within the body is below the energy flow of the subcortical brain stem and limbic networks, which in turn are anatomically below the cortex. Vertical integration honors these differentiated streams of energy, and the information they contain, and then links them to one another. One way of mediating this domain of integration is to bring the bodily sensations into awareness through the sixth sense of interoception. The body can be a deep source of intuition and wisdom.

Bilateral Integration

Careful analysis of research on the asymmetry of the vertebrate nervous system across species reveals that the left and right sides of the brain are distinct in their anatomical connections and their developmental stages. One way that this manifests itself is in the broad focus of attention of the right versus the more narrow focus of the left. In addition, the right side of the brain is dominant for direct input of bodily sensations into an integrated map as well as autobiographical memory and the sending and receiving of nonverbal signals. In contrast, the left is dominant for factual memory and linguistic language, as well as for syllogistic reasoning—the search for cause-effect relationships in the world. Each hemisphere offers important components to a life of creativity, connection, and compassion when they are each honored and then linked.

Memory Integration

Experience, the flow of energy through the system, can become encoded, stored, and later retrieved by the nervous system. There are several layers of memory, each offering a way of understanding how past experience alters the probability of future mental experience, such as emotion, imagery, or behavior. One way of classifying memory is as implicit encoding (behavioral, emotional, perceptual, and somatic sensations, as well as priming and mental models) and explicit encoding (autobiographical and factual memory). When implicit memory is not processed via the integrative limbic structure, the hippocampus, then in its pure form it can be retrieved into consciousness without any tagging that it is coming from a past experience. Unresolved trauma, especially in the form of dissociated memory, may be one example of impaired memory integration in need of the healing that is integrative processing.

Narrative Integration

As a storytelling species, we make sense of our memories of lived events by constructing the narratives of our lives—stories we can also share with others. Narrative coherence emerges with the integration of memory and our construction of meaning out of our lived moments. Unresolved states, for example, may be revealing how narrative integration is impaired; the process of diving deeply into the sensations of past events, literally making sense, helps us to construct a story of our lives that makes sense even of things that didn't make sense at the time they occurred. Narrative integration in many ways is at the heart of the embodied ways we can come to live out the coherent narratives of our resolved traumas and free ourselves to live lives of meaning.

State Integration

The embodied brain—the head's brain and its connections to the gut's brain and the heart's brain—is a parallel distributed set of networks that function in the dynamic unfolding of states of neural activity. The subjective sense of these dynamic ever-changing states is called a state of mind. We have many states. Some are fleeting in the moment; some are enduring over a lifetime. Some can define our sense of self, and we can refer to them as self-states, while others may be related to functions that are more general and fluid, such as a tennis-playing state or a romantic or intellectual state. In trauma, the boundaries between states may be quite opaque, as in dissociative identity disorder. One example of a kind of state we experience is that of being reactive, as in the fight-flight-faint-or-freeze state; compared to the receptive state of being open and calm when reactivity subsides. In everyday life, the many states that make up the individual can be differentiated and then linked to cultivate state integration.

Interpersonal Integration

Individuals are born into the world and establish connections with attachment figures early in life as the first way their differentiated self is connected with other selves—the core of linking differentiated persons in interpersonal integration. How those early attachment experiences set the stage for the unfolding of future relational connection patterns is a focus of the field of attachment research: The direct ways we experience closeness to our caregivers, and the indirect ways we then adapt to those experiences, set up strategies of interpersonal relating that may continue long into adulthood. Limitations from the integration of early attachment security may be embedded in limitations in the neural integration of the individual's brain—and the focus of therapy may be to identify those areas of chaos and rigidity and then promote the integration of the individual's relational life, which can then promote the growth of integration within the brain itself.

Temporal Integration

Integration across time involves core aspects of existence—our longing for permanence in the face of life's transiency; a longing for immortality in the face of the reality of mortality; a longing for certainty in the face of the pervasiveness of uncertainty. Temporal integration embraces these paradoxes, honoring the longing while accepting the reality. In addition, physics has identified that the one reality we live in has at least two quite distinct realms, and differentiating these from each other and then linking them within aware-ness is also a component of this domain of integration. One realm is that of large objects, which Isaac Newton studied, and therefore it is known as the macrostate, classical, or Newtonian realm. In this realm there exists an arrow of time, a directionality of change. The perception of that directionality may be what the term "time" means in our everyday usage. In contrast, the realm of small objects, the size of electrons or photons, for example, lacks an arrow of time. The subjective experience of timelessness often felt in pure awareness during meditation or other mind-state-altering experiences may be related to the capacity of the mind to experience this microstate quantum realm. Within the classical macrostate realm, there is an appearance of noun-like entities that interact with one another; in the microstate quantum realm, in contrast, there are no nouns, only verb-like events that are massively inter-connected. Embracing these two realms of our one reality is also a part of temporal integration.

Identity Integration

Born into a body, we've seen that we have an inner aspect of who we are. Connected to other people and within all of nature, we also have an inter aspect of who we are, our relational self. As integration is the honoring of differences and the cultivation of linkages, how might we integrate identity? If "me" is a term for the inner, personal, embodied self—and "we" is a term for the inter, embedded, relational self—then integrating identity could be summarized with this equation: Me plus We equals MWe. Integration entails differentiating and linking in which the linkage does not destroy the differentiation: Integration is more like a fruit salad than a smoothie. This is where the notion that the whole is greater than the sum of its individual parts comes from—the synergy of integration.

IPNB offers a framework applicable to a wide range of human endeavors.

With this set of foundations and principles, it is possible to then apply the framework of interpersonal neurobiology to a number of different pursuits that aim to promote well-being. In the remainder of this chapter, we explore how these domains, especially the integration of identity, may be able to play a fundamental role in moving beyond the psychotherapy suite into the family living room, school classroom, organizational boardroom, seat of government, meditation hall, city streets and the defense of social justice, and out into the world of nature and the movement to support environmental protection and regeneration.

IPNB Applied Beyond Psychotherapy

Parenting

A wide array of parenting education, from workshops to books, reveals how the IPNB framework can help parents cultivate the mindsight skills to offer secure attachment for their children, adolescents, and even adult offspring. At the heart of this approach is the principle of integration as the source of health and resilience. When parents learn to make sense of their own childhood histories, they are integrating their lives and offering an internal source of healing as well as a relational source of cultivating secure attachment for the next generation.

Education

Schools can offer individual classrooms or whole school systems ways of bringing IPNB into educational strategies for cultivating resilience in their students and faculty. A mindsight-informed school teaches the central role of insight, empathy, and integration—the components of mindsight—to the faculty and parents so that the students come to live within a community of compassionate learners across the life span. One of the implications of an integrative pedagogy is the cultivation of identity and belonging that enable us to move beyond the solo-self often taught in modern culture, as we discuss more in the final section of this chapter.

Organizational Functioning

Executive leadership can weave the principles and foundations of IPNB into their approach to how their organization functions, providing individuals and departments with ways to cultivate both resilience and health as well as innovation and collaboration. The idea of integration can be applied at the individual and larger systems level. One example of a set of research and practical applications of integration includes the Wheel of Awareness. This tool can be used to promote the integration of consciousness and has embedded in it the three pillars of mind training—focused attention, open awareness, and kind intention—that research reveals cultivates integrative growth in the brain and the five molecular changes of health including decreases in the stress hormone cortisol; enhancing immune function; diminishing cardiovascular risk factors; decreasing systemic inflammation via changes in epigenetic regulation; and the optimization of the enzyme telomerase, which repairs and maintains the telomere caps at the ends of chromosomes. In addition, offering access to the hub of the wheel is a practical way to help access creative thinking and collaborative mental states.

Seats of Government

IPNB has also been useful in speaking with members of the U.S. Congress and various parliamentary bodies across the globe. As a framework for understanding our world through the consilient lens of science, naturally this approach is welcomed only by governmental agencies that value science as a disciplined, self-correcting way of exploring knowledge and then applying it to pressing problems. The Wheel of Awareness practice has been of particular interest in this regard, enabling members of a range of governmental agencies to learn a personal practice that promotes resilience in the face of stress as well as to see creative ways of thinking outside the box when confronting seemingly insurmountable political divides. Not a panacea, IPNB simply offers one way of thinking anew about entrenched problems needing a fresh view and approach for resolution.

Bridging Science and Spirituality

Through an inadvertent journey to imagine how we might define the mind beyond the definition used since the time of Hippocrates that the mind is only "what the brain does," a direct immersion into mind as an emergent property of the complex system of energy flow has led to some unexpected findings. After offering the Wheel of Awareness practice to tens of thousands of individuals in workshops around the planet, it became clear that in the hub of the wheel, people experienced a shift in consciousness that was parallel to what has been repeatedly described in wisdom traditions, contemplative practices, various religions around the world, psychedelic research studies, and mystical teachings. In trying to make sense of the reports that the hub was "timeless; filled with joy, love, connection; empty yet full; full of possibility," it became evident that IPNB research needed to move beyond existing brain research to the field of physics that studies energy in its purest forms. The notion of quantum physics that energy is the movement from possibility to actuality led to a deep analysis of the Wheel of Awareness survey findings and a proposal that awareness originates from energy in the lowest place of certainty—consistent with the sea of potential or quantum vacuum. In a diagram of these findings, we call this a plane of possibility.

The physics view of a formless source of all form suggests that this location of energy's probability in its lowest point of certainty is the generator of diversity of actualities that might arise. Here let us simply state that combining the first-person accounts of the Wheel practice, the 3-P framework for the mind (plane of possibility, plateaus of enhanced probability, peaks of actuality), and reports from the wide array of wisdom, contemplative, mystical, and religious traditions reveals a remarkable potential bridge between science and spirituality. Engaging in deep discussions around these exciting overlaps and potential bridges has been a profoundly rewarding ongoing journey of consilience.

The Art and Science of Hope and Justice

IPNB has also found a role in the pressing issues of social inequities and the need to promote social justice in our modern world. With the principle that integration is the heart of health, keeping hope alive as a steward of justice emerges out of differentiating our histories from one another and then cultivating the compassionate connections that honor those differences, without losing track of them. Hope in many ways can be seen to emerge from having a goal, a sense of agency, social support networks, and a pathway with a purposeful project. IPNB keeps hope alive by supporting each of these while also channeling possible feelings of despair and hopelessness into a foundation for being helpful. Identifying the in-group/ out-group process of the primate brain for the last 50 million years of our evolutionary history is a starting place for then trying to understand the neural contribution to our social construction of caste and race. Confronting these processes is aided by the realization that when such socially constructed concepts are perpetually used to shape identity and belonging in nonintegrative ways, everyone suffers from the ensuing chaos and rigidity in society.

Intraconnected Within Nature

IPNB also helps us see that denial of the reality of how deeply connected we are, with one another and within nature, can lead not only to massive social injustice but also to environmental destruction. When we differentiate excessively as a species, we do not honor the integrity of other members of nature. The loss of biodiversity and the warming of the planet in the face of massive emissions of carbon dioxide can be traced to this denial of our being a fundamental part of nature. Yes, we are interconnected, as individuals linked to other individuals. And yes, within nature we live, not connected from outside it, but intraconnected within all of life. Intraconnection is one way of imagining how we can move forward to link each of these ways of applying IPNB to our world. One common ground that connects all these is identity and belonging.

IPNB, MWe, and the Integration of Identity and Belonging

One implication of IPNB builds on the domains of integration and suggests that the subjective-experience facet of mind that we indicate with the terms "identity" and "belonging" may play a central role in our well-being at the broad range of levels of the systems in which we are born, grow, and live our lives. In this final section of this brief overview chapter, some central aspects of this implication are explored. A more in-depth immersion in this specific application of IPNB may be found in my next book, with the tentative title *IntraConnected: MWe (Me + We) as the Integration of Belonging and Identity*.

Our first facet of mind, subjective experience, comes to be known because of our second facet of mind, consciousness. This capacity to be aware enables us to sense the subjective inner experience of who we are, what we can simply call our identity. Often that experience of identity then influences our third facet of mind, information processing, even within the mental processes that unfold without being a part of conscious experience. In this case we might say that identity can be both conscious and subjectively felt within our awareness, and aspects of identity can also be nonconscious and therefore not a part of our subjective experience—even though it shapes information processing directly—how we think, perceive, remember, and interact with the world around us.

Much of our mental processing is outside of awareness and we don't subjectively feel it, yet it shapes our decisions, our beliefs, our thoughts, our emotional reactions, and our behaviors. This is all a reminder that mind is not limited to what is in consciousness; information processing operates with or without awareness. Identity influences each of these first three facets of mind: subjective experience, consciousness, and information processing.

Our fourth facet of mind, self-organization, also does not require consciousness. As we've seen in this overview, highlighting the notion that energy is the fundamental stuff of what we call mind as a starting place, while not often stated or explored, offers us a foundation for clarifying many current issues and imagining new ways to apply IPNB to reduce suffering and cultivate flourishing in our world. The proposal that a fourth facet of mind can be defined as the embodied and relational, emergent self-organizing process that regulates the flow of energy and information provides a working foundation from which to explore how health may arise from optimizing self-organization.

Self-organization, as the term implies directly, organizes the "self" of a system's wholeness. The linkage of differentiated parts, as we've seen, is the mathematical process of complex systems (those that are open, chaos-capable, and nonlinear) that maximizes complexity—the way they optimize their unfolding. This is what we mean by optimizing self-organization to create well-being. The FACES characteristics of this optimal self-organization we've used as a guide to health: flexibility (being able to change fluidly), adaptability (effectively modifying to changing conditions), coherence (resilience over time), energy (vitality), and stability (reliability). When linkage and/or differentiation are blocked, self-organization is constrained, and chaos and/or rigidity are more likely to arise in the system's flow.

One could then posit that the "self" of self-organization has many levels. The brain in the head is a complex system; the fully embodied brain—the whole nervous system and its body—is a complex system; the individual within that body, including the experience of mind (subjective experience, consciousness, information process, self-organization), is a complex system; dyadic relationships (couples, parent-child pairs) are examples of complex systems; families, classrooms, schools, organizations, communities, nations, and even our whole living planet each exemplify the many levels in which we live and experience being a part of complex systems.

When we reflect on the reality that neither skull nor skin are impermeable boundaries blocking the passage of the flow of energy and information, we can see that the terms "inner" and "inter" serve as spatial references that orient our communication about what goes on inside or outside the brain or body, rather than limitations in how energy and information actually flow in reality within the diverse levels of our lives. Yet these terms, brain and body, can sometimes rigidify our concepts, so that we conceive that the skin-encased body or skull-encased brain are somehow the sole location for self or for mind, respectively. When we instead widen our thinking to consider that the fundamental unit of the complex systems in question is energy and its subset, information, and that this energy flows and changes in various spatially distributed locations, we can then broaden our conceptualizations about the mind and about the self. In other words, we can suggest that mind, and the self arising from it, emerge from energy and information flow within physically locatable aspects of the world we can discuss—but this flow giving rise to mind and self may in fact not be confined to simply being in, or even arising from, the skull or the body alone. The self and its mind are broader than the brain and bigger than the body.

The proposal in this approach to IPNB is that each of the four facets of mind may be emergent properties of the complex systems in which they arise. For example, our third facet of mind, information processing, can be used to reveal this more distributed nature of mind, rather than mind simply being the brain's activity. In the philosophy of cognitive science, the term "4-E" reminds us of this spatial distribution of information processing, as cognition is described as being embodied, enacted, extended (beyond the body), and embedded (in communication patterns within the cultures in which we live).

Our suggestion is that self-organization also arises at different levels of the systems in question. We can study the brain in the head and find fascinating and important discoveries about the differentiated regions and how their linkages with one another within networks reveal insights into the electrochemical energy flow of neural processing and its correlation with mental experience, such as emotion, attention, thought, memory, narrative, and morality. Those studies can be added to the exciting findings, more difficult to study in many ways, of the body as a whole and the contribution of other organs, such as the heart and the intestines, including its biome, to the information processing, self-organization, subjective experience, and perhaps even consciousness facets of mind.

If we use the term "embodied brain" to remind us that this energy and information flow of internal aspects of who we are is not limited to the contents and processes of the skull, we can then state that we have an inner energy and information flow in this embodied location and manner. This inner aspect of our existence is real, and it is really important. And in addition, this inner aspect of our existence is not the totality of who we are, of what makes us up, of what constitutes our identity.

Beginning within, we can reflect on a modern culture lesson, one that perhaps includes the 2,500-year-old statement from Hippocrates, a grandfather of modern medicine, that all our joys and sorrows, essentially all our mental processes, are outcomes of the brain in the head alone. This modern medical perspective is that mind arises only from the brain. If mind is the origin of self, then if we took this modern medical view as total truth, we would say that our self is in our head—and the body is at best a transport vehicle carrying the true "us" around. If we widen this view just a bit, extending perhaps to William James, the grandfather of modern psychology, and his acceptance of the brain origin of the mind while also focusing on the body as a whole in his writings in the late 1800s, we can see who the self is in the body as the mind originates there.

In IPNB's foundations drawn from a consilient view of all sciences, we have needed to reconcile these inner origins of mind with the equally important differentiated perspectives of fields such as linguistics, sociology, and anthropology, which view mind as relational, not embodied. IPNB then sees these findings as support for the attempt to bridge these often independent pursuits by proposing that energy and information are the stuff of mind, and that the flow of this stuff, this energy and information, arises both within the body and its brains, and in relationships with people and the planet. In this way, IPNB sees relationships as central to who we are. In my particular exploration of IPNB, as we've seen, I am offering a definition of mind that suggests that our mind is more than the important inner embodied aspect; mind is also fully relational.

The singular stuff of mind that is both embodied and relational is energy and information flow. Skull does not limit that flow; skin does not limit that flow. We share the flow of energy and information in our relationships with one another as members of a human family, and we share that flow as members of the living world of nature, of all living beings.

The term "self" is often used in a range of ways in various fields. For example, "self-regulation" is a common focus in developmental studies, and self-dysregulation is considered central to understanding psychopathology. But what is this thing we call self?

You may realize that this author, this body called Dan, has a tendency to use acronyms to recall things, and here is a third and penultimate one for this chapter: SPA. "Self" refers to a center of subjective experience, perspective, and agency. We've seen that subjective experience is the felt texture of lived life. Perspective is the point of view; the way perception is filtered by a particular way of taking in experience. Agency is the experience of being a localization for the initiative of action, the determiner of behavior in the world. Simply put, we have subjective experience, perspective, and agency, and each of these three combines to contribute to our experience of self in the world.

In developmental and relational terms, when our self is obliterated early in life, we can feel shame when our subjective experience and perspective are denied, and humiliation when our agency is destroyed. The sense of self that then arises is directly altered by these self-shaping experiences. This sense of self may indicate the compilation of the SPA of self, our subjective experience, perspective, and agency combined, and then how we become aware of these in consciousness. In this way, we may have a self-experiencing of SPA, and our awareness of that central set of unfoldings we call our sense of self.

How the self gets organized is shaped by our experience. Our genetics shape our temperament and the proclivities of our embodied brain, and directly influence the flow of energy and information within us, and how we share that with the world. In this way, our inner source of genes and of temperament shapes experience and therefore can shape our development of self. We also have our interactions with the world, especially the world of other people. Early in life, attachment figures, including our parents and others who care for us, provide the interactive experiences that shape our subjective experience, perspective, and agency. These relational connections shape the unfolding of our inner neural connections to sculpt our inner states. A simple finding is this: integrative relationships promote the growth of integration in the brain of the child. As integration is the basis of regulation of many functions, from emotion and affect to thought and memory, self-regulation depends on integration. Integration in secure attachments provides the differentiation and linkages within communication patterns across time that stimulates the growth of the integrative connections—the linkage of differentiated parts of the brain—that permit optimal self-regulation.

In this way, relational connections become inner neural connections. In turn, these integrative inner connections enable optimal function to be achieved, including participating in integrative, mutually rewarding relationships for the growing child, adolescent, and adult.

Even with optimal interactive experiences, with reliable repair when ruptures arise, the individual grows with a multitude of inner states that constitute the healthy maturing person and directly influence our experience of self.

The brain can enter many states, some shaped by intense emotions, others by skills, others by developmental period. We therefore experience many selves or self-states that are enduring patterns of subjective experience, perspective, and agency filled with particular memories, emotional tendencies, and narrative processes that make meaning out of those experiences. This multitude of selves in turn shapes the layers of identity we have; and that in turn shapes our experience of belonging.

Identity can be described as a sense of the "who" of our experience, who we are, that emerges from our inner states and our interactive relationships with the world around us. Identity is shaped by the messages we receive from the culture in which we are immersed. Yes, we have inner layers of self-states that emerge from our temperament, our neural proclivities, and our interaction with caregivers at home. And yes, we have the experience of interactions with peers and teachers at school, and then messages from the media and our interactions with the larger culture that shape our experience of identity. If we are born into a culture in which the color of our skin places us in a socially constructed category called race, and that division is a subordinate grouping in a caste system, then the feeling of belonging and being empowered within the larger culture will be severely restricted. Here we can see how family belonging may arise with a sense of identifying with one's family of origin; and at the same time there may be messages of being disrespected and discounted, of being humiliated and dehumanized, such that the experience of systemic racism gives rise to a feeling of not belonging to the larger culture.

Identity is shaped by our memories of interactive experiences that can have complex contrasts between the SPA of self in family and the SPA of self in society. Interactions that give rise to a sense of respect and inclusion, ones in which differentiation is honored and linkages established, can be viewed as the origins not only of trust, but of belonging. To be seen for one's authentic inner experience, to have one's subjective experience honored, one's perspective respected, and one's agency held with integrity and receptivity enables the self to belong in that relational world.

We can see, from an IPNB perspective, how relational integration directly impacts the experience of belonging in life. Identity, too, is shaped by our SPA experience of self molded by interactive experience, embedded in memory and narrative, and directly related to the experience of membership in a group beyond the body in which we are born—our sense of belonging.

For at least 50 million years, a fundamental in-group versus out-group process has influenced primates' interactions with one another. Our human evolution then built upon this primate heritage with complex societal messages emerging from our large collections of people living together in modern times. One example of this primate extension into human culture is the caste system mentioned above. In this intricate web of in-group/out-group distinctions, levels of legitimacy and status are offered, with the dominant group filled with privilege and the subordinate group deprived of opportunity and even a sense of belonging. Here we can see how the lessons from a caste culture teach an individual what their identity is and how they belong, or not, to the larger society in which they live.

Caste, and the related systemic processes of racism, reaffirms the view that one's experience of self does not simply come from the inside; one's identity and belonging arise in relationships with the world around us and shape the experience of self. The SPA of selfing is enhanced or diminished by the culture in which we live. Selfing is a term we can use for the verbal-like nature, as a present participle in grammar, of the process or experience of becoming self—of selfing.

We can propose that cultures that promote deep forms of integration are optimizing the self-organizational life of that society. What this means is that differentiated ways of being are not only tolerated; our unique ways of showing up in the world are respected, cherished, and nurtured. Then these differentiated, unique ways of being are linked to one another with compassionate communication and acceptance. In this setting, the many selfings that arise, ones that promote integration within the individual and within the relationships that constitute our identity and belonging, can be welcomed into the community.

When systemic racism and a caste system prevail, such integrative ways of being in the world are instead moved away from the integrative harmony, the FACES flow of flexibility, adaptability, coherence, energy, and stability, toward chaos and rigidity. This would be an IPNB view on the impact of assaults on social justice.

In addition to this form of impairment to integration that leads to social injustice, there is also the practice of ignoring or destroying the truth of our interconnected world as we excessively differentiate our human species from other species of life on earth. The chaos and rigidity we see on the planet as a whole, with the emission of greenhouse gases, the warming of the planet, and the loss of biodiversity as our ecosystems have been devastated in recent years, may each be seen as examples of impaired integration of humanity on earth. Here, too, IPNB offers a way to focus on our self, our identity and belonging, and highlight how we may, in modern times, have become excessively differentiated in what we teach each other about ourselves.

This brings us to the final notion of this chapter, and to the final acronym: SIBLING. If we imagine that we are born into the world as a brother or sister of the family of all living beings, we can see that our birthright is to belong to our family, to have an identity as an individual within our family, and to have a self—a subjective experience, perspective, and agency—that is differentiated and linked with the system of that family. Whether an only child or one of many siblings, we connect with our caregivers and enter the larger world of people and of nature ready to connect and learn who we are. In many Indigenous teachings from a range of continents and traditions, a sense of self is broader than the body; who you are is fundamentally a part of all living beings. Yet in modern culture, what used to be called the West but which more recently extends around the planet, anthropologists note an individualistic cultural teaching of a separate, solo-self. At the other end of the spectrum of identity is a collectivist sense—one emphasizing membership as a relational being.

But what would happen if both the inner, personal, individual and the inter, relational, collective could be differentiated and linked? What if the siblings of a family could be honored for their differences but fully engaged in their membership in the group?

In linguistic terms, how might we be both a "me" and a "we"? As we've discussed, the term "integration" is very specifically defined as the differentiation and then linkage of components of a system. What might an integration of identity and belonging entail? How might we cultivate an integrated self in society?

One simple way of approaching these questions is with the equation, Me plus We equals MWe. In our acronym of SIBLING, this would be highlighted in the following ways.

S: Our unfolding as a *self*, our selfing with its SPA of subjectivity, perspective, and agency, might be nurtured to retain what children often know innately, that we can feel both inner and inter, have the point of view of the body we are born into as well as that of other individuals across species, and be a source of action on behalf of a wider center of agency than merely the body we are born into. Self can be both the inner me and the inter we.

I: Our *identity* can be nurtured to have both this inner and inter localization, enabling us to widen the view of a solo-self into this integrated sense of who we are as both fully embodied and fully relational beings in the world.

B: As we integrate self and identity, we come to experience *belonging* to a much larger membership than merely the body, our immediate family, or to people who look only like us or who share only our beliefs, our nationality, or even our species. We can broaden our fundamental group of belonging to include membership in the wider world of all living beings, to the world of nature.

L: When people attempt to express the feeling of this broader belonging, this integrated identity, this synergistic self—a selfing in which the individual components give rise to something more than just the individual elements alone—the one word that repeatedly is offered is this: *love*. Though rarely sanctioned to use in scientific discussion not specifically focusing on this subjective experience directly, here this observational finding across a large population suggests a vital force of life, one that emerges both within and between, one that drives us to connect and forms the fuel for hope and justice.

I: When a sense of separation embedded in the subjective experience of a solo-self begins to dissolve and give way to an integrated identity and broader belonging, what becomes revealed is the reality of the interconnection among the many individual elements making up the wholeness of reality. When the subjective experience, perspective, and agency of this interconnected reality is breathed into the selfing of this opened experience, the term that arises is *intraconnected*. Who we are, our self, identity, and belonging, fueled by the vital force of life we can name love, is intraconnected within all living beings.

N: When we study our place in the universe, this factual view can be called *noesis*, our conceptual knowing, and lets us know that we are fundamentally a part of the whole of *nature*. Yes, we have a body, the inner facet of our selfing; and yes, we are nature; the relational facet of our selfing. Integrated, our identity and belonging are both within and between.

G: It is possible, as consistent with our contemporary understandings from physics, to become aware of a macrostate classical Newtonian aspect of reality in which the world is composed of noun-like separate entities that interact with one another; and we can come to know another realm of our one reality, the microstate quantum aspect of reality, in which there are no entities, but rather verb-like events that are deeply interconnected. The term "gnosis," is sometimes used to mean "knowledge of spiritual mysteries" or the knowing that arises from direct experience beyond factual knowledge alone. As beings born into a body, we live in a macrostate world and what we see with our eyes gives us the Newtonian view of entities. But if we embrace a different way of knowing, of seeing beyond the appearance of separation that might underlie our confusion, creating the concept of the separate solo-self, we could instead consider this systems view of our identity and belonging extended beyond the noun-like body and embedded in the web of life on the globe, on *Gaia*, our Earth. The *Oxford English Dictionary* suggests that, as James Lovelock coined its usage, Gaia means the earth viewed as a vast self-regulating organism, with synonyms of the natural world, nature, the living world, the world, the earth, the ecosystem, the biosphere, Mother Nature, wildlife, flora and fauna, the countryside, the landscape. We are siblings of nature; our integrated identity of MWe is intraconnected with all living beings on this wondrous planet.

One way to come to live within this intraconnection of a living system is to contribute to optimizing its self-organizational flow toward integration. A term we can use for this participation and systems flow is "generative." A generative system cultivates differentiation and linkage as it grows and nurtures its own harmonious unfolding.

The G of SIBLING can be anything that resonates with you as you go forward in your journey. For this body with the individual name Dan, the terms gnosis, Gaia, and generative each resonate well with the fullness of what it means to have a self, an identity, a belonging, love, intraconnection, and the facts of our noesis of nature. The feelings arising are gratitude and honored to be intraconnected with you in our journey to bring healing and wholeness, to bring integration, into life in all its forms.

IPNB offers a framework that can help support the work to reduce suffering and promote flourishing at many levels of our experience, from within these bodies we are born into as individuals within psychotherapy, to helping transform societies to address social injustice and environmental destruction. We can help life move from the states of chaos and rigidity, within and between, that emerge from impediments to integration. As we move forward in our lives together on this shared home, cultivating integration within and between can be the shared goal to keep hope and justice alive in our world.

One more acronym before we go—a kind of postscript for us all. Hope can be considered the steward of justice; hopelessness, as Bryan Stevenson (2014) states in *Just Mercy*, is the enemy of justice. A dive into the science of hope suggests this mnemonic: GASSPPP. When we are in awe, we gasp. And the awe of love can be inspired by this set of properties that promote hope in our lives: having a goal, agency, social support, and a pathway with a purposeful project. Imagine how together, MWe can work with agency and purpose toward the goal of creating more integrated ways of living for all living beings on our precious planet, this common home we call earth.

References

Siegel, D. J. (2010a). *The mindful therapist: A clinician's guide to mindsight and neural integration.* New York: Norton.

Siegel, D. J. (2010b). *Mindsight: The new science of personal transformation.* New York: Bantam/Penguin Random House.

Siegel, D. J. (2012). *Pocket guide to interpersonal neurobiology.* New York: Norton.

Siegel, D. J. (2017). *Mind: A journey to the heart of being human.* New York: Norton.

Siegel, D. J. (2020). *The developing mind: How relationships and the brain interact to shape who we are* (3rd ed.). New York: Guilford.

Stevenson, B. (2014). *Just mercy: A story of justice and redemption.* New York: Spiegel and Grau/Penguin Random House.

Wilson, E. O. (1998). *Consilience: The unity of knowledge.* New York: Vintage.

2

The Interpersonal Neurobiology of Therapeutic Mutual Regressions in Reenactments of Early Attachment Trauma

Allan N. Schore

IN MY ONGOING STUDIES, I CONTINUE TO SUGGEST THAT THE mental health field is currently experiencing a paradigm shift, in large part due to the integration of neuroscience within updated models of clinical treatment (see Schore, 2003b, 2012, 2019b). Indeed, neuroscience as a whole is now in a rapid period of growth, due to both new technology and its expanding connections with other scientific and clinical disciplines. This expansion is being fueled by the rediscovery of brain lateralization, first established in the 19th century at the dawn of modern neurology, and very recent research on the different structural and functional organizations of the right and left brains. My clinical and theoretical models represent ongoing investigations of the right brain and its adaptive body-based emotional, relational, and survival processes. That said, although we are in the midst of a paradigm shift from the cognitive, verbal left "rational brain" into the right-lateralized "emotional brain" and its unique nonverbal communicational and relational functions, there still exists a bias in the mental health field and the psychological sciences for conceptualizing the mind as solely the conscious "left mind," one that can be assessed by self-questionnaires and explicit verbal reports or observations of overt behavior. As a result, the methodology of this research generates theoretical models that are centered more in the verbal, analytical, conscious left mind, as opposed to the subjectivity and intersubjectivity of the nonverbal and unconscious "right mind."

With respect to the origins of these two lateralized self-systems, a large body of research indicates an earlier maturation of the visuospatial right brain than the left brain (see Schore, 1994, 2012, 2003a, 2003b, 2019a,b). In support of Sigmund Freud's (1923) classic formulation that the unconscious mind develops before the conscious mind, "thinking in pictures . . . approximates more closely to unconscious processes than does thinking in words, and it is unquestionably older than the latter both ontogenetically and phylogenetically" (p. 21). This proposal is supported and echoed in current brain laterality research, where Howard and Reggia (2007) conclude, "The right hemisphere develops a specialization for cognitive functions of a more ancient origin and the left for a specialization for functions of more modern origin" (p. 121). Consonant with this conceptualization, in his wide-ranging studies of the unique structural and functional specializations of the dual hemispheres, the neuropsychiatrist Iain McGilchrist now asserts that "the right hemisphere both grounds our experience of the world at the bottom end, so to speak, and makes sense of it, at the top end," that this hemisphere is more in touch with both affect and the body, and that "neurological evidence supports what is called the primacy of affect and the primacy of unconscious over conscious will" (2015, p. 44).

For the past three decades I have offered interdisciplinary research and clinical data demonstrating that the operations of the right hemisphere are centrally involved in the essential functions of the human unconscious, the deepest levels of the human mind. This right-lateralized core of the subjective self evolves in the early mother-infant attachment relationship, and over the life span this psychobiological system, at levels beneath conscious awareness, intersubjectively communicates with other right brains that are tuned to receive these communications. Applying this developmental model of the mother-infant dyad to the clinical context, I have described how the cocreated psychotherapeutic relationship acts as a dynamic intersubjective context of rapid communications of emotional states within the emerging therapeutic alliance. These spontaneous right brain-to-right brain nonverbal communications of self-states take place in the present moment, a time frame from fractions of a second to 2 to 3 seconds. Importantly, this "relational unconscious" not only communicates with but also *synchronizes* and is expanded by another relational unconscious (Schore, 1994, 2003b, 2019a, 2019b). This spatiotemporal synchronization of right brain patterns allows

the therapeutic dyad to mutually share unconscious (implicit) communicative, emotional, and regulatory functions, thereby facilitating psychotherapeutic growth and development of the right brain.

In this contribution to regulation theory, a theory of the development,
psychopathogenesis, and treatment of the subjective self, I draw upon my
two newest volumes, *The Development of the Unconscious Mind* and especially
Right Brain Psychotherapy. My latest theoretical and clinical studies continue
to demonstrate that recent discoveries in interpersonal neurobiology are
directly relevant to a more complex understanding of the underlying
mechanisms of therapeutic action in all forms of psychotherapy (Schore,
1994, 2003a, 2003b, 2012, 2019a, 2019b). In the following, I discuss the
essential roles of rapid nonconscious right brain-to-right brain communications beneath the words of the patient and clinician, and of rapid nonverbal regulatory communications embedded in intersubjective implicit
relational processes. Special attention is focused on reenactments of early
attachment dynamics and on the growth-facilitating effects of mutual
regressions in heightened affective moments of the psychotherapy session.
I shall show that these regressions are a naturally occurring process in psychotherapy. Apart from these clinical applications, I will also suggest that
psychotherapeutic reenactments and mutual regressions also shed direct
light upon the essential dynamic functions of the deepest hidden levels of
the unconscious mind, which as Freud demonstrated are centrally involved
in all aspects of the human experience.

This interpersonal neurobiological model highlights the ongoing neuroplastic development of the right brain as a primary mechanism of change
in all forms of psychotherapy, including individual child and adult, couples,
and group psychotherapy. In a special issue of the journal *Psychotherapy*
titled "Evidence-Based Psychotherapy Relationships," the editors Norcross
and Lambert (2018) assert, "decades of research evidence and clinical experience converge: the psychotherapy *relationship* makes substantial and consistent contributions to outcome independent of the treatment" (p. 313,
emphasis added). However, before I begin, I briefly offer information about
recent advances in neuroscience methodology and technology that allow
a deeper understanding of the interactions of two right brain systems in
the therapeutic relationship coconstructed by the clinician and the patient.
These advances provide a valuable opportunity for a deeper understanding of the implicit relational processes that operate between both members
of an interacting therapeutic dyad at levels below conscious awareness.

Throughout, the term "psychoanalyst" may be substituted with the term "psychotherapist," and "psychoanalytic" with "psychodynamic."

Right brain-to-Right brain Communication: Update

Over 25 years ago, in my first book, *Affect Regulation and the Origin of the Self*, I proposed that in dyadic mother-infant and patient-therapist social-emotional interactions, *brains align and synchronize their neural activities with other brains* (Schore, 1994). In this first articulation of the emergent fields of interpersonal neurobiology and neuropsychoanalysis, I offered extant neurobiological evidence to show that the early developing right brain is the psychobiological substrate of the human unconscious and described the operations of a relational unconscious, whereby one unconscious mind communicates with another unconscious mind in nonverbal right brain-to-right brain emotional communications. I further posited that regulated emotional exchanges trigger synchronized energy shifts in the infant's developing right brain, allowing for a coherence of activity within its cortical and subcortical levels and the organization of the emotion-processing right brain into a self-regulating "integrated whole." In this manner, "the self-organization of the developing brain occurs in the context of a relationship with another self, another brain." Research evidence of the two-person, two-brain model awaited an emergent technology that could simultaneously measure two interacting brains in real time.

In 2012, I cited Dumas's (2011) clarion call for a "move from a classical one-brain neuroscience toward a novel two-body approach," pointing out the parallel shift in the clinical literature from a one-person intrapsychic to a two-person interpersonal psychology (Schore, 2012). In the last decade, hyperscanning methodologies utilizing simultaneous electroencephalography (EEG), functional magnetic resonance (fMRI), magneto-encephalography (MEG), and near-infrared spectroscopy (NIRS) measurements have been created. This technological advance now allows the study of two brains synchronizing spontaneous social interactions with each other in real time, including during rapid emotional communications. The word "synchrony" derives from the Greek words *syn*, which means the same or common, and *chronos*, which means time. Thus "synchrony" literally means "occurring at the same time." The construct of synchrony, shared by both scientists and clinicians, is tightly associated with physiological linkage, affective reciprocal exchange, emotion transmission, and coregulation. Furthermore, the implicit interpersonal neurobiological mechanism of interactional synchrony lies at the core of the growing literature on the critical processes that mediate the subliminal change mechanisms implicitly embedded in the therapeutic relationship, specifically the reciprocal dynamic emotional communications between the therapist and patient.

Inspired by the developmental research of Beebe, Tronick, and especially Trevarthen on the intersubjective nonverbal communication and coordination between a mother and her infant (see respectively Figure 6.3 in Schore, 1994; Figure 8.1 in Schore, 2012; and Figure 2.3 in Schore, 2003a), Dumas and his colleagues (2010) offered a now-classic dual EEG hyperscanning study of interbrain synchronization during a spontaneous social interaction between two adults, characterized by reciprocal communication and turn-taking. They reported a simultaneous measurement of brain activities of each member of a dyad during interpersonal communications, where "both participants are continuously active, each modifying their own actions in response to the continuously changing actions of their partner" (Dumas et al., 2010, p. 1). These authors documented specific changes in both brains during nonverbal imitation, a central foundation of socialization and communication. In this relational context, both share attention and compare cues of self and other's actions.

Furthermore, these researchers described an interbrain synchronization, on a time scale of milliseconds, of the right centroparietal regions, a neuromarker of social coordination in both interacting partners (Tognoli et al., 2007), as well as a synchronization between the right temporoparietal cortex of one partner and the right temporo-parietal cortex of the other. They point out that the right temporo-parietal junction (TPJ) is known to be activated in social interactions and is centrally involved in states of attention processing, perceptual awareness, face and voice processing, and empathic understanding. Indeed, the right TPJ, a central node of the social brain, is activated in face-to-face interactions (Redcay et al., 2010) where it plays an essential role in implicit attentional functions that *operate outside of conscious awareness* (Chelazzi, Bisley, & Bartolomeo, 2018, italics added). The right TPJ *integrates* input from visual, auditory, somesthetic, and limbic areas and is thus a pivotal neural locus for self functions. This right-lateralized system is known to be fundamentally involved in social interactions and self-functions (Decety & Lamm, 2007), in allocating attention to self and other representations (Santiestaban et al., 2012), in "making sense of another mind" (Saxe & Wexler, 2005) and in "subjective judgments of humanness" (Dumas et al., 2020). The top-down view of Figure 2.1 shows this interbrain synchronization, lateralized to the right hemisphere of each member of a

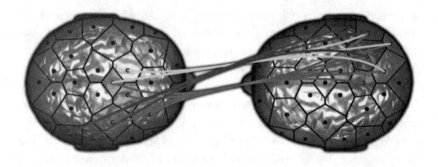

FIGURE 2.1 Top-down view of a right-lateralized interbrain synchronization of a spontaneous nonverbal communication. From Dumas (2011), "Toward a Two-Body Neuroscience," with permission from the author.

nonverbally communicating dyad. Note that the figure depicts a specifically right-lateralized interbrain synchronization and what I have called a right brain-to-right brain interaction between one subjective self and another subjective self that cocreates an intersubjective field between them (Schore, 1994, 2003b, 2012, 2019b, 2020).

This right brain-to-right brain synchronized communication model is also supported in a hyperscanning study by Stolk and his colleagues (2014). These authors generated fMRI brain images on each participant of a communicating dyad, where "both partners mutually learned to adjust to each other" (a fundamental mechanism of an evolving relationship of emotional conversations between two interacting brains). Simultaneously measuring cerebral activities in pairs of communicators, these researchers reported that establishing mutual understanding of novel signals synchronizes cerebral dynamics across both communicators' right temporal lobes. Importantly, interpersonal synchronization occurred only in pairs with shared communicative history. These researchers documented that in this nonverbal intersubjective communication, the processing of novelty and meaning is generated in the right (and not left) hemisphere.

In my earlier developmental studies, I provided extensive interdisciplinary research to show that this right brain-to-right brain emotional communication system also underlies the dyadic attachment dynamics between mother and infant (Schore, 1994; see Figure A-7 in Schore, 2003a). The evolutionary mechanism of attachment, expressed as the implicit interactive regulation of emotion, fundamentally represents the regulation of biological synchronicity between and within organisms (Schore, 1994). Attachment transactions thus directly influence the "early programming of hemispheric lateralization and synchronization" (Stevenson et al., 2008, p. 352). Within the evolving attachment relationship the more the mother tunes her activity level to the infant during periods of social engagement, the more she allows him to recover quietly in periods of disengagement, and the more she attends to his reinitiating cues for reengagement, the more *synchronized* their interaction. These mutually regulated synchronized interactions are fundamental to the ongoing affective development of the infant. Indeed, at all points of the life span, interactive psychobiological regulation supports the emotional, relational, and survival functions of the right-lateralized self system. Thus synchronized right brain-to-right brain affectively charged dynamics embedded in a co-created attachment bond act as a biopsychosocial mechanism by which humans are sociophysiologically connected to others in order to coregulate their internal homeostatic states (Schore, 2003a).

Applying this interpersonal neurobiological model of the nonverbal attachment bond of emotional communication to the psychodynamics of psychotherapy, my ongoing work describes how the rapid, dynamically fluctuating moment-to-moment state sharing between the patient and therapist represents an organized dialogue, a nonverbal conversation occurring within milliseconds. In this interactive matrix, both partners spontaneously match states and then simultaneously adjust their social attention, stimulation, and physiological arousal in response to their partner's signals (Schore, 2003b). It is this state sharing that allows each person's conscious and especially unconscious states of mind to be known to the other implicitly. More specifically, at levels below conscious awareness, the psychobiologically attuned, empathic, intuitive clinician, from the first point of contact, is learning the nonverbal moment-to-moment rhythmic structures of the patient's internal states, and is relatively flexibly and fluidly modifying her own behavior to synchronize with that structure, and thereby a context for the cocreated organization of a therapeutic alliance (Schore, 2003b). Note that this right-lateralized interbrain synchronization allows for the dyadic emergence of a right brain-to-right brain communication system. Neuroscience authors are now describing "a form of therapeutic conversation that can be conceived . . . as a dynamic interplay between right hemispheres" (Meares, 2017, p. 315) and asserting that "the right hemisphere, in fact, truly interprets the mental state not only of its own brain, but the brains (and minds) of others" (Keenan et al., 2005, p. 702).

This interpersonal neurobiological model is supported by a growing body of recent psychotherapy research on the essential role of synchrony in psychotherapy. Koole and Tschacher (2016) now argue interpersonal synchrony establishes interbrain coupling that provides "patient and therapist with access to another's internal states, which facilitates common understanding and emotional sharing. Over time, these interpersonal exchanges may improve patients' emotion-regulatory capacities and therapeutic outcomes" (p. 1). These authors conclude that the single-brain approach "falls short of explaining the dynamic interpersonal aspects of psychotherapy" and that "researchers should therefore adopt an inter brain perspective, by unraveling the interactions between the patient's and therapist's brains" (p. 12). The construct of synchrony has also been associated with emotional contagion. Dezecache and his colleagues (2013) state that an unconscious and spontaneous tendency to automatically synchronize and mimic facial expressions, vocalizations, postures, and movements with those of another person and consequently to converge emotionally is commonly activated in dyadic interactions (including psychotherapy). There is now a growing consensus in the developmental and the clinical literatures that empathy, a central construct in all forms of psychotherapy, is fundamentally a mature form of synchrony (Imel et al., 2014; Schore, 2019b, 2020). Other research shows that in the psychotherapeutic context nonverbal synchrony is associated with positively-valenced affect and better rapport within the therapeutic relationship (Ramseyer & Tschacher, 2011).

In pioneering and groundbreaking research Zhang and her colleagues recently presented the very first hyperscanning research of simultaneous recordings of a patient's brain and a therapist's brain during a face-to-face psychotherapy session in the laboratory (Zhang, 2018). In a non-invasive functional near-infrared spectroscopy (NIRS) study of cortical blood flow entitled "Interpersonal brain synchronization associated with working alliance during psychological counseling," these authors offered a psychotherapy study of college students with moderate stress or troubles in academic activities, problems in interpersonal relationships, or adaptability to their college life, but no psychiatric diagnoses. Over the videotaped 40-minute first counseling session the psychologists' focus was specifically on the clients' emotional states. As a control they used a hyperscanning context where the counselor verbally chatted with the clients about hobbies, entertainment and so on, without focusing on the client's emotional states or personal troubles. They observed increases in interpersonal brain synchronization of the right temporoparietal junction (right TPJ) in both brains during the counseling process, which were related to subjective ratings of the affective "bond or positive personal attachments between dyads."

Furthermore, they reported that the right-lateralized interpersonal brain synchronization was significantly larger in the counseling than the verbal chatting group and noted, "Although psychological counseling was conventionally called 'the talking cure' (Breuer and Freud, 1895) the establishment of a working alliance in the initial session in this study distinguished psychological counselling from verbal chatting." The authors interpreted these finding as showing that the client and the counselor form a right-lateralized interpersonal brain synchronization that plays an essential role in building a working alliance and a positive therapeutic relationship, and that this brain-to-brain coupling facilitates the development of the emotional bond of the therapeutic alliance in the first counseling session. They concluded that counselor training should now focus on how to effectively synchronize with clients, and that this important *nonverbal skill* improves the working alliance.

In a more recent publication this laboratory offered another near-infrared hyperscanning study "Experience-dependent counselor-client brain synchronization during psychological counseling" (Zhang et al., 2020).

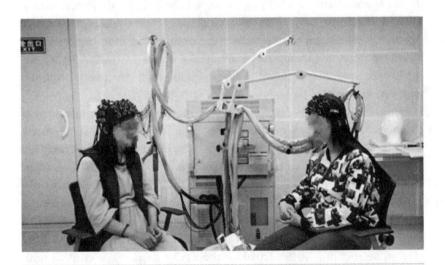

FIGURE 2.2 Experimental design. Hyperscanning NIRS study of right-lateralized interbrain synchronization between client and therapist during a counseling session. From Zhang et al. (2020), "Interpersonal brain synchronization associated with working alliance during psychological counseling," with permission from the author.

Working with a similar clinical population, during the first counseling session the therapeutic dyad focused on emotional states, and in this reciprocal communication both members observed each other's nonverbal cues, facial expressions, and gestures (see Figure 2.2 of this "naturalistic psychological counseling context" in the laboratory). They documented a counseling-induced right-lateralized interpersonal synchronization that was especially evident with clinicians who had more psychotherapy experience. The experienced therapists (psychologists) had 600–4000 hours of clinical experience and utilized an "integrative" clinical approach focusing on empathizing and offering emotional feedback to the client. The expert clinicians reported that they used "moment-to-moment cues (e.g., emotional expression, body posture) and tried to be attentive to their clients' reactions."

The authors demonstrated that in the first session the clinician's ability to specifically focus on the client's emotional states and to interpersonally synchronize with the client is an expression of therapeutic expertise. They concluded that increased interbrain synchronization over the session is associated with tighter interpersonal closeness/connectedness and better alliance/emotional interaction, and that this study confirms an interpersonal synchrony model of psychotherapy which dictates that "the more tightly the client and counselor's brains are coupled, the better the alliance" (Koole & Tschacher, 2016, p. 7). This research also supports the clinical principle that the establishment of an effective relationship is the most important criterion for measuring therapeutic expertise (Norcross, 2011), and that expertise is expressed in the clinical ability to establish an effective relationship with various types of patients (Hill et al., 2017).

Importantly, in both Zhang studies during the therapeutic session synchronous brain activity was seen in specifically the *right temperoparietal junction* of both members of the therapeutic dyad, the exact same right-lateralized brain synchronization as the Dumas pattern of a nonverbal spontaneous reciprocal communication and turn-taking in Figure 2.1. In other words, the right TPJ of the counselor is interpersonally synchronized with the right TPJ of the client, what I have termed a right-lateralized interbrain synchronization and a right brain-to-right brain nonverbal communication system, see Schore, 2019b, 2020). Note in this therapeutic context both the therapist and the patient have shifted dominance from the left to right hemisphere, a synchronized mutual regression "beneath the words." In total these hyperscanning data directly support my assertion that the right hemisphere is dominant in psychotherapy (Schore, 2014).

In another groundbreaking article overviewing hyperscanning research, Ray and his colleagues (2017), using the Dumas image of coupled, synchronized right brains (see Figure 2.1), asserted that among all forms of interbrain communications, the communication of emotion is the most important process for mental health. They offer clinical applications of this new and state-of-the-art "multibrain" functional neuroimaging methodology. These authors argue that the interpersonal perspective of between-brain functional connectivity can allow for a deeper understanding of the *relational* deficits of a wide range of psychopathologies, personality disorders, depression, social anxiety disorder, autism spectrum disorders, schizophrenia, somatic symptom disorder, sexual dysfunctions, and suicide. Most intriguingly, they see the direct application of this paradigm shift in interbrain neuroimaging to fundamental research on the therapeutic alliance, which is defined as the collaborative bond between patient and therapist and is now considered "the quintessential integrative variable" (Wolfe & Goldfried, 1988). Furthermore, they stress the need for interbrain connectivity between the patient and the therapist, especially during the early detection and repair of ruptures of the therapeutic alliance.

Applications of Interpersonal Neurobiology to Change Mechanisms of Psychotherapy

Attachment, Transference-Countertransference Communications, and Implicit Affect Regulation

At the clinical, theoretical, and research levels, the ongoing paradigm shift within the mental health field is expressed in updated models of change in therapeutic action that have migrated from left hemisphere conscious cognition to right hemisphere unconscious emotional and relational mechanisms, from a reasoned narrative to a spontaneous conversation. Over three decades I have continued to describe the underlying implicit neurobiological mechanisms of the right brain in affective communications of regulated and dysregulated attachment dynamics, stressful transference-countertransference transactions, and affect regulation, which all operate at levels beneath conscious awareness (Schore, 1994, 2003b, 2012, 2019b). My work specifically focuses on the enduring negative impacts of what I have termed developmental "relational trauma" (Schore, 2001) on the individual's right-lateralized subjective self's capacity for communicating with other minds, that is, intersubjectivity, as well as for attachment, the interactive regulation of emotion. Conscious and especially unconscious dysregulating experiences are communicated within the emotional attachment bond cocreated between patient and therapist on a millisecond time scale, right brain to right brain, especially in moments of affective shifts into and out of stressful subjective emotional states. These relational stressors of the therapeutic alliance are an essential element in dyadic rupture and repair transactions, a central relational mechanism of the treatment.

From the perspective of modern attachment theory (Schore & Schore, 2008) right brain attachment style refers not only to different strategies of emotion regulation but also to relational styles of synchronized right-lateralized nonverbal interbrain communications. In psychotherapy, as in early development, the right-lateralized attachment mechanism is interpersonally expressed in regulated and dysregulated right brain-to-right brain nonverbal facial, prosodic, and gestural emotional communications. These affective transactions can be interactively regulated, a core mechanism of the affective bond between two right brains. My clinical models focus on the treatment of various attachment disorders, where I discuss the diversity of attachment orientations and differences in attachment security, that is, personality differences in strategies of unconscious (and not conscious) affect regulation. This "subliminal affect regulation" does not rely on the limited capacity of the conscious mind and resists conscious intervention (Jostmann et al., 2005). Deep growth-promoting psychotherapy thus focuses on psychoneurobiological changes in the patient's unconscious internal working model of attachment.

In 2014 I published an article in an issue of the American Psychological Association Division 29 flagship journal *Psychotherapy*, offering clinical and neurobiological evidence that the right brain is dominant in psychotherapy (Schore, 2014). The focus of the work was on the implicit relational mechanisms of the right brain within the patient-therapist dyad that implicitly operate beneath the words of their verbal narrative. In such nonconscious moment-to-moment body-based communications, the empathic intuitive therapist can intrasubjectively attend to "barely perceptible cues that signal a change of state" in both the patient and herself, and to intersubjectively detect the patient's "nonverbal behaviors and shifts in affects." During these transactions, the psychobiologically attuned clinician, especially at moments of direct eye contact, can interpersonally synchronize with and match the patient's rhythmic patterns of emotional arousal, especially into and out of different affective states. This right brain state sharing in turn allows the therapist to enter into the patient's changing feeling state, in order to "follow the affect" (Schore, 1994) and to act as an implicit affect regulator of the patient's dysregulated emotional states. Psychotherapeutic synchronized and interactively regulated right-lateralized communications facilitate neuroplastic structural changes in the patient's right brain regulatory systems, which in turn allow for optimal treatment outcomes in both symptom-reducing and growth-promoting psychotherapies.

In addition to attachment dynamics, the clinical constructs of transference and countertransference lie at the theoretical and clinical core of psychotherapy change mechanisms. Current psychodynamic models of transference now contend that "no appreciation of transference can do without emotion" (Pincus et al., 2007, p. 634). Clinicians describe transference as "an established pattern of relating and emotional responding that is cued by something in the present, but oftentimes calls up both an affective state and thoughts that may have more to do with past experience than present ones" (Maroda, 2005, p. 134). This concept is echoed in neuroscience, where Shuren and Grafman (2002) assert, "The right hemisphere holds representations of the emotional states associated with events experienced by the individual. When that individual encounters a familiar scenario, representations of past emotional experiences are retrieved by the right hemisphere and are incorporated into the reasoning process" (p. 918). Note that both literatures emphasize the importance of accessing past emotional and relational experiences in the therapeutic process. It is important to note that transference-countertransference is now being seen as a central mechanism of not just psychodynamic but all forms of psychotherapy (e.g., see Cartwright, 2011).

In my ongoing work in neuropsychoanalysis, the science of unconscious processes, I continue to offer both theoretical and clinical models of early developing interbrain transference-countertransference transactions. This reactivation of early right-lateralized negatively valenced autobiographical memories is communicated in bidirectional, nonverbal, nonconscious, right brain/mind/body affectively stressful transactions between the patient and therapist. Transferential body-based limbic-autonomic communications are expressed in nonverbal, visual, auditory, and gestural affective cues that are spontaneously generated from the face, voice, and body of the patient. Beneath the words, the intuitive clinician's countertransferential responses to these communications of intense, negatively-valenced affects are appraised by the therapist's observations of his own visceral reactions to the patient's material. The empathic clinician's countertransferences to the patient's unconscious communications are thus experienced as subjective interoceptive autonomic responses that are reactions on an unconscious level to the patient's nonverbal messages. Stressful countertransference dynamics are manifest in the therapist's capacity to recognize and utilize the sensory (visual, auditory, tactile, kinesthetic, and olfactory) and affective qualities of imagery that the patient generates in the psychotherapist. In heightened affective moments of the treatment, these interpersonal stressors perturb the therapeutic alliance, bringing back into consciousness autobiographical developmental ruptures of the attachment bond and early dysregulated intense affective states such as fear, aggression, loss and despair, and shame. Thus, through transference-countertransference transactions the dyadic therapeutic relationship can jointly process reenactments of early stress-related attachment dynamics, including highly dysregulated states of relational trauma.

In my 2012 volume *The Science of the Art of Psychotherapy*, I offered a chapter, "Therapeutic Enactments: Working in Right Brain Windows of Affect Tolerance," in which I discussed the interpersonal neurobiology of right brain-to-right brain transference-countertransference transactions. In that work, I cited Maroda's (1998) classic definition of the term:

> Enactment is an affectively driven-repetition of converging emotional scenarios from the patient's and the analyst's lives. It is not merely an affectively driven set of behaviors; it is necessarily a repetition of past events that have been buried in the unconscious due to associated unmanageable or unwanted emotion. (p. 520)

Maroda also stated that for the patient the enactment "is his or her chance to relive the past, from an affective standpoint, with a new opportunity for awareness and integration" (p. 520).

It is important to note that therapeutic enactments are common in histories of nonverbal attachment trauma. Borgogno and Vigna-Taglianti (2008) observe,

> In patients whose psychic suffering originates in . . . preverbal trauma . . . transference occurs mostly at a more primitive level of expression that involves in an unconscious way . . . not only the patient but the [therapist]. . . . These more archaic forms of the transference-countertransference issue—which frequently set aside verbal contents—take shape in the [therapeutic] setting though actual mutual enactments. (p. 314)

In working with such patients, during a sudden rupture of the attachment bond embedded in the therapeutic alliance, both the patient and therapist are non-verbally reenacting a traumatic pathological object relation, an internal interactive representation of a dysregulated self interacting with a misattuning other.

In such *shared* stressful reenactments of attachment trauma, rupture, repair, and regulation of the patient's dysregulated affects may act as a core mechanism of therapeutic action (Schore, 2012). As the result of the nonverbal communication and implicit emotion regulation (Koole & Rothermund, (2011) within the strengthening therapeutic relationship, intense right brain emotional attachment communications can be synchronized, resonated, and amplified in both members of the therapeutic dyad. According to White-head, "Emotions are deepened in intensity and sustained in time when they are intersubjectively shared. This occurs at moments of deep contact" (2006, p. 624). In these heightened affective moments of mutual gaze, the therapeutic relationship acts as a nonverbal right brain emotional resonance system, in which right-lateralized interbrain synchronization amplifies affect, allowing affects beneath levels of awareness to come into consciousness in both. In this manner, emotionally shared and interactively regulated mutual enactments promote the integration of the patient's right brain. Thus, in neurobiologically informed psychodynamic models, not only conscious but unconscious affects can be communicated and interactively regulated.

Synchronized Mutual Regressions and Reenactments of Attachment Trauma

In addition to the attachment mechanism, transference-countertransference communications of early developmental trauma, and clinical enactments, the clinical construct of mutual regression acts as a core mechanism that can promote emotional growth and development in psychotherapy, especially in psychodynamic psychotherapy. This interpersonal neurobiological mechanism allows the patient and the empathic clinician to reexperience *together* developmentally dysregulated emotional and relational stressors in a therapeutic reenactment of early attachment dynamics, in order to provide a growth-promoting context that over time can transform an insecure into a secure attachment pattern. In order for this to be achieved, there needs to be a mechanism that can transiently shift dominance from the patient's left brain into his or her right brain, the repository of early developing attachment memories.

The neurobiological mechanism of regression from the "higher" left to the "lower" right hemisphere, acting at rapid and thereby unconscious levels, provides such transient shifts in brain laterality. Callosally mediated reversals of hemispheric dominance are known to take place at speeds between 50 and 100 milliseconds, well below conscious awareness. McGilchrist (2009) described this interhemispheric dynamic: "We must inhibit one in order to inhabit the other," clearly implying that the left prefrontal cortex must be inhibited (taken off-line) in order to bring the disinhibited right prefrontal system from the background to the foreground of consciousness. The clinical dictum "safe but not too safe" means not staying too entrenched in the left mind, which processes the familiar, but allowing access to the right mind, which processes the unexpected and the novel, essential components of new corrective emotional experiences.

Indeed, this left-right inversion of hemispheric dominance is described by the psychoanalyst Heinz Kohut: "The *deeper* layers of the analyst's psyche are *open* to the stimuli which emanate from the patient's communications while the *intellectual activities of the higher levels of cognition are temporarily largely but selectively suspended*" (1971, p. 274, emphasis added). This transient hemispheric inversion now allows the intuitive clinician to enter into what Carl Rogers termed a state of empathy with the patient: "It means entering the private perceptual world of the other . . . being sensitive, moment by moment, to the changing felt meanings which flow in the other person. . . . It means sensing meaning of which he or she is *scarcely aware* (1980, p. 142, emphasis added). Note these dynamics enable the therapist to enter into the patient's unconscious states. This sudden switch of hemispheric dominance is frequently accompanied by a rapid shift from the clinician's left hemispheric cognitive empathy, an intellectual understanding of the patient, into a right brain body-based affective empathy.

Furthermore, in light of the current two-person relational model, the construct is transformed from an intrapsychic regression within one brain to an interpersonal mutual regression shared by two interacting brains. In this manner, the therapeutic dyad can access an interpersonal synchronization mechanism that can transiently induce a callosal reversible dominance of the hemispheres in both patient and therapist, from the verbal and cognitive functions of their later-developing higher verbal left hemisphere to the nonverbal and social-emotional functions of their early-developing lower right hemisphere. This spontaneous synchronized state shift allows the therapeutic dyad to transition from "top-down" to "bottom-up" work.

In my inceptive 1994 volume *Affect Regulation and the Origin of the Self*, I suggested that a "temporal regression" represents a "downward state shift, that allows access to older memory stores of previous developmental stages" (Schore, 1994). More recently I have suggested that in terms of developmental neuroscience, this specifically refers to a regression and release of "lower" right brain structures and preverbal functions that first evolve in the prenatal and postnatal stages of early brain development, before the later-maturing "higher" left brain growth spurt of language functions in the late second and third year. These transient regressions to the psychic activities of early social-emotional maturation are clinically manifest in the aforementioned moments of the reemergence of right brain attachment and transference-countertransference dynamics. As a result of the ongoing communication and regulation of the patient's conscious and unconscious affects in the evolving therapeutic alliance, synchronized shifts in brain laterality embedded in mutual regressions can act as a growth-promoting therapeutic interpersonal neurobiological mechanism that can lead to progressions in the structural and functional complexity of the evolving right brain.

At the very beginnings of modern neurology in the late 19th century, the pioneering brain laterality studies of Paul Broca and Carl Wernicke focused on the role of different language functions of the left hemisphere. Yet shortly after, John Hughlings Jackson, the father of British neurology, was first to discuss the role of the right hemisphere in emotional processes, to articulate a model of the hierarchical organization of the brain, and to describe the role of regression from later-forming "higher," "voluntary" levels to early-forming "lower," "automatic," "primitive" levels of the brain (Jackson, 1879, 1931). Jackson thus asserted that regression from "higher" to "lower" levels represents a *"taking off of the higher"* and *"at the very same time a letting go, or expression of the lower"* (see Schore 2003b, 2012, 2019b). This downward movement into lower levels allows access into temporally earlier stages of brain development. Jackson directly influenced Freud's psychoanalytic conception of the hierarchical relation of the later-developing higher verbal ego's inhibition of lower early-developing nonverbal id processes, and his psychoanalytic model of a temporal regression as a return to an earlier stage of life and to more "primitive methods of expression and representation" (Freud, 1900). He later wrote, "unconscious processes only become cognizable . . .when processes of the higher preconscious system are set back to an earlier stage by being lowered (by regression). In themselves they cannot be cognized" (Freud, 1915, p. 186). Yet over the course of his career Freud was ambivalent about the clinical value of therapeutic regressions.

Indeed, the construct of clinical regression has been controversial. Even in the present time, a common bias still exists across the sciences that favors the "higher" left brain rational conscious mind over the "lower" right brain emotional unconscious mind. Echoing the respective differences between the non-dominant right and dominant left hemispheres, Aron and Bushra (1998) point out that "regression, the body, the woman, the child, the playful, the passionate, and the fantastic have often been positioned unfavorably behind/below progression, the mind, the man, the adult, the industrious, the cerebral, and the realistic" (p. 390). Over most of the last century, the classical psychoanalytic position viewed regression in pejorative, maladaptive terms: "pathological regression." On the other hand, for some time a large body of psychoanalytic ego psychology research has described adaptive regressions in the service of the ego that promote the growth and development of the self (Kris, 1952).

In contrast to Freud, by the second half of the last century a number of master psychoanalytic clinicians offered theoretical and case studies on the adaptive role of regression in the treatment of early-evolving growth-inhibiting maternal-infant psychodynamics. In 1958, the pediatrician-psychoanalyst Donald Winnicott asserted,

It is commonly thought that there is some danger in the regression during psychoanalysis. The danger does not lie in the regression but in the analyst's unreadiness to meet the regression and the dependence which belongs to it. When an analyst has had experience that makes him confident in his management of regression, then it is probably true to say that the more quickly the analyst accepts the regression and meets it fully the less likely it is that the patient will need to enter into an illness with regressive qualities. (p. 261)

In other writings, Michael Balint (1968) described the dangers of "malignant" (dysregulated) regressions that "overwhelm the ego," but also emphasized the value of "benign" (regulated) regressions, suggesting these are beneficial when the clinician provides an accepting atmosphere in which the patient feels safe enough to regress "for the sake of recognition" and "understanding and shared experiencing." This regression work involves encounters with emotional pain which trigger primitive psychological defenses that expose "a basic fault" or (dissociative) "gaps":

Thus, the first task of the understanding analyst, who has determined that

therapeutic regression is indicated, involves the facilitation of a trusting
therapeutic partnership that encourages the dissolution of resistances to
that regression. Once this is accomplished, the function of the treatment
is to allow the patient to experience acceptance and recognition. In this
way, the treatment provides what was unavailable during the patient's
early life. (Balint, 1968, p. 469)

In this work he recommended that the clinician be "unobtrusive and ordinary" so that a treatment environment would be created in which the patient
could experience a benign form of regression in a therapeutic context of "a
new beginning." He further concluded that these regressions allowed access
to the patient's inner world and his or her way of being in the world.

In later pioneering studies, Philip Bromberg (1979) postulated that therapeutic regressions represented "a fundamental component of psychoanalysis" that act as "the royal road to new growth." He posited that "the ego
(or self), in order to grow, must voluntarily allow itself to become less than
intact—to regress. Empirically this is one way of defining regression in the
service of the ego" (p. 653). Accordingly, "The deeper the regression that can
be safely allowed by the patient, the richer the experience and the greater
its reverberation on the total organization of the self. . . . For the deepest
analytic growth to occur, the new experience must require that the existing
pattern of self representation reorganizes in order to make room for it" (p.
654). Bromberg asserted that regression in therapy is a naturally occurring
process, if not impeded by too much interaction on the therapist's part.

In the next decade, Boyer (1990) described the importance of a "compli-
mentary regression of patient and therapist":

The analyst's awareness of his own fantasies, emotional states, and physical sensations that occur during his free-floating attention (and at times
subsequent dreams) enables him to be more in tune with his patient's
communications, and that such awareness is especially useful in working
with the regressed patient. The analyst's tolerance of the patient's primitive regressions . . . as they are relived in the analytic situation, entails his
capacity to *regress concomitantly with his patient*, while simultaneously retain-
ing the observing function of his ego. (pp. 209–210, emphasis added)

In 1996, Hamilton wrote on the value of adaptive clinical mutual
regressions:

I think in Winnicottian and Balint's terms, which are very similar . . .
that is, in terms of the basic fault and therapeutic regression where, in
the analysis, the patient gets back to much earlier states of development,
perhaps to traumatic or pretraumatic states. And working with these
states, both in terms of experiencing and in terms of interpretation. Very
often, it is the noninterpretation that is as important, the *experience* of
the analytic situation. And also it can be very important *not to interpret*
because interpretation, particularly transference interpretation, can take
the patient out of a state of regression. It is better to allow the patient to
experience what it is like to be in that state and *for you to be in the regression with them*. . . . You should do everything you can to keep yourself as
"unobtrusive," in Balint's phrase, as possible. (p. 259, emphasis added)

Note the direct allusion to a relational two-person model of mutual
regression into an early traumatic state. Also note the emphasis in these
moments of the treatment not on left hemispheric language interpretations but on shared right hemispheric emotional experience in the
synchronized downshift of state. Giovacchini described the importance
of the therapist's creative processes in these moments of the treatment,
when "a broad range of functioning . . . traverses various levels of the
psyche, frequently reaching down to the very earliest, primary process
oriented parts of the self. Ego boundaries, in turn, can become quite fluid
and permeable, even though they are ordinarily firmly established and
well structured" (1991, p. 187).

At the beginning of this century, Tuttman (2002) advocated,

The skilled acceptance of regression to the traumatic developmental
phases where something needed for growth was missing, and then facilitating understanding and growth from that point forward, via an analytical relationship that has transitional, mirroring, non-autocratic, and
synthetic qualities along with play and experimentation, are necessary
steps in such treatment if healthy individuation is to occur. (pp. 469–470)

In a 2011 article, "Progressing While Regressing in Relationships," Levine
concluded,

Regression may be a necessary means of accessing and addressing the
inaccessible parts of the self. Regressions move to different emotionally

vulnerable and unformulated points of trauma, developmental and structural weaknesses, and unresolved conflict. Regressive states may hold an
unfiltered raw, immediate way of experiencing that could be a source for
creative, inspired experience, a sense of aliveness—a regression in the
service of the ego. (p. 625)

She further observed that regressions to "more primitive interpersonal interactions . . . can sometimes provide opportunities for the development both
of a more integrated self and more mature relating" (Levine, 2011, p. 621).

In 2015, Aron and Atlas stated, "Enactments may well be a central means
by which patients and analysts enter into each other's inner world and discover themselves as participants with each other's psychic life, mutually
constructing the relational matrix that constitutes the medium of psychoanalysis" (p. 316). Most recently, Grossmark (2018) referred back to Balint's
(1968) classic work on adaptive "benign regressions": "His invaluable observation was that it was the *relationship* between the analyst and the patient
itself that was paramount for the treatment to progress and furthermore
observed that regressed patients seemed to require a form of relatedness
that was 'more primitive than that obtaining between two adults'" (p. 247,
emphasis added). Notice that therapeutic regressions are an emergent property of a strengthening nonverbal therapeutic relationship.

Further Thoughts on Surrendering
Into Mutual Regressions

In my own neurobiological studies of therapeutic regression, I have focused
on a shift of clinical focus from the left to right brain, and on therapeutic
state transitions from the left to the right hemisphere. In chapters 3 and
4 of *Right Brain Psychotherapy*, I elaborate an interpersonal neurobiological
model of mutual regressions into earlier stages of right brain emotional
development within the dynamically evolving therapeutic relationship
(Schore, 2019b). This ongoing work on the neuropsychoanalytic change
mechanisms embedded in the evolving therapeutic alliance describes how
in heightened affective moments of the treatment this instant reversal in
hemispheric dominance allows the activities of the right hemisphere to suddenly shift from the background into the foreground of psychic life, along
with a switch into an emotional subjective state of consciousness.

This transient loosening of dominance of the left over the right hemisphere is expressed in a functional regression from the verbal, cognitive, analytical, explicit functions of the conscious mind to the nonverbal, emotional-imagistic, intuitive, implicit functions of the unconscious mind. In a mutual regression, the relational unconscious of one right brain interacts with another relational unconscious, which also shifts from a left brain-to-left brain conscious verbal language communication system to a right brain-to-right brain unconscious nonverbal emotional communication system. Regression represents a state shift from "higher" left brain conscious cognition to "lower" unconscious body-based affect, from later-forming cortical to early-maturing subcortical systems, and from the central nervous system to the autonomic nervous system, what Jackson (1931) termed "the physiological bottom of the mind." In therapeutic heightened affective moments when the patient is experiencing a right brain emotional state, the psychobiologically attuned empathic therapist implicitly surrenders into a regression, releasing a shift of the reversible dominance of the left over the right hemisphere, and thereby into intersubjective contact with the patient's emotional, automatic state (see Schore, 2019a, 2019b).

In classic ego psychological writings, Reik (1948) argued that as the creative clinician *surrenders* to the regression, he instantiates a shift from (left hemispheric) secondary process cognition into (right hemispheric) primary process cognition, which is necessary for producing novel, original ideas. He observed that surrender is associated with access to an uncanny insight and a conscious intuition into the patient's dynamics. Ghent (1990) proposed that this surrender or letting go is not a voluntary activity, and it does not necessarily require another person's presence, "except possibly as a guide." Indeed, it allows for a context in which "secondary processes have receded from consciousness," thereby facilitating an experience of being *"in the moment"* and *"totally in the present"* (Ghent, 1990, p. 111). According to Ghent, this surrendering into a regression is described as a *"letting down of defensive barriers"* that potentially allows for "a liberation and expansion of the self" (p. 108, emphasis added).

Aron and Bushra (1998) have used the construct of regression to describe a particular "loosening of structure" in which the clinician "is not seen as remaining in a 'normal,' 'rational' state holding the patient who regresses to a primitive or childish state," but rather a "mutual regression" in which both move "through a wide range of states, each mutually regsulating the other's experience as the process unfolds. For this process to work, patient and analyst must differentially surrender to one another and become transformed" (p. 408). I would add that therapeutic boundaries between the patient and therapist must be firmly established and well-structured before they can be loosened and become more fluid, permeable, and flexible.

Thus, the key to an adaptive mutual regression is a synchronized shift from the patient's and the therapist's rational, verbal left minds into their nonverbal, emotional right minds, and thereby the coconstruction of a "working relationship" between their unconscious minds. Tschacher and Meier (2019) state, "Synchrony is generally defined as the social coupling of two (or more) individuals in the here-and-now of a communication context that emerges alongside, and *in addition to, their verbal exchanges*" (p. 1, emphasis added). In an article in *The Lancet*, "Psychoanalysis in Modern Mental Health Practice," Yakeley (2018) asserts,

> Nonverbal-communication, and other implicit relational and affective processes within the intersubjective relationship between patient and therapist are now recognized as crucial factors in initiating therapeutic change in psychoanalytic psychotherapy, in addition to the traditional mutative role assigned to the patient who gains a conscious insight into their difficulties. (p. 448)

Recall, synchrony is associated with physiological linkage, affective reciprocal interchange, emotion transmission, and coregulation. In the above article, "Physiological Synchrony in Psychotherapy Sessions" Tschacher and Meier (2019) show that the therapeutic alliance is *nonverbally and physiologically* grounded in autonomic nervous system (ANS) activity, which "occurs outside conscious awareness and volition" (p. 2). These authors offer a prototype for synchrony assessments in psychotherapy sessions. Four physiological signals (heart rate variability, heart rate, respiration, and electrocardiogram) were recorded simultaneously from a therapist and her patient in naturalistic psychotherapy sessions. The clinician, a female psychologist and psychodynamic therapist and four regular clients were physiologically monitored in 93 sessions with durations of up to 60 minutes. They report that the therapeutic alliance rated by the client or therapist was positively associated with physiological synchrony, which is expressed in shared patterns of autonomic arousal. They conclude that the "sociophysiological coupling" between therapist and client "speaks for the sympathetic and parasympathetic coupling between the therapist and her client and its links with ratings of the therapy process" (p. 1). This laboratory is now calling for further research on "sympathetic and parasympathetic synchronization" in psychotherapy (Tschacher, Ramseyer, & Koole, 2018).

In addition, there is a growing consensus in both the developmental and clinical literatures that empathy, a central construct of all forms of psychotherapy, is fundamentally a mature form of synchrony. Over time the emotionally empathic clinician, sensitive to even low levels of a patient's dynamic subjective shifts into and out of states of affective autonomic arousal, learns how to fluidly synchronize this shift with the patient's shifts. This right-lateralized synchronization of a mutual regression allows for intersubjective communication and interactive regulation of right brain stressful dysregulating conscious and unconscious affects, especially in reenactments of early attachment dynamics.

Furthermore, in *Right Brain Psychotherapy* I discuss the affect-inhibiting roles of the character defenses of dissociation and repression in both the patient and therapist in synchronized mutual regressions. Citing case material, I offer a clinical model for working with the defensive coping strategies embedded in adaptive clinical regressions, especially in enactments of unconscious dissociated affect in spontaneous mutual regressions, and unconscious repressed affect in voluntary mutual regressions. I suggest that dissociation acts as an early-appearing defense against preverbal traumatic affects such as terror, rage, and hopeless despair that are generated subcortically in the right brain, while repression is a later-evolving developmentally more advanced defense in which painful negative affects that are represented at the cortical level of the right brain are barred access to the left hemispheric conscious mind (Schore, 2019b, in press).

These dual affective defenses represent a major counterforce to the emotional-motivational aspects of the change process in psychotherapy, and thus a graded lowering of these defenses and release of regulatable negative affect during mutual regressions represent a stressful yet valuable opportunity for intense painful affects beneath defenses to be subjectively experienced, communicated, and interactively regulated within the co-constructed therapeutic alliance, thereby increasing the patient's affect tolerance. Such left- and right-lateralized defenses against strong affect are universal, and therefore also exist in the clinician. In heightened affective moments of relational stress within the therapeutic relationship, enactments of rupture and repair must be surrendered into and not avoided. This callosal left-right shift, a "taking off of the higher and at the same time a letting go or expression of the lower" is critical to the clinician's participation in mutual regressions. In other words, not only the patient's but the therapist's defenses must be addressed in clinical models of psychotherapeutic change. Indeed, according to Russell (1998), "The most important source of resistance in the treatment process is the therapist's resistance to what the patient feels" (p. 19).

Transient inversions of hemispheric dominance thus underly the therapist's entrance into a creative regression by intuitively surrendering out of the analytic left hemisphere, specialized for cognitive control, and into the emotional right hemisphere, specialized for both vulnerability and creativity (Hecht, 2014). The research of Mayseless and Shamay-Tsoory (2015) demonstrates that reducing left frontal and enhancing right frontal activity lessens cognitive control, allowing for more creative idea production. Within this intersubjective context, the therapist's disciplined spontaneous regression activates a shift from left hemispheric control and certainty to right hemispheric openness, vulnerability, uncertainty, humility, and authenticity. In this hemispheric transition, the empathic therapist's state switch of hemispheric dominance and reduced defensiveness allows for the implicit reception and intuitive affect regulation (Koole & Jostmann, 2004) of the patient's right brain-to-right brain nonverbally communicated negatively (and positively) valenced affective states. Note that in the moment of a left-right shift, cognitive appraisal and mentalization, which Fonagy defines as the ability to interpret the mental states of others and is associated with left hemispheric activation (Nolte et al., 2010), is deactivated.

A central goal of the interdisciplinary field of interpersonal neurobiology is to more deeply understand the underlying mechanisms by which the structure and function of the mind and brain are shaped by experiences, especially those involving emotional experiences, as well as the relational mechanisms by which communicating brains align and synchronize their neural activities with other brains. Overall, the clinical organizing principle for working with mutual regressions and relational trauma in a mutual enactment, and indeed with any disturbance of affect regulation, dictates that the psychobiologically attuned empathic therapist facilitates the patient reexperiencing overwhelming affects in incrementally titrated, increasing affectively tolerable doses in the context of a safe environment, so that overwhelming traumatic feelings can be regulated, come into consciousness, and be adaptively integrated into the patient's emotional life. In this manner, adaptive, interactively regulated mutual regressions within synchronized reenactments "generate interpersonal as well as internal processes eventually capable of promoting integration and growth" (Ginot, 2007, p. 317).

At present, there is a paradigm shift in the construct of regression, just as with the related concepts of relational trauma and clinical enactments. It is now thought that attachment reenactments are not technical mistakes of the therapist or the patient's acting out but that "the [clinician's] sensitivity, or her right brain readiness to be fully attuned to nonverbal communication, is a necessary therapeutic skill. Becoming entangled in an enactment, although at first out of awareness, is a surprising facet of such sensitivity" (Ginot, 2007, p. 297). Bass (2003) observes that enactments represent especially challenging moments for the clinician and may be decisive turning points in the therapy. He argues that these are times of both high risk and high gain for both patient and therapist. Aron and Atlas (2015) assert, "Just as we may 'get stuck' in enactments, unable to work our way out of them so too we may inhibit or avoid entering into or surrendering to therapeutically generative enactments" (p. 322). Regulated reenactments of attachment trauma represent valuable opportunities for therapeutic change, including changes in attachment patterns, yet at the same time challenge even experienced clinicians (see Schore [2019b, 2020] for clinical examples in both individual and group psychotherapy).

It is important to note that these enactments occur in the context of a progressively stable therapeutic alliance over time, one that provides increasing levels of safety and trust for the patient. As the neuroscience research indicates, right-lateralized interbrain synchronization increases in partners with a shared communication history. Interactively regulated mutual regressions embedded in an evolving, strengthening, emotional attachment bond between the therapist and patient thus represent critical interpersonal contexts which facilitate the growth of more complex emotional and relational functions that lie at the core of more intimate, loving relationships (Schore, 2019a, 2019b, in press).

Indeed, enactments are now seen as an emergent property of an evolving therapeutic relationship that provides an intersubjective context of effective communication and regulation of strong affects. The cocreation of a therapeutic alliance may take longer in patients with disorganized rather than organized attachments, and in patients who under relational stress characterologically access the early-forming primitive defense of dissociation rather than later-forming repression (Schore, 2012, 2019b). In the latter case, a central focus of the therapy is on building a relatively stable therapeutic relationship of emotional engagement with a patient who has had a long history of relationships that provided low levels of predictability, sensitivity, safety, and trust.

Across all forms of deep, long-term psychotherapy, a primary goal of growth-promoting (as opposed to symptom-reducing) treatment models is to change internal working models of attachment, which, according to the psychoanalyst-psychiatrist John Bowlby are represented on unconscious levels. This clearly indicates that the therapeutic relationship, the emotional bond between the patient and therapist, needs to access a psychoneurobiological mechanism that allows for (re)activation of the early-developing right-lateralized attachment system that operates below conscious awareness. In both development and psychotherapy, attachment dynamics shape the experience-dependent maturation of the right brain, the psychobiological substrate of the human unconscious mind. This clearly implies access to a regulatory mechanism of therapeutic action that can shift out of the higher levels of the left into the lower levels of the right brain and back again.

Over time, as interpersonal synchrony and right-lateralized interbrain coupling increases in the evolving therapeutic relationship, both members of the collaborative working alliance will nonconsciously increase the use of the word "we" in spontaneous emotionally-laden therapeutic conversations. As the dyad builds up a shared history of traveling down "the royal road to new growth" together, interpersonally synchronized and interactively regulated mutual regressions represent an adaptive social-emotional therapeutic mechanism that can not only reduce the patient's anxiety and depression symptomatology but also can potentially transform a right brain insecure attachment into an earned-secure attachment, thereby making structural maturational changes in the deep core of the personality. These therapeutic changes reflect enhanced synaptic growth in the regulatory circuits of the right brain, especially in what Kuhl, Quirin, & Koole (2015) term "the integrated self (that) is supported by parallel-distributed processing in the right anterior cortex," and its adaptive right-lateralized functions that are specifically expressed in "emotional connectedness, broad vigilance, utilization of felt feedback, unconscious processing, integration of negative experiences, extended resilience, and extended trust" (p. 115). Every one of these essential processes of the right mind are activated in the psychotherapeutic relationship. I suggest that the core clinical skills of any effective psychotherapy are directly grounded in the subliminal implicit, communicational, emotional, and survival functions of the intuitive therapist's non-verbal, unconscious mind.

In total, this work strongly supports the clinical principle that the right brain is dominant in symptom-reducing and growth-promoting deep psychotherapy. In both, but perhaps even more so in the latter, the therapist's relational and emotional expertise in forming psychotherapeutic relationships with a wide variety of patients, more than a mastery of techniques, lies at the core of the art of psychotherapy.

References

Aron, L., & Atlas, G. (2015). Generative enactment: Memories from the future. *Psychoanalytic Dialogues, 25*, 309–324.

Aron, L., & Bushra, A. (1998). Mutual regression: Altered states in the psychoanalytic situation. *Journal of the American Psychoanalytic Association, 46*, 389–412.

Balint, M. (1968). *The basic fault: Therapeutic aspects of regression.* London: Tavistock.

Bass, A. (2003). "E" enactments in psychoanalysis: Another medium, another message. *Psychoanalytic Dialogues, 13*, 657–675.

Borgogno, F., & Vigna- Taglianti, M. (2008). Role- reversal: A somewhat neglected mirror of heritages of the past. *American Journal of Psychoanalysis, 68*, 313– 328.

Boyer, L. B. (1990). Regression in treatment: On early object relations. In P. L. Giovacchini (Ed.), *Tactics and techniques in psychoanalytic therapy: Vol. 3. The implications of Winnicott's contributions* (pp. 200–225). Northvale, NJ: Aronson.

Breuer, J., & Freud, S. (1893-1895). Studies on hysteria. In J. Strachey (Ed. and Trans.), *The standard edition of the complete psychological works of Sigmund Freud* (Vol. 2, pp. 1–335). London: Hogarth.

Bromberg, P. M. (1979). Interpersonal psychoanalysis and regression. *Contemporary Psychoanalysis, 15*, 647–655.

Cartwright, C. (2011). Transference, countertransference, and reflective practice in cognitive therapy. *Clinical Psychologist, 15*, 112–120.

Chelazzi, L., Bisley, J.W., & Bartolmeo, P. (2018). The unconscious guidance of attention. *Cortex, 102*, 1–5.

Decety, J., & Lamm, C. (2007). The role of the right temporoparietal junction in social interaction: How low-level computational processes contribute to meta-cognition. *Neuroscientist, 13*, 580– 593.

Dezecache, G., Conty, L., Chadwick, M., Philip, P., Soussignan, R., Sperber, D., & Grezes, J. (2013). Evidence for unintentional emotional contagion beyond dyads. *PLOS ONE, 8*(1), e67371.

Dumas, G. (2011). Towards a two-body neuroscience. *Communicative and Integrative Biology, 4*, 349–352.

Dumas, G., Nadel, J., Soussignan, R., Martinerie, J., & Garnero, L. (2010). Inter-brain synchronization during social interaction. *PLOS ONE, 5*, e12166.

Dumas, G., Moreau, Q., Tognoli, E., & Kelso, J.A.S. (2020). The human dynamic clamp reveals the fronto-parietal network linking real-time social coordination and cognition. *Cerebral Cortex, 30*, 3271–3285.

Freud, S. (1900). The interpretation of dreams. In J. Strachey (Ed. & Trans.), *The standard edition of the complete psychological works of Sigmund Freud* (Vols. 4 & 5, pp. 1– 627). London: Hogarth.

Freud, S. (1915). The unconscious. In J. Strachey (Ed. and Trans.), *The standard edition of the complete psychological works of Sigmund Freud* (Vol. 14, pp. 159–215). London: Hogarth.

Freud, S. (1923). The ego and the id. In J. Strachey (Ed. and Trans.), *The standard edition of the complete psychological works of Sigmund Freud* (Vol. 19, pp. 12–63). London: Hogarth.

Ghent, E. (1990). Masochism, submission, surrender. *Contemporary Psychoanalysis, 26*, 108–136.

Ginot, E. (2007). Intersubjectivity and neuroscience: Understanding enactments and their therapeutic significance within emerging paradigms. The empathic power of enactments. The link between neuropsychological processes and an expanded definition of empathy. *Psychoanalytic Psychology, 24*, 317–332.

Grossmark, R. (2018). The unobtrusive relational group analyst and the work of the narrative. *Psychoanalytic Inquiry, 38*, 246–255.

Hamilton, V. (1996). *The analyst's preconscious.* Hillsdale, NJ: Analytic Press.

Hecht, D. (2014). Cerebral lateralization of pro- and anti-social tendencies. *Experimental Neurology, 23*, 1–27. doi:10.5607/en.2014.23.1.1

Hill, C.E., C.E., Hoffman, M.A., Kivlighan, D.M., D.M., Spiegel, S.B., & Gelso, C.J. (2017). Therapist expertise in psychotherapy revisited. *The Counseling Psychologist, 45*, 7–53.

Howard, M. F., & Reggia, J. A. (2007). A theory of the visual system biology underlying development of spatial frequency lateralization. *Brain and Cognition, 64*, 111–123.

Imel, Z.E., Barco, J.S., Brown, H.J., Baucom, B.R., & Kircher, J.C., & Atkins, D.C. (2014). The association of therapist empathy and synchrony in vocally encoded arousal. *Journal of Counseling Psychology, 61*, 146–152.

Jackson, J. Hughlings (1879). On affections of speech from diseases of the brain. *Brain, 2*, 203–222.

Jackson, J. Hughlings (1931). *Selected writings of John Hughlings Jackson, Vols. I and II.* London: Hodder and Stoughton.

Jostmann, N. B., Kuole, S. L., Vander Wulp, N. Y., & Fockenberg, D. A. (2005). Subliminal affect regulation: The moderating role of action-versus state-orientation. *European Psychologist, 10*, 209–217.

Keenan, J. P., Rubio, J., Racioppi, C., Johnson, A., & Barnacz, A. (2005). The right hemisphere and the dark side of consciousness. *Cortex, 41,* 695–704.

Kohut, H. (1971). *The analysis of the self.* New York, NY: International Universities Press.

Koole, S. L., & Jostmann, N. B. (2004). Getting a grip on your feelings: Effects of action orientation and external demands on intuitive affect regulation. *Journal of Personality and Social Psychology, 87,* 974–990. doi:10.1037/0022-3514.87 .6.974

Koole, S. L., & Rothermund, K. (2011). "I feel better but I don't know why." The psychology of implicit emotion regulation. *Cognition and Emotion, 25,* 389– 399. doi:10.1080/02699931.2010.550505

Koole, S. L., & Tschacher, W. (2016). Synchrony in psychotherapy: A review and an integrative framework for the therapeutic alliance. *Frontiers in Psychology, 7,* 1. doi:10.3389/fpsyg.2016.00862

Kris, E. (1952). *Psychoanalytic explorations in art.* New York: International Universities Press.

Kuhl, J., Quirin, M., & Koole, S. L. (2015). Being someone: The integrated self as a neuropsychological system. *Social and Personality Psychology Compass, 9,* 115–132.

Levine, R. (2011). Progressing while regressing in relationships. *International Journal of Group Psychotherapy, 61,* 612– 643. doi:10.1521/ijgp.2011.61.4.621

Maroda, K. J. (1998). Enactment: When the patient's and analyst's past converge. *Psychoanalytic Psychology, 15,* 517–535.

Maroda, K. J. (2005). Show some emotion: Completing the cycle of affective communication. In L. Aron & A. Harris (Eds.), *Relational psychoanalysis: Vol. 2. Innovation and expansion* (pp. 121–142). Hillsdale, NJ: Analytic Press.

McGilchrist, I. (2009). *The master and his emissary: The divided brain and the making of the Western world.* New Haven, CT: Yale University Press.

McGilchrist, I. (2015). Divine understanding and the divided brain. In J. Clausen & N. Levy (Eds.), *Handbook of neuroethics.* Dordrecht: Springer Science. doi:10.1007/978-94-007-4707-4_99\

Meares, R. (2017). The disintegrative core of relational trauma and a way toward unity. In M. Solomon & D. J. Siegel (Eds.), *How people change: Relationships and neuroplasticity in psychotherapy* (pp. 135–150). New York: Norton.

Nolte, T., Hudac, C., Mayes, L.C., Fonagy, P., Blatt, S.J., & Pelphrey, K. (2010). The effect of attachment-related stress on the capacity to mentalize: An fMRI investigation of the biobehavioral switch model. *Journal of the American Psychoanalytic Association, 58,* 566–573.

Norcross, J.C. (ed.) (2011). *Psychotherapy relationships that work. Second edition.* New York, NY: Oxford University Press.

Norcross, J. C., & Lambert, M. J. (2018). Psychotherapy relationships that work III. *Psychotherapy, 55,* 303–315.

Pincus, D., Freeman, W., & Modell, A. (2007). A neurobiological model of perception: Considerations for transference. *Psychoanalytic Psychology, 24,* 623–640.

Redcay, E., Dodell-Feder, D., Pearrow, M. J., Manros, P. L., Kleiner, M., Gasbrielli, J. D. E., & Saxe, R. (2010). Live face-to-face interaction during fMRI: A new tool for social cognitive neuroscience. *NeuroImage, 50,* 1639–1647.

Ramseyer, F., & Tschacher, W. (2011). Nonverbal synchrony in psychotherapy: Coordinated body-movement reflects relationship quality and outcome. *Journal of Consulting and Clinical Psychology, 79,* 284–295. doi:10.1037/a0023419

Ray, D., Roy, D., Sindhu, B., Sharan, P., & Banerjee, A. (2017). Neural substrate of group mental health: Insights from multi-brain reference frame in functional neuroimaging. *Frontiers in Psychology, 8,* 1627. doi:10.3389/fpsyg.2017.01627

Reik, T. (1948). *Listening with the third ear.* New York: Grove.

Rogers, C. R. (1980). *A way of being.* Boston: Houghton Mifflin.

Russell, P. (1998). The role of paradox in the repetition compulsion. In J. G. Teicholz & D. Kriegman (Eds.), *Trauma, repetition, and affect regulation: The work of Paul Russell* (pp. 1–22). New York: Other Press.

Santiestaban, I., Banissy, Calmur, C., & Bird, G. (2012). Enhancing social ability by stimulating right temporoparietal junction. *Current Biology, 22,* 2274–2277.

Saxe, R., & Wexler, A. (2005). Making sense of another mind: The role of the right temporo-parietal junction. *Neuropsychologia, 43,* 1391–1399.

Schore, A. N. (1994). *Affect regulation and the origin of the self: The neurobiology of emotional development.* Mahwah, NJ: Erlbaum.

Schore, A. N. (2001). The effects of relational trauma on right brain development, affect regulation, and infant mental health. *Infant Mental Health Journal, 22,* 201–269.

Schore, A. N. (2003a). *Affect dysregulation and disorders of the self.* New York: Norton.

Schore, A. N. (2003b). *Affect regulation and the repair of the self.* New York: Norton.

Schore, A. N. (2012). *The science of the art of psychotherapy.* New York: Norton.

Schore, A. N. (2014). The right brain is dominant in psychotherapy. *Psychotherapy, 51,* 388–397.

Schore, A. N. (2019a). *The development of the unconscious mind.* New York: Norton.

Schore, A. N. (2019b). *Right brain psychotherapy.* New York: Norton.

Schore, A. N. (2020). Forging connections in group psychotherapy through right brain-to-right brain emotional communications. Part 1: Theoretical models of right brain therapeutic action. Part 2: Clinical case analyses of group right brain regressive enactments. *International Journal of Group Psychotherapy, 70,* 29–88.

Schore, A.N. (in press). Attachment trauma and the developing right brain: Origins of pathological dissociation and some implications for psychotherapy. In M. Dorahy & S. N. Gold (Eds.), *Dissociation and the Dissociative Disorders: Past Present, Future.*

Schore, J., & Schore, A. (2008). Modern attachment theory: The central role of affect regulation in development and treatment. *Clinical Social Work Journal, 36,* 9–20.

Shuren, J. E., & Grafman, J. (2002). The neurology of reasoning. *Archives of Neurology, 59,* 916–919.

Stevenson, C. W., Halliday, D. M., Marsden, C. A., & Mason, R. (2008). Early life programming of hemispheric lateralization and synchronization in the adult medial prefrontal cortex. *Neuroscience, 155,* 852–863.

Stolk, A., Verhagen, L., Schoffelen, J.- M., Osstenveld, R., Blokpoel, M., Hagoort, M. L., van Rooij, I., & Toni, I. (2013). Neural mechanisms of communicative innovation. *Proceedings of the National Academy of Sciences USA, 110,* 14574–14579.

Tognoli, E., Lagarde, J., DeGuzman, & Kelson, J.A.S. (2007). The phi complex as a neuromarker of human social coordination. *Proceedings of the National Academy of Sciences, USA, 104,* 8190–8195.

Tschacher, W., & Meier, D. (2019). Physiological synchrony in psychotherapy sessions. *Psychotherapy Research, 30*(5), 558–573. *https://doi.org/10.1080/10503307.2019 .1612114*

Tschacher, W., Ramseyer, F., & Koole, S.L. (2018). Sharing the now in the social present: Duration of nonverbal synchrony is linked with personality. *Journal of Personality, 86,* DOI: 10.111/jopy.12298

Tuttman, S. (2002). Regression. In E. Erwin (Ed.), *The Freud encyclopedia: Theory, therapy, and culture.* New York: Routledge.

Whitehead, C. C. (2006). Neo-psychoanalysis: A paradigm for the 21st century. *Journal of the Academy of Psychoanalysis and Dynamic Psychiatry, 34,* 603–627.

Winnicott, D. W. (1958). Withdrawal and regression. In *Collected papers.* New York: Basic Books.

Wolfe, B. E., & Goldfried, M. R. (1988). Research on psychotherapy integration: Recommendations and conclusions from an NIMH workshop. *Journal of Consulting and Clinical Psychology, 56,* 448–451. doi:10.1037/0022-006X.56.3.448

Yakeley, J. (2018). Psychoanalysis in modern mental health practice. *Lancet Psychiatry, 5,* 443–450.

Zhang, Y., Meng, T., Hou, Y.Y., Pan, Y.F., & Hu, Y. (2018). Interpersonal brain synchronization associated with working alliance during psychological counseling. *Psychiatry Research: Neuroimaging, 65,* 293–303.

Zhang, Y., Meng, T., & Hu, Yi. (2020). Experience-dependent counselor-client brain synchronization during psychological counseling. eNeuro 2020; 10.1523/ENEURO.0236-20.2020

3

The Interpersonal Neurobiology of Executive Functioning

Louis Cozolino, Carly Samuelson, & Chloe Drulis

DURING THE MIDDLE OF THE LAST CENTURY, MARY AINSWORTH SET OUT TO explore the attachment theories of John Bowlby. First in Uganda and later in Baltimore, she and her colleagues observed the interactions of mothers and their young children in naturalistic settings. The overarching goal was to explore the correlations between maternal behavior and a child's attachment security. With the Ugandan mothers, researchers were impressed with the variability of parenting styles and the range of maternal abilities they witnessed.

Parenting was clearly not one thing; rather, it seemed to be an array of maternal behaviors and interactive dyadic styles. As they analyzed the data, they found attachment security in a child correlated with the mother's sensitivity to her baby's needs. These mothers were able to perceive, describe, and react to their children in a more attuned and helpful manner. Although we tend to attribute attunement to natural maternal instincts, it turned out to be highly variable, natural for many, but far from universal.

Later with mothers in Baltimore, observers noticed something else about mothers with securely attached children. When interrupted by their children while engaged in other tasks, they were readily able to shift their focus from what they were doing to their children. Using skills similar to those found in the Uganda sample, these mothers would quickly grasp what their children needed, respond in ways that satisfied their children, and then allow them to return to play when they were ready. These mothers would then turn back to what they had been doing before the approach of their child. These behaviors were in contrast to mothers who would have difficulty breaking away from what they were doing, become distressed by being interrupted, or intentionally ignore their children. Building on John Bowlby's notion of a parent as a secure base and safe haven, the early research by Ainsworth and her colleagues described its components— availability, attunement, and the freedom to return to exploration and play.

I must admit that when I read Ainsworth's articles years ago, it never occurred to me that these maternal behaviors had anything to do with executive functioning. In retrospect, I believe that I was so steeped in the cultural and professional biases of executive functioning being rational, objective, and male that the truth remained hidden in plain sight. What I want to suggest here is that good executive functioning on the part of these mothers is at the core of the secure attachment in their children. The core of my argument is that executive functioning involves at least three separate executive systems involved in top-down, bottom-up, and left-right control and that these systems exist in neurodynamic balance with one another. The caveat is that we have to update and expand our notion of executive functioning for this idea to make sense.

The Central Dogma of Executive Functioning

For most of the 20th century, executive functioning was thought to be a specific set of high-level cognitive abilities including working memory, problem solving, and abstract reasoning. It was also believed that they were completely conscious processes organized by (and housed within) the prefrontal cortex. This was certainly the go-to answer for exam questions when I was in school. The proof offered for this view was that damage to the prefrontal cortex resulted in a range of dysfunctions that undermined the victim's ability to solve problems and navigate the world. This view of executive functioning emerged primarily from the metaphor of the homunculus, a little person in our heads, who thinks and controls our behavior from a place located behind our eyes. IQ was believed to be a direct measure of both intelligence and executive capabilities.

Thinking of intelligence through the keyhole of cognition is deeply grounded in Western culture, and the prefrontal cortex has traditionally been posited by comparative anatomists as the structure that separates us from other primates. This is why most experts in executive functioning use computer analogies and flowcharts to explain neural functioning. They generally disregard the haphazard nature of our stream of consciousness and the value of input from the body, our emotions, and social relationships. (These assumptions obviously cannot stand in the face of what we have learned about the social nature of the embodied brain within interpersonal neurobiology.)

Despite the power of these cultural and neurological biases, there were many problems with the top-down, prefrontal view of intelligence. One was that significant prefrontal damage also resulted in deficits of emotional regulation, relational abilities, and social functioning. It is also clear that IQ doesn't map directly onto functional abilities or worldly success. Educational systems driven by the cognitive model of intelligence resulted in many students being told by their teachers that they would never amount to anything. Yet many of these "miserable students" went on to make revolutionary discoveries and pioneer new industries. Despite this, teachers continued to judge each new generation of students on old models of intelligence. Because the traditional model of executive functioning was held so strongly, the many gaps in its validity were treated as trivial exceptions rather than inspiring the questioning of basic assumptions of the prevailing model.

Over the past few decades, findings in neuroscience and neurology have undermined some of these more simplistic assumptions about executive functioning. Increasing awareness of key issues related to culture and gender have further shaken confidence in abstract, patriarchal, and imperialistic views of human intelligence. For these and other reasons, neurocognitive and intelligence testing are falling out of favor in education. By the end of the 20th century, the notion of emotional intelligence captured the attention of the general public, while the popularity of mindfulness added to a growing appreciation of the importance of self-awareness and self-reflective capacity as important components of navigating a successful life.

As old dogmas about intelligence and executive functioning were crumbling, a devastating blow was dealt by Antonio Damasio when he demonstrated that judgment and decision making rely on input from regions of the brain that process somatic and emotional information. It turns out that, contrary to Descartes's belief of "I think, therefore I am," somatic awareness and emotions serve as equal evidence of our existence. This has coincided with an expansion of sensory-motor-based educational interventions, somatic and emotion-centered forms of psychotherapy, and a general rethinking of both intelligence and executive functioning.

While executive systems are generally thought of as mechanisms of top-down control, why can't executive systems for more primitive functions, such as physiological states and reflexive reactions to danger, have systems of executive control that are bottom-up? How do we return a tennis ball that travels too quickly for us to make a decision about how it should be returned? How do we know when to respond to someone with our hearts rather than our minds? What is it that allows us to make a choice that feels right, instead of one that looks good on paper?

At this point in the development of our understanding of executive functioning, we have to take a fresh look at the scientific and clinical data that have been neglected for so long. For example, we now realize that our brains are social organs, and it is our ability to communicate with one another that has at least as much to do with the rise of civilization as the expansion of the prefrontal cortex. We know that our brains consist of a government of neural systems from different evolutionary periods with different areas of specialization and strategies to achieve their goals. We also realize that group dynamics and interpersonal regulatory processes impact all aspects of neural functioning.

In light of these more recent findings, we have to ask ourselves many questions: What neural systems contribute to executive functioning? What is the role of emotion in intelligence? How might sensory-motor experience contribute to problem-solving abilities? How do implicit memories in the form of attachment schema and affect regulation contribute to executive functioning? How does working in a group influence our abstract abilities, imagination, and innovation? Is intelligence an individual attribute, an emergent group process, or some combination of the two? I believe that it is within the realm of interpersonal neurobiology that we can best explore the contributions of thinking, feeling, relating, and being to a new and expanded notion of executive functioning.

The Components of Executive Functioning

As we open our minds to expanded notions of executive functioning, it seems safe to say that we should include the categories of emotional intelligence, social intelligence, and self-awareness to the mix.

Cognitive and educational psychologists have long touted the multidimensional aspect of intelligence. This is why IQ tests such as the Wechsler Adult Intelligence Scale contain a dozen or more subtests focusing on abilities like attention, memory, and abstract reasoning. While I'm not suggesting we expand these tests to include measures of social and emotional intelligence, what I can say with some confidence is that traditional IQ scores only make sense in the context of a person's life. This is why so much time performing assessments involves figuring out how to explain deficits in functioning and achievement despite high IQ scores or obvious intellectual abilities despite low IQ scores.

Emotional intelligence should include such areas as one's ability to successfully navigate stress and exhibit emotional control in challenging situations. Self-awareness would be expressed in the ability to engage in self-reflection, strike a balance between self-care and caring for others, and being able to take responsibility for one's actions. Social intelligence would include understanding things from the perspective of others, and the ability to experience sympathy, empathy, and compassion. It is clear that these social and emotional abilities are interdependent in the same way as attention, concentration, language, and memory combine to organize and drive cognitive functioning.

All three of these areas—emotional intelligence, self-awareness, and social intelligence, traditionally excluded from the conversation by cognitive scientists—have gained both scientific and cultural support. We certainly have to negotiate day-to-day survival: avoid touching hot stoves, eating yellow snow, or walking too close to the edge of the cliff. But we also have to deal with many different people, be aware of our inner experiences, keep our emotions regulated, and express ourselves in appropriate ways. We have to manage ongoing relationships with ourselves and others close to us, and engage in self-care while taking care of those for whom we are responsible. This more inclusive model accounts for many of the variables we have always recognized as relevant to successful adaptation, though we were without specific tests or a theoretical model to assess or include them in our evaluation.

While deficits in executive functioning have a negative impact on all of us, they stand out in stark relief when assessing the skills of business executives. It is clear that traditional ideas of IQ, while important, don't necessarily correlate with success. Being the smartest person in the room and letting others know it has its place, but is hardly ever the best leadership strategy. In the last decade, the tyrannical CEO has morphed from a cultural icon into a tragic character on their way to a heart attack. As businesses transition from family-run enterprises to multinational corporations, the patriarchal strategies of prediction and control are giving way to increasingly distributed models of feedback, decision making, and recalibration. What we are seeing is an emerging notion of intelligence and executive functioning as a set of cognitive, emotional, and social skills that are integrated in the way people treat others, know themselves, and drive positive and productive corporate cultures. In fact, they are more closely related to what has traditionally been called wisdom instead of intelligence—more on that later.

This is not an altogether new idea. As far back as the 1880s, the infamous railroad man Phineas Gage experienced prefrontal brain damage that turned him from a responsible, organized, and God-fearing man into an irresponsible, emotionally erratic, and immoral drifter. The century of neurology that followed Gage's case also showed that brain damage could result in emotional dysregulation and antisocial behavior as well as a loss of abstract thinking. Thus, there was always some recognition that problem solving and emotional stability were somehow related. And given that fits of rage, anger, or fear seem to shave many IQ points off our functional abilities, the connection has long been recognized even if not clearly articulated.

Looking at the case of Gage, it is clear that he lost the ability to inhibit impulses and regulate emotions, which led him to be unable to lead men or organize his own life. Given that we are social creatures and much of our intelligence is demonstrated in social situations, we need to be able to regulate our emotions and impulses while being aware of and attuned to the feelings of others. This occurs all the time in business, where people rise to the top based on their technical expertise, only to be undone by their difficulties managing others, emotional dyscontrol, or sexual impulses. It isn't enough to have good executive functioning based on old top-down information processing. Lack of affect regulation, lack of ability to put yourself in someone else's shoes, and the impact of unresolved trauma usually cancel out innate intelligence and technical know-how.

Three Interacting Executive Systems

Teamwork is a strategic decision.
PATRICK LENCIONI

While we are at the early stages of developing a neurodynamic model of executive functioning, I would like to share the model I use with my psychotherapy and executive coaching clients. I believe this model accounts for many aspects of executive functioning that are usually left unaddressed by cognitive psychologists. My proposal is that at least three interacting executive systems exist in neurodynamic balance. Further, all three networks are in executive control of different aspects of functioning and need to connect, integrate, and work together to allow optimal executive functioning.

The first executive system is centered in the more primitive areas of the brain, including the amygdala and regions of the brainstem. This amygdala network, which we share with reptiles and other mammals, is responsible for our moment-to-moment survival reactions and drives our physiological responses to the environment. The amygdala is an organ of appraisal that guides us in making basic approach-avoidance decisions. It is the source of our anxieties, tensions, and fears and guides us toward what we have experienced as safe and away from what has proven to be dangerous. It is when this primitive executive system is overly active that we experience anxiety disorders, panic attacks, and PTSD.

In a dangerous situation, the amygdala executive immediately takes over and inhibits our other two executive systems until the danger has passed. In a sense, it maintains veto power over our actions in the face of later-evolving systems of executive control. This process of invoking veto power over the other systems has been referred to as "amygdala hijack" in the trauma literature. Because this primitive amygdala executive receives input from systems of implicit memory, it can be triggered to become active by past memories similar to the experiences we are having in real time. For example, if someone has a traumatic history with authority figures early in life, the amygdala might become activated in situations with authority figures or subordinates later in life. If this remains unconscious and unresolved, it can severely impact the ability to function successfully within an organization in positions of management and leadership.

The second executive system is organized within regions of the frontal and parietal lobes and the fiber bundles that connect them. This system is primarily responsible for navigating the environment, problem solving, and abstract reasoning. This is the system usually considered to govern executive functioning (although traditionally thought to be limited to the prefrontal cortex). During evolution, the frontal lobes became specialized to process timing, sequencing, and a memory for the future (remembering the consequences of current behavior). Meanwhile, the parietal lobes evolved to develop maps of external and internal space and to integrate these maps to use for spatial and imaginal navigation. It is in these frontal and parietal lobes that we find the mirror neurons that allow us to attune with and learn from others through imitation.

Together, the parietal and frontal lobes integrate to create our sense of space and time and navigate it with minimal conscious attention. When this system is damaged or disrupted, we experience difficulties in navigating space and disturbances in consciousness, functional abilities, and other executive functions. It is important to keep in mind that although we are able to talk about space and time separately, they are not divisible—none of us has ever experienced one without the other. The fact that the frontal and parietal lobes construct a unified space-time allows us to navigate them simultaneously and seamlessly. This is also the reason why somatic experience, somatic therapies, and sensory integration techniques can have a positive impact on intellectual, academic, and social functioning.

The Three Executive Systems

	CORE STRUCTURES	MAIN JOB	ROLE IN EXECUTIVE FUNCTIONING
FIRST	amygdala	approach/ avoidance	rapid evaluation of stimuli, basic survival
SECOND	parietal frontal	navigation/ engagement	problem solving/ abstract thinking
THIRD	DMN OMPFC & cingulate	internal processing processing	self-reflection, imagination, daydreaming, empathy, compassion, attunement

The third executive system is centered around a group of structures along the middle regions of the brain and referred to as the default mode network (DMN). First detected in research subjects between experimental tasks, it was later discovered to be a coherent group of interconnected structures. Subsequent research discovered that the DMN becomes activated during reflection, empathic attunement, daydreaming, and imagination. The DMN is involved with our awareness and understanding of ourselves and others, and our capacity to create an internal world and use it as an imaginal space within which we can reflect on real-world problems, rehearse solutions, and use our creativity.

The DMN has been found to be largely anticorrelational with the other two executive systems, which means that it is inhibited by both the amygdala-centric first executive and the parietal-frontal functioning of the second executive. This means that when we are anxious, afraid, or preoccupied with some external task, it is far less likely that we will be either self-aware or empathic to others or even ourselves. This may explain why those with severe anxiety disorders have difficulty with empathy for and connection with others. It is also why, if our inner worlds are troubled and painful, we can engage in manic-type defenses, making long lists of tasks to keep us distracted from our negative thoughts and feelings. The fact that the DMN is largely anticorrelation and not completely so reflects the likelihood that the executive systems need to integrate and collaborate under certain conditions to attain certain goals. An example of this might be a simultaneous activation of the second and third executive systems to both have empathy for another's struggles and figure out ways to help them.

Think for a moment about the structures of the executive brain as they might relate to a business executive. A successful CEO is usually judged first and foremost on the ability to understand an area of expertise and make good decisions based on a deep understanding of a specific industry (second executive). In addition, she needs to be able to regulate her arousal, mood, and temper in order to interact appropriately with others (first executive). Finally, she has to be able to remain self-possessed, take her own counsel, and understand the feelings, needs, and motivations of those around her (third executive). In my experience, it is difficult to be successful in the CEO's chair without good functioning across all three executive systems.

In my coaching work with executives, I've been able to find and address problems using this three-system model. Everyone I work with has a highly functional second executive, knows their industry, and excels in the cognitive challenges of their work. If there are problems in these areas, the more appropriate assistance will come from other industry experts and not myself. The problems I am confronted with are generally in the areas of the first and third executive systems. On one hand, people who struggle with anxiety, depression, and difficulty regulating their arousal and emotions (first executive) need to understand and deal with dysregulations of their physiology and affective arousal. Emotional dysregulation and instability will keep an intelligent and competent executive (or any of us for that matter) from being able to stay on task, keep problems in perspective, and sustain focus on a goal. They will be sabotaged by their own emotional dyscontrol and fear of being judged by others.

Another group of managers and executives struggle with their ability to empathize, attune with, and understand the perspective of those they work with (third executive). For these individuals, the focus of coaching will be on attunement, empathy, and social skills requiring the involvement of the DMN. Individuals demonstrate great variability in DMN skills; some are on the autism spectrum and lack some of the innate mechanisms related to imitation, attunement, and sympathy provided by mirror neurons and emotional networks. Because these folks lack some of the basic building blocks of emotional intelligence, they need to learn these skills more by observation and rote memory. Another group with severe anxiety and unresolved trauma has highly inhibited DMN development and functioning. For these individuals, anxiety disorders need to be addressed and managed before the DMN can come back online and be available for coaching.

In reality, we all strive to become the CEOs of the business of running our lives. The same neurobiological and behavioral principles apply to working with clients and developing our selves. Every form of psychotherapy contains within it the goals of learning to better direct our minds and manage our brains. One of my favorite phone calls began when I innocently asked one of my more clever friends, "How are you?" His response was telling: "Lou, I have two problems. I'm self-employed, and my boss is an A**H***." All of us have this problem no matter what our occupation. Our brains have evolved to diminish anxiety through preoccupation with action. Winnicott, a child psychoanalyst, called this a "manic defense"; others call it ADHD or workaholism. Although this leads some of us to be more productive, we can easily lose ourselves in senseless activity that we talk ourselves into thinking is important. The deeper question in many therapeutic quests is, "How do I shift from living my life as a human doing to living my life as a human being?"

What drives our day-to-day lives? Are our motivations in line with our current needs, or simply shadows of old defenses that result in stress, unhappiness, and the symptoms for which we seek therapy? All three executive systems need to be addressed and treated for therapy to be successful. To establish an optimal therapeutic relationship, the DMN needs to become activated and engaged to allow for attunement, sympathy, and compassion. The relationship can then be utilized for affect regulation and amygdala whispering to help soothe and quiet a hyperactive amygdala executive.

Leveraging the parietal-frontal executive, we create experiments in living that allow our clients to take what they learn about connection, attachment, and attunement out into the world. As each executive system is developed and strengthened, it allows the other two to become better integrated into the collective executive suite of neural systems. Optimal executive functioning is a whole-brain activity.

Intelligence Versus Wisdom

There is a wisdom of the head, and a wisdom of the heart.
CHARLES DICKENS

Although we in the modern world tend to place a high value on intelligence, the development and integration of the three executive systems may more closely equate to what is referred to as wisdom. Although we tend to know it when we see it, defining wisdom can be a challenge. In fact, each chapter of a popular book about wisdom edited by Yale psychologist Robert Sternberg (1990) puts forth a slightly different definition. In the East, wisdom has traditionally focused on understanding and controlling one's thoughts and passions to promote inner and social harmony. In Western cultures, wisdom was reflected in good advice, codes of social behavior, and an understanding of natural science.

More recently, Eastern and Western notions seem to be combining to create a view of wisdom as a blending of knowledge and compassion expressed in the context of relationships. While knowledge gives us the capacity to understand what we are doing, wisdom helps us to attain a correct, prudent, and just application of that knowledge. Although no specific study has been done measuring brain activation while people are acting wisely, it is safe to assume that we would see more diverse brain activity with the involvement of intellectual and emotional functioning and an integration of our executive systems.

Who comes to mind when you think of a wise person? A relative, a teacher, or perhaps a political leader or humanitarian? When a group of undergraduates were asked to name well-known wise individuals, their top 10 choices included Gandhi, Jesus, Solomon, Martin Luther King, Socrates, and Oprah (Paulhus et al., 2002). You may notice that we don't see Napoleon, Einstein, or Bill Gates on this list, which suggests that power, intellect, and wealth aren't synonymous with wisdom. Instead, wisdom is

equated with the qualities of insight, vulnerability, compassion, and courage. In looking over this list, you may have an emotional reaction to one or
more of these people. Perhaps this kind of emotional reaction to another
human being, the neural networks they stimulate, and the biochemical processes they trigger are aspects of how we identify wisdom—knowledge that
comes from the heart and gut as well as from the brain.

With these thoughts in mind, I asked a group of graduate students to list
the qualities they felt made someone wise. They were quick to point out
that wisdom brings together both intellectual and emotional intelligence
in ways that maximize affiliation, compassion, and our common humanity.
They perceived wisdom as emerging in the context of interacting hearts
and minds coming together to comprehend and solve complex human problems. I jotted down some of what they said and sorted their descriptions
into three categories:

1. A broad perspective (self-awareness, seeing the big picture, and maintaining doubt)
2. Personal attributes (moral courage, resilience, and appropriate
   detachment)
3. Attitudes toward others (empathic, compassionate, and forgiving)

According to this small and informal survey, attaining wisdom involves
being able to see past the surface of things to deeper levels of meaning.
Wise individuals are also able to discard notions of a singular correct perspective and remain open to new learning while recognizing the limitations
and distortions in their own thinking.

The social science research suggests that wisdom coalesces from a complex pattern of personality variables, life experience, and inner growth
(Staudinger, 1999). Those judged as wise in any age group excel in coping
with existential issues and grasp the relativism of values (Baltes et al., 1995).
They tend to have good social abilities, with a rich internal life, and are
open to new experiences (Staudinger et al., 1998). Someone with wisdom
is capable of sustaining focus on a problem, as they consider its multiple
dimensions and meanings, and their personal responsibility in the matter
at hand (Holliday & Chandler, 1986). Given that navigating complex and
difficult relationships is one of life's most enduring challenges, much of wisdom is expressed in how people interact with and treat one another. This
requires the participation, development, and integration of all three execu-

tive systems over time. As a friend once told me, sometimes wisdom shows up with age, while other times age shows up all by itself.

If wisdom is the integration of intelligence and compassion in the service of others, it deserves a central place in the issues we address in interpersonal neurobiology. Wisdom is the coming together of those things we hold most dear in the exploration of brain, mind, and relationship. Wisdom is social glue, a sacred communication, a gift from one generation to the next. Becoming wise requires emotional regulation, minimizing ego, mindfulness, secure attachment, and being the safe base that allows others to explore, play, love, and work. The mothers of the securely attached children that Ainsworth and her colleagues observed long ago had good executive functioning, integrated and utilized their three executive systems, and were the wise elders that recede back into the depths of human prehistory.

References

Baltes, P. B., Staudinger, U. M., Maercker, A., & Smith, J. (1995). People nominated as wise: A comparative study of wisdom-related knowledge. *Psychology and Aging, 10,* 155–166.

Holliday, S. G., & Chandler, M. J. (1986). *Wisdom: Explorations in adult competence.* New York: Karger.

Paulhus, D. L., Wehr, P., Harms, P. D., & Strasser, D. I. (2002). Use of exemplar surveys to reveal implicit types of intelligence. *Personality and Social Psychology Bulletin, 28,* 1051–1062.

Staudinger, U. M. (1999). Older and wiser? Integrating results on the relationship between age and wisdom-related performance. *International Journal of Behavioral Development, 23,* 641–664.

Staudinger, U. M., Maciel, A. G., Smith, J., & Baltes, P. B. (1998). What predicts wisdom-related performance? A first look at personality, intelligence, and facilitative experiential contexts. *European Journal of Personality, 12,* 1–17.

Sternberg, R. J. (1990). *Wisdom: Its nature, origins, and development.* New York: Cambridge University Press.

4

The COVID-19 Pandemic Is a Challenge to Our Nervous System

A Polyvagal Perspective

Stephen W. Porges

THE SPREAD OF THE SARS-COV-2 VIRUS PRESENTS AN UNPRECEDENTED event that rapidly introduced widespread life threat, economic destabilization, and social isolation. The human nervous system is tuned to detect safety and danger, integrating body and brain responses via the autonomic nervous system. Polyvagal theory provides a perspective to understand the impact of the pandemic on mental and physical health. This perspective highlights the important role of the state of the autonomic nervous system in exacerbating or dampening threat reactions to the pandemic. In addition, the theory alerts us to the impact of clinical history (e.g., trauma) on autonomic regulation as an important compounding risk factor lowering the threshold to become behaviorally and physiologically destabilized in response to the pandemic. The theory provides a strategy to dampen the adverse reactions to threat (e.g., acute stress disorders) through portals of social engagement that evolved to downregulate defenses to promote calmness and connectedness.

Introduction

The pandemic is a challenging time in which we, as sentient beings, are aware of the chronic threat of infection. However, being aware of threat does not necessarily prepare us to deal effectively with the disruptive impact of the threat on our daily lives. In general, although we are well informed about the impact of viral infection on our health, we are poorly informed about how chronic threat impacts on our daily life and how it impacts on our mental and physical health.

As a species, we are biased toward explaining our life experiences, including both successes and failures, as the product of cognitive processes such as learning, effort, and intention. We are poorly informed about complementary neurobiological knowledge, including our evolutionary history, that could provide a more complete understanding of our experiences. This neurobiologically informed model, consistent with the principles of polyvagal theory, would provide therapists with insights to efficiently and effectively mitigate the disruptive impact of threat on mental and physical health.

This chapter applies a perspective based on polyvagal theory to further our understanding of the consequences of the pandemic on our mental and physical health. This perspective is built on and refines the interpersonal neurobiology approach. While interpersonal neurobiology assumes consilience based on common findings among independent disciplines, polyvagal theory focuses on emergent properties that are associated with autonomic states. The emergent properties are manifest on a variety of levels of measurement associated with and often defining disparate disciplines. These measures may include subjective reports of cognitive processes and emotional feelings and objective measurements of neurochemical, neurophysiological, and behavioral responses. Emergent properties are also observed in the features that define mental and physical illness and health.

Within a polyvagal perspective, the emergent properties are dependent on one's autonomic state. Within this model, autonomic state functions as an intervening variable, either optimizing the downregulation of defense to optimize health and social behavior or optimizing defense at a great cost to health and social behavior. For example, the primary emergent properties are social engagement and coregulation, mobilization (e.g., fight and flight), and immobilization (e.g., death feigning, shutdown, syncope, dissociation).

The theory applies our knowledge of the evolution of the neural regulation of the autonomic nervous system in vertebrates to explain the sequence and dependence of emergent adaptive functions on the autonomic state.

Impacts of the Pandemic on Our Biological Imperative to Connect

As the COVID-19 crisis challenges the fabric of our society, we look to our science to understand how the crisis is influencing our mental and physical health, how we perceive the world, and the way we interact with others. Polyvagal theory provides a neurobiological model to explain how the crisis elicits threat-related responses, disrupts our capacity to regulate our behavioral and emotional states, interferes with our optimism, and compromises our ability to trust and feel safe with another.

Like several other mammals, humans are a social species. Being a social species explicitly emphasizes that human survival is dependent on coregulating our neurophysiological state via social interaction. The dependence of an infant on the mother is an archetypical example of this dependency and even illustrates the bidirectionality of the social interaction; not only is the mother regulating the infant, but the infant is reciprocally regulating the mother. The features of coregulation, including reciprocity, connectedness, and trust, resonate through the mammalian nervous system and optimize homeostatic function, providing a neurobiological link between our mental and physical health.

Theodosius Dobzhansky (1962), a prominent evolutionary biologist, emphasized that connectedness rather than physical strength enabled the evolutionary success of mammals and redefined survival of the fittest by stating that "the fittest may also be the gentlest, because survival often requires mutual help and cooperation." According to Dobzhansky, it is this capacity to cooperate that enabled the earliest mammalian species to survive in a hostile world dominated by physically larger and potentially aggressive reptiles. Although I was unaware of Dobzhansky's major contributions at the time I developed the theory, the publication that introduced polyvagal theory was titled "Orienting in a Defensive World: Mammalian Modifications of Our Evolutionary Heritage. A Polyvagal Theory" (Porges, 1995). In retrospect, the title was a tribute to Dobzhansky's insightful statement that "nothing in biology makes sense except in the light of evolution" (Dobzhansky, 1973, p. 125).

An Integrated Nervous System Model Heightens Awareness of Bidirectional Brain-Body Communication

As we struggle with the pandemic, we need to reinterpret and reframe our reactions within an informed appreciation of our nervous system, acknowledging that our reactions to the pandemic will make sense only if informed by our understanding of evolution. This leads us to ask questions directed at our reactivity to threat and uncertainty and our needs to sufficiently coregulate our bodily state to move from feelings of fear and danger to feelings of safety and trust in others. In addition, we need to update our understanding of brain-body communication. To understand how threat changes both psychological and physiological processes, we need to accept a single integrated nervous system model (see below) rather than an antiquated model in which the central nervous system is separate from the autonomic nervous system. Functionally, the brain and visceral organs are connected by neural pathways that send signals from the brain to our visceral organs and from the visceral organs to the brain. Thus, threat reactions, through definable and measurable pathways, may have predictable effects on our mental and physical health.

The contemporary conceptualization of bidirectional communication between visceral organs and the brain is rooted in the work of Walter Hess. In 1949 Hess was awarded the Nobel Prize in Physiology/Medicine for his paradigm-shifting research on the central control of visceral organs. His Nobel lecture discussing brain control of visceral organs was titled "The Central Control of the Activity of Internal Organs" (Hess, 1949). The first sentence of his speech is both prescient and historical: "A recognized fact which goes back to the earliest times is that every living organism is not the sum of a multitude of unitary processes, but is, by virtue of interrelationships and of higher and lower levels of control, an unbroken unity." This brief statement provides the context upon which the development, application, and acceptance of neuro-autonomic disciplines, such as neurocardiology, have emerged.

This integrative single nervous system perspective encourages a better understanding of the dynamics of neural regulation of an integrated nervous system, while being constrained by the limited paradigms that are frequently used in the contemporary training of scientists and clinicians.

A Polyvagal Perspective

Consistent with Hess and Dobzhansky, our biological mandate of connectedness requires a functional social engagement system (Porges, 2009),
which through common brainstem structures coordinates the striated muscles of the face and head with the vagal regulation of the viscera, originating
in a brainstem region known as the nucleus ambiguus. Thus, the optimally
resilient individual has opportunities to coregulate physiological state with
a safe and trusted other. Ideally, this other person projects positive cues
regarding their autonomic state through prosodic voice, warm and welcoming facial expressions, and gestures of accessibility. From an evolutionary
perspective, the integration of the neural regulation of the viscera with
the regulations of the striated muscles of the face and head enable the visceral state to be projected in vocalizations and facial expressions. This also
allows vocalizations and facial expressions, modulated by autonomic states,
to serve as cues of safety or threat to others. Together these pathways connect behavior to the nervous system and form the basis for social communication, cooperation, and connectedness.

Polyvagal theory, by articulating an evolutionary hierarchy in the function of the autonomic nervous system in response to challenges, provides a
map of the state of the autonomic nervous system during any challenge. By
understanding the autonomic state of an individual, this map informs us of the
emergent behavioral, emotional, and physiological reactivity that an individual may have in response to threat, or alternatively to positive experiences.

From a polyvagal perspective, it will be helpful to investigate how the
COVID-19 crisis moves us into physiological states of threat that would
disrupt our connectedness and place our mental and physical health at risk.
But, more relevant to both clients and personal survival, therapists need to
identify and emphasize the innate resources they have available to mitigate
potentially devastating reactions to threat, which in turn can destabilize
the autonomic nervous system, resulting in visceral organ dysfunction and
compromised mental health. Awareness of the neural systems underlying
polyvagal theory informs both therapists and clients regarding the threats to
survival that can shift autonomic state, moving it through sequential neural
platforms or states that mimic evolution in reverse, or dissolution (Jackson,
1884). Functionally, as we progress through this trajectory of dissolution,
we first lose the competence of our social engagement system (a uniquely

mammalian myelinated vagal pathway involving brainstem structures regulating vocal intonation and facial expressions) to connect with others and calm our physiology. Without these resources, we are vulnerable to move into adaptive defensive states.

Our defense repertoire is first expressed as chronic mobilization requiring activation of the sympathetic nervous system and then expressed as immobilization controlled by an evolutionarily older unmyelinated vagal pathway. In the absence of an active social engagement system, the mobilized state provides an efficient neural platform for fight and flight behaviors. For many individuals, this state will reflect chronic anxiety or irritability. When mobilization does not successfully move the individual into a safe context, then there is the possibility that the nervous system will shift into an immobilized state with associated features of death feigning, syncope, dissociation, withdrawal, loss of purpose, social isolation, despair, and depression. Although both defensive strategies have adaptive values in protecting the individual, they are dependent on different neural pathways (i.e., high sympathetic tone or high dorsal vagal tone), which both interfere with interpersonal interactions, coregulation, accessibility, trust, and feeling safe with another person. Thus, defensive states emerge from neural platforms that evolved to defend, while simultaneously compromising capacities to downregulate our defenses through coregulation with a safe and trusted individual. Basically, the theory emphasizes that in the presence of cues of predictable social interactions of support, our nervous system of safety, the mammalian social engagement system, can downregulate our innate reactions to threat, whether the threat is tangible and observable or invisible and imaginable.

Compassion as Treatment: An Integrated Nervous System Polyvagal-Informed Perspective

In contrast to the frequent definitions of compassion as a psychological construct, polyvagal theory proposes that compassion is an emergent process dependent on one's neurophysiological state. Consistent with this perspective, compassion cannot be taught as a voluntary behavior or a psychological process independent of physiological state. Health care providers cannot express compassion, deliver compassionate care, or be trained to be compassionate through classic rules of learning. In a polyvagal-informed model of compassion, physiological state functions as an intervening variable between the person who is suffering and the responses to the person, which are manifest as subjective experiences and behavioral actions. Thus, compassion is an emergent process dependent on the shared subjective feelings of the patient and health care provider. These critical shared feelings are dependent on the bidirectional communication between two people involving their peripheral physiological state and brain function. Conceptually, compassion is a felt experience when the nervous systems of patients and health care providers communicate with reciprocal cues of safety and trust. Implicit in experiencing and expressing compassion is a shared feeling state that optimizes trust and dampens defenses. During the pandemic, social distancing disrupts opportunities to connect, to be present with others, and to experience compassion.

In polyvagal theory, the neural process of evaluating risk without awareness is labeled neuroception. Neuroception provides the mechanism and identifies the plausible neural pathways that downregulate defense and provide a mutual accessibility to enable the patient's nervous system to be involved in calming and in supporting health and healing. This process is linked to the human biological imperative of connectedness and trust, which would spontaneously lead to coregulation and shift the patient's physiological state to calmness, leading to enhanced homeostatic function with better outcomes.

Public Health Strategies Compound Feelings of Threat

A polyvagal perspective provides clarity in understanding how our perceived vulnerability to the SARS-CoV-2 virus and the mandated strategies of social distancing and self-quarantining impact on our nervous system. First the threat shifts our autonomic nervous system into states of defense, which interfere with the neurophysiological states needed both to coregulate with others and to optimize homeostatic processes leading to health, growth, and restoration. Thus, our nervous system is simultaneously being challenged by incompatible demands for both avoidance of contact with the SARS-CoV-2 virus and the fulfillment of our biological imperative of connecting with others to feel calm and safe. These paradoxical demands require different neurophysiological states. Avoiding being infected triggers a chronic mobilization strategy that downregulates our capacity to calm through social communication and connectedness. Although downregulating our capacity to socially engage, our nervous system intuitively is motivated to seek opportunities for social engagement in which our body would feel safe in the proximity of a safe and trusted person. However, opportunities to engage others, which throughout our evolutionary history have been an antidote to threat that moved us out of physiological states of defense and feelings of anxiety, now convey threat of infection. Thus, the resources of human contact that humans intuitively use to calm may now signal threat. This perspective places us in a quandary, since we now need to both avoid the virus and socially connect.

Mitigating Threat Responses Through Videoconferencing

There is no easy solution to this paradox. However, modern technologies provide us with tools that we can learn to use in a more mindful way. The upside of the current crisis is that although the pandemic is devastating to our nervous systems, it is occurring during a unique time in history when we have tools that enable us to connect even when we are mandated to isolate. To reduce the burden on our nervous systems, we need to retrain ourselves in the use of the portals for social communication that we have available. This will mean that we are more present and less distractible, while providing cues of safety and connectedness through spontaneous reciprocal coregulatory facial expressions and vocal intonations.

For the many clinicians who are now doing therapy remotely through video conferencing, there is a learning curve. This can be exhausting, as both therapist and client become more present while conducting online therapy sessions. Recognition of these challenges can be useful in coping. For example, we need to learn to share feelings and not just words through videoconferencing platforms. Our historic use of video technologies has been for entertainment, business, and education. We have become accustomed to video images as being personally distal, asymmetrical, asynchronous, and unrelated to our personal experiences. Thus, our neural sensitivity to video images is relatively numb through our historical adaptation to two-dimensional screens.

Given the current demands during the health crisis and potentially in the near future, while video conferencing we will need to retune our nervous systems to be more aware of facial expression, vocal intonation, and head gesture. Although in the physical presence of another, while actively involved in spontaneous face-to-face interactions, our nervous system detects these cues intuitively and rapidly without involving conscious awareness. Polyvagal theory labels this spontaneous process neuroception (Porges, 2003, 2004).

We are used to multitasking while watching television and streaming movies. This disembodiment in a social interaction does not provide the nervous system with the required reciprocity to enable and optimize coregulation and connectedness. This distinction between the real and virtual worlds functioned well as long as our nervous systems had sufficient opportunities to coregulate in a physical face-to-face world with safe and trusted friends, parents, or partners. However, with the COVID-19 crisis, the world is different. We need to embrace the virtual world of communication with our knowledge of the cues that our nervous system craves. To accomplish this, we need to become more accomplished at sharing feeling moments and not just syntax while video conferencing.

Conceptualizing Autonomic State as an Intervening Variable Leads to Understanding, Assessing Risk, and Optimizing Treatment

Polyvagal theory informs us that autonomic state functions as an intervening variable moving the individual from defensive states in response to threat to states of social accessibility when supported by cues of safety and trust. From a polyvagal perspective, the physiological state of an individual provides a portal into understanding how they will respond to the pandemic. For example, if we are in an autonomic state of defense, the threat of illness will be compounded by the lack of opportunities to coregulate. Thus, the public health strategies to flatten the curve and slow the transmission of the disease by social distancing and self-quarantining will exacerbate the negative impact that the pandemic will have on us. However, if we have access to trusting friends and family, we have opportunities to coregulate and functionally mitigate the disruptive impact of pandemic-related threat on our nervous systems.

As we grapple with the current situation, it will be helpful to gather data on how individuals are experiencing the pandemic and whether their current autonomic state is related to their reactions to the pandemic. Within this context, we conducted a survey study (Kolacz et al., 2020) in which we evaluated autonomic state using the Body Perception Questionnaire (Cabrera et al., 2018; Porges, 1993). The Body Perception Questionnaire is a survey tool that provides subjective responses of autonomic reactivity consistent with the autonomic circuits described in polyvagal theory to support mobilized (i.e., fight, flight) and immobilized (i.e., death feigning, dissociation, shutdown) defense reactions to threat. Our preliminary analyses of about 1,600 responders from the United States documented important findings consistent with the polyvagal theory.

In summary, the participants who experienced greater autonomic reactivity (i.e., the autonomic nervous system is more frequently reacting in defense) during the COVID-19 crisis also expressed greater amounts of worry about health and economic dangers and greater feelings of social isolation. Adjusting for age, gender, and the mutual associations between outcome variables, formal testing supported the mediation of autonomic reactivity in the link between adversity history and PTSD symptoms, depression symptoms, and COVID-19–related worry.

In deconstructing the role of autonomic reactivity, greater autonomic reactivity was significantly related to depression symptoms ($r = .41$) and PTSD symptoms ($r = .51$). If participants had a history of trauma, including childhood abuse, sexual assault, and physical assault, they reported higher levels of threat-related autonomic reactivity and greater symptoms of PTSD and depression in response to the pandemic. There was a strong linear regression between the number of adverse events and magnitude of autonomic reactivity ($r = .60$).

The statistical models describing the data documented that autonomic reactivity mediated the primary influence of adversity history on outcomes. For example, if the influence of autonomic reactivity was removed from the relationship between adversity history and depression symptoms during the pandemic, the correlation was greatly reduced ($r = .28$ to $r = .05$). When the influence of autonomic reactivity was removed from the relationship between adversity history and PTSD symptoms, a similar reduction in covariation was observed ($r = .40$ to $r = .14$). If the procedures were reversed to remove the influence of adversity, the relationships between autonomic reactivity and the clinical symptoms decreased only slightly (i.e., the correlation between autonomic reactivity and depression symptoms decreased from $r = .41$ to $r = .32$ and between autonomic reactivity and PTSD symptoms decreased from $r = .51$ to $r = .37$). Thus, within this study, autonomic state functions as a powerful intervening variable mediating the impact of adversity history on contemporary reactivity to the pandemic. In another study, consistent with these findings, our group documented the importance of autonomic reactivity as an intervening variable mediating sexual function of male and female trauma survivors (Kolacz et al., 2019).

Using a perspective based on polyvagal theory, we gain a new respect for how an individual's nervous system attempts to navigate through the threats and challenges of the pandemic. By conceptualizing autonomic state as an intervening variable, we have a better understanding of the underlying mechanisms that determine thresholds of reactivity. Common core symptoms of autonomic dysregulation that are captured by self-reported autonomic reactivity are regulated by the brainstem, which interacts with higher-level brain circuits that regulate emotion, attention, and cognition. The integration of these functional pathways can promote disturbance in mental well-being such as hyperarousal, vigilance, depression, and prolonged worry. Finally, these findings may help us develop strategies for using cues of safety and trust to retune the autonomic nervous system, moving both therapists and their clients into states that will support accessibility and coregulation. These results suggest that the sudden, global COVID-caused dangers of life threat, unemployment, economic destabilization, and social isolation may have particularly strong effects for those whose nervous systems may be tuned to optimize vigilance and behavioral responses to threat.

References

Cabrera, A., Kolacz, J., Pailhez, G., Bulbena–Cabre, A., Bulbena, A., & Porges, S. W. (2018). Assessing body awareness and autonomic reactivity: Factor structure and psychometric properties of the Body Perception Questionnaire–Short Form (BPQ–SF). *International Journal of Methods in Psychiatric Research, 27*(2), e1596.

Dobzhansky, T. (1962). *Mankind evolving.* New Haven, CT: Yale University Press.

Dobzhansky, T. (1973). Nothing in biology makes sense except in the light of evolution. *American Biology Teacher, 35*(3), 125–129.

Hess, W. R. (1949). The central control of the activity of internal organs. In *Nobel lectures, physiology or medicine (1942–1962).* Amsterdam: Elsevier.

Jackson, J. H. (1884). The Croonian lectures on evolution and dissolution of the nervous system. *British Medical Journal, 1*(1215), 703.

Kolacz, J., Dale, L. F., Nix, E. J., Roath, O. R., Lewis, G. F., & Porges, S. W. (2020). Trauma history predicts self-reported autonomic reactivity and psychological wellbeing during the COVID-19 pandemic [in press].

Kolacz, J., Hu, Y., Gesselman, A. N., Garcia, J. R., Lewis, G. F., & Porges, S. W. (2019). Sexual function in adults with a history of childhood maltreatment: Mediating effects of self-reported autonomic reactivity. *Psychological Trauma: Theory, Research, Practice, and Policy, 12*(3), 281–290.

Porges, S. (1993). Body perception questionnaire [Unpublished manuscript]. Laboratory of Developmental Assessment, University of Maryland.

Porges, S. W. (1995). Orienting in a defensive world: Mammalian modifications of our evolutionary heritage. A polyvagal theory. *Psychophysiology, 32*(4), 301–318.

Porges, S. W. (2003). Social engagement and attachment: A phylogenetic perspective. *Annals of the New York Academy of Sciences, 1008*(1), 31–47.

Porges, S. W. (2004). Neuroception: A subconscious system for detecting threats and safety. *Zero to Three (J), 24*(5), 19–24.

Porges, S. W. (2007). The polyvagal perspective. *Biological Psychology, 74*(2), 116–143.

Porges, S. W. (2009). The polyvagal theory: New insights into adaptive reactions of the autonomic nervous system. *Cleveland Clinic Journal of Medicine, 76*(Suppl. 2), S86.

5

Beyond Attachment

Understanding Motivational Systems in Complex Trauma and Dissociation

Kathy Steele

THE INTERPERSONAL NEUROBIOLOGY OF SECURE ATTACHMENT HAS BEEN described as the bedrock for adaptive growth and development, and the effects of serious disruptions in attachment are widely known (e.g., Cozolino, 2014, 2017; Schore, 2009, 2012, 2019; Siegel, 2010, 2020). Yet attachment is only one of several innate motivational systems that organize our relational experiences and endow us with tendencies to behave in particular ways under specific relational circumstances. Motivational systems have also been called *emotional operating systems* (Panksepp, 1998), and *action systems* (Van der Hart et al., 2006), as they are organized by primary emotions and direct us to act to achieve particular goals.

Motivational systems involve emergent properties, that is, entirely new and more complex traits that arise from the assimilation and adaptation of these systems to more evolved and integrated levels of functioning. Thus, an emphasis on motivational systems does not preclude essential psychodynamic and other psychological formulations that help us understand our clients' struggles. Indeed, these approaches can be quite well integrated (Cortina & Liotti, 2007).

A number of theorists have described motivational systems, and while there is basic agreement, there are some differences in how these are categorized (Cortina & Liotti, 2010; Gilbert, 2009, 2014; Lichtenberg, 1989; Lichtenberg et al., 2017; Liotti, 2017; Panksepp, 1998; Panksepp & Biven, 2012; Van der Hart et al., 2006). I have elected to use a combination of descriptions that seem particularly well suited to understanding relational responses in complex trauma and dissociation, primarily based on the descriptions of Liotti and colleagues.

The therapeutic tasks of managing conflicts between the attachment motivational system and the defense (sub)systems (flight, fight, freeze, and faint) in traumatized individuals are well documented (for example, Dana & Porges, 2018; Liotti, 2009; Ogden et al., 2006; Steele et al., 2017; Van der Hart et al., 2006). We explore in this chapter the impact of other motivational systems including the *collaboration/cooperation* system, the *caregiving* system, the *panic and loss* system, the *competition/ranking* system, the *sexuality* system (involving prosocial experiences beyond physical mating), and the *play* system. In addition to attachment, these are all prosocial in nature and underpin the social brain. We also consider an additional primitive and nonrelational system, the *predatory* system.

TABLE 5.1 Motivational Systems and Their Goals

MOTIVATIONAL SYSTEM	GOALS
Attachment	• Felt sense of security and safety • Secure base from which to explore the world
Caregiving	• Response to alarm and distress in offspring • Specific response to separation cry • Caregiving may be appeasing under threat
Panic/Loss	• Organized by panic at loss of connection • Grief, depression, loneliness • Separation cry—attempt to restore audiovisual connection with another • Frantic seeking of help/caretaking • Attempts to restore connection and joy
Collaboration/ Cooperation	• Mutual implicit understanding (intersubjectivity) • Cooperation involves independence, with each member acting separately, but with agreement on norms and goals • Collaboration is interdependent and involves active participation on mutually shared goals
Competition/ Ranking	• Maintenance of social hierarchy (dominant and submissive positions) • Management of limited resources (food, love, care, time with another)

	• Competitive aggression involves hot (hyperaroused) aggression to obtain something strongly desired • Submission involves denial of need of resources or appeasement to gain resources (e.g., love, time) • Submission may be a defense against threat (fawning)
Play	• Organized by joy • Exploration and practice • Social connection and learning social boundaries
Sexuality	• Organized by lust • Reproduction • Includes more advanced goals of pleasure
Defense	• Organized by fear • Flight, fight, freeze, and faint to defend against perceived danger or life threat • Fight involves hot (hyperaroused) aggression for protection during danger
Predation	• Intent to injure or kill another • Hunting, stalking • Cold (hypoaroused) aggression • May be planned and calculated • Sometimes involves sadism

Table 5.1, Motivational Systems and Their Goals, lists the systems discussed in this chapter along with the goals each is designed to direct us toward. Motivational systems can be overactivated, overinhibited, or maladaptively combined with other motivational systems in interpersonal trauma in ways that continue to disrupt the individual's relational capacities and interfere with the possibility of adaptive connection with others.

This chapter explores the motivational systems at work in the intersubjective space, how they potentially interfere with attachment and cooperation in psychotherapy, and how they can be identified and worked with to help both therapists and clients experience more adaptive and harmonious shifts between these systems.

Understanding Motivational Systems
in Traumatized Individuals

Motivational systems are products of evolution, beginning with the most primitive systems that organize our behavior and goals toward basic survival: homeostasis (eating, sleeping); hunting (predation); survival of the species (physical mating); seeking, which involves curiosity and expectancy; and responses to danger and life threat (flight, fight, freeze, and faint).

Prosocial motivational systems are later evolutionary developments, mostly emerging from and supporting neocortical functions. They have been referred to as *interpersonal motivational systems* (Liotti & Gilbert, 2011), and include *attachment, caregiving, collaboration/cooperation, competition/ranking, sexuality,* and *play.* These systems involve reflective functioning, the formation of mental representations, and the coconstruction of meaning in the intersubjective space (Cortina & Liotti, 2007). They also generally support curiosity about ourselves and others, an essential component of psychotherapy.

The *panic and loss system* (Panksepp, 1988) is a motivational system that is activated by real or perceived attachment loss and involves the *separation cry* (also called attachment cry or cry for help), a frantic attachment-seeking defense meant to elicit a caregiving response from a "stronger, wiser" other in the face of abandonment panic. It is often highly activated in traumatized individuals, particularly in the therapeutic relationship, and must be addressed thoroughly in treatment, as described later in the chapter.

The motivational system of *defense* is well known in the trauma field. It involves sympathetically activated mobilizing defenses of flight and fight, and the immobilizing defenses of freeze and faint (collapse). These are discussed only in relation to their effects on the prosocial systems in this chapter.

A primitive predatory motivational system involving cold or hypoaroused aggression does exist in humans, and in some individuals may be expressed aggressively (Meloy, 2006, 2012). This system has been discussed as relevant in a few trauma survivors and in their perpetrators (Liotti, 2017; Steele, 2018).

Motivational systems are organized by primary affects. They involve activation of innate neural (perceptual and motor) networks that, in their most nascent expressions, direct us to seek out positive experiences and avoid negative ones, helping us survive. Each organizes and limits our predictions, perceptions, emotions, sensory experiences, and behaviors in the service of achieving particular goals. For example, when the attachment system is active, we predict care, perceive safety, have positive emotions of love and joy, and engage in relational behaviors. But when the defense system is activated, we perceive danger cues, feel fear or terror, and engage in specific behaviors that help us avoid or escape danger.

When one motivational system is activated strongly, others can be inhibited. In some instances this is because the physiological expression of one system is incompatible with that of another system. For example, the several biopsychological states of defense (flight, fight, freeze, faint) are entirely different from those associated with attachment or collaboration/cooperation. However, more importantly the goals of these systems are different (as noted in Table 5.1), regardless of physiology. For example, the goals of understanding and cooperation in the collaboration system are quite different from those of competition for resources found in the competition/ranking system.

In normal development, motivational systems mediate our actions in a harmonious way, shifting seamlessly and collaboratively, appropriate to the current situation, with ongoing adaptive modifications and elaborations. Once we achieve a goal, there should be a signal to end an action and begin a new one, based on a new goal. This signal naturally inhibits the active motivational system, making room for the activation of other systems as we pursue other goals. Pierre Janet noted that an experience of pleasure or joy signals the end of well-completed actions, what he called the "act of triumph" (1925). This joy or positive affect involves an implicit or explicit sense of "Yes, I did it!" and marks the end of one action, paving the way for new goals and actions to emerge

Developmental trauma interferes with smooth shifts and adaptive transitions and combinations among motivational systems. The "act of triumph" is often missing in traumatized individuals, who go from one uncompleted action (mental, relational, behavioral) to another. It is imperative to restore a full stop at the end of an action (Ogden, 2019). Otherwise traumatized individuals can become rather fixed in particular motivational systems (and related goals) that are not adaptive to the situation. For example, one client can be fixed in the defense of fight or freeze (defense system) in the presence of the therapist; another is relatively fixed in sexual reactions (sexuality system) in the wrong situations with the wrong people; yet another might be stuck in endless contests and struggles for control (competition system) with others, always needing to dominate, or perhaps to chronically submit; another engages in persistent caregiving of others (caregiving system), eschewing his or her own needs; and another is fixated in frantically seeking care and connection (separation cry).

Neuroception and Motivational Systems

The motivational systems with which we are concerned in trauma can be divided roughly into two categories or types: more primitive ones involving defense against threat (flight, fight, freeze, and faint), and the ones arising from the neocortex that involve functioning in a social world. Neuroception, our innate neural detection of safety, danger, or life threat (Porges, 2011), is the first step in determining which type of motivational system is more likely to be activated in a given situation, as prosocial systems are inhibited when the individual perceives serious threat. To be clear, the attachment or caregiving system can be activated through the separation cry in early threat detection to seek protection from safe others, but seeking connection becomes inhibited as threat increases.

Developmental trauma interferes with the neuroception of safety and regular activation of the ventral vagal complex, favoring threat detection and associated dysregulation and difficulties with mentalizing. Seriously traumatized individuals tend to operate more often from overactivated motivational systems involving defense against danger and life threat or from maladaptive combinations or substitutions of prosocial motivational systems. For example, some individuals become excessively focused on sexual behavior to achieve love and connection, acting from the sexuality system rather than the attachment system. Others might habitually engage in freeze when relational intimacy becomes possible, acting from the defense system. Yet others might attempt to connect by creating a hierarchical structure in which one in a dyad must be submissive and the other dominant, indicating persistent activation of the competition/ranking system.

Variability in Mentalizing Among Motivational Systems

Because motivational systems both direct and restrict our attention, perceptions, and goals, our capacity to accurately reflect and mentalize the state of mind of others can be affected by the activation or inhibition of a given system (Liotti & Gilbert, 2011; Mitchell & Steele, 2020). For example, when defense is activated, prefrontal activity decreases, leaving an individual unable to reflect and mentalize except on a most primitive level, focused on threat cues, predicting dangerous states of mind in the other. Various prosocial motivational systems can also affect our capacity to mentalize. For example, an individual who is dominant or submissive (competitive system) will be less likely to accurately perceive the intentions of another regarding the desire to cooperate and collaborate on an egalitarian basis, and may make assumptions about the other that fit better with a competitive (dominant/submissive) state of mind rather than one of collaboration.

Motivational Systems in Disorganized Attachment and Dissociative Disorders

A central dilemma in the psychotherapy of individuals who suffered serious interpersonal trauma and neglect as children is that attachment is both needed and experienced as a threat. This is the core conflict of disorganized attachment.

Traumatized individuals with disorganized attachment typically have an overactivated attachment system, in which frantic attachment seeking erratically alternates with attachment avoidance and defense against threat, maintaining a high level of interpersonal dysregulation. This results in phobic avoidance of attachment on the one hand, and phobic avoidance of attachment loss on the other (Steele et al., 2005, 2017; Van der Hart et al., 2006). The neural pathways of the social brain are easily disrupted by ongoing avoidance and inability to reconcile this most basic relational conflict. Reflective capacities and ability to understand nuanced and implicit communications are lost in these states. Tolerance of minor and normal oscillations in distance and closeness and minor ruptures may become impossible.

The therapeutic relationship is meant to be a vehicle of repair and connection, yet relationship is the very experience that causes the most suffering and pain to clients. Closeness is all too often perceived as a prelude to danger and pain. The closer and more vulnerable the relationship, the more likely activation of defense will deactivate or delimit attachment in many clients. Thus, explicit bids for attachment by the therapist may increase inner conflict, despite the client's yearning for closeness (Steele et al., 2001, 2017). In response, the client may operate from other motivational systems that do not promote regulation. For example, the client may engage the therapist through control (dominance) or being controlled (submission) in the competition/ranking system, or engage in caregiving, or become fixed in attachment cry, desperately seeking the therapist outside of session.

Therefore, a major dilemma in treatment is how to develop a good-enough therapeutic relationship with clients who cannot yet engage adequately through the attachment system without intense conflict or dependency. A number of authors have emphasized the importance of avoiding further activating the already overactivated attachment system of relationally traumatized clients by adaptively utilizing other prosocial systems, in particular the collaboration/cooperation system (Brown & Elliott, 2016; Cortina & Liotti, 2010; Liotti, 2009, 2014, 2017; Steele, 2018; Steele et al., 2017). Play or cooperation may be activated in clients whose attachment system is overactivated and who do not feel safe with others, helping them to achieve an improved sense of well-being (Dana & Porges, 2018; Liotti, 2009, 2011, 2014, 2017; Steele et al., 2017). This regulation provides an initial "safe enough" interpersonal space to initiate therapy and is discussed later in this chapter.

The inherent conflict between attachment and defense in disorganized attachment may lead to developmental fractures in the sense of self of the chronically traumatized child. Several authors have proposed that disorganized attachment is a necessary prelude to the development of dissociative disorders such as dissociative identity disorder (Liotti, 1992, 2009, 2011; Steele et al., 2017; Van der Hart et al., 2006).

Dissociative identity disorder involves much more than spacing out and shutdown, symptoms commonly labeled as dissociative. This disorder involves dissociation of the personality in which there are multiple and contradictory mental representations of self and others, eventually resulting in different senses of self, some of which the client is unable to fully own.

The degree of disconnect between senses of self has a wide range in dissociative identity disorder, from "I know Little Mary must be me, but it doesn't feel like she is me"; to "I am Mary, but that disgusting child is *not* me"; to "I know Mary, but I am *not* Mary, I am Joe"; to "I am Joe and I don't know Mary"; to "I am Joe and I am going to kill Mary; we are separate people." Regardless of the severity of disintegration of self, dissociative identity disorder presents unique and complex therapeutic challenges due to profound inner conflicts combined with serious lapses in awareness and voluntary control.

It is likely that motivational systems serve as primary organizers of dissociative parts of the personality, shaping sense of self in line with particular organizations of perceptions, goals, sensorimotor components, behaviors, emotions, and cognitions (Nijenhuis, 2015; Steele et al., 2017; Van der Hart et al., 2006). This complicates therapeutic work with motivational systems since the activation of various dissociative parts of the client serves to over-activate or inhibit particular systems and thus contributes to a highly conflicted internal organization.

A common example is a client who has a child part fixed in separation cry. As the client seeks attachment when this part is activated, other parts whose function is to defend against threat are activated, as attachment is perceived as dangerous. One part, mediated by the competition system, might attempt to control how the therapist responds, ensuring the therapist will give the care that is sought. Another part organized by caregiving might be solicitous of the therapist and attempt to shut down attachment-seeking behaviors. A different part, organized by the sexuality system, confuses the therapist's care with sexual attraction. These intense conflicts can lead to a cascade of chaotic distress in the client and confusion in the therapist who is unaware of the dissociative disorder.

Dissociative parts are typically organized internally in a way similar to the original family, with victim, abuser, rescuer, and neglectful bystander dynamics (Liotti, 2017; Steele et al., 2017; Van der Hart et al., 2006). These dynamics result in persisting disorganized attachment, and each of these roles has underpinnings in motivational systems. For example, victim parts are typically organized by animal defenses against threat (flight, fight, freeze, faint) or the ranking/competitive system (appeasement, controlling punitive strategies), the sexual system (sexual behaviors to appease or gain care), separation cry (to gain care from a stronger, wiser other), or the caregiving system (controlling caregiving strategies), or sometimes even play (to distract or evoke a shift in emotional tone in a perpetrator). Hostile, angry types of dissociative parts are organized by aggression, which can be defensive (fight), competitive (gaining a desired goal through aggression), or predatory (with intent to hurt or kill). Rescuers are often external to the client and are typically organized by caregiving, often in ways that promote maladaptive dependency. Internal neglectful bystanders mimic the helpless caregiving strategies of overwhelmed parents who abdicated responsibility to care for the child.

At more complex levels, underpinned by motivational systems, psychodynamic defenses are also at play. For example, victim parts may also be organized by fantasies of rescue, or fantasies of becoming a perfect person as a defense against grieving. Some aggressive parts, particularly those that experience themselves as the perpetrator, may be defending against shame or identify with the aggressor to protect against realizing vulnerability and powerlessness.

Motivational Systems in the Therapist

The therapeutic relationship is rife with enactments of trauma, in which both therapist and client are participants (Bromberg, 2001; Chefetz, 2015; Schore, 2012, 2019). Each enactment involves a unique activation and inhibition of various motivational systems in both client and therapist that prevent secure attachment and a felt sense (Gendlin, 1981, p. 10) of well-being promoted by dominance of the ventral vagal system.

Interpersonal neurobiology places an emphasis on coregulation, necessary not only for the adaptive development of the child, but for adult relationships to flourish, and with good reasons. In fact, the regulatory effects of secure attachment promote adaptive and harmonious functioning among all motivational systems, not just attachment. As therapists, we are taught the primacy of attachment with our clients, the necessity of providing a good-enough relational experience that involves intersubjective reciprocity, consistency and predictability, compassionate intention, curiosity, high levels of mentalizing, and efforts toward repair when ruptures occur.

However, these capacities of the therapist are not always a steady state. The therapist is not always in attachment mode but can shift to motivational systems that are not adaptive to the therapeutic context at times. For example, the therapist might shift to an animal defense (flight, fight, freeze, faint) with an especially aggressive or overwhelmed client. Another therapist, feeling frustration that the client is rebuffing help, can shift to a competitive strategy of dominance, trying to force the client to accept interventions. Or a therapist may engage in submissive behaviors to appease an aggressive client. A predatory therapist might shift to the sexuality system and exploit the client's vulnerability for sexual gratification. Many therapists shift to the caregiving system, in which they feel an urgency to act and relieve the client's suffering, further activating the client's attachment seeking, resulting in maladaptive dependency, as described in more detail below. It is no easy task to have a stable therapeutic relationship with many clients, whose severe and chronic dissociation, shame, rage, dependency, entitlement, or avoidance of vulnerability and relationships are impediments to connection. Shifts among motivational systems can be identified by shifts in emotion and goals, so the therapist must be constantly attuned to nuanced changes.

Next, each motivational system is described in more detail, with some treatment implications.

The Collaborative/Cooperative Motivational System

The need to be understood, to share and cooperate with each other, is a basic motivational system (Cortina & Liotti, 2010; Lichtenberg, 1989; Trevarthen & Aitken, 1994). It is the foundation of intersubjectivity that is "dedicated to the communication of psychological states" (Trevarthen & Aitken, 1994, p. 623), based on the need to understand the intentions and emotions of others in order to live cooperatively in groups. Collaboration is both a prelanguage endeavor at a somatic, implicit level, and one that eventually involves language and explicit communication. Once safety is neurocepted, the collaborative system helps us further explore the intersubjective space that we share with another before attachment is activated. Thus, the use of the collaborative system allows for cooperative connection without additional activation of the client's attachment system that is so highly conflicted.

This motivational system is separate from, but likely underlies, attachment and care systems, for without understanding and mutual sharing we could not attach and care for each other adequately. Like secure attachment, the collaboration system activates social engagement. Attachment is directed toward safety, and caregiving is responsive to attachment-seeking behaviors, but collaboration is directed toward continual implicit and explicit understanding and sharing, allowing us to work cooperatively in our respective roles on shared therapeutic goals of treatment (Cortina & Liotti, 2010).

Treatment Implications

Engagement in collaborative/cooperative endeavors requires our active curiosity and sufficient authentic presence and self-awareness. We can then focus on process over content and careful attention to intersubjective experiences. The collaborative system in therapy can be activated by a focus on safety and mutually shared therapeutic goals for the client, and efforts to understand the client and have the client understand the therapist, with attachment taking a backseat, at least in the beginning of therapy. This allows the client to focus with more curiosity on inner experience as steps are taken in achieving goals rather than on the highly conflicted attachment dilemmas of closeness and distance. In a positive feedback loop, being cooperative supports and strengthens social engagement, which allows for the eventual possibility of attachment.

The Separation Cry:
The Panic and Loss Motivational System

The separation cry is part of the motivational system associated with panic and loss (Panksepp, 1998). It is activated by the absence of the caregiver and directs the individual to frantically seek out a (stronger, wiser) person who will provide help and comfort. The separation cry is organized by several primary affects: panic at separation, sadness at loss, and joy at reunion. It also involves a sense of profound helplessness that translates into an experience of severe dependency in some clients (Steele, 2018; Steele et al., 2017). The genuine unmet needs of the child in the absence of a responsive caregiver can lead to chronic overactivation of the separation cry, particularly in situations where clients feel distressed.

Permanent modifications in the emotional substrates of separation distress—panic, depression, grief, and loneliness—can result in lifelong struggles. The intense negative emotions of the separation cry can become chronic or inhibited in traumatized individuals, preventing the harmonious completion of this cycle (Steele, 2018). The client may become stuck in panic and frantic seeking of attachment, or in sadness and despair that prevents the resolution of grief, unable to experience the joy and safety of connection even when the therapist is physically present. It is imperative not to further activate this system in therapy.

When frantic attachment seeking (separation cry) is activated in the traumatized client, the neocortical interpersonal motivational systems are temporarily inhibited, along with mentalizing and reflective functioning. Thus, implicit regulatory communication pathways are inhibited. The singular goal of the client becomes gaining proximity to and caregiving from the therapist, rather than exploring and working with their own experiences to learn more adaptive strategies, potentially derailing therapy.

Adaptive Versus Maladaptive Dependency

Dependency and attachment cry are intertwined and can become problematic in therapy. Bowlby (1969, 1979, 1980) and Bornstein (1998; Bornstein & Bowen, 1995) have made essential distinctions between adaptive and maladaptive dependency. Adaptive or mature dependency is the ability to utilize support and help to grow and develop. In other words, the therapist's understanding, help, and support become stepping-stones for the client to make developmental strides, to learn and practice new skills, and to better explore in therapy what is painful and unresolved. The client continues to value autonomy in daily life even while leaning on the therapist to engage in therapeutic endeavors.

Maladaptive dependency involves a hyperactivated separation cry and distress, helplessness, and reliance on the therapist to increasingly manage crisis and provide comfort both in and outside of therapy (Steele et al., 2001, 2017). Trauma survivors have higher levels of dependency than other populations (Hill et al., 2000), leaving them (and their therapists) vulnerable to becoming overwhelmed by their dependency. When traumatized clients experience the therapist as unavailable for any perceived reason or when they otherwise feel alone or misunderstood, the separation cry can be activated (Steele et al., 2001, 2017).

The highly dependent client is chronically distressed, unable to reflect and engage in higher cortical functioning, necessary capacities in therapy. Such clients may make an increasing number of phone calls or send emails or texts between sessions, have escalating episodes of crisis, and request additional sessions. They may react with rage or despair—or both—when the therapist is not available. Once the therapist is reached, there is usually an initial calm and the client reports feeling better, which may reinforce for the therapist that additional contact is helping. However, in short order, these clients descend into distress once again upon separation. In these cases, the more contact the therapist has with the client, the worse the client becomes over time.

The Need-Shame-Rage Cycle

Because separation cry involves a profound sense of helplessness and vulnerability, it can also activate traumatic memories of trauma and neglect, and provoke enactments involving the inability to act on one's own behalf. The more the therapist does for such clients, the more they maintain a mental representation of themselves as incompetent and inadequate and as requiring help. This experience typically activates shame, which serves to inhibit need.

The more shame clients feel, the more aggressive or avoidant strategies they will employ to mitigate shame. They may then direct rage toward self or toward the therapist, isolate from others, or avoid inner experiences related to need and shame (Nathanson, 1997; Steele, 2018; Steele et al., 2017). In addition, closeness to the therapist in moments of caregiving may further activate mental representations associated with memories of relational danger, evoking avoidance of attachment, once again leaving the client feeling desperately alone, ultimately reactivating the separation cry in an endless cycle.

Treatment Implications

It is imperative that the therapist recognize separation cry in clients, for example, in those who consistently have difficulty leaving sessions due to dysregulation, or who make frequent requests (or demands) for contact outside of session or for additional sessions. The content of these requests may be quite real, for example, needing help with flashbacks and suicidal crises, but the underlying goal of separation cry to gain proximity to and caregiving by the therapist must always be acknowledged and worked with; otherwise clients can develop ever more crises in order to gain proximity to the therapist.

A client's distress and attachment seeking does not activate the therapist's attachment system, but rather the caregiving system, which in adaptive situations can effectively mediate the therapist's and client's attachment systems, as occurs in secure parent-child interactions (Feeney & Woodhouse, 2016; George & Solomon, 2011). Thus, from the perspective of the therapist who is unaware, caregiving feels entirely natural and intuitive and there seems no reason to question it, even when the client's dependency is maladaptive. In addition, some therapists are confused about the differences between attachment and caregiving, and the differences between adaptive and maladaptive dependency, compounding the problem.

Caregiving is generally much more focused on the actions and agency of the therapist rather than being with clients, supporting their agency, and cooperatively working with implicit relational processes. The role of the caregiver is to be a stronger, wiser other, which potentially places the relationship in a somewhat hierarchical model, with the client as the submissive, helpless, needful one and the therapist as the dominant, capable one whose role is to relieve the suffering of the client rather than to explore it and support capacity building (emotion regulation, mentalizing, activation of positive experience and emotion, capacity to grieve, etc.).

Entirely unintentionally, this dynamic may activate the competition system in the client under certain circumstances, as well as victim-persecutor and victim-rescuer dynamics. Meanwhile, the therapist may become caught in a trap of rescuing the client from distress instead of supporting curiosity, mentalizing, and self-agency in the client. This is a destructive cycle to recognize and interrupt in therapy.

When separation cry and maladaptive dependency are chronic and intense, the therapist, whose caregiving system is highly activated, may become increasingly distressed and concerned about the safety and well-being of the highly dysregulated client, resulting in what Solomon and George have termed "helpless caregiving" in a parent (George & Solomon, 2011; Solomon & George, 1999). When caregiving and compassion become fused with helplessness and urgency in the therapist, the result is either an abdication and withdrawal from the client, or continual efforts to rescue the client. In either case, the therapist feels helpless and has difficulty tolerating the distress of both client and self. The intensity of the therapist's distress reduces reflective capacities, leaving the therapist (and client) to rely ever more on action rather than on mentalizing and curiosity. The therapist has trouble holding in mind the competencies of clients and how to build on them and is unable in the moment to be curious about ways in which clients are stuck in dependency and may be using defenses to avoid painful grief.

A meta-approach, often with the help of consultation, can support the therapist in recognizing that the caregiving system has become overactivated and is part of the problem. Once the therapist has restored reflective functioning, reasonable therapeutic boundaries can be reestablished, and the client supported in understanding and managing separation panic differently. In these cases, a cooperative approach focused on specific and mutually shared therapeutic goals can be reparative (Steele et al., 2017). In a few cases, the therapist may be unable to restructure the therapy with support and cannot attain a mentalizing perspective and move to the collaborative system. Termination of therapy may be recommended as a last resort, with support for the therapist to do so in a way that ensures continuity of care for the client and ongoing consultation and therapy for the therapist. But every effort should first be made to support the therapist in shifting out of the mutual enactment with the client, as the working through these enactments is an essential part of therapy (Schore, 2012).

Development of Stable Mental Representations
The client (or certain dissociative parts of the client) may be numb and shut down during sessions or preoccupied by the next impending separation. Either state precludes a meaningful connection in the present. This is an essential problem to recognize and explore, because if the presence of the

therapist is not experienced in the moment of contact, no amount of being there will help the client.

The therapist should assess for an inability of the client to experience a positive felt sense of the therapist (and others) and have an intentional therapeutic focus on this difficulty. Clients often have great difficulty holding a stable mental representation (or internal working model) of the therapist, both in and out of session. Contradictory representations of the therapist as neglectful ("She doesn't understand or care about me") or abusive ("He wants something from me; he wants to hurt me") compete with more realistic representations, as well as unrealistic ones ("She will take care of me and be the mother I never had"). In addition, some clients are fearful that intolerable memories and emotions will flood them if they allow themselves to experience compassion from the therapist. Yet others believe they do not deserve to have connection, and so avoid it.

Many clients avoid these inner conflicts by dissociating any sense of the therapist: "When I leave session, you disappear." Even in session, the client is often so avoidant of connection or so preoccupied with losing the therapist that a felt sense of the good-enough therapist is not encoded. This results in an inability to construct a stable adaptive mental representation of a secure safe haven, leading to further activation of separation cry.

The Caregiving Motivational System

Caregiving is an innate drive to protect and care for others in distress. While it has been primarily associated with parenting, caregiving is broader and can be active in all types of relationships. Caregiving is active even in very young children and continues to be so throughout life.

The disturbed caregiving system in parents has received much attention (e.g., Feeney & Woodhouse, 2016; George & Solomon, 2011; Liotti, 2017; Solomon & George, 1999). It is relevant to our understanding of the ways in which traumatized individuals might utilize caregiving as a relational strategy, as well as behaviors in the therapist. When a caregiver is persistently frightened, depressed, or dependent, the child may develop controlling caregiving strategies that emerge from the caregiving system, as the parent views the child as the stronger, wiser, more capable one. The child is thus placed in a parentified position, and this behavior may persist into adulthood. While appeasing (submissive) behaviors may appear similar to actual caregiving behaviors in the controlling caregiving strategy, it is important to determine whether the individual is operating from the caregiving or competition system, as they involve different goals, emotions, and dynamics to be worked through in psychotherapy.

Some clients may abdicate genuine caregiving with their children or others, or pets. They lack a responsiveness to the distress of others, because they are too shut down, because they lack empathy, because they need to avoid painful memories of not being cared for themselves, or because they feel others do not deserve the care they themselves did not receive.

Many clients have overactivated caregiving systems, engaging in what is commonly called codependent behavior. These clients learned that pleasing others is rewarding in that it wards off fears of attachment loss. They may have had parents who were overwhelmed in some way: anxious, depressed, traumatized, and they felt the need to actively take care of the parent to receive minimal care themselves. They seek to please, care for, and serve others to be accepted. They tend to feel enormous guilt for real or perceived failures of caregiving and are intensely loyal. Generally, low self-esteem and a feeling of being "less than" are part of the psychological profile, and caregiving compensates to some degree for this deficit.

Treatment Implications

The overly caregiving client is typically seeking attachment and avoiding attachment loss through taking care of others, so awareness of personal preferences and needs are suppressed. In dissociative clients, these needs are often sequestered from awareness of the caregiving part of the client, along with ongoing rage that the needs are not met. The client may engage in self-punishment to further inhibit needs. The therapist can support exploration of the goals of caregiving beyond pleasing others. A punitive, controlling strategy is often implicit and hidden beneath the caregiving. When the client can be more aware of anger at not getting his or her own needs met, this strategy often emerges more clearly. Gradually the client can be supported in more balanced and egalitarian relational strategies, with the therapist modeling them in the therapeutic relationship.

The Competitive/Ranking Motivational System

The competition/ranking system evolved from the need to compete within social groups for resources that may be limited, as well as to maintain social order through hierarchical structure. Originally this was primarily focused on managing food resources or selecting mating partners, but it can also be applied to relational resources such as attention and care. Mammalian social structures are typically hierarchical, requiring strict adherence to social codes involving dominant and submissive behaviors. This hierarchy serves to maintain stability of the group and ensure an orderly distribution of food and social resources.

Competitive behaviors in humans can be either dominant or submissive. Disorganized attachment involves a collapse of attachment and defensive strategies and subsequent reorganization into generally dominant and submissive behaviors, the punitive controlling and caregiving controlling strategies (Liotti, 2011; Main & Cassidy, 1988). One important study noted that children with secure attachment histories tended to engage in cooperative relationships (the collaborative system), but those with insecure attachment tended toward either dominance and control (the controlling punitive strategies) or submission (fawning and controlling caregiving strategies) (Troy & Sroufe, 1987).

Submission

Frightening, abusive caregivers may elicit appeasing or fawning behaviors in the child, understood as the controlling caregiving strategies. These emerge from the submissive component of the competition system and are based in fear. The goal is to reduce threat from a dominant other by pleasing or calming a dysregulated—usually angry—caregiver. This is a second type of controlling caregiving behavior, with the other based on the caregiving system (see above). The goals, emotions, and dynamics involved are different, even though the behavior may be similar.

Submission and Shame
One theory of shame regards its evolutionary origins in the ranking/competition system. The functional intent of shame is to help us manage social threats and keep within the bounds of prevailing social limits (Gilbert, 1989; Liotti & Gilbert, 2011). When we perceive that we have broken the agreement or when others accuse us of doing so, shame ensues. The psychophysiology of shame is remarkably like that of submission: eye gaze down and averted, and slumped, hypoaroused posture.

While acute shame is adaptive, chronic shame is devastating, and unfortunately, it is pervasive in highly traumatized individuals. Chronic shame impedes neuroception of safety, as mental representations of others involve criticism and rejection, and representations of self involve a sense that one lacks dignity, competence, adequacy, or lovability. Thus, authentic connection with others becomes impossible. Dissociative clients are often organized by chronic shame, with inner shamers and ashamed parts in constant conflict, maintaining chronic shame. In the relational and internal worlds, dominance and submission become integral ways of relating to attempt to mitigate shame.

Dominance

Controlling punitive strategies that emerge from the collapse of attachment strategies primarily involve competitive aggression. Competitive aggression is concerned with achieving a goal: "You have something I want, and I am going to hurt or punish you in order to get what I want or need." In this case, the goal is to obtain the desired object or experience (food, love, care, attention, etc.). The aggression will cease as soon as the goal has been achieved. For example, a client may be overly aggressive with a therapist who does not, cannot, or will not give something, such as an extra session or contact between sessions.

Certainly, many other manifestations of dominance involve competition. For example, some clients are so highly competitive that they will do almost anything to win. In therapy, this may manifest in the client being unable to engage in cooperative endeavors with the therapist.

Treatment Implications

The therapist may use psychoeducation to explain the controlling strategies and help the client understand and recognize these patterns in a compassionate and nonjudgmental manner. The experience of the therapist with clients who engage in competitive behaviors is often one of feeling controlled; indeed, the purpose of controlling punitive and caregiving strategies is to control the other to gain care and love or some other resource. The solution is often to explore what clients really need to develop and grow and to find acceptable and adaptable ways to reach their goals, and to grieve when that is not possible. A shift to cooperative and collaborative work on shared goals is often the best option and renders controlling strategies unnecessary (Liotti, 2014; Liotti & Gilbert, 2011). The therapist should be aware of any tendencies toward his or her own controlling strategies, either punitive or caregiving, to appease the client.

Competitive aggression should be distinguished from defensive or predatory aggression (Liotti, 2017). Competitive aggression is an attempt to gain a desired outcome. Defensive aggression is an attempt to thwart attack and danger, with a goal of protection (fight response). Predatory aggression, which is discussed later in the chapter, has the goal of killing or injuring for its own sake.

Fawning behaviors based on fear of the therapist and others should be noted and worked through. Often this is manifested in the good client who does everything the therapist asks and reports that everything the therapist says and suggests is helpful, even though change is not occurring. Fear of attachment loss or punitive responses by the therapist should be carefully explored and worked through.

The role of chronic, pervasive shame in maintaining dysregulation and dissociation in chronically traumatized individuals cannot be overstated. There are many helpful strategies for working with shame, too numerous and complex to describe here (e.g., DeYoung, 2015; Nathanson, 1994, 1997; Steele et al., 2017). Acknowledging the role of submission in shame supports the therapist in shifting in the moment of shame to a more egalitarian position of cooperation, helping the client explore the outer boundaries of shame, how shame is managed, and entering into the experience of shame in order to transform it (Steele et al., 2017).

The Sexual Motivational System

Maladaptive sexual behaviors in traumatized individuals emerge from the combination of other motivation systems and the sexual motivational system (Liotti, 2017). The prosocial sexual system is more complex than mere mating because it is also about connection and sensual enjoyment.

Sexually exploited children may utilize sexual behaviors with or without attachment components. Some clients behave flirtatiously or seductively toward the therapist, or the felt experience of sexual energy may be more implicit in the session. The need to be loved and protected becomes fused with sexual behavior, and sex is viewed as achieving care or love. Some clients may engage in high-risk sexual behaviors, constantly seeking but never finding the safe haven and sense of love for which they so yearn. Other clients may separate the attachment and sexual systems, viewing others only as objects of sexual gratification, without meaningful emotional connection. There is no sense of warmth or care, or interest in the other person's experience. While this may seem predatory on the surface, often these individuals can be quite caring, compassionate, and responsive in nonsexual relationships. This may become a compulsive activity that wards off painful memories, emotions, or conflicts, avoiding the possibility of attachment and love.

Other systems can also be combined with the sexual system. An adaptive combination could involve play and sexuality for lovely iterations of playful sex, and, clearly, secure attachment and sexuality are important combinations. A maladaptive pairing might involve immobilizing defenses of freeze or faint with sexuality, in which the individual is unable to move. Predation and the sexual system are paired in sexual predators.

Treatment Implications

The therapist should be alert to implicit, unconscious, or conscious sexualization of the therapeutic relationship. Careful inclusion and management of any dissociative parts that are highly sexualized is essential to adequately resolve sexualized transference and maladaptive sexual behaviors. The therapist and client should explore the meaning of sexual behavior: Is it meant to gain attachment, a component of controlling behaviors or submission, a manifestation of self-punishment secondary to shame, and so on?

The Play Motivational System

Play, including sense of humor, is about social learning and social limits. When we play, we practice skills, develop bonds with others, and learn the parameters of what is fun and enjoyable versus what hurts. Play is an important component of interpersonal relationships and is essential for the development of the social brain (Kestly, 2014).

Play involves heightened positive affect, namely joy, and widens the window of tolerance for some negative emotions, such as disappointment when one loses a game. The absence of positive affect and ability to play is notable in many traumatized clients. Kohut (1971) observed that a sense of humor is an important mark of maturity that is impaired in clients with major psychopathology, and it is an important prognostic factor.

Many traumatized clients have inhibited capacities for play and playfulness. The creativity, spontaneity, and freedom of play may feel out of control to some clients, both emotionally and physically. Humor may be self-deprecating or hostile in some and may be a defense against other emotions or closer relational connections.

The inhibition of negative affect in traumatized individuals is not sufficient for treatment; rather, it is essential to develop and accentuate positive affect (Fosha, 2000; Schore, 2012). Several authors have noted that depression is due not only to the presence of negative affect but to the absence of sufficient positive affect (Panksepp et al., 2014; Schore, 2012). Play is a motivational system that activates the ventral vagal complex (Dana & Porges, 2018) and can be an important system to utilize in psychotherapy to enhance positive affect and relational regulation (Kestly, 2014). Play can be coupled with other motivational systems. For example, play and cooperation are activated among team members in sports or other group endeavors; play and competition are activated between groups; play and sex can be paired for playful sex; and play and attachment can be activated in couples and parent-child dyads.

Play and Positive Emotions as Defense

It is worth noting that play and positive emotions also can be used defensively. Laughter is an essential behavior and expression of joy but can also be used to deride or humiliate; teasing can be affectionate or cruel; play can be cooperative or sadistic (Panksepp, 2000). Thus, play can also be paired in less adaptive ways with other motivational systems. For example, play and fight can occur when a child suddenly feels belittled during play or is accidentally hurt by another child; play and competition can be paired to cheat in a game or to always need to be the best and win; and play can be involved in grooming a child for sexual abuse ("Let's play a little game of touch"). In dissociative identity disorder, playful child parts can have the function of distracting the therapist and avoiding painful memories or pleasing the therapist out of fear (Steele et al., 2017).

Mosquera (2017) observed that positive emotions more generally related to idealization can interfere with domestic violence victims leaving their partners, and Stark (2002) noted that idealization of the therapist and certain positive fantasies ("I had a wonderful childhood"; "My therapist will fix everything for me") serve to defensively avoid grieving. The defensive use of play, humor, and positive emotions should be carefully noted and explored in therapy.

Treatment Implications

The use of play in therapy has been discussed as a means to activate the social engagement system (e.g., Dana & Porges, 2018; Kestly, 2014; Ogden et al., 2006; Ogden & Fisher, 2016). This may or may not involve literal play, but often involves the judicious use of humor or simple activities like tossing a ball back and forth. Practicing grounding and regulating exercises together can be done with playfulness and fun. Clients can be encouraged to explore their reactions to fun and pleasure and try small experiments in having fun.

The Predatory Motivational System

While we are primarily concerned in this chapter with prosocial motivational systems, there is one additional system that bears mentioning. In more extreme and rare cases, aggression may not emerge from competition or from defense against direct threat, but from the predatory motivational system (Liotti, 2017; Meloy, 2006, 2012; Steele, 2018). Predatory aggression has its evolutionary foundation in hunting (Meloy, 2006, 2012), involving relatively little emotion or arousal, and thus is considered to be a cold aggression (Glenn & Raine, 2008; Hanlon et al., 2013; Raine et al., 1998). Physiologically it is quite distinct from the hot emotional aggression of jealousy or rage stemming from relational injury or a sense of injustice or unfairness, or from fighting rage in reaction to threat or shame. It is not directed toward punishment and submission for not meeting the individual's needs (competition) or to survive threat, but toward the desire to injure or kill another, to prey on the vulnerable. Predatory aggression can occur impulsively, not in reaction to perceived threat, or can be carefully planned and calculated over time. In rare cases, it can be paired with pleasure or enjoyment in sadistic individuals.

Treatment Implications

Most clients do not display predatory aggression, but a few do, and the danger posed to the unaware therapist (and others) is sufficient to make it noteworthy. Thus, therapists should be adept at recognizing psychopathy or psychopathic traits in select clients, and should be able to distinguish between predatory, threat-related, and competitive aggression, as treatment differs. When predatory aggression is activated, the therapist should not attempt to activate attachment but seek to establish a safe environment for both client and therapist. Otherwise, the therapist may be in a vulnerable position, which can further activate the predatory system in the client.

Conclusion

This chapter has focused on several motivational systems in addition to attachment that affect relationships and have a significant impact in interpersonal neurobiology. These evolutionary underpinnings of emotion and behavior are highly relevant to the treatment of chronically traumatized individuals, including those who have dissociation of the personality (for example, dissociative identity disorder). They can substitute for attachment in both adaptive and maladaptive ways. Recognition of moments when these systems are activated becomes yet another powerful tool in the hands of the psychotherapist to offer a therapeutic relationship that regulates and provides a safe intersubjective space for clients to explore their experiences, change their inner organization, and develop more satisfying lives.

References

Boon, S., Steele, K., & Van der Hart, O. (2011). *Coping with trauma-related dissociation: Skills training for patients and therapists*. New York: Norton.

Bornstein, R. F. (1998). Depathologizing dependency. *Journal of Nervous and Mental Disease, 186*, 67–73.

Bornstein, R. F., & Bowen, R. F. (1995). Dependency in psychotherapy: Toward an integrated treatment approach. *Psychotherapy, 32*, 520–534.

Bowlby, J. (1969). *Attachment and loss: Attachment*. New York: Basic Books.

Bowlby, J. (1979). *The making and breaking of affectional bonds*. London: Tavistock.

Bowlby, J. (1980). *Loss, sadness, and depression* (Vol. 3). New York: Basic Books.

Bromberg, P. (2001). *Standing in the spaces: Essays on clinical process, trauma and dissociation*. New York: Routledge.

Brown, D. P., & Elliott, D. S. (2016). *Attachment disturbances in adults: Treatment for comprehensive repair*. New York: Norton.

Chefetz, R. (2015). *Intensive psychotherapy for persistent dissociative processes: The fear of feeling real*. New York: Norton.

Cortina, M., & Liotti, G. (2007). Implicit unconscious processes, intersubjective abilities, and evolutionary models of the mind: New approaches to understanding human nature. *Fromm Forum* [English edition], *11*, 40–51.

Cortina, M., & Liotti, G. (2010). Attachment is about safety and protection, intersubjectivity is about sharing and social understanding: The relationships between attachment and intersubjectivity. *Psychoanalytic Psychology, 27,* 410–444.

Courtois, C. A., & Ford, J. D. (2015). *Treatment of complex trauma: A sequenced, relationship-based approach.* New York: Guilford.

Cozolino, L. (2014). *The neuroscience of human relationships: Attachment and the developing social brain* (2nd ed.). New York: Norton.

Cozolino, L. (2017). *The neuroscience of psychotherapy: Healing the social brain* (3rd ed.). New York: Norton.

Dana, D. A. (2020). *Polyvagal exercises for safety and connection: Fifty client-centered practices.* New York: Norton.

Dana, D. A., & Porges, S. W. (2018). *The polyvagal theory in therapy: Engaging the rhythm of regulation.* New York: Norton.

DeYoung, P. (2015). *Understanding and treating chronic shame: A relational/neurobiological approach.* New York: Routledge.

Feeney, B. C., & Woodhouse, S. S. (2016). Caregiving. In J. Cassidy & P. R. Shaver (Eds.), *Handbook of attachment: Theory, research, and clinical applications* (3rd ed., pp. 827–851). New York: Guilford.

Fosha, D. (2000). *The transforming power of affect: A model for accelerated change.* New York: Basic Books.

Gendlin, E. (1981). *Focusing* (rev. ed.). New York: Bantam.

George, C., & Solomon, J. (2011). Helpless caregiving: The development of a screening measure. In J. Solomon & C. George (Eds.), *Disorganized attachment and caregiving* (pp. 133–166). New York: Guilford.

Gilbert, P. (1989). *Human nature and suffering.* Hove, UK: Lawrence Erlbaum.

Gilbert, P. (2009). *The compassionate mind: A new approach to life's challenges.* London: Constable and Robinson.

Gilbert, P. (2014). The origins and nature of compassion focused therapy. *British Journal of Clinical Psychology 53,* 6–41.

Glenn, A. L., & Raine, A. (2008). The neurobiology of psychopathy. *Psychiatric Clinics of North America, 31,* 463–475. doi:10.1016/j.psc.2008.03.004

Hanlon, R. E., Brook, M., Stratton, J., Jensen, M., & Rubin, L. H. (2013). Neuropsychological and intellectual differences between types of murderers: Affective/impulsive versus predatory/instrumental (premeditated) homicide. *Criminal Justice and Behavior, 40,* 933–948. doi:10.1177/0093854813479779

Hill, E. L., Gold, S. N., & Bornstein, R. F. (2000). Interpersonal dependency among adult survivors of childhood sexual abuse in therapy. *Journal of Child Sexual Abuse, 9,* 71–86.

Janet, P. (1925). *Psychological healing.* New York: Macmillan.

Kestly, T. A. (2014). *The interpersonal neurobiology of play: Brain-building interventions for emotional well-being.* New York: Norton.

Kohut, H. (1971). *The analysis of the self: A systematic approach to the psychoanalytic treatment of narcissistic personality disorders.* New York: International Universities Press.

Lichtenberg, J. D. (1989). *Psychoanalysis and motivation.* Hillsdale, NJ: Analytic Press.

Lichtenberg, J. D., Lachmann, F. M., & Fosshage, J. L. (2017). *Self and motivational systems: A theory of psychoanalytic technique.* New York: Routledge.

Liotti, G. (1992). Disorganized/disoriented attachment in the etiology of dissociative disorders. *Dissociation, 5,* 196–204.

Liotti, G. (2009). Attachment and dissociation. In P. F. Dell & J. A. O'Neil (Eds.), *Dissociation and the dissociative disorders. DSM V and beyond* (pp. 53–65). New York: Routledge.

Liotti, G. (2011). Attachment disorganization and the controlling strategies: An illustration of the contributions of attachment theory to developmental psychopathology and to psychotherapy integration. *Journal of Psychotherapy Integration, 21,* 232–252.

Liotti, G. (2014). Overcoming powerlessness in the clinical exchange with traumatized patients. *Psychoanalytic Inquiry, 34,* 322–336.

Liotti, G. (2017). Conflicts between motivational systems related to attachment trauma: Key to understanding the intra-family relationship between abused children and their abusers. *Journal of Trauma and Dissociation, 18,* 304–318.

Liotti, G., & Gilbert, P. (2011). Mentalizing, motivation, and social mentalities: Theoretical considerations and implications for psychotherapy. *Psychology and Psychotherapy: Theory, Research and Practice, 84,* 9–25.

Main, M., & Cassidy, J. (1988). Categories of response to reunion with the parent at age six: Predictable from infant attachment classifications and stable over a 1-month period. *Developmental Psychology, 24,* 415–526.

McEllistrem, J. E. (2004). Affective and predatory violence: A bimodal classification system of human aggression and violence. *Aggression and Violent Behavior, 10,* 1–30. doi:10.1016/j.avb.2003.06.002

Meloy, J. R. (2006). Empirical basis and forensic application of affective and predatory violence. *Australia and New Zealand Journal of Psychiatry, 40,* 539–547. doi:10.1080/j.14401614.2006.01837.x

Meloy, J. R. (2012). Predatory violence and psychopathy. In H. Häkkänen-Nyholm & J.-O. Nyholm (Eds.), *Psychopathy and law: A practitioner's guide* (pp. 159–167). New York: Wiley.

Mitchell, S., & Steele, K. (2020, May 23). Mentalising in complex trauma and dissociative disorders. *European Journal of Trauma and Dissociation.* https://doi.org/10.1016/j.ejtd.2020.100168

Mosquera, D. (2017). Idealization and maladaptive positive emotion: EMDR therapy for women who are ambivalent about leaving an abusive partner. *Journal of EMDR Practice and Research, 11,* 54–66.

Nathanson, D. (1994). *Shame and pride: Affect, sex, and the birth of the self.* New York: Norton.

Nathanson, D. (1997). Affect theory and the compass of shame. In M. R. Lansky & A. P. Morrison (Eds.), *The widening scope of shame* (pp. 339–354). Mahwah, NJ: Analytic Press.

Nijenhuis, E. R. S. (2015). *The trinity of trauma: Ignorance, fragility and control.* Göttingen, Germany: Vandehoeck and Ruprecht.

Ogden, P. (2019). Acts of triumph: An interpretation of Pierre Janet and the role of the body in trauma treatment. In G. Craparo, F. Ortu, & O. van der Hart (Eds.), *Rediscovering Pierre Janet: Trauma, dissociation, and new context for psychoanalysis* (pp. 200–209). New York: Routledge.

Ogden, P., & Fisher, J. (2016). *Sensorimotor psychotherapy: Interventions for trauma and attachment.* New York: Norton.

Ogden, P., Pain, C., & Minton, K. (2006). *Trauma and the body: A sensorimotor approach to psychotherapy.* New York: Norton.

Panksepp, J. (1998). *Affective neuroscience: The foundations of human and animal emotions.* London: Oxford University Press.

Panksepp, J. (2000). The riddle of laughter: Neural and psychoevolutionary underpinnings of joy. *Current Directions in Psychological Science, 9,* 183–186. doi:10.111/1467-8721.00090

Panksepp, J., & Biven, L. (2012). *The archaeology of mind: Neuroevolutionary origins of human emotions.* New York: Norton.

Panksepp, J., Wright, J. S., Döbrössy, M. D., Schlaepfer, T. E., & Coenen, V. A. (2014). Affective neuroscience strategies for understanding and treating depression: From preclinical models to three novel therapeutics. *Clinical Psychological Science, 2,* 472–494.

Porges, S. W. (1995). Orienting in a defensive world: Mammalian modifications of our evolutionary heritage: A polyvagal theory. *Psychophysiology, 32,* 301–318.

Porges, S. W. (2011). *The polyvagal theory: Neurophysiological foundations of emotions, attachment, communication, and self-regulation.* New York: Norton.

Raine, A., Meloy, J. R., Bihrle, S., Stoddard, J., LaCasse, L., & Buchsbaum, M. S. (1998). Reduced prefrontal and increased subcortical brain functioning assessed using positron emission tomography in predatory and affective murderers. *Behavioral Sciences and the Law, 16,* 319–332.

Schore, A. N. (2009). Right-brain affect regulation: An essential mechanism of development, trauma, dissociation, and psychotherapy. In D. Fosha, D. Siegel, & M. Solomon (Eds.), *The healing power of emotion: Affective neuroscience, development and clinical practice* (pp. 112–144). New York: Norton.

Schore, A. N. (2012). *The science of the art of psychotherapy.* New York: Norton.

Schore, A. N. (2019). *Right brain psychotherapy.* New York: Norton.

Siegel, D. (2010). *The mindful brain: The new science of personal transformation.* New York: Norton.

Siegel, D. (2020). *The developing mind: How relationships and the brain interact to shape who we are* (3rd ed.). New York: Norton.

Solomon, J., & George, C. (1999). Attachment and caregiving: The caregiving behavioral system. In J. Cassidy & P. R. Shaver, *Handbook of attachment: Theory, research, and clinical applications* (pp. 649–670). New York: Guilford.

Stark, M. (2002). *Working with resistance.* Northvale, NJ: Jason Aronson.

Steele, K. (2018). Dependency in the psychotherapy of chronically traumatized individuals: Using motivational systems to guide effective treatment. *Cognitivismo Clinico [The Legacy of Giovanni Liotti]*, *15*(2), 221–226.

Steele, K., Boon, S., & Van der Hart, O. (2017). *Treating trauma-related dissociation: A practical integrative approach.* New York: Norton.

Steele, K., Van der Hart, O., & Nijenhuis, E. R. S. (2001). Dependency in the treatment of complex posttraumatic stress disorder and dissociative disorders. *Journal of Trauma and Dissociation*, *2*, 79–116.

Steele, K., Van der Hart, O., & Nijenhuis, E. R. S. (2005). Phase-oriented treatment of structural dissociation in chronic traumatization: Overcoming trauma-related phobias. *Journal of Trauma and Dissociation*, *6*(3), 11–53.

Trevarthen, C., & Aitken, K. J. (1994). Brain development, infant communication, and empathy disorders: Intrinsic factors in child mental health. *Development and Psychopathology*, *6*, 597–633.

Troy, M., & Sroufe, L. A. (1987). Victimization among preschoolers: Role of relationship history. *Journal of the American Academy of Child and Adolescent Psychiatry*, *20*, 166–72.

Van der Hart, O., Nijenhuis, E. R. S., & Steele, K. (2006). *The haunted self: Structural dissociation of the personality and treatment of chronic traumatization.* New York: Norton.

6

Becoming a Therapeutic Presence in the Counseling Room and the World

Bonnie Badenoch

AS I WAS SUBMITTING THE FIRST VERSION OF THIS CHAPTER, ALL OF US were finding ourselves plunged into the emergency of the COVID-19 pandemic. Ongoing uncertainty coupled with emergent crises coming hour by hour and day by day were keeping us on high alert. Images of terror and death side by side with bravery, kindness, and movement toward each other were alternately agitating and quieting our nervous systems, tightening and opening our bellies, and contracting and expanding our hearts. Wave after wave of these powerful experiences were sweeping through every system in our bodies, touching old wounds and old strengths. Adaptive beings that we are, after a time, many (but certainly not all) found their systems settling into new patterns as we began to realize we were going to be living with this virus for a long time. People told me they were taking deeper breaths again, following their need for connection by finding new ways to join with others even with social distancing.

On May 25, any sense of settling was shattered by the horrific murder of George Floyd by police officer Derek Chauvin in Minneapolis. George's words—"I can't breathe"—tore at the hearts of people around the world, men and women of all colors and nationalities. Perhaps our own fears about dying breathless because of COVID-19 rendered us more resonant with his loss of breath. Perhaps this latest outrage, coupled with the very recent murder of Ahmaud Arbery by two vigilantes, ignited 400 years of trauma embedded in the bodies of our Black citizens. Perhaps the nervous system tension brought on by ever-increasing polarization in this country because of massive injustice and inequality in so many areas of life also added fuel to the Black Lives Matter protests that bloomed even in small cities with few people of color. The experience of witnessing such an upwelling of solidarity within so much diversity awakened in me a sense of the goodness at the center of what it is to be human—empathic connection leading to strong action on behalf of others. At the same moment, rage in a few of the protesters and many of the police was ripping us in the other direction—toward fear and despair at witnessing the state of our country. While fear of the pandemic was moving into the background as the limited capacity of our minds and hearts was strained past its ability to hold multiple overlapping traumas, it nonetheless remained present in our bodies, which are capable of noticing so much more than our conscious minds.

At this moment, the pandemic continues while our traumatized nation struggles to find a coherent response because we have lost our sense of being with and for each other. There is no clear path forward for the cultural and societal changes that would move us in the direction of justice and equality. Our planetary home continues to be desecrated each day. Everything is standing on the narrow ledge between movement toward regaining an embodied sense of our deep humanity and sliding into the multiple potential catastrophes wrought by alienation from who we humans are meant to be. We are all holding our breath.

I am a white woman, coming to terms with what my whiteness means to me and to Black people in a new way. I am an old woman feeling the threat of a virus that takes refuge in bodies like mine. I am a mother and grandmother looking in sorrow and fear at the degradation of our planet. In the midst of it all, I am a student of interpersonal neurobiology (IPNB), holding its tenets close for guidance in this time of relational crisis at every level—these moments that are filled with danger and opportunity in proportions not often seen. I do believe that IPNB, when taken in slowly and embodied, provides a path toward healing the pervasive trauma that has captured all of us. By the time you read this, the immediacy of these experiences may have faded, but their effects will still be lingering in our bodies as we face whatever challenges are to come.

It is the nature of us social beings to turn toward one another for safety, reassurance, accompaniment, and meaning. We do this unless our wounds make it impossible for us to access this most essential resource—each other.

Those of us (including you) who are part of the IPNB community likely have heightened awareness of how profoundly we are interwoven with each other. My fear can become yours through the signals we exchange below conscious awareness. My safety can offer sanctuary for your frightened self. We coregulate and co-dysregulate together. My mirror neurons and resonance circuitry will ripple your internal state through my body, and I may begin to shake with you or feel compassion and care well up inside so that I am a comfort to you. In times of helplessness, we find help in each other's presence through eyes and voice (even when we can't touch, even when we wear a protective mask), and in the embodied memory of those with whom we have trustworthy and caring bonds. If my history has taught me that it is dangerous to be in connection, then I may withdraw more deeply into my isolation during this time. I may find that the isolation of others leaves me feeling less alone, or I may slide toward depression and despair. If I am terrified of those who are different than me, I may seek to protect myself by resorting to hatred and violence in the midst of this struggle for greater equality and care for each other. Or I may begin a humble and close study of what has shaped my relationships with Black people. I might be drawn to broaden that to include Indigenous people and other people of color. No matter what, we are in this together in the most profound embodied sense as we are touched by these current experiences and all that is awakening within us from our history.

The same alienation from our inborn capacity to lean into healing, supportive connection with one another is fueling the slow trauma we are all experiencing as our Earth—with whom we are inextricably intertwined and on whom we are utterly dependent—is being damaged each day. I see the pandemic, the cruelty of pervasive injustice and inequality, and the Earth's desecration as springing from the same root—our estrangement from our birthright, the felt sense of "we." This tragic departure from our nature has a powerful influence on our embodied systems, even when most of that lies outside awareness as we protect ourselves by forgetting and ignoring. When we move instead toward remembering and attending, as painful as this may be, these long-held embodied traumas can heal. Then the neural circuitry that allows us to perceive and act from a felt sense of "we" can open a different path.

What follows is the story of how the embodiment of IPNB and relational neuroscience became the foundation for a group of us to gradually experience a more profound way of being present in our counseling rooms and our daily lives. Day by day, we found ourselves becoming more rooted in the neural circuitry that is nourished by ongoing receptivity to each other. In this time of physical distancing, unrest, and the struggle not to lose the thread of possible change, the ability to see both the beauty of our diversity and our common humanity reflected in each other's eyes and to deeply attend is life-giving for the one offering to listen and the one being heard.

The word "transformational" is used so often that it has lost much of its inherent power and meaning. Perhaps we can reclaim some of that potency here by beginning with its etymology—something or someone that causes a person or situation to undergo a change of shape or form. Deepening into an embodied experience of the principles of IPNB over the past 17 years has indeed changed my internal shape to the extent that what emerges in the counseling room is a quietly yet radically different relational experience for me and for the courageous people who come to heal. Over time, I am finding that this change of perspective influences every encounter I have in the world.

Interpersonal neurobiology is more than a theory drawn from the discoveries of relational neuroscience. It is an invitation to make direct contact with the heart of our genetic human inheritance. As Stephen Porges (Porges & Phillips, 2016) says, "Connection is a biological imperative." Marco Iacoboni (2011) speaks of the importance of the interpersonal world this way: "We have created the self-other distinction in our explicit discourse, along with many other constructs that divide us. Our neurobiology, in contrast, puts us 'within each other'" (p. 57). These are powerfully relational words at a time when our society is focused much more on the values of a left-hemisphere-based worldview (McGilchrist, 2009)—self-reliance and self-regulation; the priority of tasks, behaviors, and goals over relationships; and, in our field, the importance of assessments, protocols, tools, and interventions. From its inception, IPNB (Cozolino, 2014; Schore, 2003; Siegel, 2020) has pointed us toward our interconnectedness, toward the ways we are continually shaping one another's neural firing patterns from the womb until our last breath. The emergence of our sense of being an individual paradoxically arises from how we become woven into one another. Quite literally, IPNB shows us that there is no "me" apart from "us."

There is also no expansion of the application of IPNB apart from how each of us has come into unique relationship with the principles. Many of us have been drawn into the orbit of this seminal work, so that it has become like a large tent holding the diverse ways we have applied its understanding of what it is to be human beings in relationship with each other. How we are attracted by particular aspects of IPNB likely has something to do with our own history as well as with how these principles have reshaped the ways we offer therapy. I know my own early experience of extreme attachment loss drew me to IPNB's emphasis on presence as central to any healing process. As each of us has persevered in our explorations, we have gone through a unique developmental process that has gradually changed our perception of what it is to be a human being, how we are hurt and healed in relationship, and what this means for us as clinicians and as citizens of the world.

Part of this development often involves drawing scientists and theo-reticians who are outside the Cozolino-Schore-Siegel core into our orbit because they resonate with what feels particularly meaningful about IPNB for each of us. For me, these have included Stephen Porges (2013), Iain McGilchrist (2009), Marco Iacoboni (2011), Lane Beckes and James Coan (2011), Jaak Panksepp (Panksepp & Biven, 2012), Uri Hasson (Hasson et al., 2012), and Bruce Ecker (Ecker et al., 2012). Inside me, these seminal explor-ers and thinkers have engaged with each other to become partners with the three founders to create an ever-evolving vision that supports, deepens, and enriches both the principles and application of IPNB.

Initially, each of the three progenitors gave me many pieces. Here I will mention what comes most fully to mind and heart right now. When I think of Lou Cozolino (2014), the phrase "social synapse" comes alive. That our brains are both inside us and between us keeps our attention on the rela-tional space between. Dan Siegel's (2020) formulation of the pathways of neural integration and how they unfold in the space between gave me eyes to see injury and health in terms of what had the support to integrate and what hadn't. I began to see markers of healing emerging through increases in response flexibility, emotion regulation, moral sensitivity, and more. Allan Schore's (2003) deep sense of the importance and tenderness of the earliest days of life helped me have ears to hear my clients' stories with greater attention to how their current relational struggles are linked to these earliest implicit foundations. His emphasis on right brain-to-right brain communi-cation became a constant guide to practice, remembering particularly the power of what flows between our clients and us with no words.

My own relationship with IPNB began when I heard Dan Siegel speak for about 90 minutes at a conference in 2003. At the time, I was the clini-cal director of a small group of marriage and family therapists in Orange County, California, all of us dedicated to working with people suffering from severe attachment losses and egregious abuse. The most immediate effect of hearing Dan was visceral, with the hair standing up on the back of my neck. It was as if his scientifically grounded explanation of the neurobiology of how we become traumatized and then heal began to put a different kind of foundation underneath the work we were doing with our courageous survivors. My whole body knew this was important. Today, bringing in Iain McGilchrist (2009), I would say that my left-hemisphere knowledge became a stronger support for my right-hemisphere capacity to hold a space for healing. It settled something in me, and then very soon in my interns as well. As we began to study IPNB more deeply (I was now in Dan's monthly study group), we started to be able to picture what was unfolding within our clients more clearly. I noticed I felt calmer and my interns reported a decrease in anxiety of about 50%, particularly when their clients' systems became activated. Interpersonal neurobiology was already entering the therapy room as each of us became a more regulated and therefore safer presence for our people.

I don't know that we would have talked about these changes in terms of safety then, but a couple of years later as we began to integrate Stephen Porges's (2007) polyvagal theory with what we were learning from IPNB, we were gradually becoming more aware of the sustained influence the state of our autonomic nervous system (ANS) was having on our clients' regulation. Specifically, we understood that if we were experiencing the sympathetic arousal of fear, even at a level below conscious awareness, our people were more likely to also feel unsafe. As we gained greater awareness of the neurobiological intricacies of coregulation, of our human sensitivity to even the slightest movements that might indicate disconnection, we became more conscious of how this process was unfolding in our own lives from day to day. Pendulating between theoretical knowledge and personal experience was laying the all-important foundation for embodiment of the principles. In the light of our own experiences, which we talked about regularly in supervision, our compassion for the easily aroused responses of our clients' ANS was rapidly growing. Dysregulated behaviors that once may have brought on fear or irritation in us could now be met with understanding and empathy that made room for greater coregulation. Bit by bit, our people were responding to this offering of deeper attending and greater receptivity to them, whatever their current state, by moving into the necessary trauma work with more ease and frequency. We were also less tired at the end of the day.

Without specifically trying, this new knowledge was helping us become less judgmental because we were less afraid and had fewer reasons to defend ourselves or take control with our clients. One of my interns told me that he used to feel his whole body tighten when a particular client came into the room because he knew that, at some point during the session, she was going to get angry with him. He said he would watch everything he said to try to keep her anger away while thinking what an impossible person she was. More and more, he found himself able to stay with curiosity about what might be making her feel so unsafe that she had to get angry to protect herself. He explained that the difference was mostly in his body feeling more relaxed and open, which made room for curiosity and a different perception of her. The knowledge he was absorbing was allowing his own ANS to settle, and all the rest flowed from that. He also noticed that she was needing her anger less often as he was more able to stay with her, however she was.

With more moments like these, we realized even more fully that nonjudgmental receptive presence, without imposing our own agenda, is indeed the core of safety and the foundation of healing. Without our own agenda, our people were free to move as their inner world directed, with us following their lead with whatever support we had to offer. We were joyously discovering that each person had a reservoir of inherent wisdom about what needed to happen next. Warm, wise accompaniment was becoming more important than planful doing. Being human, we were also regularly forgetting this new way of being, and taking control again as our nervous systems gave us often-subtle signals of danger. This constant reminder of our humanness was also a gift as it gave us fewer judgments when our people were also unable to sustain change in a linear manner.

Day by day, as our understanding of IPNB principles was gradually becoming more refined through study, repetition, daily practice, and conversations with each other, certain core ways of seeing what it is to be human began to emerge. One that significantly changed our presence in the counseling room was our growing realization that we each carry a bounty of inherent health, no matter how broken we are feeling in this moment. Two aspects of this were central for my group early on. The first part is that a genetically embedded need for connection is at the core of our humanness. This means that our system is always seeking the most nourishing attachments it can imagine (Siegel, 2020). It is true that our imagination is constrained by our previous relational experiences. We found that wounds in this area were central for almost everyone who came to our office in search of healing. However, it is equally true, thanks to an abundance of neuroplasticity, that if we have relationships rich in warm reflection, our anticipation of what is possible in relationship will shift in the direction of expecting this from those with whom we connect. Often this change gradually happens in the counseling relationship when the therapist can provide that kind of receptive, reflective experience consistently. Our system is just waiting for the arrival of another to partner with us in support of the emergence of our natural movement toward healthy relatedness. Standing firmly on this understanding, we could hold the vision of a system actively seeking attachment even with our most wounded people. Thanks to the power of right brain-to-right brain communication, they seemed to feel buoyed by our hope. More than one person said to me, "You believe I'm not broken, don't you?" While a quiet nod affirmed that, the person had clearly already been touched below the level of words.

The second heartening message that came early on has to do with our brains being complex systems with natural co-organizing ability (Siegel, 2020). While the capacity for neural integration is built into our system, it requires the presence of another to emerge. We would discover later how true this is for so many of our systems (ANS, midbrain emotional-motivational systems, even our belly brain's functioning). We relational people are full of inherent capacities that blossom through nourishing connection with another. This means that our system's healing capacity is innate and ongoing, needing only the accompaniment of someone who can enter with us into the vulnerable places that hold our traumas, while providing what Bruce Ecker (Ecker et al., 2012) calls disconfirming experiences. When we bring what was needed at the time of the traumatic event but not available—acceptance to the humiliated one, safety to the endangered one, presence to the abandoned one—the wisdom residing in their neural system guides integration of the experience.

With just these two pieces, we found we began to see our people differently. No matter how wounded, how disorganized, these two inherent capacities were waiting in them for support. While this matters at the level of our awareness, it matters most to what happens in the space between our people and us, often without words. What we see in our people is what is energized in them. We were attending differently, and as McGilchrist (2009) says, "In all these circumstances, you will also have a quite different experience not just of me [the one attending], but of yourself: you would feel changed if I changed the type of my attention" (p. 28). The respect and hope we felt for them began to shift their sense of themselves and supply a foundation for them so that these inherent healing capacities could awaken. This way of being seen, in itself, was often a disconfirming, restorative experience. My interns told me they were also hearing things like "You really do believe I can heal!" from some of their clients who had felt too broken to mend, while others simply settled more deeply into the hard work of recovery with greater tenacity and a stronger sense of sanctuary with their therapists.

Side by side with this burgeoning sense of inherent health, we were deepening into understanding the power of implicit memory to shape our lives at every moment (Schore, 2012; Siegel, 2020). These underground streams have been built and strengthened in our relationships over decades, patterns embodying both nurturance and embedded wounds. They shape and color every thought, feeling, action, and relationship. They mold the perceptual lens through which we experience the world. In parallel, we found that the deepening realizations offered by IPNB were also shaping our perceptual lens, helping us see our people with fewer assessments, greater understanding, and compassion for their unique current struggles. The connection between past experience and current feelings and behaviors became clearer to us and then to them, opening a pathway toward warm curiosity and exploration rather than criticism and blame for past actions and relationships from either of us.

I recall working with a young man who had come to me lost in shame because he had shaken his infant son. At one time, I feel sure judgment and aversion would have arisen in me at least briefly. His system would have been touched by that, no matter what happened next. Instead, I found myself immediately curious about what had awakened in this loving father that led him to do something so abhorrent to him. Without me saying anything in response to his admission, he met my gaze and said, "You don't hate me, do you?" I replied with reassurance, but I feel certain that those words were less important than what he had already sensed about my inner state. Day by day, we were more clearly experiencing that decreases in judgment bring increases in safety, and this opens the door to healing.

Since implicit memory is embodied memory, we also found ourselves getting more in tune with our own bodies, more aware of the implicit experiences that would awaken in us in the course of being therapists and in daily life. We were realizing that the more we could both understand (left hemisphere) and become viscerally aware (right hemisphere) of our own experience, the more what we were learning could become a living practice with our people. We were becoming more attuned to their bodies as the plate of working memory—that tiny plate of seven to nine awarenesses at a time—began to change to accommodate a more even distribution between words and sensations as we listened to ourselves and to them. We may not have been able to name it at the time, but because of the increase in listening brought on by this embodiment, we were becoming more skilled followers of their experience. Posture shifting slightly, eyes becoming a bit more tense, a face beginning to get rosy or pale—all of these signals became important communications that we could more easily feel, meet with warm curiosity, and follow as different aspects of our people announced their presence.

As we will see, we were in the early stages of developing a capacity to let go of leading, of taking charge of the therapy in favor of supporting the other person's inherent pathway and process toward health. This is not a passive stance, but one of active attention that was leading us to attune to what our people were bringing rather than formulating our own plan. Then, from the methods most familiar to us, we could offer possibilities for fostering movement toward healing. We offered these with what we might call an appropriate tentativeness, checking with our people's inner worlds to see if they felt what we proposed was the right next step. After listening for a while to whatever my person was bringing that day, I might say, "I'm wondering if it feels like moving to sand tray might be helpful. How is that for you?" Then we would pause for my person to listen as deeply as possible in that moment to the response from his inner world. Because I had no investment in whether or not we did sand tray, there was no implicit pressure for him to do it or not. Doing this, I was shown over and over again that this person's system knew a lot more than I did about what was needed next. Over time, this respectful rhythm of following and responding gradually became the bedrock of the process emerging in us as we deepened into IPNB.

Bit by bit, this deeper sense of the power of the implicit was leading us to a felt-sense understanding of this principle: Each of us is literally doing the best we can at any moment, given the state of our neurobiology and our level of support. This opens the way for radical inclusiveness of every part of a person. While our group had always cognitively believed in offering this, our growing experience of being received by each other, no matter what state we were in, was settling this idea into our bodies. As we brought this broad receptivity to our people, who were often sunk in shame, lost in anxiety or depression, or captured by self-hatred, it seemed their bodies felt our steady holding. Even though we offered words about this, it became clear to each of us that the power originated in the strength of the right-hemisphere-to-right-hemisphere communication of the value of every part. Often, eyes brightened, spines straightened a bit, and the flow of connection deepened as they lifted out of self-hatred and self-blame. This next part is difficult to capture in words. It was as though our ever-widening circle of inner acceptance of ourselves was catalyzing their capacity for finding value in all parts of themselves. As this compassionate acceptance bloomed in both of us, a circle of cohealing that was bigger than the two of us also arrived. Words like "grace" and "blessing" seem appropriate for this experience.

We began to understand that in these exchanges, more was going on than words being spoken. This perhaps goes back again to how people are changed by the way we attend to them. Over time, we had noticed we would sometimes offer thoughts about a particular IPNB understanding without the inner conviction. The other person might be touched briefly but not experience an inner change. On the other hand, we could hold an inner conviction that had become embodied in us and not have it come into words. Something would likely shift to some extent because of how we were seeing this person, but without the kind of clarity that made it more solid, more tangible. What we gradually found was that the combination of embodied conviction with words that clearly conveyed a scientifically grounded understanding seemed to reach the whole person, often in enduring ways.

We wouldn't have said it this way then because we weren't yet aware of Iain McGilchrist's (2009) work, but we eventually understood that we and our people were having a whole-brain experience. The right hemisphere was allowing for the resonant connection between us that conveyed the felt sense of the concept before words, while the left hemisphere was being the able emissary by grounding it in words. All of this was then flowing back to the right hemisphere where these experiences of communion were unfolding.

All of this is to say that the importance of slowing down and making space for new learning to become embodied was getting clearer to us. It increasingly changed the way we did training and supervision. By staying with one principle for a long time, we are making room for integration throughout our neural system. Then when we had the opportunity to share some of this learning with our people, it was not just an idea but an experience that we were offering. We stopped using the word "psychoeducation," which seemed to lead us and our clients toward a more left-hemisphere-only communication. Instead, we thought of it as a concept-supported empathic response to our people's inner request for understanding applicable in this particular moment. Couples often came in feeling bewildered about why they were fighting so much. As they talked about a particular conflict, we shared that the felt sense of unsafety with each other was provoking a pro- tective response, that no one was to blame. Understanding a little bit about how their ANSs were responding to each other made room for the three of us to become curious about how this lack of safety was arising. As curiosity bloomed, the experience of safety arrived. This weaving of concepts with experience supported an enduring change in how they saw each other. It also often gave them a perception-changing framework for exploring their relationship at home.

After spending about six years focusing mainly on core IPNB principles, we were beginning to be drawn toward other theoreticians and scientists whose work was confirming and expanding our understanding of the depth of our influence on one another's neural firings. In about 2010, we became aware of Iain McGilchrist's (2009) work. It was another of those times, as with Dan Siegel's first talk, when everything settled a little differently because of McGilchrist's seminal viewpoint on the two hemispheres of our brains. Much that we were understanding through IPNB was deepened and clarified. There is no way to do justice to his work in this small space. How- ever, his understanding of the "two people" living in our brains in the form of these two hemispheres—and particularly the need for the two of them to be in right relationship—further strengthened the foundation for understand- ing the nature of the therapeutic relationship—and really, all relationships.

McGilchrist (2009) talks about the two hemispheres in terms of how each perceives, and then creates, the world. Our right-hemisphere circuitry opens our capacity to be attentive to others, to the space between, and is taking in the felt sense of aliveness of new experience in every moment. When we are attending to our people by being present to their unique experience in this moment, without judgment and without overlaying our own perspective (as much as that is humanly possible), our right-hemisphere circuitry is in the lead. This kind of receptivity is the foundation for a felt sense of safety in the one being heard. Attending in this way communicates to people that they can be vulnerable because they will be received.

The left hemisphere, on the other hand, takes what the right hemi- sphere brings, renders it static, and categorizes it so it can create systems.

In the process, what is individual and unique is stripped away to attend to the overall pattern. When we find ourselves planning interventions based on assessment, for example, we have likely given our left hemisphere the lead. In the process, we have to some degree abandoned our people's in-the-moment experience. Because of Steve Porges's work, it was becoming clear to us that this kind of departure from attentiveness is something our people's nervous systems notice, particularly at the level of neuroception, out of conscious awareness. They will adaptively then respond by shutting down vulnerability to some degree, sometimes by joining us in the left hemisphere.

Both hemispheres are necessary and valuable, McGilchrist (2009) says, but need to be in the right relationship with each other. It is the nature of the right hemisphere to be prone to anxiety because it is attending to what is emerging in this moment and the next and the next. Everything is uncertain. For us to attend as fully as possible, we are agreeing to live in this fluctuating sea. A left hemisphere that is educated in the ways of the right and in a broader understanding of how human beings are hurt and healed can provide a stable platform of supportive knowledge to steady us as we enter more and more fully into the territory of unknowing.

For balance and health, McGilchrist (2009) suggests that the right hemisphere needs to be in the lead, creating a potentially empathic and connected experience, while the left becomes the indispensable emissary who supports but does not lead. The knowledge offered by IPNB is the richest source I have found for educating the left in the ways of the right hemisphere while providing scientifically grounded information about the human brain. At the same time, IPNB, with its emphasis on relationship, invites us into the need for embodying the knowledge, a right-hemisphere way of knowing, so that the two hemispheres can move into an optimal relationship with each other. We thrive when thinking and embodied experience match.

This kind of hemispheric integration is also crucial for us to move forward together in this time of pandemic, social unrest and the call for justice, and planetary challenge. When we are able to lead with the right hemisphere, the felt sense of "we" emerges. All beings become valued in their uniqueness. Judgment recedes while the ability to take in diversity and to suffer well expands. We are able to stay with the emerging moment as our left hemisphere provides balance and structure based on the right hemisphere's felt understanding of what is unfolding. We naturally turn toward each other for support. Without this balance, the fear inherent in these times encourages us to retreat into left-hemisphere dominance. People who feel threatening to us need to be controlled. The earth becomes a pile of resources for the taking. Our personal wants and needs take precedence over protecting others from the virus.

While this essential integrative process between the hemispheres can sound complicated and challenging, it is actually part of our inherent health. We leave this path of robust bi-hemispheric integration when our systems are challenged beyond their capacity to feel safe. When we feel afraid, one protective response is to try to take control of the situation, and this moves us into the left hemisphere. When the right is chaotic because of trauma and we aren't able to move left, we live in a sea of dysregulation. When our system is supported, when traumas are healed, we actually move in the direction of the left supporting the right naturally.

How does our personal work to move toward hemispheric integration help our people? Through resonance with our more whole-brained system, they encode more of the experience of being in healthy relationship. Uri Hasson and his colleagues' (2012) research on brain coupling suggests that in emotionally connected relationships, brains fire more and more in tandem. For this reason, the work of neural integration in our people is more supported when we are in a more integrated state. Marco Iacoboni's (2011) work also suggests that our people are internalizing us in whatever state we are in, so when left and right are working well together, we become ongoing internal coregulators and sources of comfort. We literally go home with our people.

For us to get to this state of embodied knowledge and strengthening relationship between the two hemispheres, we found ourselves slowing down to make time and space for knowledge to be experienced, sharing it with each other to anchor it in relationship, and returning to it often. We began to be much more selective about trainings we took, not because they don't each have value, but because continuing to pour new information into our brains didn't leave room for digestion leading to embodiment. Without that space for assimilation, we were relying more on left-hemisphere decisions about which interventions to offer, making us more prone to deciding on behalf of our clients which new tool to use to change this situation. When we take control in this way, safety diminishes. We are also cutting off access to our people's inherent wisdom about what they need.

The rush to learn everything new is the left hemisphere's way of accumulation, often fueled by the right hemisphere's concern that we aren't enough and do indeed always need to know more. This sense of being deficient can point us toward doing personal work in our own therapy. If at all possible, this work might unfold in a process similar to what we are learning through IPNB. In this way, doing our own work can provide support for living into these principles. In addition, gradually healing our implicit world lets our inner landscape become an increasingly robust foundation for remaining whole-brained and embodied.

From the beginning of our IPNB explorations, we had found ourselves growing in the understanding that safety is at the heart of the therapeutic relationship. McGilchrist (2009) helped us see that if we were leading with the assumptions of the left hemisphere, applying what we were calling evidence-based solutions to particular diagnoses, we were flying in the face of what IPNB was telling us. And yet our training and the culture itself were constantly pushing us in that direction. Often, new clients would come in asking us for tools and quick fixes for the symptoms arising from long-held traumas. We realized that we needed to become skilled at talking with our people about the process of healing, sharing neurobiological concepts in ways that were both accurate and understandable. Throughout, we needed to be modeling the process we were describing so at a neuroceptive level they would begin to feel the importance and life-giving value of the connection between us. We wanted to consistently convey our confidence that their own system held the keys to healing once they felt sufficiently supported. Needless to say, as we worked in this direction, the principles were becoming more embodied in us and more available to our people.

Along with McGilchrist (2009), we got immersed in the work of Marco Iacoboni (2011) on mirror neurons, resonance circuits, and the way we internalize each other. We found two primary benefits for our people. Right away, we had an increasing sense of how important their internalization of us is and explored additional ways to support conscious awareness of that in them. Over the years, I have found that many therapists feel uncomfortable in the role of primary inner supporter of healing for their clients. The reasons vary: the feeling of not being enough, the fear of being intrusive, a sense that it is arrogant to assume such a position, discomfort with the level of emotional interdependence this implies, and others. (All of this is grist for remaining in our own therapy.) As we deepened into Iacoboni's (2011) work, we began to explore how we ourselves had internalized others, noting especially the power and support provided by the inner presence of those who have nurtured us. With this inner experience, it became easier for us to support our people's desire to turn toward our inner presence. A young woman, embarrassed by feeling an inner dependency on me, was surprised to find me encouraging her to lean in. I said, "This is what was supposed to happen when you were young, but your parents were so absorbed in their own pain they could barely be aware of you. So instead of feeling a warm presence accompanying you everywhere, there has been emptiness. What a joy for me that I get to become part of you that way now."

In addition to appreciating this kind of positive entanglement, we were also learning from Lane Beckes and James Coan (2011), who were working out the fine points of social baseline theory. Their research revealed that when we are in the presence of a trustworthy person, both people's amygdalae calm. If that person is a trusted beloved, the effect is even more profound. This leaves the resources of the middle prefrontal region available for all kinds of exploration and creativity, as well as substantially reducing the perception of pain and altering our experience of the difficulty of any task. We began to imagine that after establishing a relationship with any of our people, just opening the door of our office while in a safe, receptive state was a healing interaction. Without doing anything, our neural systems were rewiring in the direction of secure attachment. If, instead, we were planning our next intervention or focusing on what happened in the last session when we opened that door, we were less present and therefore less trustworthy. Sharing this information with our people was also helping them be more present as parents, partners, friends, and workmates. It is such a relief to discover that the foundation of healing rests on being rather than doing.

Our society is so caught in the sense of needing to find ways to fix perceived problems, whether in a corporation or a nervous system, that there has been little invitation to reflect on and practice the ways that presence, on its own, is healing. It is as though Carl Rogers faded away to a dim corner of our awareness because of the cultural pressures that anchor us in our left-hemisphere way of perceiving. Our immersion in IPNB was now reanchoring us in the centrality of relationship, and the additional pieces offered by these scientists and theoreticians were fleshing out this life-giving awareness. As these satellite learnings affirmed what we had initially learned, IPNB principles became more powerful in us.

Over the years, we had become more aware of the neural pathways inhabiting our bodies: the brain in our belly signaling us about safety, the one in our heart speaking to us about connection, and now Jaak Panksepp (Panksepp & Biven, 2012) was taking us into the midbrain to encounter the roots of our emotional life. Along with keeping us focused on bottom-up processes and how they manifest in our bodies, we discovered that the seven circuits Panksepp had explored were arranged in a way that emphasized how our systems are always focused on getting connected in warm and nourishing ways. When we are out of connection, our SEEKING system lends its powerful energies to the systems that can draw others to us—SEPARATION DISTRESS, FEAR, and, if all else fails, RAGE. When we have a felt sense of connection, SEEKING is free to give its energies to CARE and BONDING, PLAY, and LUST (in adolescence and beyond) while having a lively experience of curiosity, exploration, and creativity in the world.

One day we learned that the biologically healthy response to SEPARATION DISTRESS is clinging. For the most part, our culture finds that unacceptable at almost any age. As therapists, we can't help but be touched by that societal conviction, and when it is accompanied by our own early experience of being rejected in our need to cling, we may find being with severely wounded clients almost unbearable. We may become agitated or shift left and disconnect from the person because our system responds with such a neuroception of danger. Panksepp's assertion opened a path for us to sit with our experiences of being needed in this way, helped us heal our own wounds, and take a stand for healthy clinging rather than obeying the cultural command. The effect on our clients was astonishing. As we began to welcome their legitimate need to cling to us emotionally as a sign of health, they often wept as they shed much of the shame that had been thrust upon them for being needy. It was often one of the most profound disconfirming experiences of their lives.

We therapists had many opportunities to practice this openness to emotional dependence because most of our work over two decades was with severe trauma—abuse, neglect, and early attachment wounds. Many of our clients were also parents, so their own experience of being received in their clinging as well as every other emotional state, coupled with what we could share with them about Panksepp's (Panksepp & Biven, 2012) seven systems, began to transform their parenting. I had the privilege of working with a mom whose son was quite shy. Having been timid herself, she was afraid he was going to suffer the same humiliating teasing she had experienced. Because of this, his daily clinging in the face of any new experience was intolerable to her. In the midst of exploring her own experience of being a shy girl, we began to talk about clinging as the healthy response to fear and disconnection. She remembered her parents pushing her away when what she yearned for was a place to hold on and be heard about how scared she felt, followed by quiet reassurance and accompaniment. I was able to provide those experiences for her as she began to ease her way toward nurturing her sensitive son's explorations. When these ripples of goodness spread outward, especially down through the generations, it is the most rewarding work.

Because our agency chose to work primarily with severely wounded people who had storehouses of devastating embodied implicit memories, these clients were regularly feeling overwhelmed in daily life. Making room for the felt sense of these memories changing was our everyday focus. Bruce Ecker and his colleagues (2012) have gathered the major research on memory reconsolidation, scientific evidence of the possibility of the felt sense of implicit memories shifting. We were able to apply these findings to chart out a pathway for healing. Ecker saw symptoms as protectors of implicit memories that our systems experience as too frightening or hurtful to approach. No matter how severe the symptom, our system implicitly believes that touching what it is protecting would be worse for us. The depression that is keeping me in bed is less harmful to me than risking being shunned if I go out in public. Drinking to the point of blackout is less injurious than feeling the anguish of my father's daily humiliation of me. These well-developed protections represent the best ways our system knows how to manage the pain and fear we are carrying. Coming back to social baseline theory, we can imagine that the combined resources of trust and safety between us and our people might provide what is needed for these protections to step aside so these deeper wounds could surface for healing.

We were strongly resonating with Ecker's message that there is no pathology, but only adaptive protections linked to embedded traumatic experience. It is a profoundly respectful and hopeful vision, linked strongly to IPNB's view of inherent health and natural movement toward ongoing neural integration. In this view, healing is a bottom-up process that involves deepened connection with a safe person who can provide an embodied experience of what Ecker calls disconfirmation or mismatch while the trauma is alive in the space between client and therapist. Every day, in our counseling rooms, we sought to provide enough safety for our people to drop into the strong emotions and bodily sensations of these memories. Our understanding of this process and all that we were doing in our own personal therapy helped our joined windows of tolerance expand sufficiently to hold all that was arising. Their fears could be met with safety, their grief with comfort, their shame with acceptance. The depth of these working relationships is difficult to describe as each therapeutic pair establishes a unique healing dance.

Cognitive-behavioral frameworks, which have dominated the therapy world for several decades, have a tendency to see the world from the top down. They believe that changing thoughts and behaviors can relieve symptoms. While this can be true because this process can build alternative neural pathways that provide some protection, it doesn't grant access to the subcortically held implicit memories that make trauma survivors' lives so precarious and challenging. The process of neural integration, as we were understanding it in our work with embedded trauma, begins making connections primarily from the bottom up. Vertical integration (Siegel, 2020) brings felt-sense experience into conscious awareness, a bottom-up process that opens the implicit memories to receiving the disconfirming experiences that can change the visceral sense of the trauma. Just being able to explain this to the suffering people who came to us gave them hope that they wouldn't always be tortured by awakening implicit memories of abuse and neglect.

Our dedication to the principles of IPNB was also bringing a significant challenge. As we felt more and more committed to being available and receptive, we also sometimes found ourselves becoming anxious about whether we were going to be able to be fully present often enough. Many years ago, I had heard Ed Tronick (2003) talk about how secure parents make the empathic connection with their little ones on the first try about 33% of the time. For security to emerge, all that is needed is for these moms and dads to notice the 66% of ruptures and offer repairs most of the time. As a way of understanding the limits of being human, this is very good news. As therapists, it helps us find reassuring humility in the midst of what the discoveries from IPNB and its relational neuroscience supporters ask of us. As we expected less of ourselves, we could relax into the flow of ruptures and repairs, welcoming our mistakes as compost for strengthening the relationship.

The same was true of our human tendency to be judgmental. The pull to criticize ourselves about judgments that arise in all of us can overwhelm our attempts at compassion, especially in a left-shifted society that expects us to move toward perfection. It can make cultivation of kindness a tiring and discouraging process. In light of all this, it can be hard to even remember Tronick's research, much less apply it generously to ourselves. With practice (and maybe writing a reminder in several places), we can begin to give ourselves the grace of our humanness. The beauty of this for our people is that as we are transformed in this way, the hurting ones who come to us will feel our greater relaxation (more receptive, less striving), experience that we enjoy rupture and repair (maybe they could, too), and through both the neural pathways that are fostered by these states and resonance with us, begin to take on these qualities.

At some point along the way, as we began to selectively bathe in more theories and accept our human condition with humility, we were also becoming aware that the integration of any new body of learning and experience is a multiyear process. Perhaps it is even a never-ending process, as we continue to deepen into the actual practice of what we are inhabiting— or perhaps more accurately, what is inhabiting us. This process changes us, shifts our perceptions, our beliefs, our behaviors, and, most importantly, our way of relating. We were becoming a different presence in the counseling room and the world. What was initially a trait was gradually becoming a neurally anchored state change.

This process has no end. Today, we can better articulate how we see the process of therapy, recognizing that it is built on the foundation of the initial understandings about the brain and relationships given to us by IPNB. Our particular developmental course led us toward deepening into the capacity for providing safe presence, a kind of quietness inside based on our sense of the wisdom in the systems of our people and the power of making a space in which it can manifest. Nurturing this safe, trustworthy space, we listen as deeply as we can and follow our people's lead. We offer the skills we have developed based on our deepening understanding of Dan Siegel's (2020) integrative pathways of healing. This circle of listening, following, and responding looks very much like what Allan Schore (2012) describes at the heart of early secure attachment. We dwell ever more easily in the social synapse that Lou Cozolino (2014) named, aware that this process is focused on that third thing, the relationship that constellates in the space between. We have become more aware of the signals in our bodies that tell us we are moving toward sympathetic arousal and the need to take control. We breathe, rest back into listening, and wait to feel the arising of a response. We do this knowing that about 33% of the time we will respond in a way that our people feel met on our first try, and find gratitude for the healing power of ruptures and repairs. Inner stillness grows, skill expands, and humility flowers. We feel changed in some fundamental way by all of this, not only in the counseling room but in our daily walk in the world as well. At a time when we are in the midst of so much suffering , these capacities may let us provide a healing salve for this troubled world.

References

Beckes, L., & Coan, J. A. (2011). Social baseline theory: The role of social proximity in emotion and economy of action. *Social and Personality Psychology Compass, 5*(12), 976–988. doi:10.1080/10926771.2013.813882

Cozolino, L. (2014). *The neuroscience of human relationships: Attachment and the developing social brain* (2nd ed.). New York: Norton.

Ecker, B., Ticic, R., & Hulley, L. (2012). *Unlocking the emotional brain: Eliminating symptoms at their root using memory reconsolidation.* New York: Routledge.

Hasson, U., Ghazanfar, A. A., Galantucci, B., Garrod, S., & Keysers, C. (2012). Brain-to-brain coupling: A mechanism for creating and sharing a social world. *Trends in Cognitive Sciences, 16*(2), 114–121. doi:10.1016/j.tics.2011.12.007

Iacoboni, M. (2011). Within each other: Neural mechanisms for empathy in the primate brain. In A. Coplan & P. Goldie (Eds.), *Empathy: Philosophical and psychological perspectives* (pp. 45–57). New York: Oxford University Press.

McGilchrist, I. (2009). *The master and his emissary: The divided brain and the making of the western world.* New Haven, CT: Yale University Press.

Panksepp, J., & Biven, L. (2012). *The archaeology of mind: Neuroevolutionary origins of human emotions.* New York: Norton.

Porges, S. W. (2007). The polyvagal perspective. *Biological Psychology, 74,* 116–143. doi:10.1016/j.biopsycho.2006.06.009

Porges, S. W. (2013, September). A neural love code. In M. Kern (Chair), *Breath of life conference 2013.* Symposium conducted at a meeting of the Craniosacral Therapy Educational Trust, London, UK.

Porges, S. W., & Phillips, M. (2016). *Connectedness: A biological imperative* [Webinar]. Best Practices in Therapy. *http://bestpracticesintherapy.com/silver-month-long-july/*

Schore, A. N. (2003). *Affect regulation and the repair of the self.* New York: Norton.

Schore, A. N. (2012). *The science of the art of psychotherapy.* New York: Norton.

Siegel, D. J. (2020). *The developing mind: How relationships and the brain interact to shape who we are* (2nd ed.). New York: Guilford.

Tronick, E. Z. (2003). Of course all relationships are unique: How co-creative processes generate unique mother-infant and patient-therapist relationships and change other relationships. In *New developments in attachment theory: Application to clinical practice.* Los Angeles: Lifespan Learning Institute.

7

Humiliation Is Not Just About the Intent to Shame and Degrade

Some Facets of the Psychotherapy of Trauma Related to Humiliation

Richard A. Chefetz

ACUTE SHAME CAN BE UNDERSTOOD AS LEADING TO THE DEVELOPMENT OF enduring shame-laden mental states (Chefetz, 2020). Early experiences of repetitive shame lead to chronic shame that is dyed in the wool from which the fabric of an unsuspecting child's mental life is spun, a caul of shame created so early that it has the subjective experience of a given. It is upon that kind of shame-laden fabric that the imprinting of humiliation experience looks different than what we can see printed on the emotional clothing of those with even a modicum of self-esteem.

With the presence of self-esteem, a person becomes angry at efforts to humiliate them because they feel undeserving of such treatment. When shame is implicit in the very structure of an already wounded sense of self, then humiliation may be met with acceptance, resignation, confusion, fears of annihilation, paralysis, feelings of powerlessness, depersonalization, dissociative state change (switching), unconscious or conscious rage, self-destructive behavior, or suicidality, and especially the feeling of being permanently stained, damaged, or defective, among other responses. When humiliation finds an agar to its liking—and even after only a short incubation period—feeling unlovable, defective, or bad becomes an ongoing subjective trifecta from hell. Add to this the all-too-common bullying and ridicule of childhood, or the misfortune of having any manner of physical deformity, and the tendency of peers to mock and point is unerringly wounding at the deepest levels. Righteous indignation is often not on the list of reactions to humiliation in the context of chronic complex post-traumatic stress disorder (PTSD), or its more extreme cousin, dissociative identity disorder (DID).

Humiliation deserves a close look lest we lump it too quickly with shame experience and lose track of its compelling explanatory power in the treatment of trauma. However, humiliation is indeed part of the shame spectrum of emotion, and that is a good place to start its exploration. A moment, though, might be well spent in considering how we might most beneficially think about feelings in a clinical context, especially those as complicated as the spectrum associated with shame.

Some Preliminary Thoughts About a Theory of Feelings: An Affect Theory

I need not reference the reality that many clinicians use the words "affect," "feeling," and "emotion" interchangeably in clinical discourse. However, what's routine may be a disadvantage. The vicissitudes of shame and humiliation, and the hot blush of recognition, require that somatosensory experience be included as an essential component of psychotherapeutic inquiry alongside psychodynamic and cognitive processes. There is a somatic imperative, a requirement to consider the body as part of the mind, the holder of inarticulate subsymbolic (Bucci & Maskit, 2007) contexts for lived moments when language fails in the experience of trauma (Rauch et al., 1996, 2003; Shin et al., 1997, 2005, 2006).

Feelings have a physiological basis. They are literally a physical experience, a feeling, an embodied sensing. They are described by words that assign a lexicon of parsed meaning through words signifying emotion. A more elaborate discussion of this issue is elsewhere (Chefetz, 2015). Let's consider how thinking this way adds to the vitality of a clinical discourse. The following is a statement of my clinical experience, and the interpretation of such relies heavily on understandings gleaned from the work of others who have studied affect for a lifetime and to whom I remain indebted (Lane & Nadel, 2000; Lane et al., 1990; Ledoux, 1996, 2012; LeDoux & Pine, 2016; Panksepp, 1998, 2004; Panksepp & Biven, 2012; Tomkins, 1962, 1963, 1982).

I prefer to use the word "affect" to describe the physiology that underlies the production of what eventually rises into consciousness as an embodied sensing; a feeling, something I feel in my body as a result of physiological responses to the mind's internal and external environment. These unconscious affective processes may be described by biofeedback-like measurable changes in skin conductance and may be associated with sympathetic nervous system outflow, for example, the flow of blood through small blood vessels that create the red flush in the skin of the upper chest or face associated with shame, or the release of adrenalin in response to fear that provokes muscle tension. These processes create a kind of somatic summation-vector that lead to this embodied sensing; a feeling. These physiological changes tend to be outside awareness.

My clinical observation in hypochondriasis reveals there is a hypersensitivity to affectivity and an inability to know the meaning of somatic experience. This leaves the feeler nearly terrified, often frantic, about what's happening to their body. In the clinically opposite realm of depersonalization, bodily sensation may be absent. The mind of the depersonalized person may be highly reactive to the emotion-laden scene that the non-depersonalized individual would recognize as charged, but with depersonalization the cognitive processes associated with knowing a feeling are slowed, blunted, or delayed to the point of sensing something is "off," if anything is sensed at all, without knowing what or why (Sierra et al., 2002).

Kelly (2009) opined that Tomkins's affect psychology solved the problem of stimulus confusion by sorting experience through unconscious affect. An affect was stimulated, and then experience became known. Clinically, my posttraumatic patients come to me mostly with all manner of feeling capacities decreased or absent (some do come emotionally flooded) (Lanius et al., 2010). This is secondary to dissociative numbing, redirected through dissociatively activated psychodynamic processes like denial, disavowal, and undoing, or unconsciously enacted without awareness of the meaning of their behavior (Ryle, 1999). Treatment moves people toward consciousness for emotion. However, emotional pain is a deterrent. In this context it is important to note that our somatizing patients have a neurobiological burden of a confusion between pain affect and pain sensation. Pain affect may encode in brain organs like the anterior cingulate cortex that are associated with consciousness, but not the somatosensory cortex associated with physical sensation (Rainville et al., 1997). Anxiety about pain increases pain perception and activates hippocampal networks (Ploghaus et al., 1999, 2001). Emotional pain must be resolved in order, at least in part, to reduce suicidality (Levinger et al., 2015), but beyond that, in order to tolerate the reconstruction of an accurate trauma narrative, without which healing does not occur.

Faces communicate states of feeling, and our brain is wired interactively to know what our face is showing as well as what other people's faces are showing (Gallese et al., 2007; Pizzagalli et al., 2002). In children, disgust faces may signal anger (Widen & Russell, 2010). In people with isolated self-states, as in DID, emotional reaction may be different for one self-state than for another (Schlumpf et al., 2013). The conveyance of emotion through facial expression may be crucial to emotional development (Beebe et al., 2016), and form at least part of the basis for right brain-to-right brain communication between mother and child (Schore & Schore, 2008). The bottom line here is that if a therapist can't see the client's face, or the therapist is relatively bereft of facial expression, emotional communication may suffer a great deal. (This is magnified in the culture of online psychotherapy that is part of the response to the SARS-CoV-2 pandemic. It requires, in my opinion, an additional effort on the part of the clinician not only to be conscious of this parameter, but to significantly add their own physical indicators of affective life through facial expression and especially the prosody of their voice. We do well to put the hypnotic-like qualities of good communication to work.) It is no wonder, then, that states of shame or humiliation often involve the reaction of hiding one's face. In a broader sense— closer to the feeling of what happens in shame-laden trauma—there may be an effort to hide one's mind, not only from others, but from oneself.

No clinician reading these words would fail to recognize the familiarity of the experience of hearing one of their patients describe a raw empty feeling in their belly; a kind of nearly nauseous weight of indescribable presence, associated with feeling weighed down, heavy, as if unable to find any energy in their body for no particular reason. The relief such a person can experience if the bodily feeling is correctly named, such as sadness, and the subsequent connection of the narrative of their life to this named emotion occurs, is a wonder to behold. Naming feelings is important, and if feelings are a kind of personal and interpersonal radar, then knowing feeling is essential for living a conscious life.

Physiological precursors and embodied sensings refer to affect and feelings, respectively. Emotion words have a special place in language. They are symbolized relational shortcuts that convey complex scripts (Tomkins, 1995) succinctly. The nuances of experience are perhaps best described by the poets, and yet us mere mortals must still find a way to talk with each other about our feelings. If we are not taught the words for emotions, then we are at a real disadvantage in life.

Not having words for feelings, the concept of alexithymia (Taylor, 2000), represents a body of research exploring what has been found to be a trait in many people. In my clinical practice, however, a relative alexithymia is closer to the norm in some people: They often start treatment unable to express both thoughts and feelings. But after an emotion-focused approach to their psychotherapy (Greenberg, 2004; Johnson et al., 1999; Paivio & Nieuwenhuis, 2001), their use of emotion words and their experience of being alive in their body has often increased dramatically. In my practice, alexithymia is related to state rather than trait. In parallel to this is the concept of alexisomia, not having words for sensations (Ogden et al., 2006). Providing a menu of language for a patient that helps them describe an embodied sensing in more clear terms can assist in the process of moving toward symbolization through the use of words for specific emotions.

We have emotional memory, even if we don't always have great access to it (e.g., depersonalization), and we constantly make nonconscious associations to our past experiences, both at the narrative level and the psychodynamic. My clinical approach benefits from a mostly affective neuroscience perspective for what Panksepp (1998; Panksepp & Biven, 2012) has called emotional feelings and their subcortical correlates, as well as an appreciation of the sophisticated higher-order appraisal processes described by cognitive neuroscience (Lane & Nadel, 2000). Once a library of emotional experiences is achieved, higher-order appraisals occur quickly and routinely via associative processes. These appraisal processes may influence how a person interprets consciousness for the subcortical activation of pathways associated with a particular felt experience. Dissociative processes undermine these important contextualizers of experience and may make meaning indecipherable. A clinical perspective that makes use of the clinician's consciousness for somatosensory dimensions of experience is a priori an affective neuroscience approach that benefits from an appreciation of the connection of affective dimensions of experience with subcortical structures (Lamm & Singer, 2010; Ledoux, 1996; LeDoux & Pine, 2016; Rauch et al., 1996; Shin & Liberzon, 2010).

One particular advantage in thinking about affects as a kind of protosensation, and feelings as embodied sensings, is related to special trauma treatment techniques and the use of hypnotic protocols (Spiegel & Spiegel, 1978; Watkins, 1971) as well as eye movement desensitization and reprocessing (EMDR) (Forgash & Knipe, 2012; Shapiro, 1995). The uses of bodily states, embodied sensings, and feelings as an entry point (target) for the clinical inquiry is a powerful nonverbal approach. Focusing also makes use of this affective reality (Gendlin, 1978). Traumatic experience is often without words. The creation of new narrative—reconstruction of the trauma scene—is a central part of treatment. It's nice to have some theory to undergird this effort.

The Shame Spectrum of Emotion

Shame-related emotion pivots on the experience of feeling in some way devalued or as generating action toward devaluing another. Guilt must be considered here because there are numerous clinically salient patterns of mixed guilt and shame (Tangney & Dearing, 2003; Tangney et al., 1996). However, guilt is less about feeling devalued and more about knowing that you have done something wrong and regretting it while maintaining self-esteem. Embarrassment, shame, humiliation, and mortification are each about loss of value, while contempt, disgust, dissmell (noticing a "stinker"; Tomkins & McCarter, 1995), loathing, ridicule, and bullying are about efforts to devalue another. Each of these feelings exposes core narcissistic vulnerability or injury that may generate fears of annihilation or compensatory grandiosity (Kohut, 2009; Wolf, 1988). The inward-facing experience of shame is more attachment oriented, seeking relatedness, while the outward-facing attack of contempt is about establishing a competitive ranking organization or domination-submission, and seeks to maintain distance (Gilbert, 2005). Elsewhere I have described the simultaneous activation of attachment and competitive-ranking motivational systems as an "attackment" experience (Chefetz, 2015, 2018); that is, creating an experience of confused and unconsciously simultaneous efforts at tenacious connection and desperate distancing. There is an implicit sense of needing to be close to be safe while also feeling a desperation to distance in order to be safe. Dissociative processes make this kind of constellation more intelligible as the product of relatively isolated self-states with conflicting needs and fears.

Shame-organized constellations of experience are reminiscent of Nathanson's (1992) compass of shame. Set about the points of a compass, the east-west dimension is about an attack response when feelings of shame suddenly emerge into awareness, attack self, or attack other. This bypasses feelings of helplessness and loss of efficacy associated with shame through a compensatory effort to restore agency with action. The north-south dimension is about a more passive response to shame—avoid or withdraw. Agency is restored in this case by taking charge and removing the incitement from face-to-face awareness, whether that is with a person or a physical location. An impulsively canceled psychotherapy session after a disruption in the therapeutic alliance is an example. Each of these dimensions describes a typical pattern of reactivity when suddenly feeling shame. The visibility of unexpected attacks or avoidance/withdrawal in psychotherapy predicts the potential utility of Nathanson's compass and gentle probing to locate possible shame experience at the source of this kind of behavior. At a minimum, sudden attack of self/other or avoidance/withdrawal in a treatment ought to raise consciousness in a clinician that a shame experience may have occurred.

I find it helpful to think of the sequence of embarrassment, shame, humiliation, and mortification as one of increasing intensity. Embarrassment is more about a kind of self-consciousness of personal lack or error than an acute sense of feeling devalued, as occurs in acute shame (Trumbull, 2003). Chronic shame is a much more deeply painful experience and is regularly associated with complex PTSD as well as the dissociative disorders. Chronic shame is less about single or multiple occurrences of shame and more about shame that is resident in the core construction of the sense of self, where the nearly amniotic feeling of the origin of shame takes root. Shame-spectrum experience is always relational, a feeling of disintegration of self in relation to a dysregulated other (DeYoung, 2015). Chronic shame often occupies a place of what I have called omnipotent badness, a badness that explains what happens to me in the universe (Chefetz, 2000): I am bad, and bad things happen to me because I deserve them. If anybody is to be hurt, it ought to be me since I deserve nothing better and am unlovable. I deserve to be dead. Mortification refers to the sense of needing to suffer through ascetic or penitential means in order to ameliorate the wish to sin. In less spiritual or religious contexts, the use of the word conjures a feeling that "I was so ashamed I could have died. I was mortified." This intense shame experience and the sense of a need for physical punishment in response is often part of a chronic shame or humiliation experience. Or, in other words, "what happened is so awful that my interest in living is blocked" (Kelly, 2009, p. 21).

The reader who has studied shame and humiliation experience knows how challenging it can be to separate the two. The writer's intent is to highlight those aspects of humiliation experience that may distinguish it from shame. The stuck-in-molasses-like experience of working with chronic shame and humiliation may require an exquisitely detailed exploration of these experiences in order to tease them out from the mind-numbing blankness that often obscures exploration of the shame spectrum of experience. Using highly specific language synonymous with humiliation experience allows exhuming very difficult areas of experience not otherwise accessible with only the language of shame.

Shame Experience

In the study of shame, all paths lead to two intellectual streams that eventually join and create a formidable river—the works of Sylvan Tomkins and Helen Block Lewis. Tomkins's work is extraordinary in its detail and depth (Tomkins, 1962, 1963, 1982; Tomkins & Karon, 1962), among others (Lansky, 1992; Lewis, 1992; Miller, 1985; Morrison, 1989; Nathanson, 1992; Tangney & Dearing, 2003). I have found that reading Tomkins through the keen sight of several of his interpreters is rewarding (Demos, 1995; Kaufman, 2004; Kelly, 2009). Tomkins's notion of what he called the innate affect of shame-humiliation, as described by Kelly, was that this affect motivates us to take action toward the satisfaction of enjoyment when we are suddenly deprived of interesting and enjoyable things. Kelly tries to make clear that shame occurs when our interest-excitement is blocked, and we don't want it to be so. In his discussion, he emphasizes that shame-humiliation would not occur if no interest-excitement was activated. (In Tomkins's nosology, interest-excitement is one of the primary innate affects, while shame-humiliation is an accessory affect, an affect modifier that acts upon a primary positive innate affect to downregulate it.)

I find the scientific-sounding references to stimulus, signals, and so on less congenial to my psychodynamic orientation than I would prefer. But there is a valuable punch line for the reader who stays with Tomkins's ideas: shame is inherently relational in Tomkins's formulation, too, because the disruption of interest-excitement creates a longing to reconnect and establish the positive connection that was lost (Demos, 2019). That's a big deal, and I believe it's true of humiliation experience, but in a different way that relates more to the use of power and the dynamics of domination and submission. This motivational system shift tends to make meaning flow toward the realm of humiliation experience and away from contexts of shame, a movement from attachment motivations of safety in the presence of another toward competitive-ranking motivations (domination-submission), safety in a hierarchy of power.

The clinical wisdom of Helen Block Lewis has always delighted me. "Shame is contagious. It is so painful that the witness to it ordinarily looks the other way. Contemporary psychoanalysts are no exception to this tendency. . . . Unanalyzed shame may be playing a part in 'negative therapeutic reactions' before assigning patients to an ominous 'borderline' or 'narcissistic' category" (Lewis, 1987, p. 2). Beyond this reason for shame's neglect in contemporary psychiatry, Lewis notes, "An ethical system based on the premise that human nature is evil or aggressive will emphasize guilt as its major control, whereas an ethical system that includes human sociability as a 'given' will also emphasize the shame (in one's own eyes) of losing the love of the 'other.'" This dovetails nicely with Tomkins's more scientific statements about shame as an affect modifier that activates when interest-excitement is blocked and relatedness is sought as a repair. Having reviewed some aspects of shame experience, let's look at humiliation and then see to what extent it is distinct from shame.

Humiliation Experience

Humiliation "is a relational form of human behavior stemming from interpersonal dynamics that cannot be adequately explained by individualistic, intrapsychic theories" (Hartling & Luchetta, 1999, p. 260). In shame, power dynamics may be relatively invisible. In humiliation they are right out front. In fact, in looking at the scene of international relations, there is reasonable speculation that humiliation may be considered the nuclear bomb of emotions (Hartling et al., 2013). This goes beyond the coherent arguments offered by others regarding bypassed and unacknowledged shame as a profound contributor to social violence (Scheff & Retzinger, 2001) and speaks to ongoing conflicts that have been well explored (Lacey, 2011). Bypassed shame occurs when, for example, hyperverbal activity is used to deflect and cover over experiencing shame (Lewis, 1987). Unacknowledged shame is another of Lewis's concepts that predicts the buildup of resentment and retaliatory fantasies, things that melt away when shaming experiences are acknowledged by perpetrators and apology is offered as an olive branch toward the restoration of dignity for all (Hicks & Tutu, 2011). Humiliation is more about a wish to damage or destroy a person, to render them nonthreatening, not just to tell them they are bad or unlovable.

Social-psychological views of humiliation are importantly informative in this regard (Torres & Bergner, 2010). Claims of social status inherent in a person's life may be accepted or rejected. It is the rejection of these claims that create humiliation and an ability to degrade an individual who is publicly exposed, for example, in a courtroom. Powerless rage, hopelessness, helplessness, and suicide are potential outcomes of a public humiliation. Motivation in life may be preempted by humiliation experience, eclipsing all other motivations. There may also be a loss of status as an appraiser of reality, or a loss of status to claim basic human rights that are associated with a sense of worthlessness and profound loss of self-esteem also typical of shame.

Thus, humiliation can also be seen as less of an intrapsychic event and more of an act that occurs in the world (Leask, 2013). For Leask,

> The impact of the act of humiliation will vary, in part because of the resilience built in by successful early relationships and in part because of strategies of resistance (which themselves may owe much to such early relationships). I also suggest that recognising the specific nature of humiliation has implications for the relationship between the therapist and the patient" (2013, p. 130).

He further recognizes that humiliation dynamics include unconscious factors that have led the patient to become repeatedly entangled in relationships replete with humiliation experience. Leask considers humiliation an action that makes humiliation less a matter of the victim feeling humiliated but more about being humiliated, something done to another unjustly and with apparent impunity, an active exercise of power. This act consistently demonstrates

> stripping of status; rejection of exclusion; unpredictability or arbitrariness; and a personal sense of injustice matched by the lack of any remedy for the injustice suffered. . . . Humiliation leads to a strong sense that one has been wronged, while shame involves a sense that one has done wrong and is diminished in one's own eyes or in the eyes of others. (Leask, 2013)

I'm glad that Leask identified the wielding of power in the experience of humiliation. My patients often fully recognize their sense of powerlessness in the face of feeling humiliated as well as shamed. Not only is there a loss of power as a hallmark of humiliation, but there is a profound fear of challenging the power of the perpetrator lest the act of humiliation be surpassed by annihilation. Not only does this crush a protest, but it smacks down and suppresses the rage in the victim that accompanies the experience of shame or humiliation. This effectively welds rage to shame or humiliation (Chefetz, 2015; Lewis, 1987). When this happens, going near a shame or humiliation experience in psychotherapy often quickly exhumes formerly buried rage that can overwhelm self-regulatory capacities and result in self-harm or harm to others. This is especially the case if the rage is isolated in a self-state typical of DID.

For example, Rachel, whom I have written about before (Chefetz, 2009), became actively suicidal for three harrowing weeks after the first time I speculated she might feel some anger toward her mother. Her whole internal system of some 27 self-states was organized so as to ensure that she would not be in conflict with her mother, on any count, and that nobody might even know she was anything other than aligned with her mother. While her experience of sadistic abuse from an outside male perpetrator, Mr. X, was profound, it was the relentless out-of-tune adjustment of reality that her mother insisted upon that was most profoundly damaging for Rachel.

Inevitably, as she went further and further in treatment toward full embodiment, no depersonalization, and orienting herself to living in 2020 rather than being stuck in a trauma-laden past, she felt threatened by the changes and dug in her heels. She felt herself to be at risk of being humiliated and controlled by her mother in 2020. In this place, Rachel professed to have no mind, no wants, no needs, no self, and did not know what it meant when people said they liked her. She was not allowed to accrue any value, nor was she allowed by her internal system of states to do anything that asserted she had the skills to live in the world. If this self-conception was challenged, rage of suicidal proportion was unleashed. If she did not remain humiliated and incapable of making decisions to buy food, clothing, and so on, then she feared retaliation by her mother. She had become the chief humiliator of herself, a repetition of the experience with her mother. Here, the sense of the mother of her childhood still somehow being present in her mind was a tenaciously persistent experience, only slowly giving way toward the reality that her mother had done some growing and was no longer the same as the mother of childhood. But the longevity of this perception was enough to still terrify her and leave her entrenched in self-reinforcing humiliation experience as she failed, day after day, to live a life. Rachel was always blocked by self-states guarding the way to self-actualization. She lived in despair, feeling defective, unworthy of existence, a toxic brew of shame and humiliation slathered with self-protective rage. Her repetitive rage and humiliation prevented her from growth lest she lose the narrative of nearly her entire life and experience the sadness of decades of marginal living and untold losses.

The extent to which a humiliator exercises the intent to shame, degrade, denigrate, demean, belittle, and annihilate the efficacy and esteem of another human being is a statement of the enormity of the impact of humiliation: an effort to destroy the humanity, the dignity, of another. It is an effort to damage and permanently disable, to destroy a felt threat to the humiliator, or to render the target of humiliation feeble as a way to assure the humiliator of their superiority and safety. This kind of act creates the experience of losing trust in the world (Leask, 2013). It creates a realization in the mind of the target of humiliation that nobody is going to rescue them; "nobody is coming." It's also true that because the humiliator's woes take origin in their own mind, the ghost from their very own nursery holding retaliatory sway over their adult personality, repetitions of efforts to humiliate regularly fail to reduce anxiety for more than a short period of time. As anxiety rises, acts that demonstrate domination through humiliation become more necessary, more insistent. This describes the scene in some families, some communities, and some nations as the fear of humiliation (Rothstein, 1984) infects in ways just as subtle as SARS-CoV-2, and leaves damage for years to come. It is terrifying when a head of state becomes the humiliator-in-chief. Even a donkey knows that, as the following reveals.

Yann Martel (2010) speaks of this in his chilling play within a novel, written by a taxidermist, the story of a donkey, Beatrice, and a monkey, Virgil, caught up in the extremity of Nazi Germany:*

BEATRICE: I never did tell you what happened to me, did I?
VIRGIL: What? When?
BEATRICE: When they arrested me.
VIRGIL: [uneasy] No, you didn't. I never asked.
BEATRICE: Would you like to hear about it?
VIRGIL: Only if you want me to.
BEATRICE: I should tell one person at least, so that the experience doesn't vanish without having been put into words. And who else but you?

[Pause.]

BEATRICE: I remember the first slap, just as I was being brought in. Already then, something was lost forever, a basic trust. If there's an exquisite collection of Meissen porcelain and a man takes a cup and deliberately drops it to the floor, shattering it, why wouldn't he then proceed to break everything else? What difference does it make, cup or tureen, once a man has

---

*Martel may be best known for his earlier novel, *The Life of Pi*.

made clear his disregard for porcelain? With that first blow, something akin to porcelain shattered in me. It was a hard slap, forceful yet casual, given for no reason, before I had even identified myself. If they would do that to me, why wouldn't they do worse? Indeed, how could they stop themselves? A single blow is a dot, meaningless. It's a line that is wanted, a connection between the dots that will give purpose and direction. One blow demands a second and then a third and onwards. (pp. 174–175)

The horror of Beatrice's captivity had just begun. There is much more, but for our purposes here to elaborate further would be gratuitous. What I can tell you is that in the psychotherapy of the person who brought this novel to my attention, we have referenced this section of the book numerous times as an exemplar of their childhood experience (not simply the part of Beatrice's story you have heard, but the part you'll have to find for yourself). It is too much to bear, and to be alone with the story, never to have been heard by another, as Beatrice noted, would be an affront, as if it had never happened; a kind of dissociative solution. Humiliation may create an experience of loss of trust in the world, nations, institutions, and, most importantly, people. To speak in psychotherapy of humiliation requires an extraordinary leap of trust, a tentative faith in the potential witness. I can say with authority that if a person has been betrayed and humiliated by a previous therapist, then the work in treatment is exponentially more difficult. Likewise, a betrayal or humiliation of one of my patients in treatment may fully test the relationship as no other event might.

Chronic shame often leaves a person with an omnipotent sense of badness (Chefetz, 2000), a central organizer of beliefs about the self that explains why people shame and dismiss. This is the badness that explains the reasons underlying the knowing one is unlovable. In humiliation, the experience is of being deeply damaged and becoming inherently defective. The distinction is significant. To be unlovable is a condition of the heart; it's possible to secretly hold to an inarticulate hope of being loved, one day. To be humiliated and become defective is to be without the possibility of redemption, an even more hopeless position. In the language of Tomkins, it is to become a "stinker" and to see on the faces of those around you a sneering contempt with an upturned nose (a feeling aptly named "dissmell"; Tomkins & McCarter, 1995).

Just the reality of having a trauma and then being unable to resolve the posttraumatic experience creates shame and humiliation. The stigma of mental illness is already upon a person with a significant loss of function due to a psychological problem. Shame is ubiquitous. When being judged by an outside other, humiliation experience is cemented in place. Moreover, when there is an internal harsh superego to which classical psychoanalytic theory speaks, no outside agent need speak up. There is a ready-made mechanism for an inside job fomenting humiliation experience. This is spelled out elsewhere (Chefetz, 2015) and is based upon mechanisms described earlier in psychoanalytic theorizing whereby part of the ego is taken as an object (Freud, 1917). A more recent example is in a discussion of the severe neuroses (Wurmser, 2000). Each of these earlier works is consistent with a multiple self-state psychology; a ubiquitous finding when chronic shame and humiliation have taken root. In the language of the treatment of DID, these states have been dubbed "abuser-protector" states. The use of intrapersonal (self-state to self-state) and interpersonal self-regulation strategies based upon actions and experiences that evoke dissociative detachment and numb calm often instigates the ignition of self-harming activities or harm to others in a sad reenactment of abuse (Chefetz, 2017).

Humiliation Experience in Psychotherapy

The early hours of the morning, often between 3:30 and 5:00 a.m., seem to be the time my mind often chooses to present me with preoccupying thoughts and feelings related to shame, humiliation, seemingly unresolvable conflict in my life and especially in my casework, my work with the people who hire me and then become my patients, the ones who suffer (according to the roots of the word). It is in this sleepy and then suddenly alert crucible of malleable and heart-pounding perception that some work often tries to happen in my mind. It feels like it intrudes without apparent plan or insight, just the rawness of me emerging into the unguarded, too-early morning.

One morning my consciousness blossomed with thoughts of a treatment gone awry, unwieldy as it nearly always had been, but more so, much more so, recently. There was the feeling of the inevitability of its failure, my failure, to untangle the mess. Embroiling, immobilizing, self-destructing, contemptuous, loathing, fearing, shaming, guilting, and humiliating experience seemed to swarm and swallow up all my efforts. As has been my habit in describing complex PTSD and DID, in moments like this we do not find ourselves in the paw of the lion, but in the giant maw leading to the belly of the whale—trapped, no escape, marooned, undone, depleted, and unworthy (Chefetz, 2020). Good morning to you, too.

It is challenging for me to pay attention to humiliation experience. It is an acidic, nauseous wave of crushing pain and doubt about personal efficacy. It etches deep grooves in the once-intact images of self-esteem that become like shards of broken glass waiting in the tall grass for my bare feet to be reminded of what came before. The reader may find it useful to consider how these sensory experiences I am talking about are exactly the kinds of things that I attend to when working with a person who is bereft of narrative but overflowing with sensory impressions that render them inarticulate. While the language is somewhat poetic, the earlier section on affect theory is informative of the several places I might intervene to open up access to more internal experience. "Tell me about the nausea, please. That's right. Where do you feel it? Can you focus on that and tell me what comes to mind? If you were to use the nausea as a search term in Google, and then click Enter and search, what would pop up as the first several hits?" This is an informal and conversational way to focus attention on the associative potentials hidden at the surface of the patient's productions. Attention to the somatic stirrings makes a big difference.

If a therapist asked me what kinds of images were popping up, and I told them it was an image of my mother, then without asking me for any narrative content, I could be engaged on an imagistic level to create associative links to otherwise isolated (dissociatively organized) material. "Okay, Rich, you said you had an image of your mother, right? Yes, good. Can you focus on that image please? Can you imagine the image on a TV screen? Good. Can you put the TV into split image mode and put your mother over on one side, please? Which side is she on? Good. Right. Okay, now on the left side pull up any other image of your mother that comes to mind and tell me what you see when you are ready, please." Treating the image as a sensory target, the patient stays oriented to the original image while pulling numerous other mother images from the past. Each pulled image has associative links, emotional and cognitive, even if they are consciously unknown to Rich. Within a day or so, this review of images will produce a raft of associations. Be careful not to go overboard on this. Ten or 15 minutes of this is more than enough. This is similar to a technique I call "interior decorating," which is a review of a childhood home (Chefetz, 2015). The associations come quickly after an initial delay of a day or so. Knowing that emotional life is divided up into affective and embodied sensing dimensions allows me to focus my efforts on tugging on the associable aspects of otherwise blocked emotional experience. Working with shame and humiliation is often just like this. Working with the crumbs of emotional experience can be very rewarding.

There is frankly nothing poetic in the experiences my patients tell me about of the abject power plays of humiliators who laugh at their vulnerabilities, ridicule their helplessness, and smile knowingly when their victim has been successfully tricked, once again, into believing some falsehood hiding in a carefully tailored costume of truth-like creations. While the scene I'm describing here is more about carefully planned sadistic abuse, the cloth from which humiliation is cut has many different styles when crafted into clothing that constricts, undermines, and burdens as it's worn.

My preference is always to write about a case, and yet it happens that writing about another person's sense of humiliation and asking them to vet that for publication is simply over-the-top ill-advised. Further, nearly all my patients who have powerful humiliation histories have uniformly and preemptively asserted their wish that I not publish anything about their experiences of humiliation. I can accept that, and so that just leaves my own experience to write about.

A Countertransference Analysis of the Experience of Humiliation

After several months of watching myself make a series of errors in a treatment that my patient took some passionately outraged pains to point out to me in their astonished disbelief, I had a dream: "I was talking with a patient, and they were yelling at me about how I had betrayed and injured them, how what I had done was unforgivable, and that it had destroyed any possibility for them to continue treatment."* Still in my dream, but from another vantage point in

---

*To my patients: In writing about my personal experience, something I feel is a necessity lest intensive psychotherapy for trauma treatment be a black box for the clinician's experience, I do recognize the risk that somebody might believe I am writing about my experience with one of you. I regret that possibility. I can only say that this experience is related to a time prior to 2010, and in a treatment that ended. I wish I could have had my current knowledge of myself and of treatment dynamics earlier in my career, at the time of this treatment and dream. This is an example of why I believe that essays like this one must see the light of day. Younger clinicians tell me how relieved they feel to know that senior people make mistakes and still

my mind, I noticed how upset I was, how miserable I felt. I had an odd sense of the truth in what was being said to me as well as a kind of bafflement about it that was expressed in a clear question, delivered to my struggling awareness, in a pleading tone with a feeling of astonishment, that emerged suddenly into my mind: "How did I become such a monster?" I woke up, heart pounding, upset, and I was also aware that in having asked the question I was calming down. The sun was not yet up. I was exhausted. I was not a happy camper.

It is humiliating to be found so lacking, so incompetent as to make repeated errors of a similar kind. It's also very curious, and I can say that now, with authority, some years later, all the while having worked on these kinds of issues. I'll not review those earlier treatment circumstances. However, in more recent times, the trajectory of other work prompted me to recall having my monster dream. I found my notes, and now can finally breathe some life and meaning into them. So, in the spirit of what Alice told me when we discussed whether or not my countertransference reactions should appear alongside the detailed discussion of enactment in her treatment (Chefetz, 2015), I will write about what I've come to understand about myself in relation to countertransference humiliation.

Dorahy (2017) wrote that adherence to shame helps a person to avoid the realization of humiliation experience in that the perpetrator intended to wound and diminish a person. Building on that clarity is that humiliation experience is linked to a call to action, much as with anger, because humiliation holds the knowing of the enormity of the power differential between abuser and victim. If the victim risks feeling powerful, shows their proportional rage and resentment, what one astute patient called "enragement," they are at risk of preemptive retaliation from the sadistic abuser for not masochistically accepting the abuser's dominance. An interesting dynamic arises in this context: The failure to heed the call to action in the moment of humiliation can be experienced as shameful, and a powerful self-hatred can be generated that takes the place of the threat of retaliation. There is also forbidden retaliation if the victim knows the vulnerabilities of the perpetrator well, loves them, and knows that to ruthlessly attack the perpetrator is to weaken and potentially destroy the loved person. (It is complicated, and it's at its most complicated when both perpetrator and victim have a

---

are learning even after so much learning has come before. Senior people knowingly smile and may offer a hug, virtual or otherwise, pandemically speaking.

mental construction with isolated self-states typical in both complex PTSD and the dissociative disorders. It is routine to discover that a perpetrator has the emotional footprint of DID.) The call to action is diverted and targets the weak and pathetic self who failed to respond to the provocation of humiliation. Self is attacked, rather than other, as per Nathanson's compass of shame. Thus, a vicious cycle of humiliation, enragement, shame, self-hatred, self-disgust, and self-attack (after which humiliation is often also experienced for failing to maintain safety) is entered and may be sustained, at great cost.

So when humiliation occurs for the therapist, and the patient drives it home with apparently appropriate outrage, then these dynamics are at risk of rising up in the therapist. Do I accept the proclamations of my patient regarding my incompetence? Do I make an assessment of the actual error I made and plead for a mitigating proportional response from the patient, downgrading the fact of my error to one of a lesser crime? Can I stop my internal berating for making the same error, again? What do I do with the self-disgust, the shame, the failure to maintain the consciousness that is a hallmark of the therapist providing good treatment? And how did this failure of self-monitoring occur? Why? Should I accept the consultant's assessment that the patient has gone overboard with their outrage when I know that I did make several errors?

At a second level of consultation on a different case but with similar dynamics I presented a case to my peer consultation group (a group of highly seasoned clinicians; some of us have been meeting together, monthly, since 1998 with the intent to discuss difficult casework). To say that we know each other's stuff is an understatement. It is a safe venue for case presentation. In having presented material about such a case and talking about feeling humiliated and ashamed, I was taken aback by the protests of one person about my disregard for my self-esteem: "You are a fine clinician. What are you talking about here? You are caught up in the countertransference. What is going on?" Those words stuck with me, luckily, and helped to alert me to my own inside job. Multiple consultations about difficult cases are a good thing. Nobody can tolerate doing this work alone. A clinician spouse is neither adequate to shore up the reeling clinician, nor ought they necessarily be burdened with the repetition of these miserable dynamics. The dining table and the bed are for the discourse of a marriage, not the analysis of relentless or obsessional preoccupations of a messy treatment. A word to the wise.

How Did I Become Such a Monster?

Countertransference incompetence (Chefetz, 2000) is an occupational hazard for the clinician engaged in trauma treatment. While objective countertransference is attributable to the reaction any experienced clinician would have to the interaction with a patient and their story, it is the subjective countertransference where the particular idiosyncrasies of the clinician distort the perception, responses, and interpretation of the patient's story and behavior (Gorkin, 1987). In a similar vein, enactment takes root in the fertile soil of isolated mental content (as Freud [1909] pointed out regarding isolated affect, a dissociative process). Bromberg elegantly spelled this out over the years in his books (Bromberg, 1998, 2006, 2011) and numerous papers. Dissociative processes encumber both clinician and patient, depriving them of consciousness for feelings, thoughts, and meaning that leave them prone to action as the only way left to communicate what hurts. In this context, the clinician and patient together earn the right for the clinician's self-disclosure (Bromberg, 2006; Levenkron, 2006) of their ongoing emotional context in the enactment. This is in the service of that disclosure leading to the benefit of the patient on the road to resolving the enactment and achieving relatedness (Stern, 2010) and reflective awareness (Fonagy & Luyten, 2009). It was Bromberg who made the case for the requirement for self-disclosure in the untangling of scenes of enactment as part of working through. Disclosing the therapist's shame to the patient? Disclosing the therapist's humiliation to the patient? Would you? Could you?

For the child who longs to be seen, to be known, and most of all to be loved, the parent whose capacity to love is impaired is a potential disaster. The only kinds of interpretation a small child has for the emotional unresponsiveness of a parental figure (the best predictor of adult dissociation is the emotional unresponsiveness of the parent; Lyons-Ruth et al., 2006) is that the child is invisible, does not exist, is unworthy of love, and/or is unlovable. And if the child continues to press the parent for an emotional response and fails to receive it, there is a sense of shame over the failure to get such confirmation. It is also a humiliating experience as the apparently withheld response—perhaps noticed as withheld, or noticed in the contrasting emotional aliveness exchanged with others but not the child, is not only a disconfirmation of the child's existence and value (a shaming experience)—but is taken as proof by the child of their failure to hold value and to be found defective, lacking status, importance, a humiliation. It's not just that the child is bad. It's that they are hopelessly beyond redemption.

In relation to my patient Rachel, who continues in treatment, I wrote (Chefetz, 2009, 2015) about some of the vulnerabilities I incurred in relation to my family of origin. I know that I was loved as a child. I can also say that as a child I don't think I knew what that meant because of the errors in communication that accumulated in relationships, particularly with my mother, but also with my father. These errors in communication (Hennighausen & Lyons-Ruth, 2005; Liotti, 2011) predict dissociative responses in the child and may account significantly for Type D, disorganized/disoriented infant attachment styles. It's important to be aware that Type B, secure attachment, often occurs in tandem with Type D in a family unit. While I have believed for many years that my choice of becoming a psychiatrist was related to my childhood job of helping to stabilize my mother's affectivity (Miller, 1981) and then repeating the effort later in life in 50-minute sessions, I can also see how caregiving controlling behaviors might play a role in my choice of careers and some personal habits. What if those controlling behaviors were rebuffed? What if they were declared of no value?

It is in this context that I've come to appreciate that ubiquitous shaming experiences in childhood set me up for the feeling of having become a monster in my countertransference responses to clinical scenes ripe with humiliation and shame. The alien-self (Fonagy et al., 2003) concept quickly came to mind after having reviewed my monster dream. The child may organize an unconscious alien sense of self if their fantasy superpowers, for example, are not met with markedness (Gergely & Watson, 1996) by a playful father who delightedly runs from the son who yells, "I'm going to get you!" but is instead met by the father who takes the small child's assertion as a challenge and backhands him across the face: "You little shit! Who the hell do you think you are?!" It's as if the parent fears the child's powers, and the message to the child is that they are dangerous and need suppression. The dangerous child is interpellated and felt to be alien, but undeniably present.

I can see that in my family of origin I was overwhelmed and deeply shamed by the repetitive outbursts of my frustrated mother, who—unable to manage her own anxieties and also respond to the challenges of parenting a precocious child—turned to gross shaming as a solution to clear any threats to her stability and to establish her dominance. Having been conscious in adult contexts for this activity in my mother, I can still see with my mind's eye the sneer of contempt, as in "How could you be so stupid?" or "Who would do such a thing?" or "You lousy rotten kid," in moments when she was not her usual loving self and lapsed into self-protective modes of living. I know that she was in part repeating what came at her from her own mother. An eminently controlling woman, very loving, and who would do anything for her children, my grandmother, as a child, had walked during nights across the Pale of Settlement out of Ukraine, through Macedonia, into Romania, and then by boat to Marseilles, before eventually coming to New York City by sea in the early 1900s. Oh, did I mention her having hidden in haystacks in the barns of accommodating farmers during the daytimes, while Cossacks plunged pitchforks into the stacks to find fleeing Jews? A multigenerational trauma history is at work here.

My father's background was basically the same Pale of Settlement exodus story for his parents, but his mother was the daughter of a revered rabbi— and had even been educated. Life in the United States was a humiliation for her, an enormous loss of status. My father's normal rebelliousness was met with callous rule making and physical enforcement. His early outbursts toward me were so shameful for him, I believe, that he resorted to having me write endless repetitive behavioral admonitions: "I will not hit my sister" was a typical one. I can still remember his fury when he found me writing the first 50 lines in a column of "I," followed by a column of "will," and so on. What child has not done this? On the other hand, I had already learned about the violence in him that he squashed and was reinforced by my mother's shaming. I could feel it in the way he steeled himself in holding back his rage as he instructed me on what he wanted me to do for punishment. This was, I imagine, confirmation of the alien-self construct in me.

My alien self has been the child who knows he is bad, shameful, defective, a lousy rotten kid, and was required to be nice to everybody, especially girls, and had to compensate for all this by being a good, good boy. I think of this as a tyranny of niceness. This was humorously revealed to me during my family practice residency, before I became a psychiatrist, when my attending physician was curious as to why I had misspelled one of the words (penis) I put on the blackboard at his request during a urology lecture. I had spelled it "penice." Be nice. (I was actually insistent that the textbook spelling of "penis" was in error, when I went to check it!) This is one of the better examples of a parapraxis that I've come across. But it also seems, in retrospect, to be about undoing my alien-self feelings of being bad. I could not tolerate any badness in me.

The downside of this kind of unconscious admonition, of course, as Alice and I discovered, was that with my anger inhibited, there was a way in which I was not real in response to her provocations. I couldn't be angry. I was not allowed. Of course, I did know my anger, but as a clinician I also had the conviction that getting openly angry with my patients was not useful. So I was not angry with her in response to her obvious provocations. She was desperate for my anger, which I withheld, unconsciously, while trying to be the good therapist (Searles, 1967). Of course, the more I tried to be good, the sicker she got, not only because I needed to be the rescuing hero, but especially because I denied her emotional reality, a particularly devastating thing for somebody living dissociatively. The idea that I could know I was angry and hold it, study it, learn from it, and metabolize it was known to me. I thought I did that. But it turned out that anger and an admixture of shame-humiliation was a stealth intruder invisible on my radar. Alice and I eventually figured this out. She actually was the one who tipped me off. It moved the treatment along quite nicely, finally.

It is in this context that I can still recall the emotional particulars of the failed treatment some years ago. I had come to hate my patient. She had been challenging me up one side and down the other for months. This was not a new experience. I didn't realize, though, how far under my skin she had gotten. Under the rule of unconscious law and my requirement to be nice, I didn't have the emotional freedom to know of my hate, then, even though I know it now. (I had then not yet evolved to embrace the perspective about hate provided by Winnicott, which I will describe later.) In the immediate throes of the scene where I had lashed out at my patient, the physiological response to her calling me to task, a clear shaming and humiliating, were devastating for me. Furious with me, my patient got up in a rage and walked out. Fear gripped me and left my body feeling weak. I was nauseous. At times I tasted the metallic taste of anxiety that I had not tasted since my first year in college at the first set of final exams. (This is another place in a treatment where the affect theory section earlier in this essay would guide exploration via associations to embodied sensings.) I was livid with myself for having failed to properly monitor my words. I had lashed out in response to a challenge in an unguarded moment and was pointedly dismissive and humiliating in my remark. I believed my patient was right. I was a poor excuse for a therapist. I felt inconsolable. I slammed my fist on the arm of my chair. I had done the opposite of what I had dedicated my professional life to do: to help those who had been traumatized to heal. Now I was re-creating that trauma for this person. How could I have done that?

Hate is love rejected. It is an entangled, vexed, preoccupying engagement. If it lasts for a bit, then it creates a barrier to relatedness on the basis of the previous rejection of the offered love (Balint, 1952). Indifference is the opposite of both hate and love. Hate is tenacious. I had really tried hard to meet this person where they were. Why did they continually challenge me? It was as if I were asking myself: How could they not love me? Look how good I have tried to be! Don't they know it? How can they say these things about me?

If I were secretly, unconsciously, viewing myself as a monster, that might account for the painful difficulty of "wearing the attributions" (Lichtenberg et al., 1996) when they are imbued with humiliating qualities. My alien-self organization would be loath to acknowledge its activation—and especially to own feeling defective and incompetent because it would prove the worst fears within me. Yet to be in denial about this would leave me unable to know feeling humiliated, and mounting a protest, including the possibility and freedom to feel hate toward the person attacking me. Had I the freedom to try on the attribution without risking collapse of my fantasy of being a good boy, then I could have the freedom to speak rather than to experience flushing, tachycardia, and obsessive preoccupations. I might then be able to say: "What's it like that I humiliated you?" "What's it like having a therapist who is incompetent?" "What comes to mind or happens in your body when you consider how badly I've behaved and what I've said?" "There's a look on your face that seems like hatred. Am I reading that correctly? What's happening for you, right now?"

A piece of a potential solution to countertransference humiliation is the capacity to protest, privately, and to know hate for the patient and contain it. A protest might be consistent with humiliation involving a feeling that the shaming attack is undeserved. This then requires a kind of consciousness for processes related to shame and humiliation that breeds tolerance for these feelings, as well as having core feelings of being lovable and loved.

Let's circle back to definitions and see how they resonate now. What is humiliation? Four themes are noted in a summary review of the literature: (1) being lowered in the eyes of others: losing esteem, social status, or dignity; (2) to feel psychologically lowered by somebody else through an attack reflecting hostile intent, including ridicule or torture; (3) this lowering occurs in the eyes of an audience, in public; and (4) is the humiliation related to a theme of incompetence, or is it undeserved? The last element described is inconsistently present in the literature (Elison & Harter, 2007). Like the writer, these authors group shame, embarrassment, guilt, and humiliation as members of a family of emotion with fuzzy borders: the shame family. Determining which member of the family is most prominent requires getting into the details of the experience. Of course, countertransference humiliation a priori assumes that what the clinician experiences in the relationship with the patient has at least some validity, or the patient wouldn't challenge the therapist in the first place. So it's the job of the clinician to determine the degree of validity—and to take the stance of wishing to learn from the experience. This learning is toward being both more knowledgeable about self—and to then be able to make use of that knowledge in the service of helping the patient to understand their own experience. It means that there needs to be a capacity to know and feel hate in response to efforts at humiliation. Again, it needs to be emphasized that this relies upon a solid sense of self-worth, relatedness, and the feeling of being loved and lovable as a bedrock felt knowing.

Countertransference Hate and Humiliation

Winnicott classified countertransference phenomena in three ways: (1) abnormality in feelings that are under repression in the analyst and requiring more analysis, (2) personal qualities in the analyst that provide the positive setting for analytic work and make the work different in quality from that of any other analyst, and (3) the analyst's love and hate in reaction to the actual personality and behavior of the patient, based upon objective observation. He suggests that "if an analyst is to analyze psychotics or anti-socials he must be able to be so thoroughly aware of the countertransference that he can sort out and study his *objective* reactions to the patient. These will include hate" (Winnicott, 1949). Later, "in the ordinary analysis the analyst has no difficulty with the management of his own hate. This hate remains latent." For Winnicott, it is likened to the hate a nursing mother feels toward the infant who bites her tender breast. The growing infant's behavior is hated, not the infant's essence.

The main thing, of course, is that through his own analysis he has become free from vast reservoirs of unconscious hate belonging to the past and to inner conflicts. There are other reasons why hate remains unexpressed and even unfelt as such:

(1) Analysis is my chosen job, the way I feel I will best deal with my own guilt, the way I can express myself in a constructive way.

(2) I get paid, or I am in training to gain a place in society by psycho-analytic work.

(3) I am discovering things.

(4) I get immediate rewards through identification with the patient, who is making progress, and I can see still greater rewards some way ahead, after the end of the treatment.

(5) Moreover, as an analyst I have ways of expressing hate. Hate is expressed by the existence of the end of the "hour." (pp. 70–71)

I was especially interested in Winnicott's work because the intensity of my reaction, and the way it took me over, was so reminiscent of self-state activity in me, and a multiple self-state model of mind applies to all of us, therapists included. Winnicott did not disappoint, but it occurred in a way that both surprised and then delighted me. In writing about the motives imputed by the patient to the analyst, he offered: "Would it not follow that if a *psychotic* is in a 'coincident love-hate' state of feeling he experiences a deep conviction that the analyst is also only capable of the same crude and dangerous state of coincident love-hate relationship? Should the analyst show love he will surely at the same moment kill the patient" (Winnicott, 1949). I agree with Winnicott that if we are to be the analysts of psychotic patients, then we would need to reach down to very primitive things inside ourselves. But what I didn't expect was his discussion of a healing dream and his description of his psychotic patient that told me he and I were working in the same clinical territory—dissociative processes, not psychosis.

For the sake of brevity, I will report only the second half of Winnicott's dream: "What I knew was that I had no right side of my body at all. This was not a castration dream. It was a sense of not having that part of the body" (Winnicott, 1949, p. 71). The surprise was when he reported his psychotic patient "was requiring of me that I have no relation to her body at all, not even an imaginative one; there was no body that she recognized as hers and if she existed at all she could only feel herself to be a mind." He went on to indicate that the side of his body that faced the patient was his right side.

By chance, some years ago I was invited to discuss a paper by a brilliant disciple of Winnicott, Nina Farhi, who had taught Winnicottian theory for at least 30 years (Chefetz, 2008). Farhi, following Winnicott, presented the case of a psychotic woman. Upon reading the exquisitely detailed protocol, I was taken by the descriptions there in the same way I found Winnicott's dream language clearly pointing to experiences of depersonalization, both in his patient and in his countertransference dream. In my discussion of Far-hi's work, I challenged the notion of psychosis and opined that the patient was suffering from a dissociative disorder with profound depersonalization described by having holes in her body that "birds could fly through." In her discussion, challenged by me, she nevertheless agreed with my posi-tion. She held Winnicott's perception of the particular case of her patient's depersonalization as psychosis.

I am struck by the extent to which Winnicott was describing a case of hate in the countertransference in a patient with depersonalization, in relation to which he had a healing dream, and the potential for a similar process in my experience of countertransference humiliation. My healing dream alerted me to an oddness: At a gut level I felt good about myself, but on another level, unfamiliar to me, I nevertheless believed I was a monster. (I had a multiple self-state dream in the same way Winnicott had a deper-sonalization dream.) How did that happen? Why did I believe that?

If somebody loves you and attacks you, then that is deeply wounding and confusing. The only way to understand this is to assume that the attack is because of necessity: I'm attacked because I'm bad, and the attack is needed to protect others from my badness. In the mind of the child, this is about self-hatred; the feeling of being betrayed by my essence and hating that I'm bad and stuck with that. There's also the problem the child has in noticing that they may behave in other ways that are routinely applauded by others. However, there is a lingering fear that others will discover the essential bad-ness that is hidden behind the outward goodness. The child lives in fear of being truly known and then found to be bad—a fate that destroys the felt experience of others loving them.

To be found out creates a horrible sense of foreboding and a wish to remain hidden. The alien self must be hidden lest others discover the bad-ness within. A fear of humiliation makes sense, and an intolerance of feel-ing anger, rage, contempt, or hatred puts the clinician at risk of isolating these feelings, while still a child. When this happens, the stage is set for enactment of the dissociatively organized emotional set in both patient and therapist (Bromberg, 2003). The monster in me didn't make sense, finally, and I was alert to him. With my monster out of the closet, I was no longer fearful of humiliation—no longer in need of not knowing my anger, rage, contempt, hatred, and other unwelcome feelings. Monsters are people too, and sometimes they are just scared children (Mayer, 1976).

Humiliation Is Distinct From Its Sister, Shame

The setting for the intensive psychotherapy for persistent dissociative processes, including PTSD and complex PTSD as well as the dissociative disorders, must include a place at the table for humiliation, that is, the intent to shame, degrade, damage, and leave a person believing they are defective and beyond repair or redemption, perhaps also corrupted and no longer containing goodness in any way. Sadistic abuse, in my clinical observation, is often about destroying the will to live, extinguishing the urge to fight back for survival and destroying any goodness in the victim. The sadist revels in the felt collapse of the other's mind, their will, so long as their victim is conscious of that collapse and the sadist can see it in the eyes of the victim. While most of my patients were not abused in this way, the mindless ways in which they were regarded as of no consequence, ignored as if having no value, and intentionally made to know their place at the margins of the world, wounded, damaged, and discarded, left deep scars in their minds and often on their bodies.

Speaking the narrative truth about a person's life may not be pretty, but by the time it's tolerable to do that, knowing the details of their experience, and still having my deep respect and commitment to their life and protection of their dignity can be sustaining. Yes, it's about loving and being loved in the way us humans do. But there are model scenes (Lichtenberg, 1989) in which love is not just a four-letter word (Perlin & Lynch, 2015). This is when we must rise to the occasion of defending the potential to put real love to work, and not let the perversions of love into hate and the control and destruction of other people's lives prevail. Knowing the scarred and bloodied underbelly of shame—humiliation—is important if we are to help people to emerge from the traps of their earlier lives when they seek a witness and a guide out of the primal forests in which they are often still imprisoned. It's not a pleasure, but that's never been the intent. At best it is sometimes deeply sobering. It is about showing up for somebody, often after everybody else has gone home. It's about having company on the journey, even if there are times when all you can do is sit together, exhausted but still alive, committed to going farther, and as far as necessary, until it's possible to move again.

References

Balint, M. (1952). On love and hate. *International Journal of Psycho-Analysis, 33,* 355–362.

Beebe, B., Messinger, D., Bahrick, L. E., Margolis, A., Buck, K. A., & Chen, H. (2016). A systems view of mother-infant face-to-face communication. *Developmental Psychology, 52*(4), 556–571.

Bromberg, P. M. (1998). *Standing in the spaces.* Hillsdale, NJ: Analytic Press.

Bromberg, P. M. (2003). One need not be a house to be haunted: On enactment, dissociation, and the dread of "Not-me." *Psychoanalytic Dialogues, 13*(5), 689–710.

Bromberg, P. M. (2006). *Awakening the dreamer: Clinical journeys.* Mahwah, NJ: Analytic Press.

Bromberg, P. M. (2011). *The shadow of the tsunami and the growth of the relational mind.* New York: Routledge.

Bucci, W., & Maskit, B. (2007). Dissociation from the perspective of multiple code theory: Part I: Psychological roots and implications for psychoanalytic treatment. *Contemporary Psychoanalysis, 43*(2), 165–184.

Chefetz, R. A. (2000). Disorder in the therapist's view of the self: Working with the person with dissociative identity disorder. *Psychoanalytic Inquiry, 20*(2), 305–329.

Chefetz, R. A. (2008). *Nolens volens* out of darkness—from the depersonal to the "really" personal. *Contemporary Psychoanalysis, 44*(1), 18–40.

Chefetz, R. A. (2009). Waking the dead therapist. *Psychoanalytic Dialogues, 19*(4), 393–403.

Chefetz, R. A. (2015). *Intensive psychotherapy for persistent dissociative processes: The fear of feeling real.* New York: Norton.

Chefetz, R. A. (2017). Issues in consultation for treatments with distressed activated abuser/protector self-states in dissociative identity disorder. *Journal of Trauma and Dissociation, 18*(3), 465–475.

Chefetz, R. A. (2018). *Attachments: Subjugation, shame, and the attachment to painful affects and objects.* Paper presented at the Shame Matters Conference, Bowlby Centre, London, England.

Chefetz, R. A. (2020). Shame and the developmental antecedents of enduring, self-critical mental states: A discussion and some speculations. *Psychiatry, 83*(1), 25–32.

Demos, E. V. (2019). *The affect theory of Silvan Tomkins for psychoanalysis and psychotherapy: Recasting the essentials.* New York: Routledge.

Demos, V. (Ed.) (1995). *Exploring affect: The selected writings of Sylvan S. Tomkins.* New York: Cambridge University Press.

DeYoung, P. A. (2015). *Understanding and treating chronic shame: A relational/neurobiological approach.* New York: Routledge.

Dorahy, M. J. (2017). Shame as a compromise for humiliation and rage in the internal representation of abuse by loved ones: Processes, motivations, and the role of dissociation. *Journal of Trauma and Dissociation, 18*(3), 383–396.

Elison, J., & Harter, S. (2007). Causes, correlates, and consequences. In J. L. Tracy, R. W. Robins, & J. P. Tangney (Eds.), *The self-conscious emotions: Theory and research* (pp. 310–329). New York: Guilford.

Fonagy, P., Gergely, G., Jurist, E. J., & Target, M. (2003). *Affect regulation, mentalization and the development of the self.* New York: Other Press.

Fonagy, P., & Luyten, P. (2009). A developmental, mentalization-based approach to the understanding and treatment of borderline personality disorder. *Development and Psychopathology, 21*(4), 1355–1381.

Forgash, C., & Knipe, J. (2012). Integrating EMDR and ego state treatment for clients with trauma disorders. *Journal of EMDR Practice and Research, 6*(3), 120–128.

Freud, S. (1909). Notes upon a case of obsessional neurosis. In J. Strachey (Ed.), *The standard edition* (Vol. 10). London: Hogarth.

Freud, S. (1917). Mourning and melancholia. In J. Strachey (Ed.), *The standard edition* (Vol. 14, pp. 237–258). London: Hogarth.

Gallese, V., Eagle, M. N., & Migone, P. (2007). Intentional attunement: Mirror neurons and the neural underpinnings of interpersonal relations. *Journal of the American Psychoanalytic Association, 55*(1), 131–176.

Gendlin, E. T. (1978). *Focusing.* New York: Bantam.

Gergely, G., & Watson, J. S. (1996). The social biofeedback theory of parental affect-mirroring: The development of emotional self-awareness and self-control in infancy. *International Journal of Psychoanalysis, 77,* 1181–1211.

Gilbert, P. (2005). Social mentalities: A biopsychosocial and evolutionary approach to social relationships. In M. W. Baldwin (Ed.), *Interpersonal cognition* (pp. 299–333). New York: Guilford.

Gorkin, M. (1987). *The uses of countertransference.* Northvale, NJ: Jason Aronson.

Greenberg, L. S. (2004). Emotion-focused therapy. *Clinical Psychology and Psychotherapy, 11*(1), 3–16.

Hartling, L. M., Lindner, E., Spalthoff, U., & Britton, M. (2013). Humiliation: A nuclear bomb of emotions? *Psicología Política,* no. 46, 55–76.

Hartling, L. M., & Luchetta, T. (1999). Humiliation: Assessing the impact of derision, degradation, and debasement. *Journal of Primary Prevention, 19*(4), 259–278.

Hennighausen, K., & Lyons-Ruth, K. (2005). Disorganization of attachment strategies in infancy and childhood. In R. E. Tremblay, R. G. Barr, & R. D. Peters

(Eds.), *Encyclopedia on early childhood development* [online]. Montreal: Centre of Excellence for Early Childhood Development.

Hicks, D., & Tutu, D. (2011). *Dignity: The essential role it plays in resolving conflict.* New Haven, CT: Yale University Press.

Johnson, S. E., Hunsley, J., Greenberg, L., & Schindler, D. (1999). Emotion focused couples therapy: Status and challenges. *Clinical Psychology: Science and Practice, 6*(1), 67–79.

Kaufman, G. (2004). *The psychology of shame: Theory and treatment of shame-based syndromes.* New York: Springer.

Kelly, V. C. (2009). A primer of affect psychology. *The art of intimacy and the hidden challenge of shame,* 158–191.

Kohut, H. (2009). *The restoration of the self.* Chicago: University of Chicago Press.

Lacey, D. (2011). The role of humiliation in the Palestinian/Israeli conflict in Gaza. *Psychology and Society, 4*(1), 76–92.

Lamm, C., & Singer, T. (2010). The role of anterior insular cortex in social emotions. *Brain Structure and Function, 214*(5–6), 579–591.

Lane, R. D., & Nadel, L. (2000). *Cognitive neuroscience of emotion.* New York: Oxford University Press.

Lane, R. D., Quinlan, D. M., Schwartz, G. E., & Walker, P. A. (1990). The levels of emotional awareness scale: A cognitive-developmental measure of emotion. *Journal of Personality Assessment, 55,* 124–134.

Lanius, R. A., Vermetten, E., Loewenstein, R. J., Brand, B., Schmahl, C., Bremner, J. D., & Spiegel, D. (2010). Emotion modulation in PTSD: Clinical and neurobiological evidence for a dissociative subtype. *American Journal of Psychiatry, 167,* 640–647.

Lansky, M. R. (1992). *Fathers who fail: Shame and psychopathology in the family system.* Hillsdale, NJ: Analytic Press.

Leask, P. (2013). Losing trust in the world: Humiliation and its consequences. *Psychodynamic Practice, 19*(2), 129–142.

Ledoux, J. E. (1996). *The emotional brain.* New York: Simon and Schuster.

Ledoux, J. E. (2012, January 22). Searching the brain for the roots of fear. *New York Times.* https://opinionator.blogs.nytimes.com/2012/01/22/anatomy-of-fear/

LeDoux, J. E., & Pine, D. S. (2016). Using neuroscience to help understand fear and anxiety: A two-system framework. *American Journal of Psychiatry, 173*(11), 1083–1093.

Levenkron, H. (2006). Love (and hate) with the proper stranger: Affective honesty and enactment. *Psychoanalytic Inquiry, 26*(2), 157–181.

Levinger, S., Somer, E., & Holden, R. R. (2015). The importance of mental pain and physical dissociation in youth suicidality. *Journal of Trauma and Dissociation, 16*(3), 322–339.

Lewis, H. B. (1987). *The role of shame in symptom formation.* Hillsdale, NJ: Lawrence Earlbaum.

Lewis, M. (1992). *Shame: The exposed self.* New York: First Free Press.

Lichtenberg, J. D. (1989). Model scenes, motivation, and personality. In S. Dowling & A. Rothstein (Eds.), *The significance of infant observational research for clinical work with children, adolescents, and adults* (pp. 91–107). Madison, CT: International University Press.

Lichtenberg, J. D., Lachmann, F. M., & Fosshage, J. L. (1996). *The clinical exchange: Techniques derived from self and motivational systems.* Hillsdale, NJ: Analytic Press.

Liotti, G. (2011). Attachment disorganization and the controlling strategies: An illustration of the contributions of attachment theory to developmental psychopathology and to psychotherapy integration. *Journal of Psychotherapy Integration, 21*(3), 232.

Lyons-Ruth, K., Dutra, L., Schuder, M. R., & Bianchi, I. (2006). From infant attachment disorganization to adult dissociation: Relational adaptations or traumatic experiences? In R. A. Chefetz (Ed.), *Dissociative disorders: An expanding window into the psychobiology of mind* (Vol. 29, pp. 63–86). Philadelphia: Saunders.

Martel, Y. (2010). *Beatrice and Virgil.* New York: Spiegel and Grau.

Mayer, M. (1976). *There's a monster in my closet.* New York: Penguin.

Miller, A. (1981). *The drama of the gifted child.* New York: Basic Books.

Miller, S. (1985). *The shame experience.* Hillsdale, NJ: Analytic Press.

Morrison, A. P. (1989). *Shame: The underside of narcissism.* Hillsdale, NJ: Analytic Press.

Nathanson, D. L. (1992). *Shame and pride: Affect, sex, and the birth of the self.* New York: Norton.

Ogden, P., Minton, K., & Pain, C. (2006). *Trauma and the body: A sensorimotor approach to psychotherapy.* New York: Norton.

Paivio, S. C., & Nieuwenhuis, J. A. (2001). Efficacy of emotion focused therapy for adult survivors of child abuse: A preliminary study. *Journal of Traumatic Stress, 14*(1), 115–133.

Panksepp, J. (1998). *Affective neuroscience: The foundations of human and animal emotions.* New York: Oxford University Press.

Panksepp, J. (2004). Affective consciousness: Core emotional feelings in animals and humans. *Consciousness and Cognition, 14*(1), 30–80.

Panksepp, J., & Biven, L. (2012). *The archaeology of mind: Neuroevolutionary origins of human emotions.* New York: Norton.

Perlin, M. L., & Lynch, A. J. (2015). Love is just a four-letter word: Sexuality, international human rights, and therapeutic jurisprudence. *Canadian Journal of Comparative and Contemporary Law, 1*(1), 9–48.

Pizzagalli, D. A., Lehmann, D., Hendrick, A. M., Regard, M., Pascual-Marqui, R. D., & Davidson, R. J. (2002). Affective judgments of faces modulate early activity (~160ms) within the fusiform gyri. *Neuroimage, 16*, 663–677.

Ploghaus, A., Narain, C., Beckmann, C. F., Clare, S., Bantick, S., Wise, R., Matthews, P. M., Nicholas, J., Rawlins, P., & Tracey, I. (2001). Exacerbation of pain by anxiety is associated with activity in a hippocampal network. *Journal of Neuroscience, 21*(December), 9896–9903.

Ploghaus, A., Tracey, I., Gati, J. S., Clare, S., Menon, R. S., Matthews, P. M., Nicholas, J., & Rawlins, P. (1999). Dissociating pain from its anticipation in the human brain. *Science, 284*(5422), 1979–1981.

Rainville, P., Duncan, G. H., Price, B. C., & Bushnell, M.C. (1997). Pain affect encoded in human anterior cingulate but not somatosensory cortex. *Science, 277*(August 1997), 968–971.

Rauch, S., Shin, L. M., & Wright, C. I. (2003). Neuroimaging studies of amygdala function in anxiety disorders. *Annals of the New York Academy of Sciences, 985,* 389–410.

Rauch, S. L., van der Kolk, B. A., Fisler, R. E., Alpert, N. M., Orr, S. P., Savage, C. R., Fischman, A. J., Jenike, M. A., & Pitman, R. K. (1996). A symptom provocation study of posttraumatic stress disorder using positron emission tomography and script driven imagery. *Archives of General Psychiatry, 53,* 380–387.

Rothstein, A. (1984). Fear of humiliation. *Journal of the American Psychoanalytic Association, 32*(1), 99–116.

Ryle, A. (Ed.) (1999). *Cognitive analytic therapy: Developments in theory and practice.* New York: John Wiley.

Scheff, T. J., & Retzinger, S. M. (2001). *Emotions and violence: Shame and rage in destructive conflicts.* Lincoln, NE: iUniverse.

Schlumpf, Y. R., Nijenhuis, E. R., Chalavi, S., Weder, E. V., Zimmermann, E., Luechinger, R., Marca, R. L., Reinders, S., & Jäncke, L. (2013). Dissociative part-dependent biopsychosocial reactions to backward masked angry and neutral faces: An fMRI study of dissociative identity disorder. *NeuroImage: Clinical, 3,* 54–64.

Schore, J. R., & Schore, A. N. (2008). Modern attachment theory: The central role of affect regulation in development and treatment. *Clinical Social Work Journal, 36,* 9–20.

Searles, H. (1967). The dedicated physician. In R. W. Gibson (Ed.), *Crosscurrents in psychiatry and psychoanalysis* (pp. 128–143). Philadelphia: Lippincott.

Shapiro, F. (1995). *Eye movement desensitization and reprocessing.* New York: Guilford.

Shin, L. M., Kosslyn, S. M., McNally, R. J., Alpert, N. M., Thompson, W. L., Rauch, S. L., Macklin, M. L., & Pitman, R. K. (1997). Visual imagery and perception in posttraumatic stress disorder. *Archives of General Psychiatry, 54,* 233–241.

Shin, L. M., & Liberzon, I. (2010). The neurocircuitry of fear, stress, and anxiety disorders. *Neuropsychopharmacology Reviews, 35,* 169–191.

Shin, L. M., Rauch, S. L., & Pitman, R. K. (2006). Amygdala, medial prefrontal cortex, and hippocampal function in PTSD. *Annals of the New York Academy of Sciences, 1071*, 67–79.

Shin, L. M., Wright, C., Cannistraro, P. A., Wedig, M., McMullin, K., Martis, B., Macklin, M., Lasko, N., Cavanagh, S., Krangel, T., Orr, S., Pitman, R., Whalen, P., Rauch, S. L. (2005). A functional magnetic resonance imaging study of amygdala and medial prefrontal cortex responses to overtly presented fearful faces in posttraumatic stress disorder. *Archives of General Psychiatry, 62*, 273–281.

Sierra, M., Senior, C., Dalton, J., McDonough, M., Bond, A., Phillips, M. L., O'Dwyer, A. M., & David, A. S. (2002). Autonomic response in depersonalization disorder. *Archives of General Psychiatry, 59*, 833–838.

Spiegel, H., & Spiegel, D. (1978). *Trance and treatment: Clinical uses of hypnosis.* Washington, DC: American Psychiatric Press.

Stern, D. B. (2010). *Partners in thought: Working with unformulated experience, dissociation, and enactment.* New York: Routledge.

Tangney, J. P., & Dearing, R. L. (2003). *Shame and guilt.* New York: Guilford.

Tangney, J. P., Miller, R. S., Flicker, L., & Barlow, D. H. (1996). Are shame, guilt, and embarrassment distinct emotions? *Journal of Personality and Social Psychology, 70*(6), 1256.

Taylor, G. J. (2000). Recent developments in alexithymia theory and research. *Canadian Journal of Psychiatry, 45*(2), 134–142.

Tomkins, S. S. (1962). *Affect imagery consciousness: Vol. 1. The positive affects.* New York: Springer.

Tomkins, S. S. (1963). *Affect imagery consciousness: Vol. 2. The negative affects.* New York: Springer.

Tomkins, S. S. (1982). *Affect, imagery, consciousness: Vol. 3. Cognition and affect.* New York: Springer.

Tomkins, S. S. (1995). Script theory. In E. V. Demos (Ed.), *Exploring affect: The selected writings of Silvan S. Tomkins* (pp. 312–388). New York: Cambridge University Press.

Tomkins, S. S., & Karon, B. P. (1962). *Affect, imagery, consciousness: Vol. 4. Cognition.* Cambridge, UK: Gaunt.

Tomkins, S. S., & McCarter, R. (1995). What and where are the primary affects? Some evidence for a theory. In E. V. Demos (Ed.), *Exploring affect: The selected writings of Silvan S. Tomkins* (pp. 217–262). New York: Cambridge University Press.

Torres, W. J., & Bergner, R. M. (2010). Humiliation: Its nature and consequences. *Journal of the American Academy of Psychiatry and the Law Online, 38*(2), 195–204.

Trumbull, D. (2003). Shame: An acute stress response to interpersonal traumatization. *Psychiatry, 66*(1), 53–64.

Watkins, J. G. (1971). The affect bridge: A hypnoanalytic technique. *International Journal of Clinical and Experimental Hypnosis, 19*, 21–27.

Widen, S. C., & Russell, J. A. (2010). The "disgust face" conveys anger to children. *Emotion, 10*(4), 455–466.

Winnicott, D. W. (1949). Hate in the countertransference. *International Journal of Psychoanalysis, 30,* 69–75.

Wolf, E. S. (1988). *Treating the self: Elements of clinical self psychology.* New York: Guilford.

Wurmser, L. (2000). *The power of the inner judge: Psychodynamic treatment of the severe neuroses.* Northvale, NJ: Jason Aronson.

8

Dysregulation and Its Impact on States of Consciousness

Daniel Hill

SOME PATIENTS ARE HARD TO REACH BECAUSE IT'S DIFFICULT TO GET through their defenses. Topics are off limits; therapeutic actions are thwarted. Sometimes the problem has more to do with states of consciousness that impede therapeutic progress. I'm referring to temporary, often subtle impairments in the processing of conscious experience that occur when we're dysregulated and unaware of it. Such patients may bring in the same problem, or some version of it, again and again. It's not only that they don't seem to learn from experience. They don't learn from talking about it either. Along with helping to understand the inefficiency of a treatment, appreciating such impaired states of consciousness can provide points of entry into patients' experience of being dysregulated, guide empathic responses, and help them detect and manage such states on their own.*

   In this chapter, I explore various ways that consciousness is impaired when we're dysregulated. We'll see that the impairment is starkly different depending on whether the dysregulation is hyper- or hypoarousal. However, in both cases the capacity to think and feel clearly and to reflect on and integrate our thoughts and feelings is compromised or deactivated entirely. The com-

---

*With regard to diagnosis, it has recently been recognized that getting a report of a patient's states of consciousness is critical for diagnosis and treatment of dissociative disorders (Ataria, 2014; Chefetz, 2015; Dell, 2009a), and there has been renewed empirical study of the phenomenology and conceptualization of severely altered states of consciousness (Frewen & Lanius, 2015; Vaitl et al., 2005).

plexity and flexibility of normal waking consciousness is diminished. Higher-order functions deteriorate and may collapse entirely. Agency, dependent on complex conscious processes, is reduced or disabled. The capacity to process subjective experience and to relate intersubjectively is impaired.

There is a spectrum of dysregulation and a spectrum of impaired consciousness. The greater the degree of dysregulation is, the greater the impairment and the greater the change to subjective experiencing. We tend to think of dysregulated states in the extreme. They can, however, be quite subtle and difficult to detect in ourselves and others. Damasio (1999) notes an analogous example about the temperature at which we feel comfortable (i.e., remain in a homeostatic state). It need only deviate a degree or two before we feel chilled or uncomfortably warm. I would add, by the time we become aware of it, it's already been happening. Affect represents the state of the body. Affect regulation, maintaining homeostasis by another name, also has a narrow range; for many of our patients, a very narrow range. Insecurely attached patients become dysregulated at low levels of stress (Schore, 1994). When the dysregulation is subtle, the accompanying deterioration of consciousness may go unnoticed.

In what follows, I explore what happens to consciousness when we're dysregulated: the kinds and degrees of deterioration and the accompanying changes to subjective experiencing. We will see that hyperaroused dysregulation generates states of consciousness marked by a loss of temporal perspective, over-immersion in experience, and loss of coherence accompanied by a sense of fragmentation experienced as being flooded by feelings and overwhelmed by thoughts. Hypoaroused states also involve a loss of temporal context, but, in stark contrast, there is a detachment from experience. The loss of coherence is due to a lack of mental activity, and the subjective experience is of an empty and barren inner world.

Impaired consciousness is commonly referred to as being dissociated. Let me take a moment to clarify how I use the term "dissociation." It suffers from referring to two different conditions (Allen, 2001; Cardena, 1994; Holmes et al., 2005; Meares, 2012 Putnam, 1997; Spitzer et al., 2006). It may refer to the compartmentalization of psychological structures such as traumatic memories that would dysregulate us were they to intrude into consciousness. Such sequestration is a defense against dysregulation. Although there are costs, compartmentalization preserves as much adaptive functioning as possible. Psychoanalysis calls this repression and understands it to be effected by classic ego defenses. Importantly, the sequestered content has achieved consciousness and ongoing defending is required to keep it out of awareness. Note also that it's not the thought that is disruptive. It's the affect that accompanies it that undoes us and, ultimately, it's the affect that's being defended against. While the thought and affect are linked, it is the increased tolerance for the affect, actually the modulation of its intensity, that alleviates the problem.

The other use of the term "dissociation" refers to a breakdown in the processing of affect and to the impaired state of consciousness that occurs when one is dysregulated. There is a disorganization and thus dissociation at the neurological level that severs the mind from the experience of the body and alters consciousness (see, e.g., Dell, 2009b; Meares, 2005). So one use of the term refers to a defense against and the other to a symptom of dysregulation. Compartmentalization/repression involves the effective functioning of psychological defenses against dysregulation, whereas altered states of consciousness are the result of the disruption of neural processing when dysregulated.* In what follows I use "dissociation" to refer to symptomatic impairments of consciousness and will explore it from the point of view of regulation theory and interpersonal neurobiology (Schore, 1994, 2003a, 2003b, 2012; Siegel, 1999).†

Traumatology has focused on severely altered states of consciousness such as flashbacks and depersonalization-derealization, which are sequelae of severe single-incident trauma and symptoms of severe dysregulation. However, moderately altered states of consciousness are far more common and a frequent occurrence during therapeutic sessions. My concern is with patients with avoidant and preoccupied attachment patterns. They have experienced moderate cumulative trauma and suffer moderately disordered states of consciousness due to moderately dysregulated affect states (Hill, 2015). I will propose dimensions of consciousness that describe the subjec-

---

*At this point, there are no known neural mechanisms and no generalizable neural correlates for repressive defenses (Holmes, 1990). Dysregulation-dissociation, on the other hand, has been shown to be associated with a distinct imbalance in the limbic-autonomic system and a resulting disorganization/dissociation among neural structures (Bremmer et al., 2010; Frewen & Lanius, 2015; Vaitl et al., 2005). A corresponding limbic-autonomic imbalance is proposed by Schore (1994). The neural dissociation is also addressed by Meares's (2012) research on P3a,b.
† Bromberg (2006) blends the two meanings of dissociation with his use of the term "dissociated self-states." On the one hand, these are mental structures that are compartmentalized. However, when the defenses against them fail, we become dysregulated and experience altered states of consciousness as they are enacted.

tive experience of such states and that, along with its clinical value, I hope will contribute to a taxonomy of consciousness called for by Bach (1985). I end with clinical examples and a discussion of impaired states of consciousness as intersubjective phenomena.

Trauma-Related Altered States of Consciousness

The first general study of altered states of consciousness was *The Varieties of Religious Experience* by William James (1902). He distinguished altered states of consciousness from what he called "rational consciousness," today referred to as "normal waking consciousness." Altered states represent a qualitatively different and temporary way of experiencing our inner and outer worlds. They may be drug induced, psychologically or behaviorally induced (meditation, physical exhaustion), intersubjectively induced (shared expanded states), physiologically induced (starvation, high fever), hypnotically induced, or trauma induced (peritraumatic altered states of consciousness), or they may be chronic sequelae of trauma (Vaitl et al., 2005). It's the sequelae of trauma that are the concern of this chapter: chronically disordered states of consciousness that are markers of affect dysregulation at low levels of stress due to an impairment of the capacity to regulate affect.

Beginning with Janet (1889) through Breuer and Freud (1893/1955) to the present (see, e.g., Dell, 2009b) trauma-related "hypnoid" states have been understood to accompany automatisms such as conversion symptoms.[*] They are now seen to accompany discrete hyperaroused enactments

---

[*] Janet (1889, 1901) observed that hysterical patients suffered from "narrowed" states of consciousness and that, when in what we would now call constricted states of consciousness, they were subject to losing volitional control over their bodies, manifesting involuntary gestures or paralysis. He thought of such conversion symptoms as "automatisms." Automaticity has remained a central concern of dissociative studies and is important for understanding the effects of dysregulation. It is, however, beyond the scope of this chapter. I mention it here because it is an inevitable partner to states of consciousness altered by dysregulation and must be considered along with it. Think of your own state of mind when being defensive, and you can get a sense of what Janet's constricted consciousness is like. Note also that when in this state you are relatively automated, scripted by procedural memories, operating perhaps according to some kind of algorithm. Automaticity is what we're reduced to when dysregulated and in constricted states of consciousness.

(Bromberg, 2006) that are highly automated/scripted.* I am proposing that dysregulated-dissociated states of consciousness occur not only during such events but whenever one is dysregulated.

Depicting dissociated states of consciousness requires an appreciation of higher and lower levels of consciousness and of their comings and goings. Much of what follows is drawn from Russell Meares (2000, 2005, 2012, 2016), who understands consciousness as a core phenomenon in clinical practice. He articulates the development of the increasing complexity and capacities of conscious processes, and describes how, once developed, higher-order consciousness is subject to sudden disruption.

The story begins with Janet (1901), who was the first to associate altered states of consciousness with trauma. He noticed that automaticities such as the involuntary gestures he observed in traumatized patients, then diagnosed as hysterics, occurred along with a "narrowed" state of consciousness. His theory of why this happened was based in the work of the English neurologist John Hughlings Jackson, the mid-19th-century father of English neuroscience whose ideas had a fundamental influence on an extraordinary array of theorists including Charcot, Breuer, Freud, James, Piaget, Vygotsky, and more recently Damasio, Edelman, Schore, and Meares. Jackson understood consciousness as an emergent phenomenon resulting from increases in neural complexity. As the brain increases in complexity, culminating with the development of the prefrontal cortex, there is an increase in integration and a concomitant increase in the complexity of conscious experiencing and mental operations. Since then, consciousness has been conceptualized as lower and higher.

Lower-order consciousness is understood to provide simple phenomenological awareness. One is pressed up against the present moment (Stern, 2004), essentially a biological automaton with no reflective capacity and no thought between stimuli and responses.† There is awareness, but no awareness of awareness; no capacity to reflect and operate on mental representations. One is immersed in the moment without a sense of the past or future

---

*In an article that came out as I was completing this chapter, Maroda (2020) suggests that the continuums of level consciousness with varying degrees of control may provide us with greater understanding of enactments than thinking in terms of conscious versus unconscious.

†While being in the moment is usually considered a positive experience, this is only when we allow it to happen and not the case when it's involuntary, such as during intense fear states.

(Damasio, 1999). Edelman (1989) calls this "primary consciousness," understands it to be generated by the right brain, and emphasizes that without the past and future we are without the capacity for contextualization. Consciousness is constricted, and one is stuck in the present. When we're dysregulated, we're reduced to varying degrees of constricted consciousness. A patient of mine, struggling to extricate herself from an abusive relationship, described a version of this. Referring to an incident in which she felt pressured by him, she put it this way: "When he's like that, I only see the small picture."

Higher-order consciousness is exponentially more complex. Experience is constructed by more complex processes. Compared with the constricted quality of primary consciousness, it has a spaciousness born of the reflective capacity. William James (1902) conceived of it as "dualistic," referring to the introspective capacity to take one's stream of conscious as an object. It gives birth to our inner world. Meares (2005) elaborates this more complex state, calling it "doubled consciousness," about which more below. Adding to this vertical or depth aspect of the sense of spaciousness, there is a horizontal dimension derived from the capacity to think about ourselves in the past and to imagine our future (Damasio, 1999). This allows us to escape the present and, even as we process it, provides a background awareness of a past and future. So consciousness has a sense of depth provided by introspection and breadth provided by the capacity for time travel.* I'll describe this larger consciousness more fully and the differences between it and lower, early developing consciousness in the next section. For now I want to discuss why conscious capacities come to be reduced involuntarily.

Along with his theory of the development of complex consciousness, Jackson (1931, a,b) also proposed a theory of "dissolution" in which "assaults" (stresses) to the brain lead to neural dissociation. That is, neural systems that normally exchange information become dis-associated and there is a reduction of neural integration and complexity. Importantly, the last structures to develop are the first to become disorganized. The right brain precedes the development of the left, and subcortical development precedes cortical. The loss of cortical functioning and the disruption of the integration of the left and right hemispheres when stressed results in a lower level of consciousness and loss of higher-order functions. Additionally, the greater the

---

*The sense of depth is actually a bit more complicated than introspection. The right brain's capacity to know what's implied adds to it (McGilchrist, 2009). In a subsequent publication I will suggest a third dimension of foreground and background.

assault, the greater the loss of neural integration and complexity, and the greater the degradation of conscious mental operations. Jackson saw this as a neural "regression" down the evolutionary trajectory to a more primitive form of consciousness. Janet (1901) proposed the same idea, in which "vehement emotions" led to a "lowering of consciousness." It explained the narrowed states of consciousness he observed in his patients.

Taking "assault" and "vehement emotion" to mean that the event exceeds one's tolerance for affect, we can put this in the language of regulation theory. When affect is regulated, the brain is optimally integrated. The neurobiological systems underpinning affective and cognitive operations provide optimal perceiving and thinking. However, when affect is dysregulated, the neurobiological systems contributing to consciousness become dissociated (Meares, 2012; Schore, 1994; Siegel, 1999; Vaitl et al., 2006), and we enter into a lower/constricted state of consciousness with diminished cognitive and affect-processing capacity. This can be summed up as "regulated-integrated versus dysregulated-dissociated" (Hill, 2015) and in the proposals that consciousness is affect state dependent and that disorders of affect regulation result in chronically disordered consciousness.

At the same time that dysregulation is inducing a lowered state of consciousness, the type of dysregulation, hyper- or hypoarousal, is having additional effects. These have been studied in the extreme through a comparison of different types of altered states associated with hyper- and hypoaroused types of PTSD.

The Differing Effects of Hyper- and Hypoaroused Dysregulation on Consciousness

Empirical confirmation of two types of PTSD led to a change in the *DSM-5* (Lanius et al., 2007, 2010, 2012; Stein et al., 2012; Wolf et al., 2012). PTSD had been understood as a biphasic disorder in which patients experienced periods of hyperarousal marked by chronic anxiety, sleep disturbance, hypervigilance, and irritability alternating with periods of hypoarousal marked by emotional constriction and social withdrawal.

Consistent with clinical reports, it is now empirically established that PTSD is not biphasic but rather typified by hyper- or hypoaroused symptoms including dramatically different, indeed opposite types of altered consciousness. Patients with hyperaroused PTSD experienced flashbacks—total immersion in the experience of the activated memory. Those suffering the hypoaroused type of PTSD experienced depersonalization-derealization—total detachment from experience of the present. The two types of altered consciousness were found to have distinct neural profiles.

In neuroimaging studies, Lanius and her colleagues (2007, 2010, 2012) found a subset of patients suffering from an "under-modulated," hyper-aroused type of PTSD (about 70% of their sample). It is associated with low cortical activity and high subcortical activity in response to hearing a transcript of one's trauma story. These were the patients who were vulnerable to flashbacks and other reliving experiences. In the other type of PTSD, an "over-modulated," hypoaroused type (about 30%), the response was an overinhibition by cortical structures of subcortically mediated sympathetic arousal. These patients were vulnerable to depersonalization-derealization. Note the association of hyperarousal with immersion in experience and hypoarousal with detachment from experience. We'll come back to this.

Lanius's findings of two types of PTSD are congruent with Schore's proposal (1994) that the core difference between the two types of structured insecure attachment trauma is that one is organized by hyper- and the other by hypoarousal. That is, anxious-ambivalent attachment trauma results in a sympathetic (hyperaroused/upregulated) autonomic bias, whereas avoidant trauma results in a parasympathetic (hypoaroused/down-regulated) bias. The sympathetic bias generates a hyperaroused set point, hyperaroused responses to stress, and an underregulated, impulsive personality. The parasympathetic bias results in a hypoaroused set point, hypoactivated responses to stress, and an overregulated/inhibited personality.

There are, it should be mentioned, significant differences between sequelae resulting from severe single-incident trauma occurring in adulthood and moderate cumulative trauma occurring in infancy. Single-incident traumas tend, for example, to result in discrete sequelae whereas the sequelae of early cumulative trauma tend to result in pervasive sequelae. The former may dent or warp what may have been a well-functioning personality now coping, for example, with fears of flashbacks, whereas the latter is a type of developmental trauma that arrests development and establishes the foundation of a personality disorder. However, all traumas affect the limbic-autonomic nervous system, which is the concern here. In this case, the differences have to do with the severity of the damage done and the severity of the altered states of consciousness that derive from it. That is, the key differences between PTSD deriving from single-incident traumas and the cumulative trauma of structured insecure attachment trauma are that the former suffered severe damage and episodes of severe dysregulation and impaired consciousness, whereas the latter derives from repetitive moderate trauma resulting in moderate levels of dysregulation (Hill, 2015) and, as I now describe, moderately impaired states of consciousness.[*]

Severely and Moderately Impaired States of Consciousness

The degree of dysregulation is a key factor influencing states of consciousness. Just as, according to Jackson's theory, the degree of dysregulation corresponds to the degree of neural dissolution, there are degrees to which states of consciousness are altered (see, e.g., Dell, 2009a, 2009b; Frewen & Lanius, 2015). One patient described it as follows: "When we're bickering, I can try to stand up to him a *little* bit, but when he gets really angry and yells, I'm gone—a deer in the headlights."

Perhaps because moderate dysregulation is debilitating but not disabling, the moderately altered states of consciousness that accompany it typically go unreported by patients and undetected by therapists. Although I've yet to encounter the patient who wasn't aware of them, they are rarely discussed or thought about in a constructive way. When sufficiently severe to be obvious, patients often find the states frightening and/or shameful and don't present them as a problem. When subtle, they are often undetected by patients or brushed off. In many cases, I've learned of a patient's impaired experiencing only because, cued by my own matched or reactive state or responding to their offhand comments such as, "I know I'm all over the place," I asked about it.[†] Yet, in my experience, when dysregulated-dissociated states of consciousness are recognized and mentalized, it inevitably proves helpful.

Chronic, moderately impaired states of consciousness are due to deficits in the primary affect regulation system caused by the cumulative stresses of anxious-ambivalent and avoidant attachment relationships (Hill, 2015).[‡]

---

[*] It should be noted that the trauma of disorganized attachment results in severe dysregulation. This essay concerns only the more common trauma of structured insecure attachment.

[†] Unlike the "deer in the headlights" frozen, hypoaroused response to danger in which the dorsal vagal system is activated, this hyperaroused response is more like a squirrel in the headlights frantically zigzagging this way and that and unable to organize a coherent escape.

[‡] The primary affect-regulating system, illuminated by Schore (1994), refers to the limbic-autonomic affect-regulating system that sets up by about age 18 months. Once

Due to the resulting regulatory deficits, dysregulation and the concomitant alterations of consciousness occur at low levels of stress.

Moderately altered states of consciousness may be defined in comparison with severely altered states of consciousness. For example, a full-on flashback sweeps one in and generates a degree of absorption sufficient for the activated memory to be experienced as the present—a total immersion in a memory. We see this in a more moderate form when a disturbing, compartmentalized memory is activated, intrudes into consciousness, and sweeps us into it, but is experienced as a memory—a partial immersion. The fact that, during flashbacks, representations are experienced as perceptions is correlated with the intensity of the hyperaroused affect that comes packaged with the memory.* A more moderate affective intensity and a relatively moderate assault on the neural systems contributing to consciousness result in partial immersion.

There are corresponding differences among severely and moderately hypoaroused states of consciousness. Depersonalization-derealization involves the subjective experience of extreme detachment, a severely altered state of consciousness in which we experience ourselves outside of our body and/or in which reality is experienced as distanced to the point of being unreal—full detachment. A partial form of involuntary detachment involves an objectification of and felt distance from self and objects without the extreme sense of estrangement and alteration of perception. Here too the difference correlates with the intensity of the affect, in this case the intensity of hypoarousal. Thus, the degree of hyper- or hypoaroused dysregulation determines the relationship to experience—full or partial immersion or detachment. Immersion versus detachment is one of the dimensions I propose for describing impaired states of consciousness.

---

established, this right brain system regulates affect automatically and quickly. The secondary affect-regulating system, illuminated by Fonagy as "mentalization" (2002), utilizes the reflective verbal system that regulates affect deliberately and relatively slowly. This left brain system begins development after the primary system is established and remains dependent on it for its development and ongoing functioning.
*Regulation theory suggests that this may be due to the right brain being activated in hyperaroused states and the left brain being activated in states of moderate and low arousal (Schore, 2015). Thus, immersion in experience may be due to right brain dominance and detachment due to left brain dominance. Further explanation is beyond the scope of this chapter.

Dimensions of Impaired Consciousness
Due to Affect Dysregulation

In what follows, I suggest three dimensions descriptive of the subjective experience of impaired states of consciousness.* I begin by continuing to discuss doubled/spacious versus single/constricted states of consciousness as a dimension reflecting the complexity of consciousness. I then propose two additional dimensions determined by whether the dysregulation is hyper- or hypoaroused. As we just saw, the dimension I call "relationship to experience" refers to the involuntary sense of immersion associated with hyperaroused dysregulation versus involuntary detachment from experience associated with hypoaroused dysregulation. When in regulated states, we are able to shift spontaneously and voluntarily between being immersed in the moment and a state with a measure of detachment in which we step back and assess the moment we're in or are about to be in. A second dimension determined by whether the dysregulation is hyper- or hypoaroused refers to the "incoherence of consciousness" that occurs when dysregulated: a hyperaroused type of incoherence consisting of an overwhelming amount of information being processed by a hyperactivated mind that generates an experience of being flooded and/or fragmented, and a hypoaroused type of incoherence consisting of a hypoactivated mind and a paucity of information that generates an experience of blankness or emptiness.

Complexity of Consciousness: Single/
Constricted Versus Doubled/Spacious

The difference between lower/single/constricted and higher/doubled/spacious consciousness is fundamental to understanding the effects of dysregulation on consciousness. Let me begin with the higher level. There is an array of complex/higher-order mental operations that constitute complex states of

---

*Space does not permit a discussion of another dimension of consciousness, termed subject consciousness versus object consciousness. This was first proposed by Jackson and subsequently explored by William James, Russell Meares, and Sheldon Bach (1985, 1994). It can be understood from the point of view of interpersonal neurobiology as implicit, right brain–dominant versus explicit, left brain–dominant consciousness. I intend to explore this in a subsequent publication.

consciousness and are essential to development and adaptive functioning. The jewel in the crown of these processes is what Jackson and then William James and Russell Meares focused on—the processing of one's stream of consciousness.*

At this point, let me suggest that you think about your own experience of reflecting on your stream of consciousness as it is streaming. Unfortunately, you'll only be able to do this retrospectively. Observing such introspection interrupts the lost-in-thoughtness it requires, but try to re-create it just after you've snapped out of it.† You'll find that the stream of consciousness consists of a difficult-to-describe, nonlinear, impressionistic, largely but not entirely nonverbal, associative flow of thoughts, feelings, images, and so on that are continuously changing and, as James emphasized, are experienced as "mine" and, indeed, as "me." (He noted that they come just as we expect them to and are accompanied by a "warmth.") This stream of private mentalese, decipherable only by their owner, is observed from a position that is experienced as a constant "I" that is assessing and responding to "me," which is continuously flowing and changing. James referred to this "I-me" process as the "duplex self," in which one is both subject and object.‡ The sense of complexity of this doubled consciousness is amplified when one realizes that the "I" and "me" components seem to overlap in a kind of conversation. Establishing these processes is nothing less than the development of an inner world and the capacity for introspection (Meares, 2000, 2005, 2016).§

Similarly to Fonagy and his collaborators (2002), Meares argues that this doubled consciousness supports the capacity for voluntariness. Without it, when in states of single consciousness with only an "I" and no "me," we are reduced to scripted automaticity. Recall that Jackson's theory of dissolution posits that doubled consciousness is not a given. It collapses when one is

---

*Having access to one's stream of consciousness may now be understood as having access to the spontaneous and continuous output of the right brain.

†Observing this process while it's happening would require a third level of consciousness that does not seem to have evolved.

‡Note that this process is entirely internal. Both the "I" and "me" components are experienced as inner. This is different from the doubling in which we stand outside of and objectify ourselves. The former is created by implicit processes, the latter by explicit processes. Put in terms of interpersonal neurobiology (Schore, 1994; Siegel, 1999; Cozolino, 2014), James's duplex self is right brain–dominant, the objectification mediated by the left brain in the background. Standing outside the self is left brain–dominant.

§For James, the processing of one's stream of consciousness is the process that constitutes the self. Meares (2012) has proposed neural correlates of doubled consciousness.

stressed to the point of dysregulation. Meares (2005, 2012) focuses on its development in a relationship and posits that it is undeveloped in borderline personalities.

Other important doubled mental operations constitute higher-order consciousness. Episodic memories and the general phenomenon of mental time travel also have I-me structures and also contribute to a full sense of self—one that not only has a private inner world, but also a past and future. In the case of episodic memory, one remains in the present as the constant "I" while simultaneously experiencing oneself in the past. Imagining one-self in the future also requires doubling. Working memory also involves doubled processes. Without these we are left with only with implicit/pro-cedural, recognition, and semantic types of memory; all earlier develop-ing and simpler. Analogy and metaphor are doubled processes that expand and deepen meaning. Doubled consciousness supports empathy, a state in which we remain ourselves while imagining ourselves as another; an I-me/you experience. The analytic Third (Benjamin, 2018) and self-reflexivity (Aron, 2000), in which both subject and object are appreciated as both subject and object and that are necessary for intersubjectivity, require dou-bled consciousness. Mature defenses—rationalization, intellectualization, sublimation, repression, and so on—require higher-order consciousness, whereas primitive defenses, such as avoidance, projection, splitting, do not (Salas & Turnbull, 2010). When one is dysregulated, consciousness "de-doubles" into a singled/constricted primary state, and the capacity for all this collapses.

To summarize, higher-order consciousness involves a variety of doubled processes that put events in context, elaborate meaning, provide the pos-sibility of agency, support intersubjectivity, and generate a complex sense of self. When dysregulated, we shift into a constricted, singled, primary consciousness in which we are reduced to phenomenological awareness of an automated self existing in the present. So much for the complexity of consciousness and the involuntary regression to a lower level. Let's now look at the dimensions of impaired consciousness associated with whether the dysregulation is hyper- or hypoaroused.

Relationship to Experience: Partial Immersion
Versus Partial Detachment

Recall Lanius and her colleagues' findings that the hyperaroused type of PTSD is associated with full immersion in traumatic memories (flashbacks) and the hypoaroused type with full detachment (depersonalization-derealization). On the other hand, moderately dysregulated states of hyper- and hypoarousal generate partial immersion and partial detachment. Recall also that normally we spontaneously and voluntarily generate states of immersion and detachment as called for by the situation. In moderately dysregulated states, our immersion or detachment, while moderate, is involuntary, and we lose the capacity to switch between and balance them. Additionally, in totally immersed states, doubled functioning is deactivated and we are without context. In partially immersed states, reflective functioning is compromised, but we retain an awareness of where we are in time and space. Of course, it is not only memories in which we may become involuntarily immersed, but any experience driven by dysregulated hyperarousal. For example, hyperaroused, sudden, discrete enactments that we're drawn into involve mutual states of involuntary partial immersion. This same distinction applies to the partial detachment generated in states of moderately dysregulated hypoarousal. The experience tends to involve an absence of feeling that is accompanied by an unyielding objectification of and sense of distance from self and others. Although there is diminished capacity to assess somatic experience, one does not lose the sense of being in one's body.

Types of Incoherence: Flooded/Fragmented Versus Empty/Barren

Another dimension of impaired consciousness determined by dysregulated hyper- or hypoarousal is the type of incoherence generated. I draw here from Grice's (1975) maxims used for scoring the coherence of narratives when responding to the Adult Attachment Interview. To fulfill the maxim of quantity, responses to the questions must supply enough but not too much information. States of hyperaroused dysregulation generate too much information. Thoughts speed in, and feelings flood consciousness. Integrative processes can't keep up, resulting in an experience of fragmentation. Contrasting with this, states of consciousness associated with hypoaroused dysregulation are marked by insufficient information; a lack of thoughts coming to mind, a lack of feelings, and slowed mental processes. Let's look first at hyperaroused states of consciousness.

In states of moderately dysregulated hyperarousal, patients report being overcome with thoughts and feelings that surge in, each strongly felt but fleeting and crowded out by the next. Thoughts may become distorted, one aspect becoming overly prominent while others that should be influential disappear. Overwhelmed, patients are unable to reflect on or put events into perspective. One patient referred to his thinking as "scrambled"; another to being "like a balloon you let the air out of and it darts all over the place." Another patient, with a hand choking her neck, described a sense of being emotionally flooded with thoughts that seemed "to zip in and out," and of being unable to pull back, slow it down, and make sense of what's happening.

These are highly charged, forceful thoughts, compelling because of their affective intensity. Each generates momentary absolute belief and the urge to act. Each seems to be unto itself, unintegrated with other thoughts. Reflective functioning may be compromised to the point where it is simply along for the ride. Importantly, some patients are struck by sharp jolts of affect while others report a numbing that one patient described as a "weird kind of distance, as though I don't care even though I'm crying and yelling."

Compare this pandemonium to the slowed and vacuous experience of the moderately dysregulated, hypoaroused states of consciousness associated with avoidant attachment. Hyperaroused states are expressed overtly, for example, in the rapidity of speech and breakdown in syntax. Hypoaroused states are less obvious. They are expressed by a stillness of the face and body and a monotonous vocal tone. Internally, avoidant patients report a slowed-down, grayed-out, affectless state accompanied by a sense of sluggishness. Associative activity is absent. There is a dulled or total absence of felt experience.* Whereas the overwhelmed hyperaroused patient experiences sensory overload, the underwhelmed hypoaroused patient experiences sensory deprivation and a barren inner world. One patient, experiencing incapacitating hypoarousal at a social event, reported finding it difficult to process the interactions quickly enough to keep up with conversations and that he had become "blank."

Usually such debilitated states of dysregulation go unmentioned, but appreciating the subjective experience and cognitive effects of hyper- and hypoarousal allows the therapist to empathize with and work first toward regulating the patient before setting about the business of dealing with the content. This is usually done nonverbally (Hill, 2015; Schore, 1994, 2003b). However, and perhaps especially when dysregulation is subtle, discussion of

---

*This may be due to endogenous opiods, cortical overregulation, or damage to subcortical structures that mediate affective experience.

the patient's difficulty processing experience helps sensitize them to what it's like to be dysregulated, which will serve as a starting point for autoregulation in the future. Indeed, the stopping of the action is a recognition of their distress and generates a sense of safety and well-being, which itself facilitates regulation.

Table 8.1 summarizes what I've been describing.

TABLE 8.1 **Dimensions of Normal and Impaired States of Consciousness**

	COMPLEXITY OF CONSCIOUSNESS	RELATIONSHIP TO EXPERIENCE	COHERENCE VERSUS INCOHERENCE
Normal waking consciousness	Spontaneous, balanced switching between single and doubled	Spontaneous, balanced switching between immersion and detachment	Coherence
Impaired consciousness when dysregulated	Single/constricted	Hyperarousal: involuntary immersion Hypoarousal: involuntary detachment	Incoherence Hyperarousal: flooded/ fragmented Hypoarousal: empty/barren

The Intersubjective Transmission of States of Consciousness

We have seen that when affect is dysregulated, the accompanying states of conscious are impaired and the type of impairment depends on whether the dysregulation is hyper- or hypoaroused. It follows that the ongoing nonverbal, reciprocal transmissions of affect that Trevarthen (1993) called "primary intersubjectivity" will have mutual effects on our states of consciousness. As we regulate and dysregulate one another or simply induce hyper- and hypoarousal, our states of consciousness follow suit.

Affect states are transmitted via streams of implicit communication: facial expressions, prosody of voice, postures, and gestures. These exchanges of positively and negatively toned surges and retreats of arousal evoke a continuous, spontaneous matching and adjusting to one another's affect states that is accompanied by changes in one's state of consciousness. Indeed, the first indication of a patient's dysregulation and impaired consciousness, especially at moderate levels, may be in a corresponding or counter-reactive state of consciousness induced in the therapist.

Such countertransferential states are dependent on the emotional strengths and weaknesses of the therapist. Take as an example the affective countertransference to avoidant, parasympathetically biased patients. Their diminished affect, the inertness and dreariness of their internal world, exerts a particular type of stress on the therapist; less stressful for securely attached therapists, more stressful for those who are insecurely attached and coping with their own regulatory deficits. Therapists who are sympathetically biased and have difficulty tolerating hypoarousal are prone to dysregulated hyperaroused counter-reactions; irritated, tending toward action and subject to constricted, immersed, hyperactivated states of consciousness. Therapists who are parasympathetically biased are susceptible to succumbing to the undertow exerted by their patient's lack of vitality and enter into a corresponding down-regulated, emotionally blunted, constricted, detached, hypoactivated state of consciousness.[*]

Insecurely attached therapists are also vulnerable to such counterreactive or corresponding state countertransferences when working with sympathetically biased patients. Those with sympathetic biases are vulnerable to corresponding states of hyperaroused dysregulation and to the accompanying impaired consciousness. The hyperarousal of the therapist will tend to exacerbate sympathetically biased patients' states of hyperarousal. In such mutually impaired hyperaroused states, the therapeutic couple is susceptible to hyperaroused enactments. On the other hand, faced with up-regulated patients, therapists with parasympathetic biases, who are unable to tolerate intense states of hyperarousal, will tend to react negatively. They may become defensively hypoaroused, suffer down-regulated states of consciousness, and feel anxiety about becoming overwhelmed.

Such unconsciously induced state shifts are abrupt, happening in a split second, and can be quite subtle. Moreover, reflective functioning has diminished and the capacity to be aware of one's inner states is impaired. It is of course the dysregulated therapist's responsibility to self-right and interact

---

[*]See Hill (2020) for my understanding of such devitalized patients and how I work with them.

with patients in a manner that returns them to a regulated state and full consciousness. Let's see what this looks like in clinical life as lived.

Anthony was in his late 40s when he began treatment at his wife's request. He told me in a matter-of-fact manner that she complained of his "remoteness" and that he was a "drag." He acknowledged that he wasn't "the life of the party" and had always been shy and withdrawn in groups. His mother had been chronically depressed and at one point, before he was born, had been hospitalized. Time spent with her was often of the parallel play variety—her reading and him watching TV. She often retreated to her bedroom. One of his few memories of early childhood was playing on the kitchen floor while his mother did the dishes, her back to him—a picture of benign neglect. With the exception of having been without friends in elementary school, Anthony had few memories of his childhood or adolescence. His father divorced his mother, moved across the country, and had little to do with him.

In spite of this, Anthony had excelled at school and became a successful engineer by the time he was in his mid-30s. In his second year of undergraduate school, Anthony met and soon married the only woman he had ever dated. She was unable to have children and did not want to adopt. This was fine with him. He routinely accommodated his wife, experienced little of his own needs or desires, and looked to her for guidance in how to navigate life. I saw Anthony as having a rather straightforward avoidant attachment pattern marked by his down-regulated bias, insufficient access to his own or others' affect states, thin relationships with others, and chronic, stress-induced, impaired, hypoaroused states of consciousness.

As treatment progressed, sessions were increasingly marked by an emotional flatness and my own struggle to stay interested. Even when not fighting boredom and a wandering mind, I found myself dulled, in a hypoaroused, constricted state of consciousness, without much of an inner life and unresponsive to Anthony without effort. As mentioned above, these are particularly stressful patients, and one is vulnerable to the emotional undertow of hypoaroused affect. My ongoing therapeutic task became keeping myself alert and finding ways to connect with and up-regulate Anthony to a point where he was sufficiently activated to engage in effective therapeutic processes. Helping his wife tolerate his down-regulated states was also important to the treatment.

Anthony's wife was volatile and often raged at him for "disappearing on her." This would drive him into a severely dissociated state in which, he said, "My head feels like it's in a clamp. I go blank. Just nothing. Sometimes, when she's yelling, she sounds far away. It's weird." I understood this as an example of a hypoaroused state of consciousness occasionally severe enough to induce derealization. More commonly, such incidents induced a stupor that he described as "like molasses" but in which he could feign normality. This was the state that inflamed his wife. She was acutely sensitive to his detachment, felt abandoned, took it personally, and attacked him, often with contempt. Ashamed, Anthony would deny it when she would angrily accuse him of disappearing. He had difficulty remembering the specifics of these incidents. I think it likely that the experience wasn't being processed in a way in which an episodic memory could be fully recorded. Interestingly, Anthony frequently told me things several times with no memory of having told me before, once in the same session. It may also be that there was hippocampal damage as a result of his early attachment trauma.

As therapy progressed, and as Anthony presented stressful material, we encountered varying degrees of this dazed state. I had little sense of an inner life going on behind his chronicling of events, no sense of an intermingling of his inner and outer worlds. My reactions to these down-regulated constricted states were of being numbed and without imagination, my thoughts pedestrian. It was hard to pay attention for long.

Such struggles to remain alert and vital in the face of affective inertness stand in stark contrast to the experience of working with sympathetically biased patients. If the effort with Anthony was not to succumb to his down-regulated states, the problem in working with Ellen was not to be swept away by and into her hyperaroused states. Approaching 40, she came into therapy out of concern that she might not marry or have children. She had married impulsively when young and divorced within a year. Since then she had had several relationships to which, when push came to shove, she had not committed. She could not understand why.

Poised, professionally successful, and engaging, she exuded confidence and had what she called a "bright personality" that "came naturally." Indeed, she had hypomanic character traits that defended well against depressive states and an array of repressive defenses that defended successfully against anger. The immediate precipitant for her coming to therapy was that for several months she had had unexpected "fits of tears" while alone at home. They marked moments when panic about not marrying or having children broke through her defenses. Well motivated, from the first session on, she entered the room raring to go.

Ellen had characteristics of a preoccupied attachment pattern including hyperaroused responses to stress and the above mentioned upregulated personality. She was socially adept and had many friends, but often found them burdensome in that she was always in the role of caretaker. Her relationship with her mother was enmeshed. The mother's intrusiveness included ongoing campaigns over Ellen's appearance and choice of men. She could be ferocious and would shame Ellen intensely and frequently. For her part, Ellen said it went "in one ear and out the other. That's just the way she is." She uniformly accommodated her mother's demands, offering the following rationalization: "I don't want to hurt her and it's easier this way."

Initially, listening to Ellen was pleasurable; a coherent, well-modulated flow often spiced with humor, associations, and memories told in an upbeat manner. As treatment progressed, and especially when she related the latest episode with her mother's intrusiveness, I was witness to Ellen's experience of dysregulation. Her syntax would break down, and she would speak with astonishing speed, trying to fit in an onrush of thoughts. First this, then that, each thought unto itself, crowding out whatever had just preceded it. She described this as being battered by feelings. She was the patient mentioned above who told me that she felt like a balloon with its air escaping, sputtering around in fits and starts, giving her a sense of fragmentation. (In her initial interview, Ellen told me she sometimes felt she had "no core.") When I found myself drawn into a similar state, it was a swirling tangle of thoughts and feelings. For me, and I suspect for Ellen as well, it was a blur. I had to restrain myself from being swept into the maelstrom or offering advice for dealing with her mother that would calm both of us. On top of all this, distressing stories of her mother's intrusions would be told with a smile and in a "wait 'til you hear this one!" manner. If I weren't careful, I'd be smiling too, finding it humorous, while, like Ellen, missing entirely the unconscious fear of her own and her mother's anger that was driving her hyperaroused dysregulation.

Working with up-regulated patients like Ellen can be deceptive. They tend to be engaging, emotionally expressive, interested in and good at exploring their inner world. They give the impression of a dynamic therapeutic process taking place. There often is. However, when stressed, their hyperaroused state of consciousness is incoherent. Whatever is being discussed or thought about can only be integrated when experienced in a regulated state where reflective consciousness is possible and in which one is able to think and feel clearly and fully and do the work of integration.

Summary

In this chapter, I have integrated the work of Allan Schore on affect regulation with that of Russell Meares, Antonio Damasio, and Gerald Edelman on consciousness to serve as a basis for an understanding of impaired states of consciousness that impede therapeutic growth. I have proposed that such states are markers of dysregulated affect that has disrupted the integrated functioning of neural systems underlying normal waking consciousness and higher-order mental operations. In essence, I have argued that the quality of consciousness is affect-state dependent and that disorders of affect regulation result in chronically disordered consciousness.

I have proposed a set of dimensions for a clinical appreciation of moderately impaired states of consciousness. They are: constriction, in which consciousness is without reflective functioning, complex forms of memory, or the capacity for intersubjectivity; incoherence, which may consist of hyperactivated mentation and strong affects experienced as being flooded and/ or fragmented, or hypoactive mentation and a lack of affect experienced as being empty; and the relationship to experience, which may be involuntary immersion associated with hyperaroused dysregulation or involuntary detachment associated with hypoaroused dysregulation. Such states of dysregulated affect and impaired consciousness may be subtle when moderate and sometimes detectable only through the affective countertransference and altered state of consciousness induced in the therapist. Clinically, the detection of such dysregulated-dissociated states may serve as a guide for empathic therapeutic responsiveness. Theoretically my hope is to contribute to a taxonomy of consciousness.

Figure 8.1 is an attempt to depict optimal and impaired states of consciousness and their relationship to affect states. Note the lack of a clear line between regulation and dysregulation—my attempt to portray a spectrum of altered states of consciousness that vary along with the degree of dysregulation.

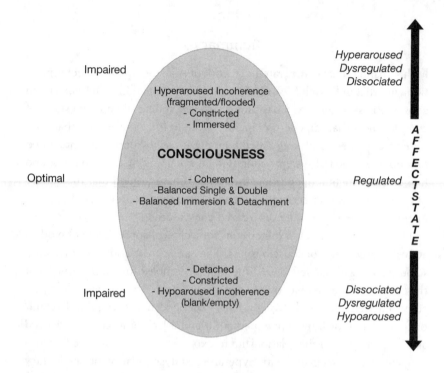

FIGURE 8.1 Consciousness is Affect-State Dependent

References

Allen, J. G. (2001). *Traumatic relationships and serious mental disorders.* New York: Wiley.

Ataria, Y. (2014). Acute peritraumatic : In favor of a phenomenological inquiry. *Journal of Trauma and Dissociation, 15,* 332–347.

Bach, S. (1985). *Narcissistic states and the therapeutic process.* New York: Jason Aronson.

Bach, S. (1994). *The language of love and the language of perversion.* New York: Jason Aronson.

Benjamin, J. (2018). *Beyond doer and done to: Recognition theory, intersubjectivity and the third.* New York: Routledge.

Bremmer, J. D., Vermetten, E., & Lanius, R. (2010). Long-lasting effects of childhood abuse on neurobiology. In R. A. Lanius, E. Vermetten, & C. Pain (Eds.), *The impact of early life trauma on health and disease: The hidden epidemic.* Cambridge, UK: Cambridge University Press.

Breuer, J., & Freud, S. (1955). Studies on hysteria. In *The standard edition of the com-*

plete psychological works of Sigmund Freud. London: Hogarth. (Original work published 1893)

Bromberg, P. (2006). *Awakening the dreamer: Clinical journeys*. Mahwah, NJ: Analytic Press.

Cardena, E. (1994). The domain of dissociation. In S. J. Lynn & R. W. Rhue (Eds.), *Dissociation: Theoretical, clinical, and research perspectives* (pp. 15–31). New York: Guilford.

Chefetz, R. (2015). *Intensive psychotherapy for persistent dissociative processes*. New York: Norton.

Cozolino, L. (2014). The neuroscience of human relationships: Attachment and the developing social brain. New York: Norton.

Damasio, A. (1999). *The feeling of what happens*. New York: Harcourt.

Dell, P. (2009a). The phenomena of pathological dissociation. In P. Dell & J. O'Neil (Eds.), *Dissociation and the dissociative disorders: DSM-V and beyond*. New York: Routledge.

Dell, P. (2009b). Understanding dissociation. In P. Dell & J. O'Neil (Eds.), *Dissociation and the dissociative disorders: DSM-V and beyond*. New York: Routledge.

Edelman, G. (1989). *The remembered present: A biological theory of consciousness*. New York: Basic Books.

Fonagy, P., Gergely, G., Jurist, E., & Target, M. (2002). *Affect regulation, mentalization and the development of the self*. New York: Other Press.

Frewen, P., & Lanius, R. (2015). *Healing the traumatized self*. New York: Norton.

Grice, H. P. (1975). Logic and conversation. In P. Cole & J. L. Morgan (Eds.), *Syntax and semantics: Vol. III. Speech acts* (pp. 41–58). New York: Academic Press.

Hill, D. (2015). *Affect regulation theory: A clinical model*. New York": Norton.

Hill, D. (2020). Vitality, attunement and the lack thereof. In *Vitality in Psychoanalysis*. New York: Routledge.

Holmes, D. S. (1990). The evidence for repression: An examination of sixty years of research. In J. L. Singer (Ed.), *Repression and dissociation*. Chicago: University of Chicago Press.

Holmes, E. A., Brown, R. J., Mansell, W., Pasco Fearon, R., Hunter, E., Frasquilho, F., & Oakley, D.A. (2005). Are there two qualitatively distinct forms of dissociation? A review and some clinical implications. *Clinical Psychological Review*, 25, 1–23.

Jackson, J.H. (1931a). Selected Writings of J.H. Jackson. Vol. 1. London: Hodder and Soughton.

Jackson, J.H. (1931b). Selected Writings of J.H. Jackson. Vol. 2. London: Hodder and Soughton.

James, W. (1902). *The varieties of religious experience*. New York: Longmans, Green.

Janet, P. (1889). L'automatisme psychologique: Essai de psychologie experimentale sur les forms inferieures de l'activite humaine. Paris: Felix Alcan.

Janet, P. (1901). *The mental state of hysterics.* New York: Putnam.

Lanius, R. A., Bluhm, R., & Lanius, U. (2007). Posttraumatic stress disorder symptom provocation and neuroimaging. In E. Vermetten, M. J. Dorahy, & D. Spiegel (Eds.), *Traumatic dissociation: Neurobiology and treatment* (pp. 191–217). Washington, DC: American Psychiatric Press.

Lanius, R. A., Bluhm, R., Lanius, U., & Pain, C. (2006). A review of neuroimaging studies in PTSD: Heterogeneity of response to symptom provocation. *Journal of Psychiatric Research, 40,* 709–729.

Lanius, R. A., Brand, B., Vermetten, E., Frewen, P. A., & Spiegel, D. (2012). The dissociative subtype of posttraumatic stress disorder: Rationale, clinical and neurobiological evidence, and implications. *Depression and Anxiety, 29,* 1–8. doi:10.1002/da.21889

Lanius, R. A., Vermetten, E., Loewenstein, R. J., Brand, B., Schmahl, C., Bremner, J. D., & Spiegel, D. (2010). Emotion modulation in PTSD: Clinical and neurobiological evidence for a dissociative subtype. *American Journal of Psychiatry, 167,* 640–647.

Maroda, K. (2020). Deconstructing enactment. *Psychoanalytic Psychology, 37*(1), 8–17.

McGilchrist, I. (2009). *The master and his emissary: The divided brain and the making of the western world.* New Haven, CT: Yale University Press.

Meares, R. (2000). Intimacy and alienation: Memory, trauma and personal being. New York: Routledge.

Meares, R. (2005). *The metaphor of play: Origin and breakdown of personal being.* New York: Routledge.

Meares, R. (2012). *A dissociation model of borderline personality disorder.* New York: Norton.

Meares, R. (2016). *The poet's voice in the making of mind.* New York: Routledge.

Putnam, F. W. (1997). *Dissociation in children and adolescents: A developmental perspective.* New York: Guilford.

Salas, C., & Turnbull, O. (2010). **In self-defense: Disruptions in the sense of self, lateralization, and primitive defenses.** *Neuropsychoanalysis, 12*(2), 172–182.

Schore, A. N. (1994). *Affect regulation and the origin of the self: The neurobiology of emotional development.* New York: Norton.

Schore, A. N. (2003a). *Affect regulation and disorders of the self.* New York: Norton.

Schore, A. N. (2003b). *Affect regulation and the repair of the self.* New York: Norton.

Schore, A. N. (2012). *The science of the art of psychotherapy.* New York: Norton.

Schore, A. N. (2015). Review of *The emotional life of your brain,* by Richard J. Davidson and Sharon Begley. *Psychoanalytic Psychology, 32*(3), 539–547.

Siegel, D. (1999). *The developing mind: How relationships and the brain interact to shape who we are.* New York: Guilford.Spitzer, C., Barnow, S., Freyberger, H. J., &

Grabe, H. J. (2006). Recent developments in the theory of dissociation. *World Psychiatry, 5*, 82–86.

Stern, D. B. (1997). *Unformulated experience: From dissociation to imagination in psychoanalysis.* Hillsdale, NJ: Analytic Press.

Stern, D. N. (2004). *The present moment in psychotherapy and everyday life.* New York: Norton.

Trevarthen, C. (1993). The self born in intersubjectivity: The psychology of infant communicating. In U. Neisser (Ed.), *The perceived self: Ecological and interpersonal sources of self-knowledge* (pp. 121–173). New York: Cambridge University Press.

Vaitl, D., Birbaumer, N., Gruzelier, J., Jamieson, G. A., Kotchoubey, B., Kübler, A., Lehmann, D., Miltner, W. H. R., Ott, U., Pütz, P., Sammer, G., Strauch, I., Strehl, U., Wackermann, J., & Weiss, T. (2005). Psychobiology of altered states of consciousness. *Psychological Bulletin, 131*(1), 98–127.

Wolf, E. J., Miller, M. W., Reardon, A. F., Ryabchenko, K. A., Castillo, D., & Freund, R. (2012). A latent class analysis of dissociation and posttraumatic stress disorder: Evidence for a dissociative subtype. *Archives of General Psychiatry, 69*(7), 698–705.

9

A Healing Context

Philosophical–Spiritual Principles of Sensorimotor Psychotherapy

Pat Ogden

*The impulse to heal is real and powerful and lies within the client.
Our job is to evoke that healing power, to meet its tests and needs
and to support it in its expression and development. We are not
the healers. We are the context in which healing is inspired.*
RON KURTZ

THE IMPLICIT CONTEXT, OR ATMOSPHERE, IN WHICH THERAPY TAKES PLACE
is the most essential and influential element of clinical practice. Every psychotherapist adheres to certain assumptions that define the quality of the
therapeutic relationship, influence the maps and strategies used, and guide
technique. These assumptions determine the overall relational climate in
the therapy room. Whether learned explicitly or implicitly, foundational
principles are established during formal training and by the characteristics
of the specific methods used in practice, commonly accepted as the "best"
or "right" way to engage with the client and to conduct therapy. They are,
in turn, uniquely interpreted and embodied in different ways and to various degrees by practitioners. Underneath these learned concepts are the
often unconscious beliefs and viewpoints of therapists themselves about
the essence of the human condition, what circumstances facilitate change,
the nature of interpersonal relationships, and the inspiration for healing.
These perspectives constitute a paradigm unique to the individual therapist

that exerts a powerful influence on clinical practice. Often unacknowledged and unconscious, myriad points of view—individual and collective, implicit and explicit, learned through education and personal experience—combine into a set of principles that determine the general climate in which therapy occurs, and are deeply felt and experienced by therapist and client alike.

Whatever the composition of a therapist's foundational principles, they provide a philosophical-spiritual ground for clinical practice. They shepherd the overall orientation of the therapist; thus the lenses or maps that inform therapeutic strategy as well as the specific time-limited interventions used in the clinical hour emerge from this orientation. By creating the overarching paradigm that shepherds the process of therapy, the foundational principles are the most critical and highly influential elements of any clinical practice, even more so when they remain unarticulated and unexamined.

The Sensorimotor Psychotherapist takes to heart a collection of six principles. Five are adapted from the work of Ron Kurtz (1990): organicity or inner wisdom, nonviolence, unity or interconnectedness, mind/body/spirit holism, and mindfulness. More recently, I expanded mindfulness to add "presence," on a continuum with mindfulness, and added a sixth principle, "relational alchemy." These principles are interrelated and overlapping: If you fully resonate with one principle, you are likely aligned with all of them. With roots in Buddhist, Taoist, and Indigenous traditions, these six principles are a credo of sorts, implicitly guiding therapeutic action and anchoring the emotional attitude and mind-set that underlie technique, not as a goal, a sequence of steps, or an end-point, and not through effort or conscious thought. Rather, they are emergent: The therapist's process of aligning with the principles inspires a particular state of consciousness that we trust will encourage the conditions in which growth is optimized, allowing clients to take their next step in their own evolution.

The foundational principles are age-old concepts that are interpreted and adapted to clinical work in explicit and implicit ways and operationalized in the process of therapy. The intention to embody these principles vitalizes a way of being in the world, with ourselves, and with each other that generates a context for healing and evolution. Thus, to align oneself with these foundations invites personal engagement. Therapists examine their affinity for each principle, curiously identify when they have transgressed the guidance of one of them, and muse on their ability to embody them in a process of self-awareness and growth.

These principles are the very heart, soul and spirit of Sensorimotor Psychotherapy. However, they do not remain static; they are emergent and aspirational in nature, held as ideals that we strive to embody, expressed differently in different contexts, relationships, and situations. As the nucleus of Sensorimotor Psychotherapy, our methodology, maps, and techniques emanate from this philosophical-spiritual base. The effectiveness and meaning of a Sensorimotor Psychotherapy session reflect first and foremost the therapist's affinity for and ability to practice within the guidance of the principles, and only second the mastery of theory and technique. This chapter describes each of the six principles, discusses their origins, and elucidates their influence on therapeutic action and technique in terms of how they are operationalized in the clinical hour.

Organicity

I can give you nothing that has not already its origins within yourself. I can throw open no picture gallery but your own. I can help make your own world visible—that is all.
HERMAN HESSE

During my life journey I've discovered an interesting thing; once you stop seeking outside you discover what already resides within.
RASHEED OGUNLARU

Deep within, there is something profoundly known, not consciously, but subconsciously. A quiet truth, that is not a version of something, but an original knowing.
T. F. HODGE

Healing is not science, but the intuitive art of wooing nature.
W. H. AUDEN

"Organicity," a term drawn from the work of Gregory Bateson (1979), conveys that all living systems possess an inherent evolving intelligence that guides their own unique unfolding. Humans, as living systems, are self-organizing, complex, and nonlinear. To be self-organizing is to naturally and without conscious intention generate a kind of order as various parts of a system interact (Bateson, 1979). This process is not linear, does not progress predictably or evenly, and may appear to advance simultaneously in various directions. The complexity of living systems is described by Prigogine (1997) as nondeterministic, rendering the future unpredictable. At the same time, this complexity also embraces the intricate relationships that can catalyze patterns. As living systems, humans are responsive to their sociocultural environment, participating in an ongoing, natural interaction with the things and people surrounding them (Kurtz, 1990).

In my beginning years as a psychotherapist in the early 1970s, I learned from Ron Kurtz that it is not the therapist's job to find answers or solutions for clients' problems; people cannot be "fixed" or healed. Doctors can set a bone or remove a tumor, but living systems heal themselves. Under the best conditions, doctors provide the support that catalyzes healing from within, but they do not do the healing. Similarly, the therapist does not cure the client; rather, the healing power lies inside each person, who is endowed with their own unique, mysterious, and emergent growth path. This wisdom is enigmatic, continually unfolding, and the form it takes cannot be fully anticipated nor forecasted. We must draw forth the needed intelligence from clients, first by recognizing and trusting in its existence and second by co-creating with them the conditions in which it can emerge.

The principle of organicity conforms to the Chinese Taoist perspective of the ancient philosopher Lao Tzu, who is credited with saying, "At the center of your being you have the answer; you know who you are and you know what you want." According to Taoist teachings, one only needs to have faith in the wisdom that resides inside oneself, and facilitate the connections so that this wisdom, which already exists, is revealed. In Sensorimotor Psychotherapy, it is the therapist who shepherds this process so that the system—the client—changes spontaneously, without force, in the progressive direction of healing and wholeness.

Organicity acknowledges that every culture inherently contains its own unique wisdom, and that the wisdom of each individual is filtered through personal and collective experiences shaped by their culture. Cultural wisdom is extremely diverse, the result of experiencing different environments and interactions, socioeconomic conditions, privilege/oppression dynamics, the transgenerational transmission of trauma and resilience, and much more. Indigenous and Western cultural wisdom are different from each other, although there is no "one" intelligence for either group. Levac and colleagues (2018, p. 4) caution that "it is easy to fall into the traps of 'homogenizing' and 'othering' by approaching these vast ways of knowing [Indigenous and

Western] in general terms." That said, there are differences between these two cultural orientations that powerfully impact personal and collective organicity. Generally speaking, the organicity experienced by Indigenous cultures is more relational and inclusive of past generations, both living and dead, than Western cultures. Indigenous knowledge emphasizes one's relationship with the Earth rather than viewing it as an object to explore or study, a more commonly held Western perspective (Smylie et al., 2014). The knowledge of many Indigenous cultures and people, across contexts, is more holistic, prioritizing relational, spiritual, and symbolic wisdom that carries across generations (Chilisa & Tsheko, 2014; Levac et al., 2018). Intelligence is considered to be a process, not an object or thing. A Western approach to intelligence is typically more fragmented, divided into separate disciplines, with an emphasis on logic and science and a rejection of metaphysical perspectives. Clearly, culture impacts our personal experience of organicity. The way in which we interact with the world and the world interacts with us, influenced by the generations before us, embraces the sociocultural values and socialization of our communities of belonging that implicitly guide us as to how to live, how to relate to others, what is possible for us, and so forth.

Organicity encompasses a non-pathologizing perspective. It challenges the medical viewpoint that is rooted in a disease model, which is focused on determining what is wrong and implementing procedures to fix the problem. The medical model attends to the parts rather than the whole, and to pathology and what is amiss. In contrast, the principle of organicity teaches that people make the best choices given the impact of their circumstances, social location, cultural conditioning (expansive and constraining), resources and information available to them. We do not see the client in terms of disease. Rather, we view clients and their presenting problems and symptoms with curiosity and compassion, understanding that each complaint, each symptom, and each problem holds within it a salubrious intent and purpose. We seek to discover the underlying adaptive function of the presenting issues, including behaviors and physical habits such as a slumped posture, as well as cognitive distortions and emotional biases.

The principle of organicity is aligned more with Indigenous perspectives that look to the natural environment and understand developmental processes as both nonlinear and emergent, linked to unknown, unseen, yet powerful intelligence that cannot necessarily be validated by the scientific method. Thus, importantly, as therapists, we cannot know what is best for our clients. As Kurtz (1990, p. 26) states, "When you embrace the organicity principle you look for and follow natural processes. You do not impose a structure or agenda on the process." We must find it in ourselves to rest in not knowing, to trust the client's unfolding process even when, and especially when, we do not understand it.

Symptoms that are usually perceived as liabilities are acknowledged as survival resources formed in attempts to regulate arousal and cope with adverse experiences, thus challenging the client's tendency to pathologize their difficulties and symptoms as shameful or as innate faults (Ogden & Fisher, 2015). Clients who come with complaints about relational issues learn to reframe them as survival resources, shaped at the intersection of one's unique developmental niche and privilege/oppression dynamics, rather than as personal deficits. Others who are dysregulated and contend with difficulties that often cause shame, such as self-harm, addictions, and so forth, can learn that these are survival resources—attempts to self-regulate and cope with their distress. For example, one young African American man was disturbed by his inability to stay calm in the face of watching reports of police violence on the media, and turned to alcohol to regulate. Through our work, he became aware of how these unsettling feelings lived in his body, and about how his earlier experiences, and those of his ancestors, propelled his dysregulation and anger. He learned that his "short fuse" had to do with a healthy protective part of himself that was both angry and grief-stricken at the injustice of racial profiling and racialized violence. He began to recognize these emotions in his body (tightness in his chest, pounding heart, clenched fists, etc.) and to channel them in more empowering ways by going for a run and putting pen to paper rather than by "exploding." By qualifying the behaviors clients are trying to change or the symptoms that destabilize them as survival resources used to cope, new options more easily open up for addressing them and finding other, more creative resources to fulfill their purpose.

A non-pathologizing perspective that trusts in a client's organicity is not meant to deny or minimize the severity of personal problems and struggles or potential risks presented by these difficulties that need attention. However, when they are understood as formed in reaction to specific circumstances and sociocultural influences with the intent to fulfill a particular function that at its core is health supporting, organicity will be revealed. We recognize that every culture has its own wisdom and that the organicity of each individual is filtered through experience and is thus shaped by social location and culture. For example, a Native American woman degraded herself for her "giving up" attitude surrounding the discrimination and oppression she and her people experience. However, this strategy can be adaptive in the context of systemic historical and current oppression when the forces of systemic oppression are perceived as too strong to fight against (Sue et al., 2019). She was able to reframe her passive attitude as adaptive and validate her capacity to take effective action in other arenas of her life. When strengths and competencies are acknowledged and embellished, difficult situations will be easier to face. Then resolving past suffering and dealing with ongoing stress and trauma will go more smoothly.

The therapist's task becomes one of being alert to the natural process of evolution, of helping clients turn inside deeply enough, in the context of an attuned therapeutic dyad, so that the right kind of information becomes available from within (Kurtz, 1990). The therapist resists being the "expert," giving advice, or controlling the session or the clients, but rather looks for their natural impulse to take the next step in their growth and guides them toward experiences that they are ready for. As this takes place, the system—the client, and often the therapist as well—changes spontaneously, without force, in a progressive direction of healing and wholeness.

To operationalize organicity in clinical practice, we recognize that all living systems follow their own path. When clients appear stuck, we assume the presence of a simultaneous impetus toward growth. We meet our clients where they are in their development, pacing to their needs, honoring their strengths, reframing their limiting beliefs and procedural patterns as salubrious adaptations and survival resources. We demonstrate faith that the client's spontaneous sensations, movements, images, emotions, thoughts, and impulses hold valuable information even when we do not understand them or the organicity that drives them (Ogden, 1986). Allowing time and space for the client to connect to their inner wisdom and refraining from giving advice are essential to operationalize organicity in clinical practice. It can be as simple as the therapist saying, "Where would you like to sit?" in response to the client asking, "Where should I sit?" at their first meeting. This implicitly communicates that the client knows what is right for them and simultaneously sets the stage for a particular kind of therapeutic relationship in which the client is encouraged to discover their own answers to their questions rather than seeking answers from the therapist.

We do not try to force clients into a direction they do not want to go or are not ready for, assume there is wisdom in resistance, and refrain from giving advice or solving problems. Even perceiving a client's symptom or issue as a problem instead of recognizing its adaptive purpose goes against organicity. Thus, we continuously help clients orient to their own locus of control within themselves, demonstrating a deep and radical respect for their freedom to be as they are and choose for themselves. The therapist learns what clients want to accomplish, validates the wisdom of their choices, and helps them turn inward to find the answers they are seeking, recognizing the value of whatever spontaneously emerges as grist for the therapeutic mill.

Nonviolence

By having a reverence for life, we enter into a spiritual relation with the world. By practicing reverence for life we become good, deep, and alive.
ALBERT SCHWEITZER

Nonviolence is not a garment to be put on and off at will. Its seat is in the heart, and it must be an inseparable part of our being.
MAHATMA GANDHI

A liberation movement that is nonviolent sets the oppressor free as well as the oppressed.
BARBARA DEMING

Every relationship of domination, of exploitation, of oppression is by definition violent, whether or not the violence is expressed by drastic means. In such a relationship, dominator and dominated alike are reduced to things—the former dehumanized by an excess of power, the latter by a lack of it. And things cannot love.
PAULO FREIRE

Nonviolence is a powerful and just weapon, which cuts without wounding and ennobles the man who wields it. It is a sword that heals.
MARTIN LUTHER KING JR.

Nonviolence operationalizes organicity in clinical practice through the active creation of a relational and emotional context in which organicity can emerge. Recognizing the natural impulse of living systems for more complex levels of organization, nonviolence taps into the natural urge to evolve, grow, and heal. It is closely related to the Taoist concept of "Wu Wei," which literally translated means "non-doing." However, Wu Wei does not mean literally doing nothing; instead it speaks to following the way of nature—the organic flow or direction that is already taking place, which proves to be the most effective and effortless course of action. By creating the right conditions, living systems change by themselves; once the soil is prepared and sun and water are provided, the plant will grow on its own. Instead of doing more, doing less easily accomplishes more because the doer is simply supporting the unfolding process that is already in motion. Therefore, efforting and trying both become unnecessary and even counterproductive. Rather than manipulating or struggling to make something happen, nonviolence means we go with the grain, with what wants to happen, the incipient next step. There is no need to work against this natural inclination or to use force, which only creates resistance when applied to living systems (Kurtz, 1990).

The concept of nonviolence can be traced back almost 4,000 years to a significant ethical tenet of Jainism, Hinduism, and Buddhism called "ahimsa," which means "non-injury" in Sanskrit. Originating in the Vedic wisdom of India (Deshpande, 2019), ahimsa advocates respect for, and restraint from doing harm to, a living being. Ahimsa is interpreted in many different ways, but it is most commonly associated with nonviolence. Although both ahimsa and nonviolence are sometimes correlated with peace and non-action, these terms more precisely refer to the absence of violent methods, or to using the least harmful method, in any situation where action is called for, rejecting the use of force to effect change.

Perhaps the most visible face of ahimsa in history, Mahatma Gandhi opposed using force and instead used nonviolent resistance to end colonialism in India, inspiring similar crusades for freedom and human rights around the globe. Influenced by Gandhi, Albert Schweitzer coined the phrase "reverence for life" as an affirmation that expressed his conviction that all living beings should be respected. Schweitzer (1965, para. 4) wrote, "Ethics is nothing else than reverence for life. Reverence for life affords me my fundamental principle of morality, namely, that good consists in maintaining, assisting and enhancing life." In keeping with this way of thinking, nonviolence as applied to therapy "is born of an attitude of acceptance and an active attention to the way events naturally unfold" (Kurtz, 1990, p. 29).

Gleaned from these traditions to become relevant to psychotherapy practice, nonviolence is expressed in therapy through a deep respect for clients' experience. The ways in which experience is organized by habits of thought, emotion, posture, and movement are based on our experiential history, shaped into patterns over time, but they outgrow their utility when circumstances change. These once-adaptive behaviors and habits are not obstacles to growth, but can become default behaviors still in effect after the conditions that shaped them are over. Rather than trying to urge or coerce change or solve a problem, emphasis is placed on how clients organize their experience physically, emotionally and mentally, which is recognized as having meaning and purpose, and as holding the keys for their personal evolution. As Kurtz said, "Clients are experiences waiting to happen, not problems to be solved." Discovering the next step in the client's evolution—what already "wants" to happen—is a task of nonviolence. Therefore, the way clients organize experience, and thus everything that emerges spontaneously in the moment, are welcomed as interesting and valuable indicators of the natural experience waiting to happen that can be explored to advantage in the therapeutic journey.

The dynamics of violence in therapy can be nuanced, revealed in critical or judgmental attitudes toward the client, in subtle dismissal of their emotions, thoughts, desires, gestures, appearance, social locations such as sexual orientation, gender expression, ability, ethnicity, and so forth. Nonviolence requires the cultivation of a nonjudgmental attitude that accepts and welcomes all parts and responses of clients with compassion, especially those aspects clients themselves cannot accept. Rather than criticizing, judging, or pathologizing behavior, we are attentive to clients' emerging experience, and help them to also become curious about their internal landscape as it unfolds, to observe and learn about themselves more fully and compassionately in relationship with the therapist.

The therapist conveys appreciation for all aspects of the client for their original adaptive and empowering function. Even psychological defenses, which Kurtz (1990) refers to as attempts to manage painful experience, are validated for their purpose, such as for their regulating capacities. Kurtz points out that calling these behaviors "defenses" conjures up images of force, as if the client were trying to fight against themselves. These management behaviors are viewed as creative, if outdated, adaptations to life events, and thus the therapist does not seek to modify or change them. Instead, the client is helped to learn about how these behaviors are organized internally, through becoming aware of present-moment thoughts, emotions, images, posture and movements, tracking for what emerges naturally or is available to change. The attention to this unfolding experience leads to fresh, in-the-moment experiential knowledge, bringing forth new information that often inspires the so-called defenses to yield by themselves.

Nonviolence should not be interpreted as passivity, allowing anything to happen, or as neglecting to act when action is needed. The therapist can be both nonviolent and an active participant in the therapeutic process. It is the therapist's job to deliberately support the client in their evolution, to bring awareness to destructive tendencies and to interrupt them when necessary. For instance, there are times when direct action is called for to prevent harm to the client or to others. But nonviolence is more concerned with how the action is executed than with the action itself. If a client is homicidal, the therapist must act to protect both the target and the client, but the way in which the therapist acts is imbued with respect, compassion, and understanding for the person and all the factors that have led them to this point in their life. The attitude of nonviolence thus renders a harmful action itself as unacceptable, but affirms the person. Similarly, if clients are suicidal, protecting them may be paramount (while honoring situations that may indicate otherwise, for example in cases of terminal illness), yet the therapist's recognition of their extreme hurt and sorrow—bearing witness to their pain—reflects the principle of nonviolence. Simultaneously, the therapist and client work collaboratively toward understanding how the client is organizing experience and toward the possibility of a concomitant, perhaps deeper, life-affirming organicity that is also inclusive and accepting of the destructive impulse.

The client's organicity is discovered and revealed through a nonviolent approach that adheres to no preconceived definitive agenda. We realize that the therapist's own agenda, even one as indirect and seemingly innocuous as the desire to be helpful, can be subtly violent, exert pressure on the client, and complicate the unfolding of the client's organicity. As therapists, we relinquish ideas of how we think the therapy is supposed to look or proceed. Even a desire for change to take place "can interfere with nonviolence by creating a subtle pressure for something to happen" (Ogden, 1986). Although we may have a treatment plan with general goals, we recognize that impromptu possibilities will emerge in the course of therapy that we could not have anticipated. We do not allow our plan to supersede opportunities that spontaneously come up in the moment. By letting go of agendas and of our desire that therapy proceed in a certain way, the door can remain open for the unexpected, and for organic unfolding.

Thus, we strive to become aware of and inhibit our hidden agendas and judgments. We recognize that lack of knowledge of culture and awareness of our own implicit bias can render aspects of clients' experience invisible to us and lead to unintended violence. The attitudes and prejudices we harbor toward others can be explicit and conscious, or implicit and unconscious. While we can challenge and inhibit our conscious biases, implicit bias, because it is outside our awareness, can insidiously wreak havoc on our intention to act nonviolently. Implicit bias often emerges in microaggressions, which verbally or behaviorally convey disrespect, hostility, or otherwise negative attitudes about race, sexual orientation, religion, and so forth (Sue, 2010). These indignities can be subtle, such as an expression of disgust when a client speaks of their sexual orientation, or a comment that reflects a stereotype, such as, "I didn't think Jewish people were good at sports" or "I'm surprised you don't like to dance, since you're African American." Microaggressions are more likely to occur when we are not aware of our bias and do not understand social locations, intersectionality, or privilege/ oppression dynamics. When bias is unconscious, we do not recognize that unintentional microaggressions inflict harm, and thus also do not recognize the need to modify our behavior. If we want to work toward embodying the principle of nonviolence, it is our responsibility to engage in an ongoing process of self-examination to learn about the impact of privilege/oppression dynamics and uncover our own implicit bias with regard to differences between ourselves and our clients, including race, culture, gender, age, economics, and so forth, as well as the impact of intersectionality.

To act nonviolently requires great awareness from the therapist, both of their own bias and propensities, and of the here-and-now experience of the client. Noticing immediate signals of aversion or distress in the client, such as a fleeting facial expression or a slight pulling back of the body, combined with the therapist's self-awareness, provide the chance to recognize indicators of violence, and recover and repair. For example, eliciting more material than the client can integrate effectively (a subtle form of violence) can be remedied when the therapist tracks the signals, names

what is noticed ("Seems like your breathing is becoming labored—maybe
this is too much"). Through such awareness and adjustment, nonviolence is
restored, and further supported as the therapist remains open to the spontaneous emergence of opportunities to follow the path of least resistance.

Mind-Body-Spirit Holism

*Being in touch with our bodies, or more accurately,
being our bodies, is how we know what is true.*
HARRIET GOLDHOR LERNER

The body is our general medium for having a world.
MAURICE MERLEAU-PONTY

*the body is wiser than its inhabitants, the body
is the soul, the body is god's messenger.*
ERICA JONG

*"The body is not a thing, it is a situation: it is our grasp
on the world and our sketch of our project."*
SIMONE DE BEAUVOIR

*With neurology, if you go far enough with it, and you keep going, you
end up getting weird. If you go a little further, you end up in the spirit.*
OLIVER SACKS

The parts of any living system are intimately connected and continually
interact with one another. Mind, body, and spirit are essential aspects of
the human organism, and each can only be understood in relationship to
the whole they constitute. All experience registers in the body, and men-
tal/emotional and spiritual components are inherent in all significant bodily
experience. The body houses the spirit in the broadest sense, and its habits
of movement, posture, and expression reflect and sustain the habits of the
mind in both thought and emotion. Our sense of ourselves, of ourselves in
relationship with others, and of our place in the world emerges from these
three ever-entwined elements that comprise the wholeness of who we are.
Well-being arises from the health of each in communication with the others.

A holistic approach to wellness considers the interrelationship between body, mind, and spirit in interaction with an environment that is constantly in flux.

Definitions and explanations of mind, body, and spirit vary enormously, and to delve into the vastness of these three dimensions is beyond the scope of this chapter. Keeping in mind that they can only be divided for conceptual purposes, working descriptions are briefly summarized as follows. Chopra (1989) wrote that our bodies are composed of energy and information that continually transforms. The mind, according to Siegel (2010), is an embodied relational process that regulates this flow of energy and information. It encompasses conscious and unconscious processes that combine thought, perception, emotion, imagination, memory, and so forth. The body as directly addressed in psychotherapy practice includes the autonomic nervous system, micromovements, and the more visible movement repertoire expressed in gestures, facial expressions, postures, and so forth. The spirit refers to the aspect of ourselves that is connected to something nonmaterial, larger than one's own existence, often associated with a sense of reverence, meaning, awe, and a greater encompassing purpose. For many, spirit includes an experience of or belief in the sacred. Although these dimensions carry their individual definitions, it bears repeating that they do not exist independently from one another and cannot be fathomed without considering their relationship to the whole.

For thousands of years, the unity of mind, body, and spirit has been reflected in the worldview and teachings of Indigenous people of various cultures, who have long understood that the health of each of these dimensions is mutually interdependent (Mark & Lyons, 2010). Gleaning wisdom from ancestral voices, animals, plants, and the land itself, drawing upon the spirit as a powerful healing force, and so much more, Indigenous people consider the communication between mind, body, and spirit as essential in wellness (McCabe, 2008). However, "proponents of Western science look at most indigenous knowledge as anecdotal at best and witchcraft at worst" (McCabe, 2008, p. 143). This rejection of holism can be traced back to the 1600s, when Descartes proposed that mind and body are distinct entities. Previously, even the Christian perspective had viewed humans as spiritual beings with a unified body and mind (Mehta, 2011). Their separation ushered in the beginning of modern science and its study of anatomy and physiology, doing away with the notion that disease was caused by nonphysical elements, such as personal or collective misconduct. But it closed the door to the unity of mind, body, and spirit in the Western world. Today, many Indigenous people have preserved their faith in holism, although the predominance of colonialism and Western science has "had the influence of sending traditional practices underground, and in some instances traditional healing practices were eliminated from the cultural vernacular altogether" (McCabe, 2008, p. 144). Conventional allopathic medicine still primarily focuses on treating parts of a person instead of considering the whole or taking into account the influence of the mind and spirit on the body. Although this is beginning to change, ailments of body, mind, and spirit are largely treated separately in the Western world.

Merleau-Ponty refutes the rejection of holism with his notion of the "lived-body," "that experience of our body which cannot be objectified" (in Gold, 1985, p. 664). The lived body holds an evolving wisdom that is already moving toward healing and health, and as therapists we intend to recognize and capitalize on this innate somatic intelligence. Our intention is recognized in Sensorimotor Psychotherapy's vision statement, "to harness the wisdom of the body to liberate human potential." This potential includes a sense of freedom and choice in body and mind, as well as the freedom and capacity to establish connection with that which is bigger than ourselves. As Gold (1985, pp. 664–665) states, "Human bodies...far from being Cartesian reductionist organ systems, can be better and more realistically envisaged as multiphasic, experiential beings of finite freedom.... [The body] is, most essentially, the centre of one's experiences, moods, expressions and thoughts: the very nexus of intentionality." Who we are, what we feel, and what we believe are intrinsically connected to our bodies.

Because the body is valued as the source of primary intelligence, intention, information, and change, it is an avenue to explore in therapy. It helps therapists and clients identify and address themes arising from spiritual, mental, and emotional realms. Sensorimotor Psychotherapy explores cues from the body that point to the strengths, spiritual connection, beliefs, emotions, and past hurts that show up in present-moment experience. Thus, the language of the body becomes a target of therapeutic action and a vehicle for understanding mental, emotional, and spiritual realms. The therapist seeks to experientially elucidate the intelligence of clients' sensations, postures, gestures, and movements with the intent to unveil an innate knowledge that goes beyond cognitive understanding.

The fact that the movement, posture, and physiology of the body adjust automatically, without conscious intent, to its environment to ensure survival and optimize resources is a potent indication of its intelligence. These adaptations result in patterns of tension, movement, gesture, posture, breath, rhythm, prosody, facial expression, sensation, physiological arousal, gait, and other action sequences. Developed in a sociocultural context, the effects of both negative and positive experiences, trauma and relational strife, spiritual communion and existential angst are held in bodily patterns. A crisis of spirit, for example—when people are "unable to find sources of meaning, hope, love, peace, comfort, strength, and connection in life or when conflict occurs between their beliefs and what is happening in their life" (Anandarajah & Hight, 2001, p. 84)—is reflected in the lived body through its posture, movement, expression, and physiology.

The story told by the body—the "somatic narrative" of gesture, posture, prosody, facial expressions, eye gaze, movement, and so forth—reflects both personal and sociocultural history. We keep in mind that culture has a powerful influence on one's perspective and experience of their own and others' bodies. Different cultures attribute more or different value to mind, body and spirit (e.g., logical thinking might be esteemed over emotions or vice versa; the body may be denounced or appreciated; spiritual life may be more or less emphasized and valued). The body from a Western perspective is usually perceived as lesser than the mind and its objectification is reflected in norms of physical attractiveness in terms of size, age, color, shape, and so forth (Hancock et al., 2000). These prejudices can lead those whose bodies do not conform to these standards to be viewed negatively, or to view their own bodies negatively. The determination of which bodies should be restrained or policed is also evidence of the norms of Western culture, particularly the perspective that diminishes Black and Brown bodies and elevates white bodies. Founded on inaccurate and harmful bias that bodies of color need to be controlled (Menakem, 2017) and white bodies need to be protected, this dangerous prejudice has contributed to and even sanctioned the incarceration and murder of Black and Brown people.

It is essential to address one's own bias toward the body so that we can challenge ourselves and not unwittingly enact our prejudice. Culture strongly influences the meaning we make from various movements and postures (Moore & Yamamoto, 2012). When movement patterns are familiar to us, we feel more security, but when they are not, we may sense discomfort or even threat. Burgoon, Guerrero, and Floyd (2010) point out that culture has a strong influence on duration of eye contact, proximity, and touch. These nonverbal patterns of communication, learned in one's particular sociocultural context, can reflect interpersonal dominance and subordination (Johnson, 2015). For example, dominance can be expressed by expansive movements and postures (Johnson, 2015) or by prolonged direct eye contact (Ellyson & Dovidio, 1985). Touch is used with more ease and frequency by those of privileged status, while those deemed to have lesser status learn to refrain from initiating touch in an asymmetrical relationship (Henley & Freeman, 1995). If we are unaware of the norms we have learned through our own sociocultural context, we are at risk of perpetuating privilege/oppression dynamics through our own movements and postures as well as through how we interpret and respond to the movements and postures of others. At the same time, we seek to respect that different individuals and groups have different relationships with and traditions concerning the body, and we seek to recognize and honor these differences in clinical practice.

When we grasp that our physical habits—the way we move, stand, sit, and so forth—are shaped by our personal and sociocultural histories, and these habits are also adjusted to our immediate internal state and external context, we understand that the body's wisdom is not static. It emerges from the constantly fluctuating interactions with others, the world, and our own internal experience. Our bodies shift from moment to moment depending on the state of our mind, emotions, spirit, who we are with, and so forth. Sometimes this shift is obvious and on a large scale, like a change in posture or gesture. Other times, this shift is subtle and almost negligible, but no less profound, like a micromovement or internal opening that may not be apparent to the observer.

The body is not only a resource for the client but a laboratory for self-awareness for therapists. When we are curious about the organization of our own bodies, we discover our physical habits, how they reflect the mind and spirit, and through this awareness we are more able to develop and model an expansive movement vocabulary. Implicitly, the therapist's own somatic resonance and awareness contribute to a safe, collaborative atmosphere in which to explore the body in interaction with the mind and spirit. We help clients to identify and understand their body as a powerful and honest avenue to self-knowledge, and to view its physical habits as intelligent adaptations. We support clients to expand their own movement vocabulary and, in doing so, to experience a corresponding expansion in mind and spirit, especially when physical patterns have become default behaviors over other actions that would be more integrative in current contexts. By developing a resilient, expansive, innovative, flexible, and fluid movement vocabulary, the overall vitality in all three dimensions of being also expands.

The intelligence of our bodies emerges out of our ever-changing experience with others, the world, and ourselves. To reveal the emergent wisdom of the body, mind, and spirit calls for a trust in the unknown and an orientation to process rather than outcome. With curiosity and willingness to explore the body, along with compassion and appreciation for ways the body adapted in the past, as well as awareness of sociocultural patterns of expression, we can better draw upon its wisdom. In Sensorimotor Psychotherapy, this means harnessing mindful awareness of the body and its relationship to emotion, cognition, and spirit, and discovering new movements and postures to support expansion in all three realms. The intelligence of the body, integrated with mind and spirit, is an emergent property, not a fixed one. Since the emergent knowledge of the body is always in transition, learning from the body is a continuous endeavor. The unity of body, mind, and spirit has different things to teach at different times as we go through various life processes, stages, and challenges. Over a lifetime, we can continue to tap the emergent intelligence of the body, allowing it to guide us beyond comfort and familiarity to reach for expansion in mind and spirit, and in all dimensions of our life.

Unity

The fundamental delusion of humanity is to suppose
that I am here and you are out there.
YASUTANI ROSHI

Pull a thread here and you'll find it's attached to the rest of the world.
NADEEM ASLAM

What if we all stopped fighting to belong
and realized that we already do?
VIRONIKA TUGALEVA

We are one, after all, you and I. Together we suffer,
together exist, and forever will recreate each other.
PIERRE TEILHARD DE CHARDIN

If you have come to help me you are wasting your time.
But if you recognize that your liberation and mine
are bound up together, we can walk together.
LILA WATSON

The unity principle underscores the fundamental interrelationship between all aspects of the universe: We exist in a constant state of being joined with all that is. Unity rejects the idea that we are separate and embraces interconnection and interdependence; it can be thought of as a beneficial force of nature that organizes disparate parts into wholes (Kurtz, 2004). Though individuals, we do not and cannot exist in isolation, but within a complex organic web of relationships. Each distinctive part of this web of self-organizing systems is generated in relationship to the whole and subsequently generates the whole. Without the activity of the whole, the parts would not exist, and vice versa. Thus, the universe is participatory: "All of us are embedded as co-creators, replacing the accepted universe 'out there,' which is separate from us" (Chopra & Kafatos, 2017). Each of us is an integral part of one unified, organic process that encompasses the whole of nature and the universe. Nothing exists outside of this complex web of relationships, and the individual cannot be separated from all that is. In the words of Thich Nhat Hanh (2001, p. 56), "'To be' is to inter-be. You cannot just be by yourself alone. You have to inter-be with every other thing."

Living systems carry within them an intelligence that cannot be explained by reductionist views that scale down complex dynamics to simple cause and effect. Advocates of reductionism propose that processes, even psychological processes, ought to be described according to science, such as through physiology and chemistry; in this view, a mental disturbance can be attributed to a chemical imbalance (McLeod, 2008). Dividing a living system into its parts, and then describing the whole in terms of the parts it contains, is the essence of reductionism, which unity contradicts. Unity acknowledges that a living system cannot be explained or understood in terms of its various parts.

The complexity of emergence in living systems is the process of something novel coming into being, which can be analyzed in retrospect, but cannot be fully predicted. Emergence occurs when a living system has attained a certain degree of complexity and then exhibits spontaneous intricate behaviors that arise from the interactions of its parts. Unanticipated behaviors or capacities are generated that the individual parts do not have on their own. Thus, emergent properties can come into being only when the parts interact with, and are reciprocally influenced by, all the other parts interacting within the larger whole. According to the principle of unity, living systems cannot be reduced to simple explanations, because multiple influences, known and unknown, seen and unseen, interact in initially mysterious ways that lead to unforeseen emergent properties. What is brought into being cannot be reduced to or explained by the components.

Unity has roots in Indigenous, Taoist, and Buddhist teachings. The Buddhist concept of "dependent origination" teaches that everything exists because of everything else—nothing can be born, created, or survive on its own because all things are interdependent, and everything impinges upon all that is, and vice versa. A multitude of circumstances, elements, and interactions are needed for something to come into existence. As Thich Nhat Hahn (2001, p. 55) wrote, "you will see clearly that there is a cloud floating in this sheet of paper. Without a cloud, there will be no rain; without rain, the trees cannot grow; and without trees, we cannot make paper." Everything and everyone emerges and exists in parallel association with everything and everyone else; thus the sense of an isolated, independent self is an illusion.

Indigenous cultures also understand that each person is an integral part of all that is, summed up in the Native American expression "All My Relations," which means, "I cannot exist without you and you cannot exist without me. What I do affects you and others and what you do affects me. Everything we do has an effect on others and on our world" (Jansen, 2018, para. 4). Closely related is the South African concept of Ubuntu, which, loosely translated, means, "I am because we are," which recognizes that "we are all bound together in ways that are invisible to the eye; that there is a oneness to humanity" (Obama, 2013, para. 9). Transmitted through oral traditions for hundreds of years, Ubuntu is an ideology in which other people are seen as reflections of the self, thus recognizing that we are joined; our joys and our suffering are bound together. It "suggests to us that humanity is not embedded in my person solely as an individual; my humanity is co-substantively bestowed upon the other and me. Humanity is a quality we owe to each other. We create each other and need to sustain this otherness creation" (Eze, 2010, p. 191). With Ubuntu comes a sense of belonging to a larger whole; thus affirmation of other beings is naturally forthcoming. We rejoice in their joy and share in their pain and suffering, which is painful also to us (Tutu, 2000).

At the same time, the principle of unity recognizes individual and group differences. Kluckholn and Murray (1953) wrote that each person is, concurrently, like no other person, like some other people, and like all other people. Unity recognizes and celebrates differences within interconnectedness. Though nothing in nature is truly separate, to exist is also to have boundaries, whether we consider the membrane of a cell, the outer skin of an organism, or the borders of a nation. People also construct and maintain boundaries to be viable, healthy, and capable of experiencing fully the unity of which they are individual parts. The concept of unity acknowledges, respects, and values differences and boundaries. In unity, we become simultaneously aware of our differences and those of others, while also experiencing a sense of connectedness to others and to the universe.

Validation of both differences and interconnectedness is described by the term "unity in diversity," which can be traced to North American Indigenous people and Taoism (Lalonde, 1994). Unity becomes a felt reality when each person can safely and with acceptance participate in the whole, offering their unique talents and inspirations to contribute to local and global communities. This requires a felt sense of interconnection, a phenomenological recognition that injury inflicted upon one person or group of people harms everyone, and that joy experienced by one person adds to everyone's joy. But all too often the illusion of separation usurps an interconnected sensibility, bringing about boundless suffering and strife, seen in rampant exploitation, oppression, and violence. Manifestations of the denial of unity occur at every level of existence—in individual, collective, human, ecological, global, political, and sociocultural contexts. Racism, racialized trauma, war, sexism, and prejudice in all its forms reflect a painful and devastating inability to live the reality of our interconnectedness.

Unity itself becomes a lived reality when parts communicate; thus, although ever-present, it is recognized and experienced more fully through communication. A central goal of therapy is to facilitate communication interpersonally and intra-personally: communication between therapist and client and communication among parts, bringing special attention to those parts that are lost, hidden, or isolated. To operationalize unity collectively, bridges and affiliations need to be built that move beyond the interests of nationality, gender, race, ethnicity, and so forth, and effort needs to be made to discourage conceptualizations of the present-day dominant culture as better or universal (Lalonde, 1994). To actualize unity in diversity for all individuals and groups is described as "the highest possible attainment of a civilization, a testimony to the most noble possibilities of the human race. This attainment is made possible through passionate concern for choice, in an atmosphere of social trust" (Novak, 1983). Unity and freedom, therefore, are found within the choices we can make when we understand our undeniable interconnectedness within parts of ourselves and within the larger whole, and live from awareness of mutual interdependence, not by denying or trying to rise above it.

Thus, as therapists, we "work to get parts communicating, whether it's members of the family, the body and mind, or parts of the mind. It's an art, full of high skill, to coax these parts out of hiding, to help them speak openly and directly" (Kurtz, 1990, p. 32). Recognizing that all aspects are part of a larger whole, a central aim is to facilitate the communication between these parts—between each of us and within each of us. We help each person discover both how communication breaks down between internal parts and with external elements and how communication is supported and enhanced. When communication is restored between mind, body, and spirit, "me" and "not-me" self-states, emotion, thought, and body, implicit and explicit selves, and so forth, differences are resolved, integration is bolstered, one's connection to the greater whole is experienced more fully, and the energy used to maintain separation is freed for other endeavors.

Janet (1925) stated that therapists must encourage as much collaboration with the client as possible. To foster a felt sense of unity, collaborative communication between therapist and client is essential. In the therapy hour, a sense of co-creation or "being in it together" decreases separation, builds connection, and shifts responsibility for what occurs from the individual to the dyad. Unity is reflected in simple ways; for example, therapists use the collaborative language of "we" and "us" ("Maybe we could explore…") rather than "I" and "you." Instead of making therapeutic decisions on our own as therapists, we share our thinking and include our clients in the conceptualizing and decision-making process. We use psychoeducation to make sure we are on the same page with the client, check out our assumptions, honor our differences, and support the client's internal locus of control. We think out loud ("I wonder if….") as we appropriately convey our perceptions and intentions and we resonate with clients to share in their joy and pain.

We embody a sense of connectedness to others and the universe while also holding the simultaneous awareness of our separateness and our difference. We aim to be aware of and speak to our own biases and social locations, to be sensitive to those of our clients, and to bring these into the therapy hour as appropriate through honest communication. We remain receptive to all parts of ourselves and our clients in a stance of "radical openness," which entails an ongoing effort "to notice, question, and relinquish presumptions about oneself and the other" (Hart, 2017, para. 6).

In operationalizing unity, the therapist recognizes that everything that emerges in the therapy hour—thoughts, emotions, postures, movements, gestures, sensations, images, and so forth—are a part of the greater whole. They are "holons"—elements that "behave partly as wholes or wholly as parts, according to the way you look at them" (Koestler, 1967, p. 48). By understanding and experiencing each part, each element as a holon, as being a whole and a part at the same time, we recognize unity in everything that emerges in therapy. With this recognition comes a sense of choice and freedom. As Feldman (1999) states, "Understanding how things come together, how they interact, actually removes that sense of powerlessness or that sense of being a victim of life or helplessness" (para. 14). Through unity, we can act in accordance with the experience of our own and our client's relationship to all that is.

Relational Alchemy

An honorable human relationship is a process—delicate,
violent, often terrifying to both persons involved. A process of
refining the truths they tell one another. It is important to do
this. It breaks down self-delusion and isolation and does justice
to our own complexity. It is important to do this because we
can count on so few people to go that hard way with us.
ADRIENNE RICH

She is a friend of mind. She gather me, man. The pieces I am, she
gather them and give them back to me in all the right order. It's good,
you know, when you got a woman who is a friend of your mind.
TONI MORRISON

The most empowering relationships are those in which each
partner lifts the other to a higher possession of their own being.
PIERRE TEILHARD DE CHARDIN

My love has two lives, in order to love you: that's why I love you
when I do not love you, and also why I love you when I do.
PABLO NERUDA

Relational alchemy, in alignment with the unity principle, appreciates that the distinctive and emergent qualities of each relationship spawn something greater than the individual components. The word "alchemy" describes an idiosyncratic process that brings about change by means that are not fully understood. Considered the forerunner of chemistry, alchemy was founded on the supposition that everything that exists is imbued with spirit and can be transformed. But when two or more substances are combined, the transformation that occurs is often unexpected. The same holds true for when humans interact. Relational alchemy describes the enigmatic transformation of two or more people that is inspired by their distinctive synchrony in the way in which they are connected. Because each person and each moment in time are unique, so is every human interaction. Thus, when people come together, novel and unexpected outcomes that cannot be understood by the rational mind are brought about.

Every human affiliation contains its own original and distinctive characteristics that bring forth content, communications, and outcomes that would not occur in any other interaction. Not only are human interactions impacted by each party's background, emotional valence, personality, perspectives, strengths, challenges, and so forth, but also by particular aspects of each person that are brought forward at discrete times, and in different relationship, generating an array of capacities, aha moments, struggles, and growth possibilities in every interaction. As living systems, relationships are self-organizing, self-directing, and self-correcting (Bateson, 1979)—thus constantly changing. Relational alchemy recognizes the mysterious forces that fuel these changes and transformations.

Human relationships are rife with opportunities for profound intimacy and expansion as well as for devastating miscommunications and ruptures, and everything in between. Relational alchemy encompasses the wonder of healing that occurs naturally, without effort, through the synergy of the dyadic dance of the therapeutic relationship. It also embraces the implicit, unformulated elements of both client and therapist that dovetail exquisitely to collide in therapeutic enactments that are incipient in any interaction but tend to blossom in long-term relationships. Powerful healing emerges from well-negotiated enactments, including collisions not only of family history but also of culture and social location. Each healing scenario—those that seem to happen magically on their own and those that are hard won through facing the challenges of enactments—holds awesome potential for transformation and liberation.

We humans have an essential and deep need for recognition, which Benjamin (1988, p. 12) defines as "that response from the other which makes meaningful the feelings, intentions, and actions of the self." Akin to what Schore (2009) calls the "interactive 'transfer of affect' between the right brains," and to what Stern (2004, p. 75) describes as when "two people see and feel roughly the same mental landscape for a moment at least," recognition is a mutual experience, a function of relational alchemy. Relational alchemy fuels both misrecognition and mutual recognition, which is as gratifying as misrecognition is painful (until it is relationally negotiated and transforms into recognition). Both can be profound change agents.

Therapy itself is "a nonlinear process [induced by relational alchemy] that endows both their relationship and their individual self-states with an ever-evolving experience of wholeness that is the primary source of healing and growth" (Bromberg, 2012). A shared moment of recognition is nourishing and growth enhancing to both therapist and client. Recognition is alchemical—a seemingly magical moment of expanding the capacity for self-other wholeness in which something spontaneous and novel is unexpectedly experienced: a "new reality is co-constructed and infused with an energy of its own" (Bromberg, 2006, p. 12). From these moments, new options are revealed, and new possibilities never before conceived spontaneously emerge.

Kurtz (2007) set the stage for acts of recognition in his initial orientation to a client: "My first impulse is to find something to love, something to be inspired by, something heroic, something recognizable as the gift and burden of the human condition, the pain and grace that's there to find in everyone you meet" (p. 13). Looking out for "something to love" instead of deficits or problems primes the pump for recognition of aspects of the client that need to be coaxed out of hiding and seen by another. Recognition can be thought of as occurring on a continuum from significant to profound. All along the spectrum are relational moments that are meaningful or significant. Such a moment might occur when a traumatized client tells their story of abuse for the first time to an attentive, attuned therapist, or when distorted limiting beliefs (e.g., "I am unworthy" or "No one will ever accept me"), learned in the context of early caregiving, are revised in an act of recognition that relationally challenges such beliefs so that the client experiences a felt sense of value and worth. Recognition can throw open the door to new possibilities, providing what is known as a corrective emotional experience that heals long-festering wounds. These moments are replete with "emotional attunement, mutual influence, affective mutuality, sharing states of mind," and an array of meanings may infuse them—validation, acknowledgment, affirmation, acceptance, understanding, appreciation, and so forth (Benjamin, 1988, pp. 15–16).

Approaching the extreme of the continuum, even more profound acts of recognition emerge as moments of heightened awareness in which both parties experience an expanded state of consciousness—a sense of spaciousness, beingness, love, reverence, gratitude, peace, or an encompassing sense of belonging (Ogden, 2007). Sometimes called "sacred moments" (Lomax & Pargament, 2011), these remarkable manifestations of relational alchemy may encompass, but are not confined to, a felt sense of spirit, holiness, blessedness, higher power, or divinity. Taylor (2013, p. 29) eloquently describes such a moment in her work with an African American adolescent in the juvenile carceral system:

> He often struggled to imagine his own future so I asked him to imagine what he thought I wished most for him. He inhaled deeply as his eyes rose slowly to the ceiling welling up with tears. He smiled and exhaled the word "freedom." All the air suddenly left the room. Something sacred and otherworldly had come to join us. Together we sat in silence.

"Freedom," particularly significant in an ancestral context of chattel slavery, was overflowing with layer upon layer of depth and meaning. Cultural history and spiritual practices, called "cultural kindling" (Cassaniti & Luhrmann, 2014), influence the meanings and connotations of such alchemical moments, and affect the nature of the unique relational alchemy in every therapist-client dyad. Cultural history and context may also prime physical experiences (such as trembling, spontaneous dancing, suspension of a sense of physical boundaries, tingling, or feelings of leaving the body), interpretation or meaning (such as liberation, safety, union), or the presence of other forces (God, spirit, ancestors, or totem animals) ascribed to a profound moment of recognition. For many clients and therapists, these experiences are "a source of meaning in life, feelings of connectedness with a larger community, and a sense of continuity bridging the past, present, and future" (Pargament et al., 2014).

These expansive experiences are life affirming, infusing clients and therapists alike with a sense of profundity that extends beyond mundane limitations. Pargament and Mahoney (2005) delineate four different categories of sacred moments. Transcendent experiences are extraordinary, rather than everyday, occurrences, such as the feeling of a greater presence. Boundlessness pertains to no longer being limited by temporal or dimensional boundaries, like the sense of time stopping or space expanding. The felt sense of an undeniable, ultimate truth refers to experiences like an unquestionable feeling of being blessed. A profound interconnectedness might be experienced in a rare depth of reciprocal understanding, attunement, and resonance between therapist and client. These various moments of heightened or sacred awareness may be accompanied by a sense of mystery, awe, humility, joy, serenity, being uplifted, peace, or other spiritual emotions (Pargament et al., 2014). However, as in the example described above, words and interpretation are often absent, for language itself is inadequate to describe these shared moments, and in fact can detract from their lived experience (Ogden, 1992/2007). Such numinous occasions are to be savored, not necessarily described.

The implicit elements or parts of both therapist and client that participate in relational alchemy exist in the depths of the unconscious, and may hold different versions of reality, beliefs, agendas, and predictions of relationships. In a reciprocal interchange between these unsymbolized elements of both participants, powerful therapeutic interchanges encompass both profound recognition and profound misrecognition. The same mysterious relational forces that lead to the recognition and sacred moments illustrated above also underpin the equally meaningful interpersonal conflicts and struggles that therapist and client come up against. As a function of relational alchemy, the implicit histories—recent, distant past, and intergenerational—of each person are reenacted through painful collusions, collisions, and enactments. These relational clashes reflect personal history, privilege/oppression dynamics, sociocultural contexts, and intersecting social locations, or all these factors combined. Mutually created, the enacted reliving of one person's relational experience calls forth a matching counterpoint in the other that reflects historical failures of relational transactions and resolutions for both. Because these historical events and their impact are not always available for contemplation and revision, and are thus enacted unawares, they have an even more potent and bewildering impact on the therapeutic relationship. These mutual enactments cause painful misrecognitions on both sides but also hold the possibility for extraordinary expansion when well negotiated (Bromberg, 2006; Ogden, 2013).

When a particular aspect of the client comes forward, a corresponding part of the therapist is drawn out to meet it, and vice versa, in an emergent process. There are infinite possibilities of enactment scenarios, all related to aspects of each person that are indirectly crying out to be heard and recognized. The alchemy that is forged as each part comes forward in interaction with its counterpart in the other usually leads relentlessly to aggravating degrees of misrecognition on both sides. If one person is needy, the other pulls away or resentfully takes care of them; when one is intrusive, the other withdraws or submits; if one is blaming, the other feels shame; if one becomes critical, the other feels inadequate or defensive, and so forth.

These relational systems also reflect the intersectional identities and sociocultural histories of therapist and client that exacerbate asymmetrical circuits of power and privilege/oppression dynamics. Oppressed and marginalized people—ethnic and racial minorities, migrants, refugees, Indigenous people, those with disabilities, the LGBTQ+ community, women and girls, the poor, and others who are persecuted by the privileged culture—suffer misrecognitions and nonrecognition in personal and sociocultural contexts that can have disastrous repercussions for generations to come. In an appalling and terrifying example, the abject lack of recognition of Black Americans as human beings with human rights during the time of chattel slavery in the United States is enacted today in incidents of police brutality and ongoing systemic oppression. The relational alchemy that brings people of different social locations together in the therapy room provides the opportunity to challenge deep-seated implicit and explicit sociocultural misrecognitions as client-therapist intersectional identities unconsciously come up against one another in a struggle experienced very differently by those of privileged locations and those of oppressed locations. These misrecognitions can manifest in ignoring difference ("We're all alike; we have the same opportunities"), emphasizing difference ("We will never really understand one another"), or misinterpreting difference ("Your anger stems from your interactions with your mother, not from systemic oppression"; "Your empathy is because you feel guilty because you are more affluent than I am"). As noted, each misrecognition brings about a corresponding reaction in the other, and vice versa. These nonconscious mutually created systems can escalate into full-blown enactments because the unresolved historical relational dynamics of one person fit together with the other's past in a way that exacerbates each one's current position. Because of this, a tremendous opportunity for healing of past and present is there for the taking if the enactment can be negotiated and implicit parts recognized.

Enactments are inevitable. Bromberg (2006) asserts, "...there is no way to avoid these clashes of subjectivity without stifling the emergence [in both therapist and client] of dissociated self-states that need to find a voice" (p. 24). If these voices are to be heard, relational safety will necessarily and inevitably be compromised or lost, at least temporarily. Large and small enactments lead to smoldering feelings of boredom, frustration, resentment, disappointment, or anger that can erupt into hostility and therapeutic impasses, even leading therapist or client, or both, to look for a way to exit the therapy. Enactments will percolate beneath the surface in misrecognitions, misattunements, and degrees of discomfort from slight to intense for both parties, communicated in body-to-body, emotional exchanges beneath the surface of consciousness while verbal content is addressed. The enactment will continue until one of the participants "wakes up" (Bromberg, 2006) to the fact that something is relationally not quite right. From there, an acknowledgment that the difficulty lies within the relationship, not solely in either person, can be nourished and the relational meaning coaxed forth from their reflective communications. If therapist and client persevere to search for mutually constructed meaning, the "failures in recognition can be addressed, acknowledged, and either repaired or mourned" (Benjamin, 2006, p. 120). The relational negotiation of an enactment, once it is realized that something is amiss, is the source of meaningful acts of recognition, and even of profound moments of transformation. Acknowledgment of a misrecognition and the hurt it inflicts, as well as active mutual mourning within the relationship, are both necessary before repair, but if done well, lead to something more than mere repair: a larger transformation that would not have been possible without the enactment. Although the unconscious collusions and collisions that emerge from the relational alchemy between the implicit patterns of therapist and client can defeat therapeutic progress, they can also lead to transformational acts of recognition when well negotiated. A well-negotiated enactment can legitimize each one's personhood, needs, and rights that have been invalidated in past relational and sociocultural contexts. Therefore, misrecognition and enactments are not errors but rather products of a deeper initiative within each person and within their relationship that seeks a higher level of communion and expansion.

In any relationship, the explicit verbal exchange pales in significance to the one that takes place implicitly, through prosody, body language, emotions, innuendo and so forth. Relational alchemy emerges from the interaction of implicit selves that hovers beneath the words, typically unrecognized and unarticulated by the conscious mind. This nonverbal communion is the elusive symphony of relational alchemy, enacted unawares through an implicit body-to-body emotional communication. Relational alchemy, the emergent and mysterious force that brings people together and guides their interactions, is the source of profound and unexpected sensations of being genuinely seen, whether emerging from spontaneous recognitions and sacred moments or from the hard struggles of negotiated enactments. Relational alchemy generates an intersubjective process of dis-covery—of knowing the other and being known by them—that occurs in a way that is neither predicted nor expected, and thus appeals to each person for the courage to step into unknown territory and trust what the journey will bring.

Presence and Mindfulness

*Maybe journey is not so much a journey ahead, or a
journey into space, but a journey into presence.*
NELLE MORTON

*...to be lost is to be fully present, and to be fully present is
to be capable of being in uncertainty and mystery.*
REBECCA SOLNIT

Beauty is the harvest of presence.
DAVID WHYTE

*The mind is a drama queen that gets too embarrassed to continue acting
up, after only a few seconds of getting our undivided attention.*
MOKOKOMA MOKHONOANA

*Stop traveling to the past and future and come home to the
present moment. That is the only place you actually live.*
AKIROQ BROST

Although sometimes conflated, mindfulness and presence can be dif-ferentiated in terms of dual and nondual states of consciousness. For our purposes, in a simplistic distinction, mindfulness is conceptualized as a divided state and presence as a unified one. Mindfulness entails being aware of something in the here and now and thus encompasses both an observer who is aware and that which is observed. In contrast, presence is a participatory state of "being" rather than observing, of engagement with rather than awareness of an object or even noticing the engagement itself. As soon as we think about or observe our presence, our consciousness shifts to a dual state, and the full nondual consciousness of presence is compromised. The distinctive characteristic of presence is a wordless, unconsidered, direct sense of the present moment, whereas the hallmarks of mindfulness are noticing and accepting what is occurring in the present moment.

Presence is a felt sense of merging with each fleeting moment and participating completely. It has to do with "being" rather than "doing," and with being one with the doing. Presence exists only in the here and now rather than in the progression of linear time, as there is no time in the present moment. Thus, presence is not defined by the past nor impaired by expectations of the future. It is contrary to reacting through habit, or continuing to perceive things in familiar, comfortable ways. In a direct, unfettered experience of the here and now, we feel a sense of immediacy, as if we are residing inside the experience instead of being aware of it. We are immersed fully and completely with a sense of being "the very awareness, the very consciousness, that is present, that exists, in this very moment" (Almaas, 2008, p. 136). Describing presence as an "ability"" diminishes its all-encompassing nature.

In its most desirable, unadulterated form, presence means we can circumvent the many permutations of mental constructs, conditioning, learned beliefs, and biases about ourselves, others, and the world that impinge on our expectations, predictions, and behaviors. Ideally, presence is a fresh and new experience in the here and now, independent of past conditioning and of future expectations, and thus open to and welcoming of novelty. Almaas and Johnson (2013, p. 39) describe it as "an actual sense of here-ness— beyond our emotions, beyond the mind, beyond our ideas. In presence, we can know ourselves in a way that is authentic, which means that we are knowing what is real in us." For thousands of years, various traditions have described compatible concepts: as "grace" or the "Holy Spirit" in Christianity; as "vital energy" or "chi" in Taoism; as "cessation" or the dissolution of boundaries between self and world in Buddhism; as wholeness or oneness in Hinduism; and as "opening the heart" in Islamic traditions such as Sufism (Senge et al., 2004).

In its essence, presence carries with it a sense of non-doing, as if we are one with what immediately surrounds us and with all that is. Senge and colleagues (2004, p. 14) describe it as generating a feeling of "letting come," receiving what is and engaging with a larger whole. Bortoft (quoted in Scharmer, 1999, p. 7) says it this way: "If the whole presences within its parts, then a part is a place for the presencing of the whole. ... a part is special and not accidental, since it must be such as to let the whole come into presence." We are able to sense the greater whole and experience our own unique place within that wholeness. This requires relinquishing control, habits, and preconceived ideas of things and letting go into a deep, attentive listening beneath what is on the surface, embracing a receptivity to the essence of things. When actions arise from this experiential and immediate sense of both the whole and the significance of each part within the whole, they can be made in service of whatever spontaneously comes forward in the moment in conjunction with how this fits into the greater picture.

When we are governed by habits formed from our history, or by "'machine age' concepts such as control, predictability, standardization, and faster is better" (Senge et al., 2004, p. 9), we will re-create the past in the present. Instead of being present, we "react" to the moment, which is "governed by 'downloading' habitual ways of thinking, of continuing to see the world within the familiar categories we're comfortable with" (Senge et al., 2004, p. 10). The brain's main function is often described as anticipation, enabling it to continually predict what will happen next so that we can make decisions and take appropriate action. Based on these forecasts, our unconscious decision-making process is an autopilot mechanism that is linked to our default mode network, by which we can make quick, timely decisions in predictable contexts in which we understand the rules of our environment (Vatenssever et al., 2017). The default mode network is related to making intuitive decisions, however intuition is often predicated on our past experience rather than the present moment, and thus our conditioning is a dominant influence.

When our minds wander, which they do about 50% of the time, our default mode network is active (Killingsworth & Gilbert, 2010), along with areas of the brain correlated with self-referential activity (Brewer et al., 2011). Half of our waking hours, we remove our awareness away from the present moment without knowing we are doing it. Even when we are engaged in pleasurable activities (except when making love), our minds will jump around (Killingsworth & Gilbert, 2010). While letting our minds wander may enhance creative problem solving and planning (Moondyham & Schooler, 2013), it can also lead to errors, poor decision-making, missing essential elements and so forth. As well, spending so much of our time on autopilot instead of being present seems to contribute to unhappiness, even when our minds gravitate toward thinking of positive things. Killingsworth and Gilbert (2010, p. 1) conclude that "a human mind is a wandering mind, and a wandering mind is an unhappy mind. The ability to think about what is not happening [in the moment] is a cognitive achievement that comes at an emotional cost."

Jha (2017, para. 20) asserts, "the opposite of a stressed and wandering mind is a mindful one." Concentration practices like mindfulness and music can help to train our minds to focus, and wander less, and thus can be a bridge from autopilot to presence. It should be acknowledged that to fit into a Western context, mindfulness practices have been altered from their original Buddhist meaning and intent. Through appropriation, Westerners, who have more resources, have adapted the symbols, practices, philosophy, spiritual intent, and so forth of primarily Buddhist mindfulness practices to suit Western purposes. In this way, mindfulness has become decontextualized from its initial cultural meaning and has lost much of its connection with its origin to benefit the group that has appropriated these practices (Kirmayer, 2015; Purser et al., 2016). When modifying mindfulness practices from Buddhism, it is honorable to reference their origin and to acknowledge that in appropriation, practices change their purpose. The Western adaptation of Buddhist mindfulness practices has turned away from the original intent of spiritual exploration and evolution, and from "the realisation of 'emptiness' and liberation from all attachments" (Anderson, 2015) and has redefined it as paying attention to the present moment with a nonjudgmental attitude of acceptance (Williams et al., 2007).

In this adaptation of mindfulness, we can begin to familiarize ourselves with our cognitive, emotional, and physical tendencies, and to learn how to let these go to return awareness to the present moment. But these endeavors still take place in dual awareness, as long as there is an observer and that which is observed, evident in most practices such as paying attention to the breath or sensation. However, over time, these efforts can act as an intermediary step that move us toward "being" and foster deepening our presence. Through mindfulness practices, we can become aware of ourselves, our thoughts, emotions, and body sensations, but in contrast, through presence we simply "be" ourselves, fully in the moment. Often in mindfulness exercises, practitioners experience a transition from observation to presence—to becoming one with the experience. But the moment they notice the oneness, they have reverted to dual consciousness, becoming the observer who notices experience.

Nevertheless, presence and mindfulness are not viewed as absolute sep-arate states of consciousness. They can be conceptualized as occurring on a continuum with full presence or unified consciousness at one end, and mindful dual consciousness at the other. Our consciousness may lean more toward one end or the other moment by moment. On autopilot, our minds are wandering somewhere off the continuum, and mindfulness brings us back. But through practice, we learn that there is a choice in every moment to return to the here and now. We begin to identify thoughts, emotions, and body sensations as temporary and ever changing, rather than identify-ing with them (Ogden & Minton, 2000). Gradually we might naturally start to prefer a more prescient state over autopilot. If so, when we move away from being present, we will start to self-correct, returning to the state of mindfulness and developing a natural inclination to come back to the pres-ent moment more and more quickly when we wander, eventually to return to the unified consciousness of presence. With practice, presence becomes increasingly stabilized, "a state to which the system will, of itself, return after being perturbed away from it" (Naft, 2011, p. 172), which can mitigate the automaticity of the default mode network. For example, the default mode networks of experienced meditators are found to be consistent with less mind wandering, and to be more present in the moment as compared to non-meditators (Brewer et al., 2011).

However, presence cannot and should not be unchanging or consistent. For example, it is imperative that we therapists are aware of our own and our client's individual and transgenerational history in relation to social location, culture, and larger contextual events, and how privilege/oppres-sion dynamics are played out in the therapy room. This requires us to be aware of our triggers and mindful of our internal reactions that interrupt presence, especially in working with clients who are "other"—of a different race, gender, socioeconomic status, sexual orientation, ethnicity, and so forth. Especially in the United States, but also throughout the world, to varying degrees we live in a culture where white supremacy and systemic oppression are the status quo, and conditioned bias toward difference is inescapable. Therefore, mindful awareness of the present-moment effect of this conditioning on our own internal patterns and processes is essential in order to dismantle implicit bias so that we do not unconsciously act on this conditioning, which would be inevitable without mindful attention. Addi-tionally, when we are aware of differences and of the impact of privilege/oppression dynamics, we can address these issues directly with the client.

Thus, in clinical practice, therapists move back and forth along the continuum of mindfulness and presence. At times, we are more mindful of our own impulses, emotions, thoughts, and how our own history relates to that of the client, and at times we are more present. As we are aware of our effect on the client, we are also mindful of the effect the client has on us (Kurtz, 1990; Ogden, 1992/2007). However, if our attention is consistently divided (regularly too mindful and thus not present), we run the risk of hindering the dyadic dance of participation, synchronicity, and presence with our client. So primarily we lean toward the "presence" end of the continuum, in a deep resonance with the client, in an open state that is conducive to responsiveness and inspiration rather than analysis, interpretation, or logical thought. Through presence, the client senses we are with them, and we find ourselves acting without premeditation. Through mindfulness, we become aware of our own internal reactions that inform our embodiment of the foundational principles that guide therapeutic action.

Principles Determine Technique

Nature does not hurry, yet everything is accomplished.
LAO TZU

You can't do what you want until you know what you're doing.
MOSHE FELDENKRAIS

Be brave. Be free from philosophies, prophets and holy
lies. Go deep into your feelings and explore the mystery of
your body, mind and soul. You will find the truth.
AMIT RAY

The most perfect technique is that which is not noticed at all.
PABLO CASALS

Therapy is complex. Determining clinical intervention with any given client at any given moment in time is not simple and rarely obvious. These principles offer the context from which to understand what treatment progress looks like for a client. Progress is less about pace and more about the emergent process; sometimes the change is slow and sometimes it happens quickly. In both cases, the principles help a therapist understand change and make it stick for clients because growth is a felt experience that emerges from their own awareness, in relationship to the therapist, within a context that is inherently health promoting. Without a strong intention to cultivate an atmosphere that is conducive to growth and evolution, and implement interventions in alignment with this atmosphere, true and lasting, self-generated healing within relationship does not occur. In Sensorimotor Psychotherapy, all technique is created from a firm grounding in the context generated by the study of, commitment to, and alignment with the principles.

In keeping with the concept of organicity—that living systems are intelligent, self-organizing, and self-correcting—the therapist helps clients learn about how they organize their experience in the present moment. Kurtz (1985, p. 7) states, "Perception is always an act of creation," constructed through habits that translate current events into experiential meaning, feeling, and action. "It is at the level of feeling and meaning [and bodily responses] that the conversion of events into experience becomes highly individual, creative, distinctly human, and sometimes unnecessarily painful and limiting" (Kurtz, 1985, p. 3). When the habits of conversion are discovered through mindfulness, therapists and clients together tap into the habitual meta-level of organization that underlies and shapes the quality of current experience. Although discussion can and does effect change through understanding and insight, it does not directly or explicitly target the habits that organize experience and ascribe significance to events, as mindfulness of these habits does. Focusing on how experience is constructed in the here and now represents a paradigm shift away from conversation and requires that talking about and focusing on content is suspended in favor of mindful awareness.

Mindfulness is gently (nonviolently) directed by the therapist in collaboration (unity, relational alchemy, presence) with the client toward the five building blocks of present experience—body sensation, movements, five-sense perception (e.g., internal images, smells, tastes, touch, and sounds), emotions, and thoughts (organicity, mind/body/spirit holism). These building blocks constantly fluctuate in response to internal and external stimuli in habitual patterns of organizing experience. Present-day reminders of the past can alter our internal experience in ways that abruptly bring our history into the experiential present, but generally we are not aware of the changes in the building blocks. If we do not notice these shifts, we are likely to respond as if the past were occurring in the present, which is usually at the root of why clients seek therapy. Discovering the internal habits of how events are converted into meaning begins with mindful awareness of one of the building blocks that is considered to be significant in the construction of experience. For example, instead of discussing the client's current conflict at work, the therapist directs attention to the tensing of the legs that occurs when the client talks about the work situation, and slowly, associations emerge: The client senses an impulse to run, sees in their mind's eye an image from childhood of being "bossed around" by their caregiver, hears the words, "I can't be myself," experiences feelings of anger, and so forth. These elements usually remain just under awareness, but they are indicative of powerful habits of thinking, feeling, and action, shaped by the past, that are imposed upon current events to convert them into meaning, albeit outdated.

Mindfulness as an intervention is passive, meaning that the intention is to notice internal experience rather than manipulate, change, interpret, or analyze it. The therapist and client suspend making meaning and forming conclusions in favor of simple observation, to stay with what at first may seem like unrelated bits of internal experience. Through mindfully sitting with these bits and noticing how experience unfolds by following the fluctuations in the building blocks, new elements that had not been noticed previously are discovered; new learning takes place, and unexpected meaning is revealed. In this way, within the context of the principles, the therapist helps the client turn inside deeply enough, toward important habits revealed in present-moment experience that convert events into meaning. Novel information becomes available from within. Because organicity is greater than what we can consciously know, "we trust that the [client] will take the new information and spontaneously incorporate it to the best advantage," (Ogden, 1986, p. 2), generating a natural internal reorganization.

Mindfulness adapted in Sensorimotor Psychotherapy is not a solo endeavor, but is embedded within the therapeutic dyad (Ogden, 2015). Instead of being taught as a meditation practice or solitary exercise, mindfulness entails therapist and client together becoming aware of the client's building blocks in the present moment. The therapist uses a specific set of skills or techniques to facilitate this, adapted from the work of Ron Kurtz (1990). Embodying the principles is the "being" part of the work, generating the skills that are the "doing" part—the specific, time-limited interventions that are used for a distinct purpose. These techniques can be observed by an outsider (except for tracking) and described.

The first skill—to track—is to be aware of the client's present-moment experience, reflected in the five building blocks as they fluctuate in response to certain stimuli—such as talking about a difficulty, remembering a trauma, sharing a recent incident of import, and so forth. Therapists do not "try" or struggle to notice anything specific, but through presence and the non-doing of nonviolence, maintain a receptive stance and find that certain elements jump out at them.

With the second skill—to make contact—the therapist then draws the client's attention to a building block considered (often implicitly) to be significant by naming it. For example, if the therapist notices that the client's shoulders tense as the topic of marriage is discussed, the therapist might say, "Seems like your shoulders are tightening as we talk about marriage." Therapeutic action does not emerge from efforting, analyzing or interpreting. Tracking and making contact reflect the principles in many ways: They emerge naturally from the absence of effort (nonviolence) and the synchronicity in the relationship (unity, relational alchemy, presence); the object of the contact statement is inherently acknowledged for its value (organicity), and as representing one aspect of mind/body/spirit holism. Tracking and making contact draw awareness to the client's present-moment experience, which initiates mindfulness. Additionally, qualifiers or adjunct clauses are used, such as "seems as if" or "looks like," to invite collaboration and modification by the client and ensure that therapist and client are in sync (unity, organicity, nonviolence).

When the client is interested in what has been named, the third skill—to frame—follows up on the contact statement by collaboratively defining the focus for exploration. The frame might be tension ("Let's stay with that tension in your shoulders"), thoughts ("How about we start with these thoughts you have about marriage?"), emotion ("Maybe we could explore this feeling of aversion to marriage"), and so forth. Note the collaborative, pensive tone and language of "we" (unity, relational alchemy, nonviolence, presence), the open-endedness of the frame inviting revision (organicity, unity, nonviolence), and the implicit acknowledgment that the frame will expand to include much more (mind/body/spirit holism).

If the client agrees to the frame, mindfulness questions are asked that directly focus attention on the target of the frame ("What do you notice as you stay with that tension?" "How is it pulling...in, up, back, or...?" "Are there any thoughts or feelings that go with the tension?"). To answer such questions, clients must become aware of present experience (mindfulness). The organization of experience is expanded as information related to the frame is gathered—the tension might hold fear, images of caregivers, sounds from the past, impulses such as to hide, thoughts and beliefs, and so forth. Mindfulness questions operationalize all the principles as a direct, collaborative, gentle, resonant inquiry into the organicity of each moment.

The fifth and final skill—to conduct experiments—guides mindful awareness to the internal fluctuations in response to a stimulus, and is prefaced by the phrase, "What happens when...?" Examples might be, "What happens when you exaggerate the tension?" "What happens when you see that image of your father yelling?" "What happens when you think about marriage?" "What happens when you sense this sadness?" The options are endless. Experiments are gentle investigations (nonviolence) into present experience (mindfulness) that elicit organicity, are adjusted as needed (unity, relational alchemy, presence), and are intended to reveal mind/body/spirit holism.

The application of these skills emerges organically as what action to take becomes apparent. The decision to intervene is not made rationally but from being receptive to what is revealed, until an action becomes obvious. In other words, action emerges from alignment with the principles, especially presence. The economist Brian Arthur (quoted in Senge et al., 2004, pp. 84–85) speaks of a "different way of knowing," claiming that,

> In a sense, there's no decision-making....What to do just becomes obvious. You can't rush it. ... You need to "feel out" what to do. You hang back, you observe. ... You don't act out of deduction, you act out of an inner feel, making sense as you go. You're not even thinking. You're at one with the situation.

So it is with "deciding" what skills of embedded relational mindfulness to implement at any given moment. Therapeutic action takes place within a context created by the principles, without which it would be a rote exercise rather than a deep relational exploration into the client's internal landscape. Through this approach, the organization of experience is unveiled; new territory is discovered and mined for its intelligence and meaning. As this takes place, the system—the client, and often the therapist as well—changes spontaneously, without force, in a progressive direction of healing and wholeness.

Conclusion

We work in the dark—we do what we can—we give
what we have. Our doubt is our passion and our passion
is our task. The rest is the madness of art.
HENRY JAMES

The principles call for us to dwell in a place of uncertainty, of not know-ing, to access a state of being that is open to the innovation of emergence. As Capra (2004, p. 41) writes, "Emergence results in the creation of novelty, and this novelty is often qualitatively different from the phenomenon out of which it emerged." We must relinquish the familiar so that we can experience something new. But this is not without risk. The quest to discover or, more precisely, to surrender to and receive, emergent wisdom and processes within ourselves, our relationships, and much more calls for the courage to step out of our comfort zones of what we think we know into unexplored, uncharted inner and outer domains without the security of being able to predict what might happen. Instead of seeking answers, we cultivate the ability to be with the questions, letting our minds and bodies become spacious and open to innovation, wonderment, and adventure. Instead of being task oriented, we are attuned to emergence, to what happens by itself. In relationship with oth-ers, stepping wholly and unabashedly into the fullness of the moment engen-ders what Tronick (2003, p. 476) calls a "dyadic state of consciousness [which] leads to feeling larger than oneself." If we can allow the principles to coax us into relinquishing the futile effort of trying to control a future that cannot be controlled, in our lives and with our clients, we might discover something infinitely more valuable than what we had expected or dreamed possible.

Every structure and every organism needs to exist within a context or foundation that will support its emergence and sustain its existence. This is true for physical structures, mental processes, people, relationships, life activities, spiritual pursuits, and everything else. In Sensorimotor Psycho-therapy, this sustaining foundation is made up of the principles that provide guidance for how to "be" as a therapist. However, they not only guide us in clinical practice but also offer a kind of road map for thriving in relation to ourselves, to others, and in the world at large. As therapists, one of our tasks is to help clients bridge the gap between therapy and life so that the expansion and growth that blossom in the therapy room do not end there, but carry forward into full bloom in the real content and experience of daily life. The foundational principles provide the context and direction that allows this to happen for our clients, and for ourselves. They inspire an increasingly higher consciousness as we engage in the emergent process of aligning with their teachings. In their purest form, taken together, the principles are a map for love.

References

Almaas, A. H. (2008). *The unfolding now: Realizing your true nature through the practice of presence.* Boston: Shambhala.

Almaas, A. H., & Johnson, K. (2013). *The power of divine Eros: The illuminating force of love in everyday life.* Boston: Shambhala.

Anandarajah, G., & Hight, E. (2001). Spirituality and medical practice: Using the HOPE questions as a practical tool for spiritual assessment. *American Family Physician, 63,* 81–89.

Anderson, L. (2015, June 5). Mindfulness has lost its Buddhist roots, and it may not be doing you good. *The Conversation.* https://theconversation.com/mindfulness-has-lost-its-buddhist-roots-and-it-may-not-be-doing-you-good-42526

Andrews-Hanna, J. R. (2012). The brain's default network and its adaptive role in internal mentation. *Neuroscientist, 18*(3), 251–270. https://doi.org/10.1177/1073858411403316

Bateson, G. (1979). *Mind and nature: A necessary unity.* New York: Bantam.

Benjamin, J. (1988). *The bonds of love: Psychoanalysis, feminism, and the problem of domination.* Toronto: Random House.

Benjamin, J. (2006). Two way streets: Recognition of difference and the intersubjective third. *Differences, 17*(1), 116–146. doi:10.1205/10407391

Brewer, J. A., Worbunsky, P. D., Gray, J. R., Tang, Y. Y., Weber, J., & Kober, H. (2011). Meditation experience is associated with differences in default mode network activity and connectivity. *Proceedings of the National Academy of Sciences, 108*(50), 20254–20259. doi:10.1073/pnas.1112029108

Bromberg, P. M. (2006). *Awakening the dreamer: Clinical journeys.* Mahwah, NJ: Analytic Press.

Bromberg, P. M. (2012). Credo. *Psychoanalytic Dialogues, 22*(3), 273–278.

Burgoon, J. K., Guerrero, L., & Floyd, K. (2010). *Nonverbal communication.* New York: Routledge. https://doi.org/10.4324/9781315663425

Capra, F. (2004). *The hidden connections: A science for sustainable living.* New York: Anchor.

Cassaniti, J., & Luhrmann, T. (2014). The cultural kindling of spiritual experiences. *Current Anthropology, 55,* S333–S343. doi:10.1086/677881

Chilisa, B., & Tsheko, G. N. (2014). Mixed methods in indigenous research: Building relationships for sustainable intervention outcomes. *Journal of Mixed Methods Research, 8*(3), 222–233.

Chopra, D. (1989). *Quantum healing: Exploring the frontiers of mind/body medicine.* New York: Bantam.

Chopra, D., & Kafatos, M. (2017). Why you and the universe are one. Chopra Foundation. https://www.choprafoundation.org/consciousness/why-you-and-the-universe-are-one/

Deshpande, R. (2019, November 8). What is ahimsa? *Yoga Journal.* https://www.yogajournal.com/lifestyle/what-is-ahimsa

Ellyson, S. L., & Dovidio, J. F. (1985). Power, dominance, and nonverbal behavior: Basic concepts and issues. In S. L. Ellyson & J. F. Dovidio (Eds.), *Power, dominance, and nonverbal behavior* (pp. 1–27). New York: Springer Verlag.

Emily. (2015, January 12). All my relations teachings. *Traditional Native Healing.* https://traditionalnativehealing.com/all-my-relations

Eze, M. (2010). *Intellectual history in contemporary South Africa.* New York: Macmillan.

Feldman, C. (1999, spring). Dependent origination. *Insight Journal,* 37–41. https://www.buddhistinquiry.org/article/dependent-origination/

Gold, J. (1985). Cartesian dualism and the current crisis in medicine—a plea for a philosophical approach: Discussion paper. *Journal of the Royal Society of Medicine, 78*(8), 663–666. https://doi.org/10.1177/014107688507800813

Hahn, T. N. (2001). *Essential writings.* Maryknoll, NY: Orbis.

Hahn, T. N. (2012). *Awakening of the heart: Essential Buddhist sutras and commentaries.* Berkeley, CA: Unified Buddhist Church.

Hancock, P., Hughes, B., Jagger, E., Paterson, K., Russell, R., Tulle-Winton, E., & Tyler, M. (2000). *The body, culture and society: An introduction.* Philadelphia: Open University Press.

Hart, A. (2017). From multicultural competence to radical openness: A psychoanalytic engagement of otherness. *American Psychoanalyst, 51*(1). https://apsa.org/apsaa-publications/vol51no1-TOC/html/vol51no1_09.xhtml

Henley, N., & Freeman, J. (1995). *The sexual politics of interpersonal behavior in women: A feminist perspective.* London: Mayfield.

Janet, P. (1925). *Principles of psychotherapy.* London: George Allen & Unwin.

Jansen, G. (2018). Living into all our relations. *Viewpoints, 22*(12). https://canadianmennonite.org/stories/living-all-our-relations

Jha, A. (2017, June 16). The science of taming the wandering mind in mindfulness: Healthy mind, healthy life. *Mindful.* https://www.mindful.org/taming-the-wandering-mind/

Johnson, R. (2015). Grasping and transforming the embodied experience of oppression. *International Body Psychotherapy Journal, 14*(1), 80–95.

Killingsworth, M. A., & Gilbert, D. G. (2010). A wandering mind is an unhappy mind. *Science, 330*, 923.

Kirmayer, L. J. (2015). Mindfulness in cultural context. *Transcultural Psychiatry, 52*(4), 447–469.

Kluckhohn, C., Murray, H. A., & Schneider, D. M. (Eds.). (1953). *Personality in nature, society, and culture* (2nd ed.). Knopf.

Koestler, A. (1967). *The ghost in the machine*. London: Hutchinson.

Kurtz, R. (1985). The organization of experience in Hakomi therapy. *Hakomi Forum*, no. 3, 3–9.

Kurtz, R. (1990). *Body-centered psychotherapy: The Hakomi method*. Mendocino, CA: LifeRhythm.

Kurtz, R. (2004). Principles and practices. Unpublished manuscript.

Kurtz, R. (2007). Readings on the Hakomi method of mindfulness-based assisted self-study. Unpublished manuscript.

Lalonde, R. (1904). Unity in diversity: Acceptance and integration in an age of intolerance and fragmentation. Bahai Library Online. https://bahai-library.com/lalonde_unity_diversity

Levac, L., Baikie, G., & Hanson, C. (2018). Learning across indigenous and western knowledge systems and intersectionality: Reconciling social science research approaches. University of Guelph. doi:10.13140/RG.2.2.19973.65763.

Lomax, J. W., & Pargament, K. I. (2011). Seeking "sacred moments" in psychology and in life. *Psyche and Geloof, 22*(2), 79–90.

Mark, G. T., & Lyons, A. C. (2010). Maori healers' views on wellbeing: The importance of mind, body, spirit, family and land. *Social Science and Medicine, 70*, 1756–1764.

McCabe, G. (2008). Mind, body, emotions and spirit: Reaching to the ancestors for healing. *Counseling Psychology Quarterly, 21*(2), 143–152.

McLeod, S. A. (2008). Reductionism and holism. *Simply Psychology.* https://www.simplypsychology.org/reductionism-holism.html

Mehta, N. (2011). Mind-body dualism: A critique from a health perspective. *Mens Sana Monographs, 9*(1), 202–209. https://doi.org/10.4103/0973-1229.77436

Menakem, R. (2017). *My grandmother's hands: Racialized trauma and the pathway to mending our hearts and bodies*. Las Vegas, NV: Central Recovery Press.

Mooneyham, Benjamin & Schooler, Jonathan. (2013). The Costs and Benefits of Mind-Wandering: A Review. Canadian journal of experimental psychology = Revue canadienne de psychologie expérimentale. 67. 11-8. 10.1037/a0031569.

Moore, C. L., & Yamamoto, K. (2012). *Beyond words: Movement observation and analysis* (2nd ed.). New York: Routledge.

Naft, J. (2011). *The sacred art of soul making* (2nd ed.). Baltimore, MD: I.F. Publishing.

Novak, M. (1983). Epigraph. In C. L. Birch (Ed.), *Unity in diversity: An index to the publications of conservative and libertarian institutions* (p. 263). Metuchen, NJ: Scarecrow.

Obama, B. (2013, December 10). Remarks by President Obama at memorial service for former South African president Nelson Mandela. White House, Office of the Press Secretary. https://obamawhitehouse.archives.gov/the-press-office/2013/12/10/remarks-president-obama-memorial-service-former-south-african-president-

Ogden, P. (1986). *The principles and bodywork*. Boulder, Colorado [Unpublished manuscript].

Ogden, P., & Minton, K. (2000). Sensorimotor psychotherapy: One method for processing trauma. *Traumatology, 6*(3). www.fse.edu/-trauma/v6i3a3.html

Ogden, P. (2007). *Training for the treatment of trauma manual*. Boulder, CO: Sensorimotor Psychotherapy Institute. Unpublished manuscript.

Ogden, P. (2015). Embedded relational mindfulness: A sensorimotor psychotherapy perspective on the treatment of trauma. In V. Folette, J. Briere, D. Rozelle, J. Hopper, & D. Rome (Eds.), *Mindfulness-oriented interventions for trauma: Integrating contemplative practices* (pp. 227–239. New York: Guilford.

Ogden, P., & Fisher, J. (2015). *Sensorimotor psychotherapy: Interventions for trauma and attachment*. New York: Norton.

Ogden, P. (2013). Technique and beyond: Therapeutic enactments, mindfulness, and the role of the body. In D. J. Siegel & M. Solomon (Eds.), *Healing moments in Psychotherapy* (pp. 35-47). New York, NY: W. W. Norton & Company.

Ogden, P., Minton, K., & Pain, C. (2006). *Trauma and the body: A sensorimotor approach to psychotherapy*. New York: Norton.

Pargament, K., Lomax, J., Mcgee, J., & Fang, Q. (2014). Sacred moments in psychotherapy from the perspectives of mental health providers and patients. *Spirituality in Clinical Practice, 1*(4), 248–262.

Pargament, K. I., & Mahoney, A. (2005). Sacred matters: Sanctification as a vital topic for the psychology of religion. *International Journal for the Psychology of Religion, 15*(3), 179–198. https://doi.org/10.1207/s15327582ijpr1503_1

Prigogine, I. (1997). *The end of certainty: Time, chaos and the new laws of nature*. New York: Free Press.

Purser, R. E., Forbes, D., & Burke, A. (Eds.) (2016). *Handbook of mindfulness: Culture, context and social engagement*. New York: Springer.

Scharmer, C. O. (1999). Imagination becomes an organ of perception: Conversation with Henri Bortoft. McKinsey & Company and Society for

Organizational Learning. https://www.presencing.org/assets/images/aboutus/theory-u/leadership-interview/doc_bortoft-1999.pdf

Schore, A. N. (2003). *Affect regulation and the repair of the self.* New York: Norton.

Schore, A. N. (2009). Right-brain affect regulation: An essential mechanism of development, trauma, dissociation, and psychotherapy. In D. Fosha, D. Siegal, & M. Solomon (Eds.), *The healing power of emotion: Perspectives from affective neuroscience and clinical practice.* New York, NY: W.W. Norton and Company. pp. 112–144.

Schweitzer, A. (1965, September 4). Schweitzer's struggle to find life's meaning: Doctor wrote of search. *Midland (Michigan) Daily News.* http://home.pcisys.net/~jnf/mdnstory.html

Senge, P., Scharmer, O., Jaworski, J., & Flowers, B. S. (2004). *Presence: Exploration of profound change in people, organizations, and society.* New York: Doubleday.

Siegel, D. J. (2010). *Mindsight: The new science of personal transformation.* New York: Random House.

Smylie, J., Olding, M., & Ziegler, C. (2014). Sharing what we know about living a good life: Indigenous approaches to knowledge translation. *Journal of Canadian Health Libraries Association, 35,* 16–21. doi:10.5596/c14-009

Stern, D. N. (2004). *The present moment in psychotherapy and everyday life.* New York: Norton.

Sue, D.W. (2010). *Microaggressions in everyday life: Race, gender, and sexual orientation.* Hoboken, NJ: Wiley.

Sue, D. W., Sue, D., Neville, H. A., & Smith, L. (2019). *Counselling the culturally diverse: Theory and practice.* New York: Wiley.

Taylor, S. (2013). Acts of remembering: Relationship in feminist therapy. *Women and Therapy, 36*(1–2), 23–34.

Tronick, E. Z. (2003). "Of course all relationships are unique": How co-creative processes generate unique mother-infant and patient-therapist relationships and change other relationships. *Psychoanalytic Inquiry, 23*(3), 473–491. https://doi.org/10.1080/07351692309349044

Tutu, D. (2000). *No future without forgiveness.* New York: Doubleday.

Vatanssever, D., Menon, D. K., & Stamatakis, E. A. (2017). Default mode contributions to automated information processing. *PNAS, 114*(48), 12821–12826. https://doi.org/10.1073/pnas.1710521114

Williams, M., Teasdale, J., Segal, Z., & Kabat-Zinn, J. (2007). *The mindful way through depression: Freeing yourself from chronic unhappiness.* New York: Guilford.

10

Addiction Recovery in a Time of Social Distancing

Oliver J. Morgan

The most powerful buffer in times of stress and distress is our social connectedness; so let's all remember to stay physically distant but emotionally close. Reach out and connect.
BRUCE D. PERRY

THIS IS A TIME OF TURMOIL. BATTERED BY MULTIPLE CRISES, INCLUDING A global pandemic, our society is stretched and faltering. Anxieties and adversities surround us, creating stresses at every level. Individuals susceptible to substance use and addictive disorders are particularly at risk in times like these. Stress is fertile ground for addictions. Below I examine some dimensions of our current predicament and offer recommendations for sustainable addiction care and recovery.

Addiction, Attachment, Trauma, and Recovery: The Power of Connection (Morgan, 2019) describes a holistic, attachment-sensitive, trauma-informed view of substance-related and addictive disorders. The full spectrum of addictive disorders—misuse and dependence on substances (nicotine, alcohol, and other drugs), on compulsive behaviors (gambling, gaming, sexual excess), on destructive attachments (to wealth, celebrity, power)—is seen as a stress-related adaptive solution gone awry and energized by adversity. When an individual feels stressed, she or he turns to substitutes for human connection. Each attempted solution begins innocuously as a temporary fix for suffering that is rooted in trauma and disconnection. Anxieties are soothed;

stress dampened. Over time, however, substitutes replace real relationships; temporary expedients supplant human connections.

Use of substitutes may begin for a variety of reasons, but it continues and deepens as the individual learns and develops neurochemical, emotional, and relational bonds with the process of substitution and the means of addiction, such as drugs or gaming (Koob & Volkow, 2016; Volkow et al., 2016). These surrogates have what it takes (psycho-activity, regulatory capacity) to help people manage the effects of adversity. For a time they work and serve a purpose. Resorting to alcohol or other drugs, gambling, or attachment to wealth and power helps to distract or numb the pain of adversity. What begins as a few drinks, lines of cocaine, or exercise of power becomes the preferred way to manage living. This process is deeply motivated, and the individual clings to it with tenacity.

Prevalence of Adversity

People can and do experience many adversities in the course of living. Most people in the United States experience some form of adversity or trauma, with lifetime prevalence approaching 60% for men and 50% for women (Najavits, 2007). A 1998 study using *DSM-IV* criteria found the actual exposure to a qualifying traumatic event to be closer to 89% overall (Ouimette & Brown, 2003). Post-traumatic stress disorder (PTSD), the diagnostic entity at the extreme end of stress experience, is 10 times (10×) more prevalent than cancer (Bremner, 2002)!

We have learned over the last 30 years that adversity, and specifically child adversity, is much more common than we knew (Anda et al., 2006; Magruder et al., 2016). Combined with societal forces that deeply affect us, individual adversities are amplified and create the seed ground for substitute relationships that can buffer the stress of living. But linked individual, developmental, and social forces are often hidden from view; they operate below the surface and create multiple health and behavioral vulnerabilities. Physiological diseases, psychological maladies, and behavioral and addictive disorders are related to these vulnerabilities. They are common but covert frailties, unevenly distributed among the population.

The range of adversities is quite large, including child abuse, physical or sexual brutality, parental strife and divorce, loss, and neglect, in addition to natural or man-made disasters (Morgan, 2019). Wider systemic adversities (family and household dysfunction, health disparities, economic hardship, racial discrimination, and collective tolerance for social deterioration), however, can also become part of a toxic social ecology surrounding individuals who struggle with addictions and substitute attachments. Societal adversities and social disconnection "get under our skin," mirroring and exacerbating individual fragmentation, reinforcing the kind of alienation and dis-ease (poverty of spirit) that create "desperate substitutes" (Alexander, 2008/2011). Trauma, adversity, disconnection, and fragmentation become the mothers of addiction.

We have also learned that adversities increase risks to physical, mental, and behavioral health. And it is not just the mere existence of adversity that can produce these outcomes; the timing, developmental background, and surrounding social ecology—the when, where, how, and potential buffers—of these occurrences also have an impact (Hambrick et al., 2019). As a consequence, many in our society experience persistent- (pTSD) as well as post-traumatic stress (PTSD). A child experiencing parental divorce, for example, will suffer different impacts than one living in a home environment with chronic fighting and discord. When, as often happens, neighborhood violence, bullying, or racism are added, the cumulative adversities can be overwhelming.

Adversity Science

There is powerful basic science underneath the impact of relational interactions and adversity. We know that babies are born experience dependent and require developmental experiences that facilitate ongoing healthy growth. Over a lifetime, we need connected environments filled with attachment and liberal doses of nourishing interactions for healthy development. As a social species, we are nourished and buffered by environments rich with attachment throughout our lives. This is a central tenet of affective neuroscience and interpersonal neurobiology.

Healthy relations with individuals and systems provide resources and skill sets that are crucial for living. They are also major factors in resilience and healing from trauma. Positive overall neural development and enhancement of stress regulatory systems depend upon both one-to-one interactions and a kind of constructive "relational density" (individuals and systems) that surrounds us. Development relies upon social ecology (Ungar & Perry, 2012).

Interactions that provide positive encounters (reliable care, affirmations, touch, looks, caresses, and so on) assist in both facilitating healthy development and stimulating empathy. Neural and emotional development anticipates and depends on repetition of these attachment encounters. Repeated experiences wire neurons and social expectations; repetition establishes neural and relational patterns for a lifetime. Neural systems adapt and learn to reflect the experienced world. This drive toward adaptation is a survival mechanism built into neural structures.

Alternatively, negative encounters can over-sensitize stress responses, cripple neural regulatory systems, and form negative expectations. With repetition of negative events, the baseline levels of our reactions and physiological responses can be altered over time. Adversity can both alter the organization of the brain and modify the physiology of the body (Perry, 2006, 2009). Negative interactions on a persistent basis and a pervasive impoverished environment lead to higher levels of stress, which in turn can lead to sensitized stress responses, inadequate neural and emotional regulation, and vulnerability to physiological, emotional, and behavioral disease.

Because we are born seeking and anticipating positive interactions with others, when these do not occur, the lack of positive encounters as well as adverse interactions can be experienced negatively. The lack of positive encounters is not a neutral occurrence. Unmet anticipation is experienced as a relational deficit and can lead to a sense of "relational poverty." Neuroscientist Bruce Perry states:

> While each child has unique genetic potentials, both human and animal studies point to important needs that every child has, and severe long-term consequences for brain function if those needs are not met. The effects of the childhood environment, favorable or unfavorable, interact with all the processes of neurodevelopment. (2002, p. 79)

While nourishing and supportive relationships underlie positive human development, extreme, prolonged, or chaotic stress triggers the stress response and over time can wear out many systems. Profound or ongoing stresses can sensitize the stress response and change its baseline activation setting. Individuals then become more reactive and vulnerable because they are already carrying a higher allostatic load. Even without encountering specific traumatic or adverse events, persons can struggle with relational deficits and ongoing relational poverty that is itself a powerful adversity. Relationally impoverished contexts can have deleterious effects developmentally and in the here and now; this mirrors the powerful impact of "relationally enriched" environments (Hambrick et al., 2019).

Put simply: Fostering and maintaining healthy social connections is essential for growth and healing. Positive relational experiences and rich interpersonal contexts within families, schools, or peer ecologies will facilitate development and likely buffer negative outcomes. This is particularly true in times of high stress. But for many, relational poverty is their surrounding ecology, even without specific events. Disruptions in social connectedness can occur and are traumatic at any age, but especially at earlier phases in living. Illness and addiction are likely outcomes.

The Current Situation: A Toxic Environment

Below I list some of the major societal challenges facing the United States today. Our current circumstances are a direct threat to health. Social connectedness is necessary for health, but our contemporary predicament with multiple co-occurring crises creates a toxic social ecology that generates and feeds addiction. COVID-19, a foundering economy, social polarization, and civil-political instability join other factors to create chaos and social anxiety. When people ask why there is so much addiction, it is relevant to consider stimuli that are usually overlooked.

Of course, many factors enable addiction: genetics, epigenetics, family and social factors, comorbidity with trauma, co-occurring mental illness, and so forth. Here I focus on upstream factors, that is, the social ecological adversities that create an addiction-enhancing environment. A systemic assessment and approach are needed. Addiction-enhancing environments create ecological risks for substance misuse, addiction, and relapse; recovery-enhancing strategies must include community-based and systemic remedies. This will take us deeper than simple prevention, treatment, and recovery strategies. The chapter finishes with recommendations for environmental improvement.

Current health and social factors in the U.S. aggravate the overall toxicity of our environment. A population already staggering under acute public health challenges (for example, the opioid and prescription drug crisis, vaping-related lung disease, prevalence of pain, chronic gun violence) and becoming aware of longer-term and stubborn illness factors (adverse childhood experiences, excessive alcohol consumption, widespread health inequities and disparities) was confronted with additional and unexpected threats that also brought anxieties and toxicity in their wake. Long-simmering hazards were aggravated.

By any measure, this is an alarming situation. Right now, we in the U.S. and around the world are living in a time of overwhelming adversity that has been characterized in certain ways. Metaphors of overlapping crises, of recurring COVID-19 waves and spikes that wash away and leave many things exposed, and more recently of a "forest fire" that burns "wherever there is wood (or human hosts) to burn" now dominate the headlines (Papenfuss, 2020). Many current and future challenges are revealed. Addiction recovery must compete with these forces as well:

- A global pandemic has radically changed the picture of illness and health, revealing health care system inadequacies, ethnic, racial, and social disparities, and many other social determinants that underlie health vulnerabilities. Many are realizing the extent of health susceptibilities such as cardiovascular deficits, diabetes, obesity, and advancing age, while the more covert vulnerabilities of race, ethnicity, poverty, poor nutrition, the ubiquity of stress, loneliness, and isolation, even geography and location are also coming to light (Graham et al., 2017; Iton, 2005). We were already at a public health disadvantage prior to COVID-19. Now our health care situation is even more precarious.

  COVID-19 is an evolving crisis. It first hit elderly and vulnerable victims, including essential health care workers, with respiratory illness. It seemed confined to select hot spots along both coasts. Now it has spread to different geographical locations (southern and western U.S.) and a more varied victimology. Much younger people are being infected and with a larger profile of illnesses. Shifting presentations of the illness (such as multisystem inflammatory illness, random blood clotting, and covid "long-hauling"), create further anxiety and uncertainty.

  At this time of crisis, the best advice for self-care seems to be at loggerheads with what we need more widely. Social distancing, social isolation, mask wearing, avoidance of touch, hand-washing, all are essential public health strategies that nevertheless prohibit social creatures from making the connections that can ameliorate stress and anxiety. We strain just to maintain the connections we already have. Mental health and addiction recovery are fundamentally challenged by the need for medical and public health self-care. Face-to-face, in-person contact had been deemed essential to substance disorder recovery. Now adaptations are required.

- With the pandemic has come economic fragility and uncertainty as months of job loss, sharply rising unemployment, loss of pay and financial resources, and growing deficits and debt, as well as ongoing economic stagnation and market instability leave many individuals and families under water (Ingram & Lindborg, 2019; Signé, 2020). Homelessness, evictions, and bankruptcies loom.

  Here again, the business and financial measures required to manage this pandemic aggravate the economic predicament. Consumer and business lockdowns, along with necessary social distancing, have brought an economic downturn that is the catalyst for anxiety and stress on a grand scale, with no signs of abatement. Leaving one's front door has never seemed riskier. This inhibits consumer confidence and activity, and threatens overall financial assurance. How do we calm individuals, businesses, and markets to begin any kind of fiscal recovery, let alone provide social stability for emotional and financial recovery?

- The COVID-19 pandemic came quickly on the heels of a prescription drug, opioid, and fentanyl overdose crisis, which had not yet been sufficiently addressed. This crisis, along with an urgency to confront the prevalence of pain and high-impact chronic pain, was already ravaging many pockets of American society when the pandemic hit (Dahlhamer et al., 2018; Institute of Medicine, 2011). Multiple, simultaneous health and economic crises compounded the perception of societal collapse and depression-era uneasiness. Society-wide stress fed the dis-ease that can promote addiction.

  Both the opioid crisis and the pandemic overmatched society's ability to respond. Both revealed the power of stress-related vulnerabilities. Basic health care delivery remains rife with challenges for the general and underserved populations. Providing addiction care and fostering recovery often relies on outmoded strategies and a paucity of concrete, evidence-based approaches (Institute of Medicine, 2006). The lives of those at greatest risk (racial minorities, the poor, the already sick, and the elderly) reveal systemic deficiencies and failures. "We don't have specific data for substance use disorder patients, but we know that due to their lack of housing, mental issues, isolation and other struggles, they are at higher risk for COVID morbidity and mortality" (Levins, 2020). As more data becomes available, we see an uptick of addiction illness due to COVID concerns (Ehley, 2020). More cases of substance misuse and addiction call for more effective recovery models.

- The combined pandemic, economic, and overdose crises revealed fault lines in our health care systems that were already laboring to cope. While politicians and health care leaders have long touted the excellence of American health care, we are slowly coming to understand that high-end and specialized medical procedures are the forte of U.S. health care for those who can afford it and have access, but the overall system of public health is woefully inadequate (Trust for America's Health, 2020). Health risks and disparities remain stubborn, upstream burdens for many citizens. And it is important to note that COVID-19 poses severe public mental health challenges as well (Campion et al., 2020). The co-occurrence of mental and addictive health problems is a fact of modern life and requires urgent action.

- Select segments of the population have been exposed as living with unacceptable health risks. Persons of color, particularly African American, Hispanic, Native American, and Pacific-Islander citizens, quickly became high-profile victims of the pandemic. Persons with risk profiles include elders, the homeless, health care workers, first responders, and those already struggling with chronic health conditions (advancing age, pulmonary disease, diabetes, obesity).

  It is important to note that social-ecological conditions (e.g., unsafe housing and living conditions, tenuous work circumstances, loss of paid sick leave, loss of child care and access to health care and insurance) intensify the public health risk for vulnerable populations and disconnect them from resources they need to address outbreaks (Centers for Disease Control and Prevention, 2019). Those at highest risk—as well as, for some, their ignorance or resistance to accepted public health strategies (politicizing of mask wearing and social distancing)—are a special challenge (Metzl, 2019; Metzl et al., 2020).

- The inadequacies of current political and governmental systems have been exposed in these turbulent times through the inadequacy of resources and supply chains, scarcity, and lack of coordinated action to relieve the pressures on health care and the economy.

  In this witches' brew, an uprising of racial animosity, prejudice, and a search for justice has found a place. Inflammatory social forces like intolerance, racism, rising authoritarianism, police brutality, and lack of preparation for the difficult work of monitoring social change and challenges all exacerbate the problem. Issues of racial discrimination and policing, crystallized in the Black Lives Matter movement, have come to the fore. Civil unrest and threats of political oppression are roiling the social situation, creating fear and added social polarization. Stigma of "others" runs rampant. These challenges are not going away and inflame social anxieties.

- The manifold dilemmas catalogued above intensify concerns over a preexisting and growing global climate crisis, accelerating a growing public awareness of (and therefore anxiety about) the dimensions of the challenge. Initial reports suggested that COVID-related changes in carbon dioxide levels and the atmosphere might improve with less use of fossil fuels (Crawford, 2020; Green, 2020). However, there is no guarantee that climate change will abate. Reports indicate, for example, that many parts of Arctic Siberia, the vast Russian region that is larger than the entire United States, have been experiencing abnormally high temperatures for several months accompanied by widespread wildfires. Temperatures have reached over 100° Fahrenheit, almost 30 degrees above normal (Georgiou, 2020).

Overall, a kind of oppressive pessimism darkens our national mood. It creates a toxic and anxious environment that can trigger addictive disease. It is difficult to plan or act in its wake. Yet, there are grounds for optimism.

Sustainable Recovery: Challenges and Opportunities

Sustainable progress requires understanding and consensus around all the factors involved in a situation. Our social health and the challenges of addiction require a comprehensive and consilient view that provides a way forward. We need a wider lens.

"According to the evidence compiled by social epidemiology, the most influential determinants of health fall outside what is traditionally thought of as the health sector" (Crammond, 2017).

We are so accustomed to thinking about health and illness in purely medical, biological, or psychological terms that we often skirt or give short shrift to social forces, social determinants, and a role for social justice (Farrer et al., 2015). However, downstream medical and psychiatric outcomes (epidemics, infections, disease, anxiety/depression, psychobehavioral disorders like addictions) can be (at least partially) explained and addressed by upstream social conditions, burdens, and toxic stresses. We need greater awareness, better research, and more effective action regarding the social determinants of health (Marmot & Wilkinson, 2005; WHO Commission on Social Determinants of Health, 2008). Meaningful action regarding social and ecological health factors must be part of a comprehensive approach to overall health, including addiction. Comprehensive and sustainable addiction care must address upstream ecological change.

In a time of multiple and seemingly insurmountable crises, this chapter is a search for understanding as well as discovery of effective and sustainable solutions in addiction recovery during a time of social distancing. There is now considerable evidence linking social conditions to population-based health; paradigmatic social and political change is required to increase effectiveness (Farrer et al., 2015). And we must remember that we still know relatively little about COVID-19 and even less about its intersection with substance use disorders. Addiction-specific strategies must be augmented with public health and wider societal action.

Let's make no mistake. COVID-19 has made substance use, misuse, abuse, and recovery much more challenging (Collins, 2020, a & b). Current increases in toxic stress significantly impact addiction-related factors, namely:

- Support services for individuals and families;
- Difficulty of access to hospital emergency rooms (a major point of contact with recovery resources);
- Difficulty of access to, and funding for, treatment programs;
- Increases in incidents of relapse;
- Loss of face-to-face social connections for recovery and relapse prevention (e.g. methadone and suboxone clinics)

In addition substance use disorders and addiction, whether light, moderate, or severe, present a variety of risks that people bring to encounters with the COVID-19 virus. These risks are pharmacological, structural, and social/ecological (Collins, 2020a).

Drugs (*pharmacology*) affect multiple bodily systems in a negative way (think smoking or vaping, or opioids), weakening pulmonary, respiratory, metabolic, and cardiovascular functions. *Structural* strains are creating havoc. Substance disordered patients are already being dislodged from vital resources, such as screening and treatment, by a tsunami of COVID patients within the healthcare system. Jail and prison systems, where many substance disordered patients are housed, have become hotbeds of COVID as well. And, early release without social supports (safe housing, recovery supports, employment) may be putting at-risk inmates at even greater risk. In addition, lack of health insurance often accompanies those with chronic medical conditions who are also at prime risk for COVID-19.

Social-ecologically, it is important to note that stigmatized individuals, like those struggling with substance disorders and addiction, often delay help-seeking and in a competitive scramble for limited medical resources may be left behind or excluded altogether. Nevertheless, there are some opportunities revealed by the pandemic, even in the. substance disorder arena.

First Steps

Perhaps the most important first step in our present situation is simply to acknowledge the complex and toxic social ecology that affects those predisposed toward mental health and addictive problems. Appreciation of the social context and environment surrounding those struggling can lead to several outcomes.

At the individual and one-on-one treatment level, empathy and flexibility are required therapeutic attitudes. Compassion needs to be informed by realistic appraisals of dangers and risks. As a society, awareness of the problem is also a first step, along with acceptance of the toxic predicament that encompasses those who struggle toward recovery. However, as individuals and as a society, we shy away from accepting our current social-ecological dilemma. We deny or rationalize hard truths. The entire country is living in a time of heightened anxiety; we are all fellow travelers in an uncertain and perilous venture. This can be good news! Normalizing the status quo can establish a sense of shared safety and common effort. Indeed, we are all in this together. Standing together with one another can be a powerful supporting intervention.

At the beginning of the pandemic, many experts feared that precautions like quarantines and lockdowns, combined with economic instability and social anxiety, would aggravate the addiction crisis. "Necessary coronavirus containment measures, like physical distancing and closures of public spaces, are making it harder for people with substance use disorders to seek help, keep up their treatment regimen, or access social supports" (Arsenault, 2020). Addiction thrives in an atmosphere of isolation, stigma, and heightened stress. A present-day 11% year-to-year increase in drug-related fatalities confirms these fears (Ehley, 2020). At the same time, a "whole-government approach" to the pandemic has put addiction research and development, treatment, and exploration of racial disparities on hold, even though overdose and death rates jumped among minority groups (Ehley, 2020). COVID-19 forced us to look away from other priorities and competing needs. But we can reorient our attention.

Addiction recovery is an arduous journey of personal reform and reintegration. No one is free of adversity; the ubiquity of trauma (individual, social, societal) is a fact of life, particularly in the current situation. But this truth can also be good news. Vulnerable and struggling people do not need to stand alone or isolated. Where do recovery seekers turn for assistance and support?

At this critical time, patients and providers must access resources of emotional regulation so that calm and determination can be brought to bear. Skills such as awareness, balanced living, mindfulness, regular nutrition and exercise, prayer, yoga, and many others are essential. These can help to buffer the stress response and provide a kind of tranquil resolve. A regular regimen of recovery activities (group meetings, reading, accessing sponsors, and so forth) is also needed. But these can be difficult to maintain in a time of crisis. Communal encouragement and support are essential.

At first blush, we can see how COVID-19 might have been a daunting hurdle for addiction treatment. Providers and systems could have been frozen in place, repeating the same old solutions and stuck in tried and true (but inadequate) approaches. It appears, however, that something different occurred.

Positive Signs

Adversity became the catalyst for seeking novel and sustainable solutions. COVID-19 and connected challenges brought specific opportunities. And some addiction treatment providers seized the moment. In *Addiction, Attachment, Trauma, and Recovery,* I argued for a number of changes that were needed in addiction treatment:

- Empowerment of a growing public recovery movement that facilitates a sense of community and connectedness, replacing stigma with hope and strategic action
- Greater appreciation of continuing care and recovery management models of treatment (versus outdated acute care) to aid in extending recovery into regular living and lifestyle
- Implementation of recovery-oriented systems of care, that is, an array of professional, nonprofessional, and volunteer networked services and relationships supporting long-term recovery for a wider group of seekers
- Complementing narrow drug-centric outcomes (abstinence, moderation, harm reduction) with concerns for overall wellness and community participation, reimagining recovery as a more fulfilling lifestyle
- Revisioning of the treatment-community relationship and positioning of professionally facilitated and specialty treatment providers and structures, such as drug courts and transformed police departments, within broader health care and communities of wellness
- Acceptance of alternative means of initiating and maintaining recovery, including medication-assisted recovery models (methadone, suboxone) as well as widespread recovery coaching
- Integration of the recovery capital revolution into traditional treatment (Morgan, 2019)

Paradigmatic changes were already beginning in recovery science. These have been expanded and further integrated.

Further Changes

Interviews and conversations with addiction treatment providers, along with other anecdotal evidence, suggest that the treatment community is adapting remarkably well.

First, Alcoholics Anonymous and other 12-step recovery support groups, such as Al-Anon, Cocaine, Narcotics, and Co-dependents Anonymous moved quickly to providing virtual services and meetings online. Other support groups (LifeRing Secular Recovery, SMART Recovery, and YPR (Young People in Recovery) also took up the challenge. All these groups provide rich social contexts for seeking support, regulating anxiety, and buffering impulsivity. Recovering people themselves organized new ways to meet their needs. They adapted services to include virtual and other distance resources. They remained connected while distancing physically.

Second, the internet developed a number of online tools (virtual meetings, online search engines, help lines, and treatment practice guidelines) for recovering people, providers, and others needing help. These resources, along with other essential sober spaces (outdoor clubhouse and advocacy activities), need to be celebrated and expanded; they are ideally positioned toward the future for the likely resurgence in addiction we will see over time. Recovery from COVID and financial traumas is likely to be slow. Treatment providers will need to incorporate remote case management services and help steer patients to complementary virtual resources.

Third, we know that alcohol misuse, drug use, relapse, and suicide tend to increase in times of economic recession, unemployment, and psychological distress. Additional forms of addictive substitution, such as compulsive behaviors or destructive attachments, are available as well. Other risks for increased drug use and addiction include physical distancing (without commensurate social connections), family quarantining with potential abusers and increased childhood trauma, spousal abuse, boredom, and extended screen use (computers, smart phones, etc.). We need creative thinking and reimagining of substance use and addictive services that will endure.

Fourth, we know that individuals with substance misuse and addiction risks—particularly those who smoke nicotine or marijuana, use methamphetamines or opioids, or vape—face risks to their respiratory, pulmonary, and cardiovascular systems. They also face discrimination and stigma without adequate access to medications or treatment. Social and financial support can be wanting, and the longer-lasting effects of COVID-19 are unknown at present.

Fifth, we need new follow-up services for those in posttreatment and early recovery in order to prevent relapse and promote timely reintervention when needed. We also need robust community-based awareness and effort to institute psychological supports for the unemployed, for families, for the addicted, and for their children.

Sustainable Changes

System reforms addressed in *Addiction, Attachment, Trauma and Recovery* (Morgan, 2019) must be implemented and extended. Recovery services must continue their transformation from a model of acute care to a focus on recovery management and continuing care (White et al., 2003).

A number of traditional recovery and treatment settings have undergone significant structural change. Others can learn from their experiences. Attempting to meet recovering patients where they are fostered a reimagining of how addiction services are offered and enhanced. Online and telehealth service provision has become essential. Whether through video or telephone sessions with counselors, or working in virtual group settings, those seeking addiction treatment and recovery now have new menus of virtual services to access. Treatment centers and providers are finding that these changes open up access to new and expanded populations, a good indicator of future sustainability.

These changes required a host of adaptations by providers. Untethering counseling and support services from clinical offices, learning to work from home, reconfiguring basic protocols, adapting reimbursement and insurance protocols and forms, even clarifying issues of leadership and supervision became essential. One large health system realized that its residential and outpatient addiction centers and services were awkwardly organized under a reporting line for hospitals, but with a little effort realigned all its mental health and addiction services under different leadership and reporting relationships that now include psychology services, medication assistance, and outpatient treatment; a better fit. Mental health and addiction services joined forces, adding relevant medication services and addressing pain as well. Realignment and streamlining proved to be efficacious.

Further to Go

One way to move forward flexibly is to allow multiple crises to stimulate insight and understanding of the societal changes we need. Take the problem of substance use and addictive disorders. For decades, the best antidrug measures available were utilized but with limited success: law enforcement, drug interdiction and eradication, drug awareness education, prevention, treatment, and family and individual recovery programs. The successes are worth celebrating, but they are insufficient. More of the same will not provide greater benefits, especially in the current situation.

To complement rational drug policies and prevention, we need to reboot and reimagine societal change and restructure the ways in which we live. We must confront our upstream vulnerabilities. COVID has revealed our social inequalities, economic fragility, health disparities, and divisions in our attitudes toward one another. This is not a sustainable course. Significant transformation and leadership are required.

We must embark on an even more ambitious journey, creating a society in which all human beings are valued, not commoditized; where compassion and creating genuine community guide our choices; where each person can belong and make a contribution. We need to reimagine ourselves as a human community of "radical kinship" (Boyle, 2011). All those suffering must become part of a "circle of compassion from which no one is excluded" (Boyle, 2011; Szalavitz & Perry, 2011), in a society in which all persons are treated as kin rather than other. For now, try to imagine such a society, and how we and so many of our troubles would be held by an inclusive community of care and compassion. But be careful. Such a vision can be intoxicating. Nothing less than a full transformation of human society will do.

References

Alexander, B.K. (2008/2011). *The globalization of addiction: A study in poverty of spirit.* New York: Oxford University Press.

Anda, R. F., Felitti, V. J., Bremner, J. Walker, J. D., Whitfield, C., Perry, B. D., Dube, S. R., & Giles, W. H. (2006). The enduring effects of abuse and related adverse experiences in childhood: A convergence of evidence from neurobiology and epidemiology. *European Archives of Psychiatry and Clinical Neuroscience,* 256(3), 174–186.

Arsenault, S. (2020, March 26). Why COVID-19 is a perfect storm in the addiction world. *Shatterproof. https://www.shatterproof.org/blog/why-covid-19-perfect-storm -addiction-world.*

Boyle, G. (2011). *Tattoos on the heart: The power of boundless compassion.* New York: Free Press.

Bremner, J. D. (2002). *Does stress damage the brain? Understanding trauma-related disorders from a mind-body perspective.* New York: Norton.

Campion, J., Javed, A., Sartorius, N., & Marmot, M. (2020, June 9). Addressing the public mental health challenge of COVID-19. *Lancet Psychiatry,* 7(8), 657–659. *https://doi.org/10.1016/S2215-0366(20)30240-6*

Centers for Disease Control and Prevention. (2019). COVID-19 in racial and ethnic minority groups. National Center for Immunization and Respiratory Diseases, Division of Viral Diseases. *https://www.cdc.gov/coronavirus/2019-ncov/ community/health-equity/race-ethnicity.html https://www.cdc.gov/coronavirus/2019-ncov/ need-extra-precautions/racial-ethnic-minorities.html*

Collins, F. (2020, August 11a). Addressing the twin challenges of substance use disorder and COVID-19. NIH Director's Blog. National Institutes of Health. Directorsblog.nih.gov

Collins, F. (2020, August 21b). Coping with the collision of puslic health crises: COVID-19 and substance use disorders. NIH Director's Blog. National Institutes of Health. Directorsblog.nih.gov

Cozolino, L. (2010). *The neuroscience of psychotherapy: Healing the social brain* (2nd ed.). New York: Norton.

Crammond, B. R., & Carey, G. (2017). Policy change for the social determinants of health: The strange irrelevance of social epidemiology. *Evidence and Policy: A Journal of Research, Debate and Practice,* 13(2), 365–374.

Crawford, V. (2020, March 31). How COVID-19 might help us win the fight against climate change. World Economic Forum. *https://www.weforum.org/agenda/2020/03/ covid-19-climate-change/*

Dahlhamer, J., Lucas, J., Zelaya, C., Nahin, R., Mackey, S., DeBar, L., Kerns, R., Von Korff, M., Porter, L., & Helmick, C. (2018). Prevalence of chronic pain and high-impact chronic pain among adults—United States, 2016. *Morbidity and Mortality Weekly Report,* 67(36), 1001–1006. doi:*http://dx.doi.org/10.15585/mmwr .mm6736a2.*

Ehley, B. (2020, June 29). Pandemic unleashes a spike in overdose deaths. *Politico. https://www.politico.com/news/2020/06/29/pandemic-unleashes-a-spike-in-overdose -deaths-345183*

Farrer, L., Marinetti, C., Cavaco, Y. K., & Costongs, C. (2015). Advocacy for health equity: A synthesis review. *Milbank Quarterly,* 93(2), 392–437.

Georgiou, A. (2020, June 26). Siberia is on fire with Arctic temperatures reaching 100 degrees: Why? *Newsweek*. *https://www.newsweek.com/siberia-fire-arctic -temperatures-1513721*

Graham, C., Pinto, S., & Juneau, J. (2017, July 24). The geography of desperation in America. Brookings Institution. *https://www.brookings.edu/research/the-geography -of-desperation-in-america/*

Green, M. (2020, May 7). Could Covid-19 mark a "turning point" in the climate crisis? World Economic Forum. *https://www.weforum.org/agenda/2020/05/green-recovery -can-revive-virus-hit-economies-and-tackle-climate-change-study-says/*

Hambrick, E. P., Brawner, T. P., Perry, B. D., Brandt, K., Hofmeister, C., & Collins, J. O. (2019). Beyond the ACE score: Examining relationships between timing of developmental adversity, relational health and developmental outcomes in children. *Archives of Psychiatric Nursing*, *33*(3), 238–247.

Ingram, G., & Lindborg, N. (2019, July 25). *Implementing a fragility strategy*. Washington, DC: Brookings Institution.

Institute of Medicine. (2006). *Improving the quality of health care for mental and substance-use conditions* [Quality Chasm Series]. Washington, DC: National Academies Press.

Institute of Medicine. (2011). *Relieving pain in America: A blueprint for transforming prevention, care, education, and research*. Committee on Advancing Pain Research, Care, and Education. Washington, DC: National Academies Press.

Iton, A. (2005). Tackling the root causes of health disparities through community capacity building. In R. Hofrichter & R. Bhatia (Eds.), *Tackling health inequities through public health practice* (pp. 95–115). New York: Oxford University Press.

Koob, G. F., & Volkow, N. D. (2016). Neurobiology of addiction: A neurocircuitry analysis. *Lancet Psychiatry*, *3*(8), 760–773.

Levins, H. (2020, May). COVID-19 meets the opioid crisis, creating disruptions and opportunities. Leonard Davis Institute of Health Economics. *https://ldi.upenn .edu/news/covid-19-meets-opioid-crisis-creating-disruptions-and-opportunities*

Magruder, K., Kassam-Adams, N., Thoresen, S., & Olff, M. (2016). Prevention and public health approaches to trauma and traumatic stress: A rationale and call to action. *European Journal of Traumatology*, *7*(10), 3402. *https://doi.org/10.3402/ ejpt.v7.29715*

Marmot, M., & Wilkinson, R. (Eds.). (2005). *Social determinants of health*. New York: Oxford University Press.

Metzl, J. M. (2019). *Dying of whiteness: How the politics of racial resentment is killing America's heartland*. New York: Basic Books.

Metzl, J. M., Maybank, A., & DeMaio, F. (2020, June 4). Responding to the COVID-19 pandemic: The need for a structurally competent health care system. *Journal of the American Medical Association*, *324*(3), 231–232. doi:10.1001/ jama.2020.9289

Morgan, O. J. (2019). *Addiction, attachment, trauma, and recovery: The power of connection.* New York: Norton.

Najavits, L. M. (2007). Seeking safety: An evidence-based model for substance abuse and trauma/PTSD. In K. A. Witkiewitz & G. A. Marlatt (Eds.), *Therapist's guide to evidence based relapse prevention: Practical resources for the mental health professional* (pp. 141–167). San Diego, CA: Elsevier.

Ouimette, P., & Brown, P. J. (Eds.). (2003). *Trauma and substance abuse: Causes, consequences, and treatment of comorbid disorders.* Washington, DC: American Psychological Association.

Papenfuss, M. (2020, June 22). COVID-19 will rage "like a forest fire" in unprepared America, top doc warns. *Huffington Post.* https://www.huffpost.com/entry/michael-osterholm-covid-19-forest-fire_n_5ef02d05c5b60f58759876e7

Perry, B. D. (2002). Childhood experience and the expression of genetic potential: What childhood neglect tells us about nature and nurture. *Brain and Mind, 3*(1), 79–100.

Perry, B. D. (2006). The Neurosequential Model of Therapeutics: Applying principles of neuroscience to clinical work with traumatized and maltreated children In N. B. Webb (Ed.), *Working with traumatized youth in child welfare* (pp. 27–52). New York: Guilford.

Perry, B. D. (2009). Examining child maltreatment through a neurodevelopmental lens: Clinical applications of the neurosequential model of therapeutics. *Journal of Loss and Trauma, 14*(4), 240–255. doi:10.1080/15325020903004350

Signé, L. (2020, April 21). *A new approach is needed to defeat COVID-19 and fix fragile states.* Washington, DC: Brookings Institution:

Szalavitz, M. & Perry, B.B. (2011). *Born for love: Why empathy is essential and endangered.* New York: William Morrow.

Trust for America's Health. (2020, May 5). What we are learning from COVID-19 about being prepared for a public health emergency. Washington, DC: Trust for America's Health. https://www.tfah.org/wp-content/uploads/2020/05/TFAH2020CovidResponseBriefFnl.pdf

Ungar, M., & Perry, B. D. (2012). Violence, trauma and resilience. In R. Alaggia & C. Vine (Ed.), *Cruel but not unusual: Violence in Canadian families* (2nd ed.). Waterloo, ON: Wilfrid Laurier University Press.

Volkow, N. D., Koob, G. F., & McLellan, A. T. (2016). Neurobiologic advances from the brain disease model of addiction. *New England Journal of Medicine, 374*(4), 363–371.

White, W., Boyle, M., & Loveland, D. (2003). Behavioral health recovery management: Transcending the limitations of addiction treatment. *Health Management, 23*(3), 38–44.

WHO Commission on Social Determinants of Health. (2008). *Closing the gap in a generation: Health equity through action on the social determinants of health: Commission on Social Determinants of Health final report.* Geneva: World Health Organization.

11

Birds of a Feather

The Importance of Interpersonal
Synchrony in Psychotherapy

Terry Marks-Tarlow

*At the heart of the universe is a steady, insistent beat: the sound of cycles
in sync. It pervades nature at every scale from the nucleus to the cosmos.*
STEVEN STROGATZ

THE TROPE "BIRDS OF A FEATHER FLOCK TOGETHER," FIRST APPEARING IN
the 16th century, alludes to how people of similar culture, interests, backgrounds, and ideas tend to congregate and that we humans are not alone
in such impulses. Birds also congregate in flocks, while other animals live
in herds, packs, swarms, caravans, or colonies, plus a host of other social
groupings. Like-minded creatures not only live together but also move to
the beat of a similar drum. While this is an old observation, our understanding of underlying neurobiological mechanisms is relatively new. Only
during the past several decades has a complexity approach to nonlinear
science identified how spontaneous, coordinated order emerges, often from
underlying chaos.

This chapter explores the concept of interpersonal synchrony, the idea that
synchronized dynamics reside at the heart of emergent human order. Synchrony, or sync for short, refers to order in time, which at its simplest means
things happening at the same time, or simultaneity (see Vrobel et al., 2008).
In his classic book *Sync*, mathematician Steven Strogatz (2008) suggests that
when events are only briefly synchronized, this is probably a coincidence, as
when your windshield wipers briefly align to the music of your car radio. By

contrast, if coordinated activity persists over an extended period, this is likely no accident. Such synchronized tendencies are easy to spot within the arts, as humans from all cultures move to the same beat through dance, song, and various forms of music making. From shared culture, to coordinated behavior, to synchronized autonomic nervous system fluctuations and coupled neural oscillations, we humans demonstrate an extraordinary degree of sync with one another. Whether in people or other animals, the very foundation for a social brain involves synchronized dynamics.

The pages to follow highlight the significance of interpersonal synchrony for psychotherapy. I examine the importance of synchronized timing from macro levels of shared belief, rituals, language, and culture to micro levels of coupled physiology, posture, facial expressions, body movements, and neural dynamics. I address how synchrony during therapy often operates below conscious levels to coordinate unconscious aspects of being. My primary thesis is that interpersonal synchrony between therapist and patient is the primary mechanism by which clinical intuition operates, in both ordinary and extraordinary ways.

The chapter begins with brief examples of sync in nature, including bottom-up models for understanding the emergence of coordinated dynamics. Next, I explore the importance of interpersonal synchrony for secure attachment during early development. I then provide evidence for synchronized physiology within psychotherapy. I introduce Koole and Tschacher's (2016) model of interpersonal synchrony as a pan-theoretical foundation for the therapeutic alliance. I offer a clinical case to demonstrate how subcortical levels of synchrony open possibilities for unconscious information sharing, resulting at times in uncanny knowing. The final section speculates about implications of interpersonal synchrony for teletherapy, now widespread during the coronavirus pandemic and mandate to shelter in place.

Sync Through Self-Organization

Have you ever sat outside on a summer night to listen to Nature's music as a group of crickets chirp all in unison? Have you snorkeled underwater and witnessed Nature's dance as a huge school of fish glides simultaneously in one direction, only to change course suddenly? In early springtime, have you noticed that trees and bushes growing near one another tend to blossom on the very same day? Or perhaps you have lived among a collection of women who wind up with coordinated menstrual flows.

Each of these phenomena is evidence of synchrony or sync in nature; each takes place without the direction of an external guiding hand. Each involves coupled dynamics, which means that some physical, chemical, emotional, or other informational exchange exists, allowing for mutual influence among the constituents. In the words of Strogatz (2008, p. 2):

> Fireflies communicate with light. Planets tug on one another with gravity. Heart cells pass electrical currents back and forth. As these examples suggest, nature uses every available channel to allow its oscillators to talk to one another. And the result of those conversations is often synchrony, in which all the oscillators begin to move as one.

So too in psychotherapy, where results of emotional exchanges and non-verbal signals, plus verbal conversations, bring the therapist-patient dyad into multiple levels of sync. In each example above, the underlying constituents differ hugely, yet the coordinated dynamics do not. This holds true whether or not the dynamics arise from purely inert underpinnings or from complex life forms.

An early observation of synchrony was recorded during the 17th century by Dutch scientist Christiaan Huygens, who noticed that two pendulum clocks hanging on the same wall eventually beat in unison. Huygens speculated that unity was achieved through physical vibrations traveling through the shared wall. The presence of shared vibrations may explain simple mechanical processes, but what about living creatures—how does a flock of birds manage to soar as a single entity? The answer waited hundreds of years, becoming accessible only with the advent of high-speed computer simulations within the multidisciplinary field of complexity science.

In 1982 a program called Flock of Boids was developed by Craig Reynolds to represent one early success in the nascent field of complexity science. In order to simulate the complex, collective behavior of a real flock, Reynolds needed only three simple rules, or algorithms, to guide each bird's interactions: (1) cohesion (each bird tries to stay close to its neighbors), (2) alignment (each bird orients based on the direction of immediate neighbors), and (3) separation (each bird maintains an ideal distance and avoids crowding). The self-organized complexity that emerges from these three simple principles is extraordinary. Not only do the rules account for unified flight, but they also enable the flock to separate and later rejoin to work around obstacles in its path.

Flock of Boids is only one among a host of other computer models revealing self-organization in Nature—how complex order emerges globally, unpredictably, and spontaneously from a few simple interaction rules applied locally to a group of similar agents. In all such computer models, complexity is emergent, arising through bottom-up processes. This same general principle of bottom-up self-organization applies to the human mind/body/brain as a unified system. Within humans, emergent self-organization works through nested time scales that operate simultaneously at multiple levels of development: how the genetic code gets implemented from a simple set of underlying nucleotides; how cell differentiation occurs in the zygote; how various organ systems emerge and begin to coordinate in the developing fetus; how hormones and neurotransmitters get released into the brain and bloodstream throughout life; and how the autonomic nervous system regulates emotional arousal while interacting with others.

Not only does bottom-up self-organization coordinate how a single mind/body/brain develops and functions throughout life, but it also guides how one brain/body/mind interfaces and coordinates with other brain/body/minds. In each case, cycles become structurally and/or functionally coupled to mutually influence one another, resulting in spontaneous, emergent order in the form of self-organized, coordinated dynamics.

Top-Down Versus Bottom-Up Processing

Advanced computation was necessary to simulate the emergence of complex order from simple bases, yet there may be another reason why complexity science was late to appear in the Western history of human understanding. Science as an enterprise favors top-down (head to body) rather than bottom-up (body to head) information processing. The scientific method is a rational affair beginning with a hypothesis that is then systematically tested using objective measures.

With respect to psychotherapy, I have previously described top-down processing as follows (Marks-Tarlow, 2012, pp. 8–9):

> When we process clinical material in "top-down" fashion, abstract concepts represent a "higher" level than concrete details supplied by minute-to-minute emotional and sensory data. During top-down processing, we do not look with open minds; we look instead to confirm our starting assumptions and presumptions in reductionist fashion. I might approach

clinical work with a fixed idea about the meaning of certain symptoms. Perhaps every time I encounter the following cluster within a patient— hypervigilance toward others, enhanced startle reactions, intense preoc- cupation with whatever could go wrong—I assume that somewhere in the past history of my patient's life there exists a traumatic life event. Next I am likely to "look for" the source of trauma in my patient by probing for a specific event. If I fail to find what I am looking for, I may persist in my conviction anyway. I might assume my patient has repressed a troubling memory. While this theory is reasonable, it precludes other possibilities just as likely, if not more. Rather than indicating one big trauma, the same symptoms often arise out of relational trauma (Schore, 2001) borne of a myriad of tiny emotional misattunements, often extending back to early infancy. Another alternative is that these symptoms indicate second- generation posttraumatic stress inherited through social channels.

At its inception, psychotherapy began as a set of top-down operations, perhaps because Freud's practice began in 1886 within the Western medi- cal model of Victorian Vienna. The Western medical model is both linear and reductive, involving a stepwise progression from diagnosis through prescription to treatment. Once Freud hit upon the idea of aligning clinical practice with the Oedipus myth, early psychoanalysts became equipped with a single developmental theory as the foundation for implementing treatment. All children were understood to pass through the same psy- chosexual stages of Oedipal development. For boys, murderous impulses to kill one's father accompanied fantasies of copulating with and marry- ing one's mother. With these violent and incestuous impulses considered forbidden, they became repressed within the unconscious mind, where pathological symptoms originated. The job of the analyst was to treat the resulting neuroses through top-down, verbal interpretations designed to render the unconscious conscious.

As psychoanalysis has progressed over the past 100 years, it has evolved on multiple fronts. It has moved from a one-person, intrapsychic stance to a two-person, relational perspective. A one-person stance is hierarchical: psychotherapists sit much like medical doctors as authorities outside the subjectivity of patients. From this bird's-eye view, they are poised to objectively observe and interpret truths about their patients' inner lives. By contrast, a two-person perspective is more egalitarian: psy- chotherapists sit as equal partners inside their own subjective experience.

By attending to all that arises, both verbally and nonverbally, meaning is cocreated and spontaneously emergent in light of the subjective experience of both participants.

This shift toward fully relational approaches within contemporary psychoanalysis also corresponds to a shift from linear to nonlinear approaches (Marks-Tarlow, 2008, 2011, 2015). Within contemporary open-ended, growth-oriented psychotherapy, stages of psychotherapy are neither stepwise, culturally universal, nor clearly delineated. Within highly complex trauma cases, diagnosis is often the outcome of treatment rather than its starting point. Meanwhile, the treatment itself is not implemented from outside the therapeutic dyad but instead emerges from increasingly coordinated dynamics between therapist and patient.

Changes from objective to intersubjective methods and from linear to nonlinear approaches coincide with shifts in technique from top-down to bottom-up processing. Rather than starting treatment with preestablished notions that are systematically or universally applied, the relational psychotherapist begins with moment-to-moment perceptions, sensations, emotions, images, and thoughts processed in bottom-up fashion, which allows higher-order understanding, meaning, and change to emerge spontaneously and mutually out of the present context.

In contemporary practice, top-down approaches remain popular within short-term, symptom-reducing psychotherapy. One example is the cognitive-behavioral model, often considered the gold standard of psychotherapy because it is empirically validated plus packaged and implemented systematically and predictably. This satisfies a host of third-party parties and payers. Yet from the standpoint of interpersonal neurobiology, many top-down assumptions are incorrect, including its central assumption that thought regulates emotion. Thought can regulate emotions at times, primarily in individuals with secure attachment and strong self-regulating capacities.

For thought to regulate emotion, limbic system connectivity must be strong from higher, cortical areas to lower, subcortical structures, while levels of emotional arousal cannot be too high (Schore, 2012). Yet these conditions do not hold for most trauma cases. Either people have backgrounds of insecure attachment or autonomic arousal is too high, or both. Whatever the cause, when emotion is highly dysregulated, thought cannot regulate emotion, because under these conditions everyone "flips their lids," as Daniel Siegel likes to say, as prefrontal areas of the cerebral cortex responsible for executive functioning (rational decision making, sound judgment) go offline. And when this occurs, the primary way to calm down involves inter-active, not auto, regulation, through attuned, empathic relationships.

Clinical Intuition Involves Bottom-Up Processing

In contrast to left brain, top-down methods of psychotherapy, bottom-up approaches work differently. In place of fixed, prefabricated techniques, clinical intuition is highlighted within open-ended psychoanalysis and other bottom-up methods (Marks-Tarlow, 2012, 2014a, 2014b). Each ses-sion begins by putting aside higher-order processes of memory, plans, and expectations. The idea is to achieve a present-centered stance with soft eyes, a broad focus, and open attention. This facilitates attunement to what the patient is feeling, sensing, imagining, and thinking while simultaneously attending to feelings, perceptions, images, and thoughts evoked in response within the therapist. In this way, intuition serves as the embodied founda-tion for clinical perception and response.

My previous writings highlight the importance of clinical intuition as a set of bottom-up processes, unique to each clinician, that fill the gap between clinical theory and practice within moment-to-moment perception and response. Some therapists feel their way into patients primarily through their bodies, as gut feelings. They may feel this as a tightening up or loosen-ing of their stomachs in various conditions of danger or safety. Other ther-apists receive hunches in the form of words. But here, the thought arrives in whole form, from an unknown source, beyond conscious formulation. Others receive information as flashes. A visual picture or image in the form of another sense arises spontaneously in the therapist's imagination. I have heard of therapists using smell (think of "smelling danger") and have even written about one colleague, also a musician, whose clinical intuition arrives in the form of musical snatches—ominous refrains for emotional danger, minor chords for sadness, upbeat melodies for joyous moments (Marks-Tarlow, 2012). Clinicians differ in precisely which intuitive channels they use at precisely which moment to receive clinical information. I suspect that different patients inspire different openings at different times. Yet all of these intuitive channels involve bottom-up processing in service of con-veying understanding, empathy, and guidance to patients, all of which rep-resents the art of psychotherapy. This chapter expands upon my previous writings on clinical intuition by suggesting that moment-to-moment attune-ment to self and other is made possible by synchronized timing. Before exploring the role of sync within psychotherapy, let us examine the role of sync within healthy development.

Foundations of Attunement

From the beginning of life, we humans are deeply wired to be interconnected with each other via body, brain, and psyche. During gestation this is obvious, since the fetus begins life tethered to the organs and brain of the mother through the placenta, such that coupled physiology provides a bath of nutrients, hormones, and neuropeptides. Yet coupled physiological processes extend well beyond pregnancy. Mothers and other caregivers must coordinate their own cycles to work with the sleep, hunger, and arousal rhythms of babies to provide proper care. This is little wonder, since virtually all mammals, including humans, are herd animals with social minds, bodies, and brains that have evolved to care for the young while living in "tribes," as Louis Cozolino (2002, 2017) likes to say, for comfort and safety. Until recently, the degree to which humans remain deeply interconnected throughout life has been partly obscured by Western individualistic biases that privilege autonomy over connection, a trend being counteracted by research within the burgeoning field of interpersonal neurobiology.

To understand the role of synchronized physiology, action, and being in early childhood, consider the research of Ruth Feldman and colleagues (2011). Three-month-old infants and their mothers were examined. Cardiac output was collected in both mother and baby during face-to-face interactions that were videotaped and microanalyzed. Episodes of mutual gaze, affect, and vocal synchrony were noted and recorded. Results indicated strong evidence for sync, which emerged within the concordance of mother and infant biological rhythms. The lab found that when mother and child are synchronized in affect and vocalization, then their heart rhythms also synchronize; by contrast, when affect and vocalization are nonsynchronous, so too is heart rate. Feldman's research points to the mutual openness of the autonomic nervous system to social influences.

Feldman et al.'s (2011) findings build on the research of others who identified three main channels of nonverbal synchrony within mother-child interactions. Kaye and Fogel (1980) examined how gaze synchrony enhances social relatedness and cognitive growth. Cohn and Tronick (1988) researched the role of affect synchrony in the development of self-regulatory capacities in children. Jaffe and colleagues (2001) identified how vocal synchrony between parent and child during what Trevarthen (1989) dubbed the earliest "proto-conversations" builds language skills, while resulting in attachment security. These studies, among a host of more contemporary others (e.g., Atzil & Gendron, 2017; Nguyen et al., 2020), point to the importance of biobehavioral synchrony during development.

Given extensive research indicating synchronized timing between mother (or other primary caregiver) and child, perhaps it is no surprise that the very language of attuned response points toward coordinated timing, especially critical during the earliest years to build secure attachment. Allan Schore (e.g., 2005, 2012) has written extensively about the centrality of mother-child attunement for healthy right brain development during the first two years of life, which provides a solid foundation for subsequent left brain development. In the beginning of baby's life, attuned response is completely nonverbal; even if mother uses words, baby understands only the emotional melody and not the content. Attuned response involves downregulating negative emotions and high-intensity arousal while upregulating positive emotions and low states of arousal. To soothe distressed babies, primary caregivers rhythmically rock, pat, and stroke them, while utilizing musical tones of voice, including bursting into spontaneous song and lullabies, especially when wishing to induce sleep. During periods when baby is calm and emotionally available, primary caregivers instinctively use play to stimulate positive states of joy and excitement through rhythmic tickling and turn taking, using games like peek-a-boo, while attending to baby's natural cycles of social engagement and availability versus needs for disengagement and rest.

Here is how Allan Schore describes these early interactions:

> In recent writings I have contended that attachment theory is, in essence, a regulatory theory. More specifically, in such attachment transactions the secure mother, at an intuitive, nonconscious level, is continuously regulating the baby's shifting arousal levels and therefore emotional states. Emotions are the highest order direct expression of bioregulation in complex organisms (Damasio, 1998), and attachment can thus be defined as the dyadic regulation of emotion (Sroufe, 1996). As a result of being exposed to the primary caregiver's regulatory capacities, the infant's expanding adaptive ability to evaluate on a moment-to-moment basis stressful changes in the external environment, especially the social environment, allows him or her to begin to form coherent responses to

cope with stressors. It is important to note that not just painful experiences but novel events are stressors. This means that the capacity to orient towards not only the familiar but to approach, tolerate, and incorporate novelty is fundamental to the expansion of a developing system's adaptive capacity to learn new information and, therefore, to move towards more complexity. (2001, p. 14)

Around three months old, during Trevarthen's period of primary intersubjectivity, babies move from a more body-based, somatic sense of self to increasingly social stages of engagement. Subcortical limbic connectivity shifts from activation only at the deepest level of the amygdala to include the middle level of the anterior cingulate (see Schore, 2012). As this occurs, attachment structures are starting to come online to establish more extensive feedback loops between mother and child. Attachment to mother (or other primary caregiver) at this stage is often accompanied by rejection of others, or stranger anxiety. During this period, baby gazes intently into mother's eyes to "find" herself there. The proto-identity of "me" is the baby's experience of herself as reflected in the eyes, emotional responses, and bodily reactions of mother and other primary caregivers.

These relational circuits involve coupled dynamics that function as positive feedback loops to amplify positive emotion, joy, and the exuberance of simply being together while exploring one another's contours. Every time baby finds herself in the glint of her mother's eye, a big squirt of dopamine is the reward, priming the seeking circuit, the granddaddy of all motivational systems (Panksepp, 1998). The hormone oxytocin is also released as trust and intimacy build. Babies' universal urges to seek themselves within the eyes of others set them up for the implicit, emotional feel of synchronized dynamics. In this way, babies establish inner identity while internalizing outer relationships, rules, and roles.

During these early intersubjective encounters, if the infant encounters the eyes, face, and body of a mother who is attuned and filled with love, admiration, and understanding, who can respond with sensitivity to her changing feelings and needs, then baby's proto-identity or nascent sense of "me" will be filled with feelings of goodness, warmth, continuity, and self-worth. By contrast, if the eyes, face, and body of a misattuned mother instead are filled with fear, resentment, or hate, then baby's proto-identity becomes wracked with fear, pain, and isolation, eventuating in shame or feelings of badness or unworthiness. Worst of all, if mother's eyes, face, and body are vacant and completely unresponsive, then baby's proto-identity will run the risk of turning up empty, which can lead later to shattered identity, fragmented perceptions, and/or dissociated emotions, what Philip Bromberg (2006, 2011) calls "not-me" states.

The importance of interpersonal synchrony cannot be underestimated during early development. Indeed, even a short delay in caregiver responses can be perceived as noncontingent by baby and becomes highly disruptive to these synchronized dynamics if repetitively encountered. Because caregiver-child interactions during the first years of life are primarily nonverbal and somatically based, their effectiveness relies on coordinated timing much more precisely than during later stages of development, when verbal exchanges can more easily bridge gaps in time. Yet even in these subsequent years, when left brain processes obscure the importance of timing, synchronized dynamics persist well beyond early stages.

Independent scholar Ellen Dissayanake (2017) speculates that the very origin of the arts themselves, in all their variegated forms, derives evolutionarily from the coordinated exchanges of mother-child interactions. Consider the abstract to an article in the *American Journal of Play*:

> The author considers the biological basis of the arts in human evolution, which she holds to be grounded in ethology and interpersonal neurobiology. In the arts, she argues, ordinary reality becomes extraordinary by attention-getting, emotionally salient devices that also appear in ritualized animal behaviors, many kinds of play, and the playful interactions of human mothers with their infants. She hypothesizes that these interactions evolved in humans as a behavioral adaptation to a reduced gestation period, promoting emotional bonding between human mothers and their especially helpless infants. She notes that the secretion of opioids, including oxytocin, that accompany birth, lactation, and care giving in all mammals is amplified in human mothers by these devices, producing feelings of intimacy and trust that engender better child care. The same devices, exapted and acquired culturally as arts, she argues, became prominent features of group ritual ceremonies that reduced anxiety and unified participants, which also offered evolutionary advantages. (Dissayanake, 2017, p. 144)

Atzil and colleagues (2012) examined how biobehavioral synchrony relates to oxytocin and vasopressin in the maternal versus paternal brain.

The group examined synchrony in mothers' and fathers' brains in response to ecologically valid infant cues during a home visit and parent-child play. Parents underwent fMRIs while watching films of their own versus other babies at play. In response to watching their own babies, results indicated that mothers showed higher amygdala activations, with correlations between amygdala response and oxytocin. By contrast, fathers showed greater activations in social-cognitive circuits as correlated with vasopressin. Parents synchronize activity in social-cognitive networks that support intuitive understanding of infant signals and planning of adequate caregiving by engaging motivational-limbic activations that are gender specific.

In general, greater parent-child behavioral, affective, and physiological synchrony are associated with many positive outcomes (e.g., Gray et al., 2018; Healey et al., 2010; Woody et al., 2016). Conversely, reduced affective synchrony is related to problem behaviors (Im-Bolter et al., 2015) and psychopathology (Criss et al., 2003; Deater-Deckard et al., 2004). Importantly, numerous studies suggest parent-child synchrony plays a role in the coregulation of emotion (Reindl et al., 2018) and enhances a child's ability to self-regulate emotion (Suveg et al., 2016), thereby reducing future risk.

Whereas secure attachment appears related to higher maternal-child inter-brain synchrony, significant psychopathology is associated with the absence of synchrony. Woody and colleagues (2016) studied mother-child interactions by comparing mothers with and without a significant history of major depressive disorder. These researchers extended previous findings of a lack of mother-child synchrony at behavioral levels to examine the impact of maternal depression on physiological synchrony using respiratory sinus arrhythmia (RSA). Evidence revealed that physiological synchrony is disrupted in families with a history of maternal major depression. Along similar lines, James et al. (2020) found that children with suicidal ideation exhibit reduced synchrony of normative positive expressions during mother-child interactions.

Li et al.'s (2020) lab examined parent-adolescent physiological synchrony in the parasympathetic nervous system by also employing RSA measures of physiological arousal. Results indicated a significant positive concurrent synchrony between adolescents and their mothers, as well as between fathers and mothers, on a minute–to–minute basis. No RSA synchrony was found between adolescents and their fathers. Furthermore, adolescent emotional insecurity significantly moderated mother–adolescent RSA synchrony. Whereas adolescents with low emotional insecurity exhibited positive synchrony with their mothers, no synchrony was observed when adolescent emotional insecurity was high. In general, emotions are limbic events within the central nervous system (brain and spinal cord), while fluctuations in arousal are the territory of the autonomic nervous system (ANS; sympathetic and parasympathetic branches). Because arousal levels are particularly important for stress management, research that taps into the ANS appears particularly sensitively attuned to the ANS of significant others.

Sync Throughout the Life Span

Given that the literal meaning of the word "attunement" means to harmonize in time, perhaps it is not surprising that the origin of the arts may derive from the way babies entrain to nonconscious psychobiological rhythms and conscious intentions and feelings in caregivers. Clearly, synchronous rhythms help to shape the earliest stages of human development. Does the same thing hold true for adults, or does the development of agency and autonomy in later stages signal the end of sync? When children start marching to the beat of their own drums, do they continue to synchronize to the beat of others?

Research indicates that structural coupling of affective, cognitive, and motor systems is as natural to adults as to children. Culturally, this is evident in the frequency of huge crowds doing the wave in large sports arenas and the popularity music and dance throughout the life span. Adults, alongside children, love to partake in rhythmic activities that harmonize with their emotions while uniting them with others. In an essay titled, "Emotional Sounds and the Brain: The Neuro-affective Foundations of Musical Appreciation," Panksepp and Bernatzky (2002) state:

> Our overriding assumption is that ultimately our love of music reflects the ancestral ability of our mammalian brain to transmit and receive basic emotional sounds that can arouse affective feelings which are implicit indicators of evolutionary fitness. In other words, music may be based on the existence of the intrinsic emotional sounds we make (the animalian prosodic elements of our utterances), and the rhythmic movements of our instinctual/emotional motor apparatus, that were evolutionarily designed to index whether certain states of being were likely to promote or hinder our well-being. (p. 133)

As brain imaging techniques have advanced, contemporary neural scientists are better able to measure the degree to which adults partake in sync. Neuroscientist Franciso Varela (2006) wrote about the importance of neuronal synchrony for binding cognitive operations in the brain, while anticipating the potential for brain imaging to merge subjective and objective levels by capturing first-person perspectives using third-person techniques (Shear & Varela, 1999). In recent decades, brain scanning has taken a huge leap by overcoming limitations of noisy, cumbersome machinery that initially required a subject to be still and isolated. Researchers can now capture minute-to-minute, embodied encounters between people as they occur within context.

One ground-breaking study was conducted by Princeton University neuroscientist Uri Hasson (Stephens et al., 2010). After solving previous difficulties with the noise and physical clumsiness of fMRI machinery, Hasson's lab created an artificial way to sync up two brains during real-time communication. The group tracked the electrical activity in the brain of a speaker who told a story, which they then synced in time to the brains of subjects while listening. This experimental paradigm revealed widespread neural resonance between the brains of speakers and listeners. Interestingly, the occurrence of neural synchrony extended well beyond the parietal and premotor areas that contain mirror neurons (specialized to fire whether a person makes an action or watches someone else making the same action). Interbrain synchrony also extended beyond the cortical areas related to speech production and reception. Results indicated that the greater the understanding displayed by the listener, the greater the interbrain synchrony. Remarkably, in response to the same story, those listeners who displayed the greatest understanding of all revealed areas of neural resonance that actually anticipated the brains of speakers.

During excellent communication, not only do we follow the words of other people, but we also tune into every nuance so as to forecast what is to come. Hasson et al. (2012) believe brain-to-brain coupling is the primary mechanism for creating and sharing social worlds. Here is how psychologist Barbara Frederickson (2013) described Hasson's work:

> Far from being isolated to one or two brain areas, really "clicking" with someone else appears to be a whole brain dance in a fully mirrored room. . . . Brain coupling, Hasson argues, is the means by which we understand each other. He goes even further to claim that communication—a true meeting of the minds—is a single act, performed by two brains. (pp. 44–45)

That shared communication may be more primary than events in either the speaker or listener alone runs parallel to concepts from contemporary relational psychotherapy, such as Thomas Ogden's (1994) notion of the "analytic third." During successful psychotherapy, when both therapist and patient are totally engaged and open to one another's input, something novel emerges in what Donald Winnicott (1971) termed the transitional space between self and other. It is here, in what contemporary relational therapists call intersubjective space, that the relationship takes off, taking on a life of its own while crafting the identities of the participants.

The New Technique of Hyperscanning

Whereas Hasson's research used artificial means to sync up speakers and listeners, a particularly exciting line of research now exists called hyperscanning (e.g., Babiloni & Astolfi, 2014; Dumas et al., 2010; Liu & Pelowski, 2014). Whether by EEG, fMRI, or other brain scanning techniques, hyperscanning involves simultaneous measurement of two or more brains in real time, which allows for more naturalistic forms of coupled brain measurements. Especially within the field of social psychology, a wealth of hyperscanning data now exists. Dikker and colleagues (2014) confirmed Hasson's earlier work by studying the degree to which speakers and listeners exhibit similar brain activity patterns during human linguistic interaction as correlated with communicative success. Results indicated that a listener's ability to predict a speaker's utterance was associated with increased neural coupling in the left posterior superior temporal gyrus between speakers and listeners.

Riley and colleagues (2011) examined neural substrates of cooperative tasks between people. Whether involving turn taking or simultaneous action, they concluded that movement systems in different actors become coupled to form low-dimensional reciprocally compensating synergies. Similar results extend beyond motor systems and behavioral cooperation, applying to emotional responses to others, and especially to crescendos and descents in arousal. Cho and colleagues (2018) examined the effectiveness of rituals among ethnic Chinese religious believers using simultaneous EEG measurements. Participants rated the perceived efficacy of spirit-medium rituals presented as video clips recorded in group and individual settings. Neural oscillatory patterns were analyzed according to subjective perceptual judgments of rituals categorized as low, medium, and high efficacy.

Distinct neural signatures and behavioral patterns emerged between the experimental conditions, such that arousal levels predicted ratings of ritual efficacy. Results from the individual setting showed increased within-participant phase synchronization in alpha and beta bands, while the group setting enhanced between-participant theta phase synchronization, reflecting group participants' orientation toward a common perspective and social coordination. The authors interpreted both intra- and interpersonal neural synchrony patterns to reveal how collective rituals have both individual and communal dimensions.

Emotional arousal has been found to synchronize cortical networks for visual attention and emotional processing across individually tested participants (Nummenmaa et al., 2012). Anders et al. (2011) identified a mirror representation of another person's affect in the perceiver's brain. Interbrain synchronization appears especially strong in people who are emotionally engaged with one another versus detached observers (Dumas et al., 2010). Dumas examined mother-child interactions by comparing mothers interacting with their own children versus with the children of strangers. Results indicated much stronger interbrain synchrony with relatives. In support of this idea, a hyperscanning study by Pan et al. (2017) examined a cooperative task in lover dyads versus friend and stranger dyads. Results indicated increased interbrain synchronization in the right superior frontal cortex of lovers compared to the other groups, which was also accompanied by higher levels of cooperative behavior.

Reindl and colleagues (2018) used hyperscanning to examine children playing both a cooperative and a competitive game with a parent (mostly mother), as well as with an adult stranger. Results indicated that during cooperation, the parent's and child's brain activities synchronized in the dorsolateral prefrontal and frontopolar cortex, which proved predictive for cooperative performance in subsequent trials. No significant brain-to-brain synchrony was observed either in competitive conditions or in stranger-child interactions. Furthermore, parent-child compared to stranger-child brain-to-brain synchrony during cooperation in the frontopolar cortex mediated the association between the parent's and the child's emotion regulation, as assessed by questionnaires. The authors conclude that brain-to-brain synchrony may represent an underlying neural mechanism of the emotional connection between parent and child, as linked to the child's development of adaptive emotion regulation. Indeed, research indicates (Isabella & Belsky, 1991) that interactions of parent-child dyads in the process of developing secure attachment relationships are characterized by disproportionately high interactional synchrony compared with dyads who go on to develop insecure relationships.

While neural synchrony appears highest among people who are emotionally invested with one another, it nonetheless also exists between strangers. Kinreich and colleagues (2017) compared romantic couples and strangers interacting during a male-female naturalistic social interaction. Under both conditions, brain-to-brain synchrony was associated with behavioral synchrony. Research indicated that brain-to-brain synchrony is linked to degree of social connection among interacting partners and grounded in key nonverbal social behaviors, such as social gaze and positive affect. The authors conclude that human attachment provides a template for two-brain coordination of all sorts.

These are but a few of the many studies now being conducted. The introduction of simultaneous measurement of brain activity allows neural technology to venture ever more deeply into intersubjective space, approaching what Dumas (2011) calls "a two-body neuroscience." Schilback et al. (2013) compares this remarkable progress in social neuroscience to the discovery of dark matter in physics.

Sync Between Patients and Therapists

As hyperscanning technology gets applied to the exquisite intimacy of psychotherapists engaged with patients during highly charged emotional moments, imagine the possibilities for capturing those unpredictable, spontaneous moments of meeting in psychotherapy. We might finally be able to operationalize the subtle and complex realms in which clinical intuition operates. Indeed, the degree and quality of interbrain resonances might one day serve as a sensitive gauge of effective psychotherapy. Hyperscanning techniques offer possibilities for illuminating bottom-up, spontaneous emergence, while lending a unique neural stamp for each idiosyncratic therapeutic dyad during each novel moment. Perhaps one day we will literally visualize the containing and germinating functions of psychotherapists. And if deep empathy includes anticipating the brain frequencies of patients, physical evidence may soon be available for how psychoanalysts succeed in "downloading" higher complexity into the psyches of patients.

It may seem controversial that interpersonal synergies span organisms by extending beyond the boundaries of skin. Yet, from a neural perspective, there appears to be little difference between transmission of information between two areas within a single brain and transmission of information between two individuals (Hasson et al., 2012). This makes sense given how important neural synchrony is in the development of cortical networks within a single brain in the first place (Uhlhaas et al., 2009). On the one hand, information is communicated from one part of the brain to another via nested frequencies, such as higher-frequency gamma waves that sync up with the lower-frequency theta band (Buzsáki, 2006). On the other hand, synchronized gamma oscillations across broad areas of the brain are one possible mechanism to solve what's been called the binding problem—how discrete perceptions from different sensory areas get unified into an unbroken sense of consciousness. While we can easily detect the presence of sync behaviorally, such as two people walking, talking, and moving in lockstep, much of the synchronized action occurs on very rapid time scales existing beneath the surface of consciousness.

The field of interpersonal neurobiology has helped to illuminate the importance of unconscious, body-to-body communication within psychotherapy. This is exemplified by Allan Schore's concept of right brain-to-right brain communication. Evidence mounts that during long-term, growth-oriented psychotherapy, patient and therapist become increasingly coupled over time at multiple, especially nonverbal levels (Ramseyer, 2020; Tschacher & Meier, 2020). At conscious levels, therapists can also attest to the experience of increasingly shared speech and greater knowledge of the other, plus anticipation of relational sequences during long-term therapy. Neural synchrony based on emotional resonances and coupled dynamics at both intrapsychic and interpersonal levels may be the foundation for nonconscious, somatically based information exchange.

Ramseyer (2020) suggests that idiographic assessments help to broaden our conception of synchrony in psychotherapy. This fits nicely with the variety of clinical intuitive techniques available to each clinician and spontaneously employed as called for within each moment. Tschacher and Meier (2020) examined physiological synchrony in naturalistic psychotherapy by analyzing the electrocardiograms and respiration behavior of a single therapist across 55 dyadic therapy sessions. They found evidence for sympathetic and parasympathetic coupling between the therapist and her clients that was linked with self-report variables.

Tschacher and Meier's study provides preliminary evidence for Koole and Tschacher's (2016) earlier interpersonal synchrony model of the therapeutic alliance. Consider the abstract from this article:

During psychotherapy, patient and therapist tend to spontaneously synchronize their vocal pitch, bodily movements, and even their physiological processes. In the present article, we consider how this pervasive phenomenon may shed new light on the therapeutic relationship—or alliance—and its role within psychotherapy. We first review clinical research on the alliance and the multidisciplinary area of interpersonal synchrony. We then integrate both literatures in the Interpersonal Synchrony (In-Sync) model of psychotherapy. According to the model, the alliance is grounded in the coupling of patient and therapist's brains. Because brains do not interact directly, movement synchrony may help to establish inter-brain coupling. Inter-brain coupling may provide patient and therapist with access to each other's internal states, which facilitates common understanding and emotional sharing. Over time, these interpersonal exchanges may improve patients' emotion-regulatory capacities and related therapeutic outcomes. We discuss the empirical assessment of interpersonal synchrony and review preliminary research on synchrony in psychotherapy. Finally, we summarize our main conclusions and consider the broader implications of viewing psychotherapy as the product of two interacting brains. (Koole & Tschacher, 2016, p. 1)

Unconscious Information Sharing

If Koole and Tschacher's (2016) model of the therapeutic alliance is correct, then interpersonal synchrony is the broad underpinning for shared understanding, trust, and communication during psychotherapy. This aligns with my own suggestion (Marks-Tarlow, 2011, 2015) that during long-term psychotherapy, the therapist and patient become increasingly coupled over time, such that successful treatment moves closer and closer to the edge of chaos, where novel structure and greater complexity can then emerge spontaneously and unpredictably.

Given how much communication as well as interpersonal synchrony occurs beneath conscious awareness, in this chapter, I also suggest that interpersonal synchrony is the mechanism by which higher-order information is shared at nonconscious levels. The metaphor of the therapist as "tuning fork" (Stone, 2006) suggests the unconscious capture of information through interpersonal resonances. If the widespread existence of interpersonal synchrony allows for bottom-up emergence of clinical information from unconscious to conscious levels, then this could provide the foundation not only for the ordinary varieties of clinical intuition, wherein therapists read subtle facial, vocal, and postural cues available from within face-to-face contact, but it also opens possibilities for the more extraordinary kind of uncanny knowing that at times appears to span large gaps in space and/or time while crossing through unconscious-to-unconscious channels.

Many, if not most, clinicians have experienced this kind of extraordinary knowing in the form of unconscious-to-unconscious information sharing, yet the subject remains largely taboo in public discussion. Only recently, with the advent of interpersonal neurobiology as a means for modeling these kinds of idiosyncratic events, have possibilities arisen for bringing such events out of the realm of the mystical, magical, or supernatural and well into the naturalistic sciences (see Marks-Tarlow, 2012). In the next section, I present the case of Abe (with patient permission and review, as adapted from Marks-Tarlow and Shapiro [in press]) to demonstrate a recent, quite extraordinary example of how unconscious resonances can lead to extraordinary information sharing accompanied by a significant change point in treatment.

The Case of Abe

Abe is a young attorney in his early 30s who grew up in a very tumultuous household with a billionaire father and a much younger mother, 30 years his junior. Abe's parents fought continually, while his father had multiple affairs he didn't even try to hide. When the boy was in early grade school, Abe's mother left her husband yet grew so distraught because of the divorce that she took to drinking heavily. During the next several years, she became unpredictably abusive toward Abe, both emotionally and physically. During these frequent episodes, Abe's father remained distant, pretending the abuse was not happening. The boy's only refuge was time spent with the young bodyguards hired to maintain the family fortress.

Whereas Abe's sister identified heavily with their mother, Abe identified more with his father and spent as much time with him as he could. Yet Abe feared his powerful father at the same time. Whereas Abe's sister reveled in the family fortune, Abe was uncomfortable with how the family's wealth and fame set him apart from others and tended to hide his personal background whenever possible. As a teenager, Abe joined the military in search of a "level playing field."

When Abe began depth psychotherapy nearly five years ago, he was just about to graduate from law school and embark on a career as an attorney. He had recently started up a romantic relationship with a fellow law student—a young lady who had ruthlessly pursued Abe. She made all the moves in a very one-sided way, even moving into Abe's apartment without his consent. It was the emotional violence of this relationship that brought Abe into psychotherapy with me, despite having been turned off to therapy in the past by multiple bouts of unproductive sessions as a child.

During early stages together, Abe and I repeatedly worked on boundary issues with his girlfriend. Yet Abe was too scared of her quick temper and irrational, unpredictable style, so similar to his mother's, to implement any insights. Instead, Abe would fall into dissociative states similar to his childhood, where he felt frozen and unable to speak out. Eventually these dynamics got so out of hand that one evening when Abe and his girlfriend were out to dinner, his girlfriend attacked Abe physically outside the restaurant. He was so seriously injured, with blood soaking profusely through his white shirt, that a random bystander called the police and the girlfriend was arrested. Abe finally hit a breaking point, ending the abuse by ending their relationship.

After the breakup, psychotherapy centered on the early family history that gave rise to these dynamics, combined with work struggles as Abe was coming into his own as a litigator in court. After being at his first job for a couple of years, Abe decided to pursue new opportunities for more money and additional learning. Immediately upon starting this second job, Abe felt emotionally drawn to a coworker, an attractive attorney named Stephanie. The two began talking more and more at work. Either Abe would go into Stephanie's office or vice versa. They would discuss any and everything, often losing track of time.

The same dynamic continued day after day. Abe was clearly attracted to Stephanie and fantasized internally about starting a romantic relationship. From Abe's description of circumstances alone, the attraction appeared to me to be mutual. Yet what was going on between the two young people relationally was one subject they never broached. One day, Abe described a recent encounter with Stephanie at the law offices. The two had talked without any food or other break until the wee hours of the night—2:30 a.m.

I inquired, "Weren't you hungry?"

Abe responded, "I didn't think about it."

"Did you consider suggesting the two of you might continue talking outside the office, where you could get something to eat?"

"That didn't occur to me either."

To me, what was going on between the two young people was so obvious, yet neither had addressed the emotional truth of these marathon encounters. As Abe was responding to my queries, a clear image began forming itself in my imagination: I visualized an ostrich with its head buried in the sand. Immediately upon seeing the image, I felt compelled to shared it with Abe.

Without a beat, he responded, "I can't believe it! That's exactly what my father used to say about his intimacy struggles with women—that he's an ostrich!"

This was a powerful clinical moment for us both. For me, the experience of unconscious information sharing is always daunting and thrilling. For Abe, this image not only hit his own central dynamic squarely on the head, but it also captured an intergenerational pattern that implicated his beloved and now deceased father. After the divorce, Abe's father had continued to be a womanizer. He literally had scores of young women lovers who continuously demanded wining and dining. While still alive and talking with Abe, his father frequently declared himself "an ostrich" in recognition of being taken advantage of. He had literally squandered most of his fortune buying houses for each of his lovers.

The emergence of the ostrich image proved to be a change moment in Abe's psychotherapy. Following the session described above, the very next week he garnered the courage to ask Stephanie on a date outside of the office. She readily accepted and the two went to dinner and addressed complications of an office romance. In the process, Stephanie shared feelings of interest and attraction to Abe but also clarified that she wanted him to take the lead in moving forward. For several weeks after, Abe's self-confidence flourished. Meanwhile, the huge differences between Stephanie and Abe's previous girlfriend allowed him to counteract his inner passivity, partly by fleshing out the ostrich as a central, guiding metaphor.

Not only was the emergence of the ostrich image remarkable in itself, but the timing of its emergence proved equally remarkable, especially in retrospect. The ostrich image entered Abe's treatment three weeks before the onset of the coronavirus pandemic. This was just enough time to establish their relationship outside of the work context. Had the two not taken their relationship outside the office prior to sheltering in place, chances are good that either their relationship would not have taken off at all or, at the very least, its onset would have been delayed for months if not years.

The emergence of the ostrich not only fit Abe's style of emotional hiding perfectly but also provided evidence for an intergenerational pattern that was unconsciously passed from father to son. As mentioned, Abe's father repeatedly described himself as an ostrich emotionally. He sidestepped emotional issues in his marriage by repeatedly having affairs. He ignored his ex-wife's abuse of his own son. He remained helplessly manipulated in his relationship to women, such that by the end of his life he wound up squandering much of his fortune. Fortunately, Abe's hard work in psychotherapy combined with the timely emergence of the ostrich brought him to an important change point, allowing him for the first time to break the pattern of freezing and hiding with women. Not only did Abe meet a different kind of woman from his mother, but he also became able to counteract his tendencies toward passivity and unconscious feelings of deserving abuse.

Behind closed doors, psychotherapists are more likely to admit how frequently instances of uncanny knowing occur. These episodes arise most often during emotionally charged moments when arousal levels are high. Indeed, to anticipate danger with respect to survival or procreation enhances the survival of our species (Bem, 2011). I suggest that conditions of high-intensity autonomic arousal likely increase possibilities for expanded realms of interpersonal synchrony. We see evidence for this among animals when they appear to anticipate earthquakes or other natural disasters, or in the jungle in the presence of predators, when fear contagion causes shrieks to spread the news rapidly to fellow animals. Perhaps during psychotherapy similar dynamics occur, such that high-arousal moments facilitate unconscious information sharing between therapists and patients. Whether or not this is the case awaits empirical validation.

Teletherapy in the Age of Coronavirus

If interpersonal synchrony is the cornerstone of the therapeutic alliance, which itself appears to be the cornerstone of effective psychotherapy (Norcross & Lambert, 2019), then what are the implications for virtual platforms of psychotherapy? This is a timely issue. At the time of writing this chapter, the coronavirus pandemic combined with quarantine not only changed Abe's relationship to Stephanie, but it also changed Abe's relationship to me as our therapy transitioned abruptly from in-person sessions to a virtual platform, where it remains today. In fact, I am currently seeing all of my patients online.

Whether or not similar levels of sync can be achieved virtually is an important avenue for future research since telehealth is the new normal that appears here to stay, with or without a pandemic. Even before the onset of the coronavirus, teletherapy was recognized as an important adjunct to in-person work. For example, Jill Savage Scharff (2013) compiled an edited volume comparing online with in-person platforms for conducting psychoanalysis. Chapters explored differences within the analytic frame, and transference and countertransference issues, alongside ethical considerations.

A *New Yorker* article by Adam Gotnik (2020), titled "The New Theatrics of Remote Therapy: How Does Treatment Change When Your Patients Are on a Screen?," is suggestive. Gotnik claims that although the ritual of psychotherapy may go on, its intimacy and efficacy appear to be affected. According to Gotnik, therapists are doing more coaching plus day-to-day problem solving as opposed to plumbing the depths of the psyche in ways traditionally considered to facilitate structural changes. Whether this is due to the medium being used or the fact that so many people are currently consumed with survival-level physical and economic concerns remains to be parsed out.

I would like to end this chapter with some personal speculations based upon my own recent experience of teletherapy, combined with anecdotal reports of close colleagues. Nearly every clinician to whom I have spoken states a preference for in-person over virtual sessions. They too experience virtual sessions as less intimate and deep, plus much more tiring, and likely to induce screen fatigue. The computer monitor clearly separates one person from another; it is a constant reminder of limits to intimacy as compared to in-person, face-to-face sessions where there is no obvious barrier between people. When conducting teletherapy, because only the head and upper torso are in view, fewer nonverbal cues are available to therapists. This may require greater attention to stay focused, both explicitly at the level of content and implicitly at the level of nonconscious signals. Although ordinarily outside of awareness, therapists continually use posture and whole-body micromovements to gauge tiny shifts in our patients' current emotional and self-states. With fewer cues available, greater attention may be needed to empathically read inner states of patients.

When utilizing the computer to interact with patients, I personally find it more difficult to get into states of flow. Prior to the pandemic, I regularly achieved a comfortable rhythm of between 8 and 10 sessions a day, one after another, during three straight days a week of clinical practice. While not every session was easy, I often found myself so engaged in the process that I could lose track of time, looking up just in time to end the session smoothly. This cadence could be exhilarating, leaving me fresh if not ener-gized by the end of the day. Unfortunately, the feeling of flow is no longer a regular occurrence for me, and I am not alone in this struggle. Many colleagues report seeing fewer patients in a day while spacing out sessions with longer breaks between. While I have kept to the same schedule, I too notice more fatigue at the end of the day. Online therapy has an addi-tional complication that may contribute to fatigue and shallower focus—we therapists are not used to watching ourselves work. Virtually every online platform includes an image of all participants. To watch ourselves watch our patients automatically instills an outside perspective that feels distracting as it dampens intimacy.

Another factor that can dampen intimacy is the loss of privacy, especially for patients who live with others, as it remains challenging to achieve the hermetically sealed environment afforded by a therapist's office. This prob-lem is compounded when patients need to talk about the very relationships with spouses and children with whom they cohabit. At times this forces patients into the awkward position of engaging in sessions from the roof, the basement, a closet, the car, or even the bathroom.

A final dimension to teletherapy I would like to comment upon is cap-tured by a telling cartoon that accompanied Gotnik's *New Yorker* article: A male therapist sits before a female patient on his computer screen. The top half of his body is properly dressed and even formally attired in a button-down shirt and tie. The therapist's lower half is garbed only in underwear and slippers. This image tickled my funny bone due to resonances with my own behavior. These days, I too sport a deep divide between how I dress on top versus what I put on bottom. During sessions, the hidden lower half of my body often goes rogue, as my legs become fidgety. I change the positions of my hips and legs much more frequently than before; at times, I even wind up straddling the computer. The two halves of my body feel quite disconnected from one another. Meanwhile, the fact that my patients have no idea what is happening down below leaves me feeling like I'm har-boring a secret.

All of these factors clearly affect intimacy. Yet I find that the loss of intimacy in some ways is counteracted by a gain in intimacy in other ways. Something about sitting with my head looming within inches of the looming head of my patient reminds me of the earliest period of parent-baby mutual gaze. In the first couple weeks of life, infants cannot see past about 24 inches, such that the mother or other primary caregiver's face occupies baby's entire universe. Neurobiologically oriented psychologist Stan Tatkin capitalizes upon the magic of this close-up frame of reference in his training protocol for therapists who do couples work. When sitting face-to-face, we rarely sit close enough to patients to be able to work within this highly intimate zone of separation.

Another source of enhanced intimacy emerges from experiencing the home environment of patients during teletherapy. I have met the pets, spouses, and children of patients, so often discussed but never encountered. I can see their apartments, houses, artwork, and other possessions. I can experience patients' aesthetic choices in the design of their spaces. I have even conducted sessions with patients who are sick in bed. And this highly personal view is a two-way street. Stay-at-home orders during the pandemic have forced many therapists to abandon their offices. While home offices have always been in fashion, teletherapy expands patients' opportunities to catch glimpses of uncurated aspects of therapists' personal lives.

In sum, there are clear trade-offs to conducting teletherapy. While working virtually has benefits by avoiding office expenses, eliminating commuting time, and fitting more easily into one's personal life, the work can also be more tiring, less intimate, less private, and less conducive to dipping under the surface of everyday life. The increases in exhaustion, distraction, and difficulty achieving flow might arise from technological factors, including frequent and distracting glitches in the system, combined with difficulties attending to the screen. Yet, in light of this chapter's subject matter, an alternative hypothesis is likely—that many of these factors are at least partially the outcome of reduced interpersonal synchrony. Not only do we lack visual cues about posture and body movements, but we are also deprived of smells, pheromones, and other in-person sensory information that helps us to align our breathing and heart rate alongside other forms of physiological synchrony. By residing in different environments, we also lose the synchrony of orienting to a common external context. This is one reason why talking on the phone when driving is so much more dangerous than talking to a passenger sitting beside us.

Meanwhile, preliminary evidence supports these ideas. Jiang and colleagues

(2012) used hyperscanning to examine differences between face-to-face communication and communication without the benefit of visual cues. They found reduced synchrony when visual cues were absent. These researchers concluded that neural synchronization between partners may underlie successful face-to-face communication. When working virtually, what if each member of the dyad also synchronizes to the flickering of their own computer screen? How would this affect interpersonal synchrony? If interpersonal synchrony truly forms the foundation for the therapeutic alliance, as Koole and Tschacher (2016) suggest, then future research should ascertain whether there are significant differences in interpersonal synchrony between live and virtual platforms. It would be fascinating indeed to compare hyperscanning studies of the psychotherapeutic process in face-to-face versus virtual platforms.

References

Anders, S., Heinzle, J., Weiskopf, N., Ethofer, T., & Haynes, J. D. (2011). Flow of affective information between communicating brains. *NeuroImage, 54*, 439–446.

Atzil, S., & Gendron, M. (2017). Bio-behavioral synchrony promotes the development of conceptualized emotions. *Current Opinion in Psychology, 17*, 162–169.

Atzil, S., Hendler, T., Zagoory-Sharon, O., Winetraub, Y., & Feldman, R. (2012). Synchrony and specificity in the maternal and the paternal brain: Relations to oxytocin and vasopressin. *Journal of the American Academy of Child and Adolescent Psychiatry, 51*(8), 798–811.

Babiloni, F., & Astolfi, L. (2014). Social neuroscience and hyperscanning techniques: Past, present and future. *Neuroscience and Biobehavioral Reviews, 44*, 76–93.

Bem, D. J. (2011). Feeling the future: Experimental evidence for anomalous retroactive influences on cognition and affect. *Journal of Personality and Social Psychology, 100*(3), 407–425.

Bromberg, P. M. (2006). *Awakening the dreamer: Clinical journeys*. Hillsdale, NJ: Analytic Press.

Bromberg, P. M. (2011). *The shadow of the tsunami: And the growth of the relational mind*. London: Routledge.

Buzsáki, G. (2006). *Rhythms of the brain*. Oxford, UK: Oxford University Press.

Cho, P. S., Escoffier, N., Mao, Y., Ching, A., Green, C., Jong, J., & Whitehouse, H. (2018). Groups and emotional arousal mediate neural synchrony and perceived ritual efficacy. *Frontiers in Psychology, 9*, 2071.

Cohn, J. F., & Tronick, E. Z. (1988). Mother-infant face-to-face interaction: Influence is bidirectional and unrelated to periodic cycles in either partner's behavior. *Developmental Psychology, 24*(3), 386–392.

Cozolino, L. (2012). *The neuroscience of human relationships: Attachment and the developing social brain* (2nd ed.). New York: Norton.

Cozolino, L. (2017). *The neuroscience of psychotherapy: Healing the social brain* (3rd ed.). New York: Norton.

Criss, M., Shaw, D., & Ingoldsby, E. (2003). Mother-son positive synchrony in middle childhood: Relation to antisocial behavior. *Social Development, 12,* 379–400.

Deater-Deckard, K., Atzaba-Poria, N., & Pike, A. (2004). Mother- and father-child mutuality in Anglo and Indian British families: A link with lower externalizing problems. *Journal of Abnormal Child Psychology, 32,* 609–620.

Dikker, S., Silbert, L. J., Hasson, U., & Zevin, J. D. (2014). On the same wavelength: Predictable language enhances speaker-listener brain-to-brain synchrony in posterior superior temporal gyrus. *Journal of Neuroscience, 34*(18), 6267–6272.

Dissayanake, E. (2017). Ethology, interpersonal neurobiology, and play insights into the evolutionary origin of the arts. *American Journal of Play, 9*(2), 143–168.

Dumas, G. (2011). Towards a two-body neuroscience. *Communicative and Integrative Biology, 4*(3), 349–352.

Dumas, G., Nadel, J., Soussignan, R., Martinerie, J., & Garnero, L. (2010). Interbrain synchronization during social interaction. *PloS One, 5*(8), e12166.

Feldman, R., Magori-Cohen, R., Galili, G., Singer, M., & Louzoun, Y. (2011). Mother and infant coordinate heart rhythms through episodes of interaction synchrony. *Infant Behavior and Development, 34*(4), 569–577.

Frederickson, B. (2013). *Love 2.0: How our supreme emotion affects everything we feel, think, do, and become.* New York: Hudson Street.

Gotnik, A. (2020, May 25). The new theatrics of remote therapy: How does treatment change when your patients are on a screen? *New Yorker.* https://www .newyorker.com/magazine/2020/06/01/the-new-theatrics-of-remote-therapy

Gray, S.A.O., Lipschutz, R.S. & Scheeringa, M.S. (2018). Young children's physiological reactivity during memory recall: Associations with posttraumatic stress and parent physiological synchrony. *Journal of Abnormal Child Psycholology, 46,* 871–880.

Hasson, U., Ghazanfar, A. A., Galantucci, B., Garrod, S., & Keysers, C. (2012). Brain-to-brain coupling: A mechanism for creating and sharing a social world. *Trends in Cognitive Sciences, 16*(2), 114–121.

Healey, D., Gopin, C., Grossman, B., Campbell, S., & Halperin, J. (2010). Mother-child dyadic synchrony is associated with better functioning in hyperactive/inattentive preschool children. *Journal of Child Psychology and Psychiatry and Allied Disciplines, 51,* 1058–1066.

Im-Bolter, N., Anam, M., & Cohen, N. (2015). Mother–child synchrony and child problem behavior. *Journal of Child and Family Studies, 24,* 1876–1885.

Isabella, R. A., & Belsky, J. (1991). Interactional synchrony and the origins of infant–mother attachment: A replication study. *Child Development, 62*(2), 373–384.

Jaffe, J., Beebe, B., Feldstein, S., Crown, C. L., Jasnow, M. D., Rochat, P., & Stern, D. N. (2001). Rhythms of dialogue in infancy: Coordinated timing in development. *Monographs of the Society for Research in Child Development, 66*(2), 1–149.

James, K. M., Kudinova, A. Y., Woody, M. L., Feurer, C., Foster, C. E., & Gibb, B. E. (2020, March 10). Children's history of suicidal ideation and synchrony of facial displays of affect during mother-child interactions. *Journal of Child Psychology and Psychiatry*. doi:10.1002/dev.21893

Jiang, J., Dai, B., Peng, D., Zhu, C., Liu, L., & Lu, C. (2012). Neural synchronization during face-to-face communication. *Journal of Neuroscience, 32*, 16064–16069.

Kaye, K., & Fogel, A. (1980). The temporal structure of face-to-face communication between mothers and infants. *Developmental Psychology, 16*(5), 454.

Kinreich, S., Djalovski, A., Kraus, L., Louzoun, Y., & Feldman, R. (2017). Brain-to-brain synchrony during naturalistic social interactions. *Scientific Reports, 7*(1), 1–12.

Koole, S. L., & Tschacher, W. (2016). Synchrony in psychotherapy: A review and an integrative framework for the therapeutic alliance. *Frontiers in Psychology, 7*, 862.

Li, Z., Sturge–Apple, M. L., Liu, S., & Davies, P. T. (2020). Parent–adolescent physiological synchrony: Moderating effects of adolescent emotional insecurity. *Psychophysiology, 57*(9), e13596.

Liu, T., & Pelowski, M. (2014). Clarifying the interaction types in two-person neuroscience research. *Frontiers in Human Neuroscience, 8*, 276.

Marks-Tarlow, T. (2008). *Psyche's veil: Psychotherapy, fractals and complexity*. London: Routledge.

Marks-Tarlow, T. (2011). Merging and emerging: A nonlinear portrait of intersubjectivity during psychotherapy. *Psychoanalytic Dialogues, 21*(1), 110–127.

Marks-Tarlow, T. (2012). *Clinical intuition in psychotherapy: The neurobiology of embodied response*. New York: Norton.

Marks-Tarlow, T. (2014a). *Awakening clinical intuition: An experiential workbook for clinicians*. New York: Norton.

Marks-Tarlow, T. (2014b). The interpersonal neurobiology of clinical intuition. *Smith College Studies in Social Work, 84*, 219–234.

Marks-Tarlow, T. (2015). The nonlinear dynamics of clinical intuition. *Chaos and Complexity Letters, 8*(2–3), 1–24.

Marks-Tarlow, T., & Shapiro, Y. (in press). Synchronicity, acausal connection, and the fractal dynamics of clinical practice, *Psychoanalytic Dialogues*.

Nguyen, T., Schleihauf, H., Kayhan, E., Matthes, D., Vrtička, P., & Hoehl, S. (2020). The effects of interaction quality on neural synchrony during mother-child problem solving. *Cortex, 124*, 235–249.

Norcross, J. C., & Lambert, M. J. (Eds.). (2019). *Psychotherapy relationships that work: Vol. 1. Evidence-based therapist contributions*. Oxford, UK: Oxford University Press.

Nummenmaa, L., Glerean, E., Viinikainen, M., Jaaskelainen, I. P., Hari, R., & Sams,

M. (2012). Emotions promote social interaction by synchronizing brain activity across individuals. *Proceedings of the National Academy of Science, U.S.A.*, 109, 9599–9604.

Ogden, T. H. (1994). The analytic third: Working with intersubjective clinical facts. *International Journal of Psycho-Analysis*, 75, 3–19.

Pan, Y., Cheng, X., Zhang, Z., Li, X., & Hu, Y. (2017). Cooperation in lovers: An fNIRS–based hyperscanning study. *Human Brain Mapping*, 38(2), 831–841.

Panksepp, J. (1998). *Affective neuroscience: The foundations of human and animal emotions.* Oxford, UK: Oxford University Press.

Panksepp, J., & Bernatzky, G. (2002). Emotional sounds and the brain: The neuro-affective foundations of musical appreciation. *Behavioural Processes*, 60(?), 133–155.

Ramseyer, F. (2020). Exploring the evolution of nonverbal synchrony in psychotherapy: The idiographic perspective provides a different picture. *Psychotherapy Research*, 30(5), 622–634.

Reindl, V., Gerloff, C., Scharke, W., & Konrad, K. (2018). Brain-to-brain synchrony in parent-child dyads and the relationship with emotion regulation revealed by fNIRS-based hyperscanning. *NeuroImage*, 178, 493–502.

Riley, M. A., Richardson, M. J., Shockley, K., & Ramenzoni, V. C. (2011). Interpersonal synergies. *Frontiers in Psychology*, 2(38), 1–7.

Scharff, J. S. (2013). *Psychoanalysis online: Mental health, teletherapy and training.* London: Karnac.

Schilback, L., Timmermans, B., Reddy, V., Costall, A., Bente, G., Schlicht, T., & Vogeley, K. (2013). Toward a second-person neuroscience. *Behavioral and Brain Sciences*, 36, 393–462.

Schore, A. N. (2001). The effects of early relational trauma on right brain development, affect regulation, and infant mental health. *Infant Mental Health Journal*, 22(1–2), 201–269.

Schore, A. N. (2005). Attachment, affect regulation, and the developing right brain: Linking developmental neuroscience to pediatrics. *Pediatrics in Review*, 26(6), 204–217.

Schore, A. N. (2012). *The science of the art of psychotherapy.* New York: Norton.

Schore, A. N. (2019). *The development of the unconscious mind.* New York: Norton.

Shear, J., & Varela, F. J. (Eds.). (1999). *The view from within: First-person approaches to the study of consciousness.* Upton Pyne, UK: Imprint Academic.

Stevens, G., Silbert, L., & Hasson, U. (2010). Speaker-listener neural coupling underlies successful communication. *Proceedings of the National Academy of Science USA*, 107, 14425–14430.

Stone, M. (2006). The analyst's body as tuning fork: Embodied resonance in countertransference. *Journal of Analytical Psychology*, 51(1), 109–124.

Strogatz, S. (2008). *Sync: How order emerges from chaos in the universe, nature and daily life.* Paradise, CA: Paw Prints.

Suveg, C., Shaffer, A., & Davis, M. (2016). Family stress moderates relations between physiological and behavioral synchrony and child self-regulation in mother-preschooler dyads. *Developmental Psychobiology, 58,* 83–97.

Trevarthen, C. (1989). Development of early social interactions and the affective regulation of brain growth. In C. Trevarthen, C. von Euler, H. Forssberg, & H. Lagercrantz (Eds.), *Neurobiology of early infant behaviour* (pp. 191–216). London: Macmillan Education.

Tschacher, W., & Meier, D. (2020). Physiological synchrony in psychotherapy sessions. *Psychotherapy Research, 30*(5), 558–573.

Uhlhaas, P., Pipa, G., Lima, B., Melloni, L., Neuenschwander, S., Nikoli, D., & Singer, W. (2009). Neural synchrony in cortical networks: History, concept and current status. *Frontiers in Integrative Neuroscience, 3,* 17.

Varela, F. (2006). Neuronal synchrony and cognitive functions. In B. Feltz, M. Crommelinck, & P. Goujon (Eds.), *Self-organization and emergence in life sciences* (pp. 95–108). Dordrecht: Springer.

Vrobel, S., Rössler, O., & Marks-Tarlow, T. (2008). *Simultaneity: Temporal structures and observer perspectives.* Hackensack, NJ: World Scientific.

Winnicott, D. W. (1971). *Playing and reality.* Middlesex, UK: Penguin.

Woody, M., Feurer, C., Sosoo, E., Hastings, P., & Gibb, B. (2016). Synchrony of physiological activity during mother– child interaction: moderation by maternal history of major depressive disorder. *Journal of Child Psychology and Psychiatry, 57,* 843–850.

12

Synchronizing Neurological States of Emotion in Family Therapy While Online

Daniel Hughes

ALISON KAPLAN JUST HAD A MEETING WITH A COLLEAGUE REGARDING A referral. He was changing his practice and could no longer treat a 10-year-old boy, John, and his parents, Gail and Simon. John struggled in his relationships with his parents, teachers, and peers. He was frequently angry and oppositional. He would make demands and was not content even when he seemed to have what he wanted. His parents were quite motivated to help their son, and their own relationship appeared to be strong. They did have difficult times during the first three years of his life, and at that time they both were often tense, withdrawn, and unable to provide each other with the support that they needed. With the pandemic the challenges within the family became more intense.

The family relational patterns appeared to be a challenge to Alison, but to make matters worse, she needed to become engaged with this family through online therapy. Due to the pandemic, for the foreseeable future she would not be able to meet with the family face-to-face. She gave careful thought to how she might engage the family online. She concluded that the relational processes that informed her model of therapy would be the same processes that she needed to rely on if she were to successfully meet with the family online. The synchronization of her affective state with the states of the family—as well as their states with one another—was all the more important if the online connection was to have an impact on all family members. I first present the nature of this relational process and then note how it might be modified somewhat to incorporate the demands of developing a therapeutic engagement online.

Since Alison held a developmental perspective that she relied heavily on while trying to understand the origins and challenges of family relationships, she initiated treatment by first speaking with Gail and Simon prior to meeting with the three of them together.

During this initial session, they agreed that the chronic stress of the early years might well have created relationship patterns between John and them that impeded his ongoing social and emotional development. These patterns also left them uncertain about how best to relate with their son when he did not seem to want to respond to them.

Alison's therapeutic approach is known as dyadic developmental psychotherapy (DDP) (Hughes et al., 2019) and is influenced by knowledge of the structure and functioning of the infant's brain as described by Allan Schore, Daniel Siegel, and Louis Cozolino as interpersonal neurobiology (Siegel, 2012). The infant's brain is actively searching for and quietly attentive to the brain of her parents so that their brains may synchronize their core neurological activities. The infant readily engages in moment-to-moment interactions with her parents that are contingent, nonverbal (bodily), reciprocal, and highly synchronized. These interactions are crucial for the development of her sense of self as well as the relationship patterns emerging between herself and her parents.

These contingent behaviors of the infant (or parent) occur because of a prior behavior of the parent (or infant). The initiation of these cycles of interaction begins at birth (if not before) at the moment of eye contact, where the eyes of each demonstrate in an instant that the other is interested and responsive. Many of the subsequent cycles in a given moment are initiated by the infant, while many other ones are initiated by the parent. Because of the prior cycles that occurred, both parent and infant anticipate that in this moment similar contingent actions are about to occur. These interactions are intentional, not random or accidental. Within months the infant is able to know what the parent's intentions are in initiating many gestures and vocal and facial expressions. Long before that, the infant can anticipate that when he initiates a bodily expression, his parent will change her own behavior. He can influence his parent. His parent notices him, and he matters to his parent!

As Dan Stern clearly described years ago, the emergent sense of self as it develops in the infant is nonverbal. It emerges from body signals experienced as "the continuous music of being alive," which he described as "vitality affects." As this affective state stretches toward intentional objects (most notably his parents), this ongoing experience of primary consciousness enters awareness as the emergent self (Stern, 2000).

The infant has no words that she can use to communicate, but she does not need them. She has her face with its many nuanced expressions. She has her voice, with many varieties of intensity and rhythm. And her body has many movements, gestures, and ways of holding itself in particular postures. She communicates with all of these bodily expressions, and her parents notice them. They take delight in making sense of them, working out what they mean, what she wants from them or wants to tell them. They guess and then respond in a way that is based on their guess. Sometimes, no matter what they guess, their infant is pleased since all she wanted was to be so engaged. Other times she does want something specific, and her face, voice, and motions continue to express her efforts to communicate with them, possibly becoming more intense until they guess right.

What is happening is that the bodily expressions of both parent and infant are becoming synchronized. They are doing a tango with their bodies, and their voices are engaged in forming a lovely melody. Momentum moves their engagement forward, where one synchronized movement leads to the next to the extent that they are not two individuals taking discrete turns, but rather a ball of twine now unwinding. This shared moment is being organized just as the joining selves of the two beings are being organized. The self of the infant is rapidly developing, while the self of the parent is also integrating the delightful new experiences emerging from being a parent.

Much of the synchronization involves their affective states. When the parent matches the bodily expression of an emotion (distress, fear, excitement, contentment) with a bodily expression with a similar rhythm and/or intensity, the infant's affective expression is being coregulated. The infant is not able to self-regulate those emerging states and needs to rely on the parent to coregulate them.

These moment-to-moment strings of engagement are having an impact on both infant and parent. The impact is reciprocal. Each is learning about the self and about the other. Each is developing—the infant is developing an emerging sense of self, and the parent is developing an emerging sense of self-as-parent. The impact on the infant of the parent so engaged is quite evident when we focus on the infant's development and we observe the deficiencies or distortions in development when these synchronized bodily actions are not sufficiently present. The impact on the parent of the infant so engaged is also evident if we focus on the sense of self of the parent being affected by her part in the success or failure of her infant's development (Hughes & Baylin, 2012).

Thus, the same experiences that organize the infant's sense of self also have an impact on the ongoing reorganization of the parent's sense of self (Beebe & Lachmann, 2014). They are having a reciprocal impact on each other. Through having this impact, the infant is not only discovering qualities of self—such as worth, sociability, and the ability to learn—but also is discovering his sense of agency, his ability to initiate actions in the world that affect the world. What he does matters! Yes, the infant is seen, felt, and known. And the infant is also joined and followed, and is the source of joy, pride, surprise, and love in his parent. The infant is receiving a great deal from his parent as well as giving a great deal to his parent.

The draw of these reciprocal states is irresistible to the developing infant. There is no other way to begin the process of organizing his great varieties of experience into a sense of self. As Beebe and Lachmann so emphatically state: "It is *not* possible *not* to be affected (by these synchronized states) on a moment-to-moment basis" (2014, p. 76).

For the integrated and coherent sense of self to fully develop, the infant relies on the readiness and ability of the parent to provide these synchronized interactions, which are continuously being fine-tuned (repaired) by the parent's response to the infant's response to the parent's initiatives. When the parent struggles with providing this attuned interaction, the infant struggles in developing an integrated sense of self. The parent needs to notice when her initiatives are not being received by her infant and then change her initiative accordingly.

The frequent fine-tuning that occurs within the call-and-response cycles of parent-infant interactions are known as interactive repair. Through these, the infant notices that how she responds to the parent matters to the parent, who responds to the infant's lack of response to one initiative by changing the next initiative. Through these cycles the infant and parent are engaged in mutual regulation of their affective states (Tronick, 2007).

These communications involve joint affective, cognitive, and intentional states. In these states, the infant is seen, felt, and known by the parent and from these experiences comes to see, feel, and know himself. The infant and parent focusing on each other is known as intersubjectivity (Stern, 2000; Trevarthen, 2001).

These intersubjective experiences involve various joint activities in which the infant's experience is being coregulated by his parents; the infant and parent are resonating with one another, are aware of being together in the presence of each other, and are discovering themselves with others in the family. These ongoing experiences are conversations that involve affective expressions of many emotions such as joy, sadness, excitement, and fear. When the parent resonates with the affective state of her infant, it is described as attunement. As the parent "gets" the infant's emotional state, the infant more clearly experiences that state within himself. The affective experience of parent and infant resonate as they are sharing the same experience. Both the parent and infant express joy, and both are joyful. As they show interest in each other, they are interesting. As they show love, they are lovable. It is within these synchronized conversations the infant is having with his parents that his sense of self begins to develop.

This complex dyadic relationship between infant and parent facilitates all aspects of the infant's neuropsychological development. Allan Schore (2012, p. 29) describes this central developmental role as follows:

> The rich intimacy of an integrative theory of neurobiology and attachment links brain, mind, and body and encompasses the essential elements that allow us to comprehend and treat attachment-related disorders of self and affect regulation more effectively. There is currently both an experimental and a clinical focus on how affective bodily based attachment processes are aroused, communicated, and regulated within the mother-infant dyad.

Some leading researchers in human development, Alan Sroufe and colleagues (2005, p. 285), noted that psychological disturbances in early childhood are best characterized as a relationship disturbance, not a disturbance within the infant or toddler. The nature of this relationship disturbance is crucial in determining the nature of the developmental challenges that the child faces.

In many dyadic states, the contingencies are not optimal (Beebe & Lachmann, 2014). Beebe and Lachmann refer to these synchronized processes as intentional action sequences between parent and infant. These action sequences create procedural expectancies that produce a sense of both self and other. Sometimes, rather than showing the optimal "serve and return" cycle, the parent and child may instead be locked into a "chase and dodge" cycle. The infant develops an action sequence marked by vigilance regarding his parent's movements while then inhibiting his response to her initiatives. The more she chases, the more he dodges, activating even greater chasing sequences, and so on.

Another action sequence leads to the development of a disorganized attachment pattern involving the parent who only recognizes her child when he is happy and does not become engaged with him when he is in distress. His distress is neither seen nor felt by the parent, which tends to evoke an infant's action sequence that is either dysregulated or frozen at the onset of states of distress. Such infants tend to have difficulty coming to know themselves, as is seen in their decreased touching themselves as well as their tendency to both smile and whimper at the same time. Their action sequences become unpredictable, as if they are at a loss as to what they (and their parent) are likely to do next. Both the mind and the behavior of the infant are at risk of not becoming organized. These sequences create procedural understanding and memories, not symbolic ones. At its core, the self is organized (or not) and develops presymbolically. For this reason, Allan Schore (2019) refers to psychotherapy as a dialogue between the right hemispheres of the client and therapist.

For Alison, our understanding of these dyadic parent-infant patterns of engagement has many therapeutic implications. So far, they are as follows.

1. She should build her therapeutic relationship on contingent, nonverbal communications, being aware of how the development of the emergent self and the core interpersonal self occurs within the nonverbal communications of the parent-infant dyad. Her nonverbal expressions should be clear (possibly exaggerated as they are with infants) so that they represent nonambiguous communications about how the child is affecting her. She can expect to be affected by the possible meaning of the child's behavior much more than the behavior itself.

2. She should focus on establishing a synchronized rhythm as she enters into a conversation with the child about all aspects of his life. This conversation should develop a momentum, which can increase the child's ability to allow stressful themes to emerge. She should avoid speaking with a monotone that emphasizes facts and reason. She should resonate with his affective expression of his emotional states and match his affect in order to coregulate these expressions. The goal is to remain regulated across all affective states rather than being calm.

3. She should be aware that the interactions need to have a reciprocal influence on both herself and the boy, as the impact on the boy alone will be less if she is not also affected by their time together. This is the nature of intersubjectivity, and it should be the stance that she embraces, rather than adopting a neutral stance.

Upon this foundation of the nonverbal sense of self, the toddler begins to add verbal communications, again primarily within the intersubjective context with her parents. These words are embodied within rich, nuanced nonverbal communications. All children are not likely to remain engaged with words for any period of time unless these words are closely associated with resonating bodily communications. Adding words to nonverbal communications enables the child to enter into conversations with her parents that are more comprehensive and complex than she could have done previously. They enable their joint attention to move into the past and future, exploring memories from the past as well as hopes and fears about the future. Words also enable the child to explore with her parent more fully her inner life of thoughts and feelings, wishes, and intentions. With words, combined with lived nonverbal experiences, the child is able to develop the meanings of her actions and those of her parents. Joining meaning with action, past with present and future, the child is able to begin to develop stories about the events of her life. These events become integrated into organized experiences, leading to stories that become integrated into her sense of self. These nonverbal-verbal conversations greatly facilitate the child's ability to develop her autobiography, a narrative of the self that is being coconstructed to a great extent by the child and parent's intersubjective experiences.

With her understanding of how the toddler develops her conversations with her parents by adding to her nonverbal communications, words and the realms of experiences that they are able to open up for her, Alison develops further implications for her therapeutic work with all children, including John.

4. Holding onto the need to have conversations that make full use of both nonverbal and verbal expressions, she should focus on helping John (and his parents) to understand the meanings of the events of his life. Her focus should be on understanding—not evaluating—the meanings that John is experiencing involving the events being explored. These meanings should involve all aspects of his life, not just the presenting problem. These meanings will link the past and present to build comprehensive stories about his life.

5. As she begins to enter into these synchronized conversations with the child, she should then ensure that the parent(s) also enter into these conversations. First, she should take the lead with John to ensure that the conversation is based on the same elements that exist in the secure parent-infant conversation. She should model and coach the parents to be so engaged, fine-tuning their expressions to John's developmental age. Then she should withdraw a bit, enabling the primary intersubjective experience to be between the parent and child in the session, at which point she will become more of an affectively resonating witness to their engagements. She should then reflect on it in a manner that will deepen their experience of each other.

When Alison first spoke with Gail and Simon, she established a level of trust while she explored what brought them to her. They were both able to express their current worries and doubts while also following her into an exploration of possible origins of these problems during the years following their son's birth. She realized that their interactions with John during his infancy were more predictably contingent than those with children who have disorganized attachment. Still, as she came to understand the challenges that they faced, she realized that they were too often inconsistent in providing John with the synchronized intersubjective experiences needed to best support his emotional and interpersonal development. They expressed regret when they recalled how often the tension that they felt in handling their substantial challenges made it difficult for them to remain openly engaged with each other and with their son. Gail spoke of times when she felt that she too frequently went through the motions of attending to her son while her mind was elsewhere. Simon spoke of finding excuses not to engage with John and turning away when his son wanted him to attend to him. Often, they were slow to respond to him when he was crying, and when he began to crawl they became impatient quickly when he did not do what they wanted him to do. With sadness, they recalled his tantrums and their angry responses. They were not coregulating his affective states. He had to try to regulate them alone, and often he was not able to do so.

As their external world had begun to stabilize, Gail and Simon realized that their own relationship was not going well. They initiated couples therapy that they thought was very helpful. From there, when John was about four years old, they worked hard to improve their relationship with their son too. However, he did not seem to respond the way that they had hoped. He often seemed content to play alone rather than do things with them. He did not often show signs of distress and seldom seemed to want comfort. He had difficulty accepting limits and consequences, and seemed to look for things to argue about. When Alison spoke with them about how John may well have begun to organize his sense of self around relying on himself and trying to be in control of both his emotions and his relationships with them and others, they concurred. John and his parents seem to have developed relationship patterns where they did not share affective states, seldom had similar interests, and had difficulty finding ways to cooperate. When his parents finally took the lead in trying to change these patterns, John seemed slow to follow. As they gradually lost confidence in how they were relating with John, they focused more on his behavior and less on their relationship, and they developed a self-protective pattern described as blocked care (Hughes & Baylin, 2012).

In addressing the challenge of providing therapy for the family online, Alison kept in mind the five factors just mentioned as she considered modifying her interventions when she would not be face-to-face with the family. Alison approached online therapy in the following way:

1. She placed even greater emphasis than usual on developing a sense of trust that all members of the family needed to have with her. Because Alison had not met the family before and due to the ambiguity often present in online conversations, she demonstrated her interest and acceptance of them through clear facial expressions and voice prosody. They needed to sense that she was with them in their distress, with compassion and acceptance, not judgment, so that they could trust her with aspects of their family life that often left them experiencing anger, discouragement, and shame. She focused a great deal more on their process of becoming engaged in a reciprocal conversation than she did on the actual content of the conversation. She acknowledged her own uncertainty about engaging in therapy online to create a sense that "we're all in this together."

2. She realized that online, not only would she be ambiguous in her communications with them, they also were likely to seem unclear to her. As a result, she focused more attention on noticing and responding to the nonverbal communications of both parent and child with her and each other, while at the same time being consistently sure that she was quite clear in her own nonverbal expressions. She realized that in highlighting her own voice prosody, facial expressions, and gestures, she was also facilitating their nonverbal expressiveness due to the natural tendency to become synchronized in our affective expressions.

3. When she initiated any nonverbal communication, she was especially aware of whether the parent or child she was conversing with entered into a synchronized rhythm with her in their voice, face, and gestures. If the interaction seemed to be lacking in symmetry, she repeated herself, paused, and made it clear that she was reflecting on how to better say what she wanted to convey. In doing so she built a bit of suspense as to where she would lead the conversation, followed by a more animated verbal expression that all were likely to be fully focused on. Her affective expressions most likely then evoked a matching affective response from the family members. If they did not, she wondered if her initiative was creating either discomfort or disagreement in the other who was not entering the rhythm with her and she gently addressed it in order to facilitate interactive repair.

4. She facilitated a greater engagement by ensuring that they entered into a conversation about all aspects of their lives, rather than just the challenges. She showed clearly that she was interested in trying to understand the various meanings of all the events that they were experiencing. Her attitude conveyed that she was interested in discovering who they were as individuals and as a family, and not focused on evaluating their behaviors.

Therapeutic Interventions

Because she was aware of how these synchronized parent-infant interactions were central in the development of John's sense of self and his manner of relating with his parents, Alison used this knowledge to guide her therapeutic interventions, whether in the context of face-to-face or online engagement. The following is a summary of how her therapy was influenced by key aspects of synchronized infant-parent interactions.

1. Alison first met with Gail and Simon alone for two sessions. She suggested that they choose a place in their home where they felt comfortable and which also was private. She shared with them the nature of developing parent-child relationships. She described how they might become engaged with their son now in ways that would help them all to experience the closeness that they missed out on during the first three years. Alison spoke with them about how she would be relating to John with an attitude characterized by playfulness, acceptance, curiosity, and empathy (PACE) and then would support them in efforts to relate with him in a similar manner. PACE involves qualities of interacting that are very consistent with the features of parent-infant reciprocal engagements. This attitude would assist her in keeping her mind on the mental state that underlay John's behaviors. This would enable her not to react to his behavior but rather to accept, wonder about, and understand the meaning of the behavior. It would also help her to be affectively engaged and regulated across a continuum from light and hopeful playfulness to empathy for the difficult aspects of his life. Without judgment, she would become consistently curious about as well as experiencing empathy for the meanings of his behavior.

She planned to help them all to discover the meanings under his challenging behaviors, and help him to convey those meanings in a manner that they might better understand and support. At the same time, Alison would be helping Gail and Simon to explore how the relational patterns that they developed in their own childhoods were likely to influence how they related to their son (i.e., how their son's behaviors might be activating their own relational histories).

In these first sessions, she also helped them to understand the nature of therapy sessions—how she would first establish a synchronized nonverbal-verbal conversation with John and then bring them into it. She would help him to become vulnerable over the doubts that he had about himself and his relationships with his parents and then facilitate his turning to them for comfort, while helping them to respond with PACE.

She indicated that if they thought that she misunderstood something that John said, they should tell her in front of John so that she could understand him better. They should not disagree with John, just clarify what they thought he meant.

2. When she then met John with his parents, Alison became engaged with him in synchronized nonverbal communications. She suggested that he might have more online experience than she did and asked if he would help her if she got something wrong. Her facial expressions, voice prosody, gestures, and movements, as they become synchronized with his, very clearly demonstrated the impact he was having on her affectively and reflectively. Without words, she demonstrated that she enjoyed and was interested in getting to know him—unconditionally. Without words, she demonstrated that she saw and accepted all aspects of him and that he was safe knowing that he would not be judged (though some of his behaviors might be evaluated). This way of engagement is best described as having a conversation, rather than teaching or giving advice. While she was so engaged with John, his parents were experiencing this intersubjective way of being (promoted with PACE) with the expectation that—through her modeling and coaching—they began to engage him in this manner themselves.

3. She was interested in all of John. There was no aspect of his self that was invisible to her, nor any aspect of his self that she rejected. She did not privilege the problem but rather was deeply interested in all that he was communicating (verbally or nonverbally) as well as aspects of his self and his history that he seemed not to be sharing or even to be aware of. When she was exploring the problem, her voice and face retained the same relaxed, conversational tone that she showed around lighter themes. It was crucial that when she transitioned into more difficult themes, her nonverbal communications remained continuous. While being so focused on John, she was also aware of his parents, assisting them in remaining open and engaged with their son if they were becoming defensive. Her primary intention was to facilitate the relationships between John and his parents, and she related with them all with PACE.

4. The moment that John disengaged from the conversation, she became aware of his nonresponse and the lack of a joint rhythm, accepted that, and followed him. She invited him to reengage if he chose around another theme, or she turned her attention to his parents, or she simply reflected out loud to herself. Since her attitude always attempted to convey acceptance, his disengagement was not experienced as resistance. He consistently found himself becoming safely engaged with Alison, again and again.

5. Her mind highlighted the wish to understand the meanings of his behaviors, his inner life, their moment-to-moment engagement, and his experience of his parents' engagement with him, as well as the meaning of similar features of his parents. As the conversation moved forward, uncovering deeper and/or more complex meanings of the events being explored, her intent was to maintain an open and engaged connection without evoking a defensive reaction. When he did become defensive, she would engage in relationship repair with PACE, and his defensiveness very often faded. When it did not, that too was accepted as being a natural occurrence in any close relationship.

6. She was aware of the power of the nonverbal expressions of delight, amazement, suspense, surprise, wonder, empathy, gratitude, and similar affective states to generate a sense of mutual understanding and joint experience while holding John's attention. She worked not to inhibit the expression of these affective experiences.

7. She was aware that John and his parents' intersubjective experiences of each other were biased toward negative meanings, leaving them often unable to see much of the positive in each other. Knowing that, she communicated her witnessing of positive qualities in both child and parents as they became present in order to facilitate their having similar experiences of each other and beginning to trust these experiences.

With these principles in mind, below is a transcript of an interactive sequence involving Alison, John, and his parents. This sequence occurred in the third session. Prior to the session, Alison spoke briefly with his parents alone. They told Alison of an interesting event that had occurred since the last session as well as one that involved a hard time for John. This latter event involved how angry he became at them two days before the session when they would not let him speak online with a friend until he first did 30 minutes of homework. He basically ignored them the rest of the evening.

At the beginning of the dialogue recorded below, John had just told

Alison with some enthusiasm about a planned virtual tour of the Boston Aquarium with his class. He expressed excitement about seeing the aquarium, since he had never been there, telling her a few things he had heard about it. Alison matched his animated affect with her facial expressions and vocal exclamations as he spoke.

ALISON: What a great opportunity you're going to have! I'm really happy for you. Will you let me know, John, what you see and discover about it?

JOHN: I guess. . . . But I don't think you're really interested.

[John seemed hesitant to accept her excitement, not wanting to believe that what he did mattered to her.]

ALISON: John, thanks for telling me that! If I'm not interested, of course you wouldn't see any reason to tell me.

JOHN: You're just talking to me so my parents will be happy.

ALISON: That must not feel good, John, if you think I really don't care about you; maybe you think I pretend to care so I can get you to be the way you think that your parents want you to be.

JOHN: They're not really interested in what I do. Why should you be?

[Even though this was a stressful theme, John remained in the conversation with the same degree of engagement that he had shown when talking about his upcoming virtual tour. Alison's continuing conversational tone facilitated this.]

ALISON: Oh, John, so it seems to you that I'm not interested in you, and your parents aren't interested either! How hard that must be!

JOHN: I'm used to it. . . . It doesn't bother me.

[John's voice went from being challenging to being resigned, speaking with less intensity. Alison followed him affectively, matching his nonverbal cadence.]

ALISON: It doesn't bother you. . . . It doesn't bother you. That would be painful . . . if your parents were not interested in what is important to you . . . and you found a way to not let it bother you. I'm glad you did, John, if you had to.

JOHN: Yeah, right. That's good. . . . You're glad that I'm not important to my parents!

ALISON: [Matching his increased intensity] John, I'm sorry if you heard me say that. I thought I said that if you feel your parents are not interested in you, it would be painful, and I'm glad that you found a way to make the pain go away. I'm sorry if I said that poorly, and you thought that I said that you were not important to your parents. Really sorry.

JOHN: Whatever . . . it doesn't matter.

ALISON: It matters to me, John . . . but you say, not to you. Ahh . . .does it seem like that a lot, John, that you're not important to your parents?

JOHN: All the time! What I want is never important!

ALISON: It seems like what you want is *never* important!

JOHN: Like yesterday! I just wanted to see my friend. Like it would be the worst thing that ever happened if I had some fun with my friend rather than doing some lousy homework.

ALISON: You wanted to spend time with your friend online, and they said no. And it sounds like you got angry. . . . You got angry, not just because they would not let you contact him, but because it seemed to you that they would not let you because what you want to do is not import- ant to them.

JOHN: That's right!

ALISON: And it even seems to you that *you're* not important to them.

JOHN: I'm not. [Said more quietly, again moving from annoyed and chal- lenging to being resigned.]

ALISON: [Again matching John's quieter affective expression] Oh, John. . . . It seems to you that you're not important to your parents. . . . If that's so, John . . . if that's so . . . why would that be? Why wouldn't you be important to your parents.

JOHN: [After a pause] because I'm not the kid they want. . . . They're dis- appointed in me. [Now there is a clear tone of sadness in John's voice.]

ALISON: [With a similar pause] Because you think that . . . that they are dis- appointed in you. Oh, John, what a hard feeling to have.

JOHN: [Very quietly] But I'm used to it. [Now with a few tears.]

ALISON: [Also speaking very softly] It might be hard to get used to a feel- ing like that. A feeling that you're a disappointment to your parents. . . . Maybe that you're not that special to them.

JOHN: I'm not. [With more tears.]

[Alison notices that Gail is starting to say something, and she quickly but gently asks her to wait, to listen. She fears that they will feel a need to reassure John, which would most likely convey that they do not understand the depth of his feeling or they don't want him to have such an experience of them.]

ALISON: Ahh . . . I guessed right. . . . You don't believe you're special to your parents. . . . You must feel so alone.

[Now Alison has some tears too. She glances to see that John's parents also seem to have been touched by his vulnerability. It is crucial that their experience of their son be similar to her intersubjective experience. She wants to seek their responses now but cannot do so if they show any negative bias that might prevent them from experiencing his vulnerability.]

ALISON: John, would you tell your parents what you just told me . . . or if you'd rather not, is it okay if I tell them for you?
JOHN: I do feel that I'm a disappointment to you. [John seems to want to look at his parents but struggles and cannot.]

[Alison quietly reminds Gail and Simon to respond with empathy prior to expressing any reassurance, something she had spoken with them about when she saw them alone.]

GAIL: It must be so sad for you if you think that we are disappointed in you. . . .
SIMON: Yes, it would be so hard. . . .
GAIL: I can understand now how alone you must feel.
SIMON: And you said that you think you're not special to us. That must also make you feel all alone.
GAIL: I am so sorry, John, that you feel that you disappoint us. I can understand why you might because we argue so much. I wish we didn't.
SIMON: I agree with your mom, John. You are very special to us, and you are not a disappointment to us. I guess we have not done a very good job of helping you to trust us. We have to get better at having conflicts so they don't make you think we're disappointed in you.
ALISON: Oh, John . . . your parents really seem to understand how hard it has been for you. The arguments that you three have been having really

have made you not trust that you're important to them. That you are special to them. [Close to a minute of silence follows as the family reflects on the experience that they are having.]

ALISON: John, do you want to say anything to your parents now?

JOHN: I try not to get so mad! Why do I! I don't want to be fighting all the time! [He now cries. With their own tears, Gail and Simon move closer to him and embrace him.]

GAIL: I don't know why we fight so much either, John. I don't want to either. Maybe Alison can help us to work things out better.

SIMON: I'd like that a lot. Would you too, John?

JOHN: [Very quietly] Yeah.

ALISON: What a family you are! You all want the same thing! To find ways to be closer, to show how special you are to each other. I am glad to be able to get to know you and to work with you on your journey together.

[Alison has just witnessed joint vulnerability and emotional closeness, something that the family has seldom experienced together. Her intersubjective experience of them will deepen their experience of this emerging quality of their relationships with each other.]

SIMON: What do we need to do, Alison? [John looks expectantly at Alison, showing in his eyes how much he wants her to be able to help them.]

ALISON: Great question. Well, I don't think we'll be focusing on how you all might control your anger better. Nor how to listen to each other better. At least not now. I think that John might have had uncertainties about whether or not you were glad that he was your son even before all the arguments started. I'd like all of us to meet next week and spend the time together thinking about the hard times that all three of you had during those years after John was born. I think those hard times made it hard for you all to build a strong sense of safety and awareness that you are important to each other. If you had been better able to trust that you are all important to each other, then the conflicts that you have been having would not have become so frequent, and you'd have worked them out better.

GAIL: I know we had hard times back then, Alison, but do you think that those still affect us now?

ALISON: I do, Gail. I know you said that you and Simon had to see a therapist for the two of you to figure out how those times affected your marriage. And you were able to build the closeness in your marriage again.

I'm saying that it might have been a good idea back then to also have some family therapy to help the whole family get close.

SIMON: We didn't think of that back then. John was so young.

ALISON: Yes, he was young. And maybe because he was so young he was not able to find the words for his sadness and loneliness and for being able to say that maybe you were unhappy with him . . . with who he was. Little kids feel those things at least as strongly as do adults.

GAIL: Do you think we can make it work out now? It's not too late?

ALISON: The little that I know about the three of you gives me confidence that the answer is yes. Definitely yes! You all want this, and you're all smart and good people. And I'm a great family therapist! What do you think, John?

JOHN: Yeah, but I don't know about the part about you.

Taken by surprise at Alison's final sentence, the family started laughing together. It brought some relief to the intense emotion that they were all experiencing. And it brought a sense of closeness as they joked about this know-it-all therapist who better know what she's talking about or they'd all be angry with her, not each other!

By working relationally, using the synchronized parent-infant manner of relating as a guide, Alison was able to provide a setting where the family could engage in the process of exploring the meanings of their interactions, their sense of who each of them were, so that they had a context where they might more easily address any behaviors as needed, without anger, fear, or shame.

In spite of the fact that the sessions were online, Alison was able to help the family feel safe enough to be open to the affective tone created by her attitude of PACE, which led them to be open to their emerging affective experience, which was synchronized with hers. The lighter conversations of the first two sessions enabled John to trust Alison enough so that in the third session he was able to express his vulnerabilities associated with the conflicts with his parents. This manner of relating remained stable, with a few brief periods of defensiveness mostly initiated by John's anxiety and shame, throughout the remaining therapeutic sessions.

Relying on the relational patterns that are central in the infant's development of a secure attachment with her parents, DDP strives to develop synchronized, reciprocal, nonverbal communications between therapist and members of the family. These then serve as the relational core of the conversations that emerge, which give expression to the underlying attachment-based intentions that lead to the resolution of family conflicts and the creation of trust and new learning.

References

Beebe, B., & Lachmann, F. M. (2014). *The origins of attachment: Infant research and adult treatment.* New York: Routledge.

Hughes, D., & Baylin, J. (2012). *Brain-based parenting: The neuroscience of caregiving for healthy attachment.* New York: Norton.

Hughes, D., Golding, K., & Hudson, J. (2019). *Healing relational trauma with attachment-focused interventions: Dyadic developmental psychotherapy with children and families.* New York: Norton.

Schore, A. N. (2012). *The science and art of psychotherapy.* New York: Norton.

Schore, A. N. (2019). *Right brain psychotherapy.* New York: Norton.

Siegel, D. J. (2012). *The developing mind: How relationships and the brain interact and shape who we are* (2nd ed.). New York: Guilford.

Sroufe, A., Egeland, B., Carlson, E. A., & Collins, W. A. (2005). *The development of the person.* New York: Guilford.

Stern, D. (2000). *The interpersonal world of the infant.* New York: Basic Books.

Trevarthen, C. (2001). Intrinsic motives for companionship in understanding: Their origin, development, and significance for infant mental health. *Infant Mental Health Journal, 22,* 95–131.

Tronick, E. (2007). *The neurobehavioral and social-emotional development of infants and children.* New York: Norton.

Credits

Index

315